ECONOMIC SURVEY METHODS

John B. Lansing

and

James N. Morgan

1971

Code No. 3276-71

DEDICATION

We dedicate this book to the memory of John Lansing, a warm personal friend, creative colleague, and careful scholar. It was his sense of obligation to science, and of the need for system and order, which led us to undertake the writing task. His concern for methodological investigation and improvement—while always pushing ahead with substantive research in the meantime—shows up throughout the book. And his willingness to look for something potentially useful in many alternative procedures has broadened its scope, has kept it from being parochial. We shall miss him, and hope that those who benefit from this book will appreciate his contributions.

James N. Morgan

PREFACE

Economics is both a social and a behavioral science. It deals with the inter-relationships among economic units, the ways in which the decisions of house-holds, business firms, and legislatures interrelate and the outcome for the whole economy in terms of resource allocation, economic growth, employment and stability. It is becoming increasingly apparent that the sophisticated models cur-rently being used require better behavioral information if they are to be useful for either prediction or policy making. And the behavioral relations must in-creasingly be at the level of individual households or firms where they can be in-vestigated and understood. Hence the need for economic survey research, where economic behavior can be related to financial, demographic, psychological and sociological variables.

Survey research is multidisciplinary, since it focuses on understanding hu-man behavior, but it can be organized to some extent on disciplinary lines ac-cording to the behavior being studied. And the problems and procedures do differ somewhat depending on the kind of behavior being studied. Although we are also concerned that surveys be economic in the sense of prudent with resources, this book focuses rather on economic survey methods, meaning using the tool of surveys to study economic behavior.

We felt this book had to be written, even though it adds to an already overwhelming flood of printed paper. As the amount of survey research on economic behavior expands, it becomes increasingly clear that old mistakes are being repeated, and methods are all the time being rediscovered. This is so pri-marily because the accumulated experience of the past has not been systematical-ly summarized and therefore principles generalizeable from it could not be ap-plied to future research. If the availability of this book assists people in avoiding the same old mistakes, if it perhaps reduces the number or seriousness of new ones, it will have served its purpose.

The authors started doing survey research more than twenty years ago when there was little experience to go on, and most of it in different substantive areas, particularly sociology. We have learned a great deal from our colleagues at the Institute for Social Research, as well as from our own mistakes and experi-ences. When we found ourselves occupied with training staff, trying to convince research sponsors about what was good study design, and teaching a graduate seminar on economic survey methods, the paucity of appropriate written ma-terial became painfully evident.

Leslie Kish's writings left the theory and practice of sampling in excellent shape; hence we include here only a few examples showing the implications of alternative sample designs. Statistical literature on data analysis is voluminous, but much of it is still in the hypothesis testing tradition, or focused on small data sets like time series, so that it tends to be not relevant or even misleading. The peculiar problems of searching large masses of data for the structure of relationships have been tackled, but often at scattered sites and with unconnected developments, and by procedures whose formal mathematical justification is incomplete. This book brings together in one place a discussion of several strategies for analyzing such data.

There are books on questionnaire design and on field procedures, which the present volume supplements and translates into the problems of economic surveys. The processes of content analysis, scaling, generation of conceptual variables, and analysis, are a warring battlefield of competing methods, none of them completely satisfactory and most of them poorly explained or justified. However, we do discuss methods and techniques that have proven satisfactory for us.

All in all, the field is neither systematic nor orderly enough so that a set of general principles will provide guidance. Yet a case-study approach is limited, and it induces uncritical imitation of less-than-optimal designs. So we try to steer a middle course, applying *some* general notions about resource allocation, and about the motivation of respondents, for instance, but also giving examples from which other generalizations may be drawn.

With the impending explosion of quantitative behavioral studies in economics, some parts of this book should soon get out-of-date, and the need to incorporate the new experience will increase with time. The reader is encouraged to supplement this book with the reports of both the methodology and substantive findings of current surveys, and ask himself whether they illustrate, add to, or contradict what we have said.

We are grateful to a large number of present and former colleagues, and in particular to George Katona, Charles Cannell, Leslie Kish, John Scott, and Angus Campbell. The Institute for Social Research and the University of Michigan funded assignments to off-campus duty for John Lansing in 1967-68 and for James Morgan in 1969-70 that allowed this to get written. Doris Thackrey edited the manuscript and William Haney saw it through the publishing. Anita Ernst typed most of it, several times.

TABLE OF CONTENTS

Chapter I

A NEW TOOL AND ITS USES

Historical Development

Although getting facts by interviewing people has a long history, starting with politicians and journalists, scientific survey research differs from this in very important ways. Simply asking someone questions tends to develop what Professor Daniel B. Suits refers to as "a man-who statistic," as in the phrase "I know a man who. . . ." This kind of survey, covering in some cases substantial groups of people, has been done for quite some time. Surveys were done in Germany in the 19th century on such things as the attitudes of workers in factories. Unfortunately, the political interests of those who conducted such surveys overwhelmed their scientific interests, and objectivity rapidly got lost.[1] Later on, largely in England and France, surveys were used to document the plight of the poor. Many of them focused on one industrial community, documenting the horrors of the industrial revolution and the urban slums. These were followed early in the 20th century by a number of surveys whose major purpose was to collect expenditure data. Such data were used largely for establishing the weights for cost-of-living indexes, but also for estimating income elasticities of various kinds of expenditures.[2] Starting in the 1940's, economic surveys expanded to cover a relatively wide range of subject matter.[3]

The Development of the Scientific Tool

It has only been in the last twenty-five years that survey research has become a scientific tool, that is, able to produce quantified, reproducible information that can be used to test hypotheses or to provide unbiased measurement of quantities or relationships. There were three scientific breakthroughs required for this. First was the development of techniques for selecting probability samples of human populations. This allowed inferences to be made about the whole population on the basis of the samples and allowed these inferences to be tested by computation of sampling variances. Second was the development of techniques for eliciting quantified reproducible information from people. And third was the development of techniques for analyzing fairly large, rich masses of data, mainly by computers.

The first two of these essentially involved tricks. Why was it so difficult to develop a probability sample of human populations? In the first place, in most cases there was no list or "sampling frame" from which one could sample people. Second, and perhaps more important, people are scattered all over the country. A purely random sample would have involved so much costly traveling to find the people that it would not have been feasible to do much survey research. What was necessary was some means of reducing travel cost while still preserving a sample that was basically a probability sample. The trick was to sample not people but the map. One can divide the map into sample areas and then fairly small subareas within those, and either interview everyone within small subareas or a sample within them of two, three, four, or five households.

Here we have an example of a straight economic problem in design: The larger the clusters in the sample, the less information per interview, but the less money one spends getting the interviews. There must be some point where the information per dollar reaches a maximum. The problem is complicated, of course, by the fact that the effect of clustering on the amount of information one gets depends on what one is asking. We shall return to this in Chapter III, where sampling is treated in more detail. Suffice it to say that sampling is a very complex science today, involving elaborate designs and interlaced controls to achieve the maximum information per dollar spent.

The second requirement was the development of procedures for eliciting information from people in such a way that one could have some confidence in it. These procedures are still being worked out, but certain important developments have vastly improved their quality. Perhaps the most important of these was the standardization both of the stimulus that was given to the respondent in the field and the procedures under central office controls for quantifying his replies. Interviewing looked at in this way is essentially a stimulus-response process where it is very important that the stimulus be controlled. In the case of attitudinal questions and even of factual questions, controlling the stimulus meant training interviewers to ask questions exactly as they were written (including questions which called for "open answers") and to write down the answers fully, and then having a controlled central office procedure by which those answers were interpreted. For attitudinal information, these procedures permitted some confidence that the proper frame of reference was being used by the respondent and that cases where he really was not answering the question could be discovered. For factual or demographic information also, open answers often revealed situations where the respondent was answering the wrong question. One example may suffice: in one pretest, a question was inserted, "Do you have any stock?" One respondent answered, "Yes, I have two cows and a horse." Clearly the question was inadequate. In more recent studies, we have had similar problems with questions about food stamps. To some people, food stamps are the commodity stamps issued to poor people by which they get food at less than market prices.

To others, food stamps mean S & H Green Stamps which they get when they buy food and which are exchanged later for premiums.

We return to the process of quantification in Chapter V in the discussion of data processing. But it is important to remember that science requires proper quantification, and proper quantification requires some kind of reproducibility. If answers are written down, at least the process of making them numerical and machine-readable can be rechecked at the time and again later if necessary. In the case of trends or reinterviews, it is possible to go back and requantify earlier information to make sure the procedures have not changed. So area probability sampling made reasonably sure that we had a representative sample of something and fixed-question open-answer procedures with central office control over the interpretation made reasonably sure that we had good information about what the respondent said.

But a rich matrix of information for a substantial sample of people would have been of very little use if we had not had computers to enable us to analyze the data. When we come to discuss analysis methods in Chapter VI, we shall discover that the most modern computers are freeing the researcher from various constraints more adequately than the previous generation of computers, allowing him to make flexible use of the matrix of data that he can collect in a survey. Actually the most recent improvements have been not so much in statistical analysis as in file management, the ability to generate new and complex variables, more in keeping with analytical models one may want to use. And, furthermore, computers have opened the possibility of using survey data in simulation to say more about their dynamic implications in elaborate economic models. It is important to keep in mind just how rich the set of data that one can get from a survey really is. Not only does one have a representative sample of families or individuals, but he also has a wide variety of information about each individual in the sample. This opens up elaborate possibilities for analysis, and also, of course, tempts the researcher into trying to collect too much information in any one interview.

For those sensitive to disciplinary boundaries, we should point out that much of the early development of survey research came from sociology rather than economics. In this book, however, we will focus on the development of the use of surveys in economics and on the possible future uses of survey research in economics.

Appropriate Purposes for Economic Surveys

Any new tool tempts us into what Abraham Kaplan in his book *The Conduct of Inquiry*[4] calls the law of the instrument, a law illustrated by the child who, given a hammer, discovers that a great many things need pounding. It is going to require continued restraint to use surveys only where they are appropriate.

While the ultimate purpose of survey research may often be prediction or explanation or evaluation, much of it seems to involve description or measurement. In a sense, description is subordinate to the other purposes. The analyst seeks to describe as a preliminary step toward subsequent prediction, explanation, or evaluation. Description is often a *necessary* preliminary. It may be necessary to know something about a phenomenon to consider what type of explanation may be appropriate. There is a tendency to regard description as a low level of professional activity and, hence, economists hesitate to admit that they are engaged merely in describing a phenomenon. Part of the low prestige associated with description results from a failure to distinguish between good and bad description. Description necessarily is based on some point of view. There is no such thing as describing a phenomenon without introducing the mind of the observer between the phenomenon and his report of it. He necessarily selects and organizes what he observes. He does the job well if he facilitates the subsequent processes of prediction, explanation, and evaluation. He does the job poorly if he fails to assist these processes. One description may be better than another, therefore, because of choice of point of view, it makes use of more relevant concepts to organize the report of the phenomenon described. The most useful method of description, however, cannot be ascertained until it is known how the description will be used. A description never used may be a mass of unrelated information, a sandpile of facts.

Much descriptive survey research is the responsibility of the government because it is needed not only for the nation as a whole but also for states and counties in some areas. The Census Bureau, in particular collects data on employment, distribution of income, home ownership, and frequency of moving. These descriptive data are useful not only to *measure* inequality or to look at differences in some parts of the population but also to analyze the impact of taxes or of other government policies on different groups in society. Furthermore, if such data are collected repeatedly over time, they produce information on *trends* in income, in inequality, in unemployment, in prices. Indeed, we are moving in the general direction of more such trend measurements, or "social indicators." There has been much interest recently in the problems and possibilities of improvement of "social indicators."[5] While some of the data for monitoring social change can come from public records, most of the improvements in and additions to social indicators will require surveys repeated with reasonably stable procedures so that the trends are valid.

Economists are often frustrated in their attempts to study alternative tax and spending policies by the lack of adequate distributional survey data from which they could infer the impact of these policies on different groups of individuals. Surveys with or without trend data can also study such things as the acceptance of innovation—the spread of TV, the use of seat belts, or early retirement.

But surveys lead immediately to the possibility of studying relationships. Who are the people who do one thing or another; who are the people with debt, or with high incomes; and what is the relationship between income and expenditures? Such analysis may sometimes lead immediately into explanations, but it may only be the search for relationships without attempting to provide elaborate explanations. Efforts to analyze the so-called "consumption function" made use of survey data particularly in attempts to estimate the marginal propensity to consume, the relation of consumption expenditures to income. Much was written over what now appears to be a technical issue—the discrepancy between cross-section and time series estimates of the marginal propensity to consume. It now has been seen that the permanent income hypothesis is just a statement about errors in variables, and the biases that were created when errors occurred in one explanatory variable.[6]

Economic experiments with human populations have been quite rare, because they are expensive and difficult to design. They often require the use of surveys to monitor the impact of the experiment. For instance, if one wants to know the effect of changing the welfare laws, as in a negative income tax experiment, it becomes necessary to follow the behavior of the experimental groups and of a control group over a period of time to find out how changes in the welfare laws affect people's behavior.

But, inevitably, almost any use of survey data ends with attempts to explain "why." It is not always obvious what constitutes a satisfactory explanation. Abraham Kaplan distinguishes two basic types of explanation which he designates as the deductive model and the pattern model.[7] In the deductive model an event is explained by subsuming it under general laws. An analyst knows the reason for "x" if he can deduce it from other facts. The other facts in turn may require explanation which the analyst may or may not be able to provide. Ability to explain "x" is not the same as the ability to explain the facts which explain "x." It is also possible, and in economics it is usually true, that the explanation is in probabilistic terms. What is known is that the *probability* of "x" depends on other facts in a certain manner. The pattern model is perhaps less familiar. An analyst knows the reason for "x" if he can put it into a known pattern. He relates "x" to a set of other elements so that together they constitute a unified system. No deduction is involved. Explanation consists in recognizing a pattern for what it is—it fits.

The broad purpose of most economic surveys is to explain or contribute to the development of explanations of economic phenomenon. Thus, results of the surveys are to be evaluated in terms of the quality of the explanation to which they lead. The quality may be evaluated in statistical terms. The analyst is concerned with the precision of his estimates, the absence of bias in procedures, and the like. There is sometimes disagreement about the importance to be attached to different statistical criteria. For example, how important is it for a statistician to estimate accurately the regression coefficient for income in an explanation of some expenditure, and how important to explain a high proportion of the variance of the dependent variable, or to estimate the probability that his hypothesis is false? Such choices, with the stress to be placed on specific criteria, clearly should depend on the purpose of the inquiry. We come back to this in Chapter VI when we discuss the analysis and interpretation of survey data.

The quality of explanation may also be considered in terms of the relation between the explanation and the general body of knowledge. At a minimum, explanation should be consistent with other knowledge.

Surveys are used in several ways to explain why something happened. Sometimes we ask people directly why they did something. And sometimes we use indirect projective questions, where we hope that a person will tell us indirectly what he thinks. For example, some people say that *other* people do not fly because they are afraid, while at the same time they might refuse to admit they are afraid themselves (even though they are).

It is often said that the ultimate purpose of any scientific inquiry is prediction. In the case of economic studies, this is the purpose as well. The simplest example is the attempt to predict the impact of changing aggregate income on the pattern of consumption by estimating different income elasticities from budget data, the Engel curves.[8] Or one may want to predict changing patterns in consumption by noting that more and more people are moving from the country to the cities, and when people move to the cities their consumption patterns change. One may also want to describe the impact of particular policies by simply knowing *who* is likely to be affected by them. But more important, one may want to predict the responses to policies by finding patterns in people's attitudes, preferences, or behavior. Indeed, in many cases of public policy, one may want both to monitor the current responses to an on-going policy *and* to understand and predict future responses on the basis of the same data.

Another kind of prediction from economic surveys is the prediction of discretionary expenditures. In an affluent society where large masses of consumers have a great deal of flexibility in their spending, they are able to postpone or speed up their expenditures, particularly those for durables bought to replace other durables. Hence it may well be that surveys can measure the current state of consumers' optimism, confidence, and willingness to spend their money. Moreover, the data from a series of such surveys can be used to investigate further what kinds of events and understandings of events caused consumers to change their propensity to consume over time.[9] Here, as in other parts of scientific endeavor, the purposes of prediction, explanation, and understanding all mingle together, and the same data that are used in the short-run for prediction can be used in the long-run for understanding and improving the predictions of the future.

A long-range possibility involves the use of survey data in simulation models to predict changes in whole systems. Major developments in this area were started some years ago by Guy Orcutt.[10] He pointed out that one way to go from information about the behavior of individuals to inferences about dynamic responses in the aggregate was to build a simulation model where representative groups of consumers moved iteratively month by month, the basic behavioral input being relations between initial state and subsequent behavior. The aggregate dynamic implications could then be dredged out of the computer in the course of the simulation. This process requires both a tremendous quantity of data and tremendous resources in computer and analytic expertise and is not moving very rapidly; but it does say something about the kinds of survey data that will be needed in the future. Survey data need to be collected which are at least dynamic enough to related initial states to subsequent actions, and to test whether such relations are stable over time.

The final purpose of economic surveys is evaluation, both of the impact of policies and of the potential uses of various kinds of new investments and, perhaps most important, of the need for certain kinds of collective consumption. There are a growing number of areas where government policies affect the individual and where voting is an ineffective way of deciding which of several policies is best overall. This problem is particularly crucial in the case of the provision of social goods like parks, hospitals, and highways. Surveys can provide important information on the patterns of individual preferences. How else can the technicians and policy makers compare the *benefits* to drivers of better highways and parking lots with the *losses* to those who use public transportation? The literature on urban problems is rife with assumptions about the relative importance of privacy, space, quick journey to work, and scenic beauty, without any evidence as to how people feel other than the author's casual empiricism. Therefore, surveys are needed to help evaluate the social benefits of such things as parks and clean air, things that cannot be priced and sold on the market. Even where a major investment results in something to be sold in the market place, surveys may avoid vast misallocations of resources by providing some evidence as to whether people are likely to be willing to spend their money on the new product or service when it is available.

It should be made clear, however, that surveys are *not* to be used to make public policy directly. They provide the basic input into discussions of public policy in the same way that they provide the input into the econometric models. They may keep policy makers aware of the existence of diverse groups, with strong desires requiring some diversity of public policy.

Inappropriate Purposes for Economic Surveys

Some years ago Leonard Salter wrote a book called *A Critical Review of Research in Land Economics.*[11] In it he pointed out that a very large number of research projects in his field, many of them involving surveys, were useless because they started with no particular hypothesis, went through no particular organized structure and, hence, could not come to any particularly useful conclusions. Salter was correct in asserting that it is inappropriate to conduct surveys unless there are some particular, explicit purposes connected with them beyond simply asking interesting questions. But even some clear purposes are not appropriate. Surveys are not good for estimating national aggregates, particularly of skewed distributions where a few people account for a large fraction of the aggregate. They are not useful for estimating total assets of a country, for instance, or even its aggregate income. They are not useful for studying illegal or illegitimate activities since, obviously, the respondents usually cannot be sufficiently sure of the confidentiality of their answers. They are clearly not appropriate for use in law enforcement since the respondent would have to be deceived about the purpose of the survey. Nor should surveys be used to collect data for the exclusive use of some particular client, whether government or private, since such data could be used to manipulate people without their knowledge. Although the whole popular controversy over privacy in survey research is focused on the issue of dossiers and the availability of such information to persons other than those for whom it was intended, another issue is equally important—the potential misuse of survey data when important facts about the attitudes, behavior, and preferences of masses of people are available only to some people and not to others. There is more opportunity to use surveys to manipulate people if the data are available to only certain people.

Surveys are also not useful to study uncommon phenomena. For instance, it is very difficult to use surveys to study fraud against consumers, not only because those who have been defrauded may not like to admit it, but because such fraud is a fairly rare thing and difficult to locate in a population. Surveys are probably not useful to estimate price elasticities or substitutional elasticities since prices do not change much in short periods and price differences in some areas are often associated with other differences. Nor are surveys useful to make precise estimates of income elasticities. For instance, there was a great deal of interest during the tax cut of 1964 in the possible measurement of what might be called the marginal propensity to spend the tax cut. This would have required measuring income during relatively short periods to the nearest percentage point and measuring consumption to the nearest 1/2 percentage point of the truth in order to be able to talk about a marginal propensity to spend part of a small change in income. What *is* possible in connection with such a change is to study the way people see such tax cuts, their level of information, whether they see themselves as having made major, discretionary expenditures either before their take-home pay actually went up or after they noticed they were accumulating the funds. One can study differential responses by people who did or did not have income increases other than those resulting from the tax cut.

Finally, surveys are probably not appropriate for testing elaborate hypotheses which require for their testing very high precision; indeed, as we shall see later, it is often unwise to think of a survey as testing a particular hypothesis rather than allowing the analyst to select among several alternative hypotheses. Very sophisticated methods of analysis assuming a particular causal structure prove to be nearly useless for determining the proper structural assumption.

Conclusion

Recent developments in scientific sampling, eliciting and quantifying information, and data processing have provided a new scientific tool to economists. It must be used with discretion. It has a wide range of potential purposes but also opens up temptations to use it where it is not appropriate. In using economic surveys, economists should keep in mind that in the process of explaining economic behavior, noneconomic variables may be important, and in the process of estimating and predicting the things economists are interested in, the same data may be very useful to other social scientists for purposes other than those for which the original survey was designed. There is a great deal of symbiosis possible in survey research, and a promising future for interdisciplinary cooperation.

A study design that proposes to test a single complex hypothesis is inappropriate, in most cases. There are usually a number of competing hypotheses and the design should allow one to rank them. At the other extreme are many studies which do not have enough theoretical structure behind them, and hence are not set up either to test one hypothesis or to select among competing explanations. Sometimes there is not even a single thing (situation, behavior) to be explained. The study may purport to study tenant farmers, or the poor, or home owners, but unless it is trying to explain something about the situation or behavior or plans of some group, the result is likely to be useless description.

How does one steer between the narrow rigidity of the "hypothesis testing" approach on the one hand, and the grab bag data collection with no structure on the other?

One way is to be sure there are clear answers to two questions:

What situation, or behavior, or set of them, is to be explained?
How will it be possible to show that the explanation given is superior to likely alternative explanations?

Footnotes to Chapter I

1. Anthony Oberschall, *Empirical Social Research in Germany 1848-1914,* Mouton and Co., Paris, 1964.

2. Faith Williams and Karl Zimmerman, *Studies of Family Living in the United States and Other Countries,* U.S. Dept. of Agriculture, Washington, D.C., December 1935. See also George Stigler, "The Early History of Empirical Studies of Consumer Behavior," *Journal of Political Economy,* 62 (April 1954) pp. 95-113.

3. James Morgan, "A Survey of Recent Empirical Research on Consumer Behavior," in *Consumer Behavior,* Lincoln Clark, Ed., Harper and Brothers, New York, 1958; James Morgan, "Repeated Surveys of Consumer Finances in the United States," in *Family Living Studies,* International Labour Office, Geneva, 1961.

4. James Morgan, "Contributions of Survey Research to Economics," in C. Y. Glock, editor, *Survey Research in the Social Sciences,* Russell Sage, New York, 1967, pp. 217-218.

4. Abraham Kaplan, *The Conduct of Inquiry: Methodology for Behavioral Science,* Chandler Publishing Co., San Francisco, California, 1964.

5. Raymond Bauer, Ed., *Social Indicators,* M.S.T. Press, Cambridge, Massachusetts, 1966; see also U.S. Dept. of Health, Education, and Welfare, *Toward A Social Report.* U.S.G.P.O., Washington, D.C., 1969.

6. Nissan Liviatan, "Tests of the Permanent-Income Hypothesis Based on a Reinterview Saving Survey," in *Measurement in Economics: Studies in Mathematical Economics and Econometrics in Memory of Mehuda Grunfeld,* Stanford University Press, Stanford, California, 1963.

7. Abraham Kaplan, *op. cit.* - Chapter IX.

8. S. J. Prais and H. S. Houthakker, *The Analysis of Family Budgets,* Cambridge Univ. Press, Cambridge, 1955. See also Harold Lydall, *British Income and Savings,* Oxford, Basil Blackwell, 1955.

9. George Katona, *Mass Consumption Society,* McGraw-Hill, N.Y., 1964.

10. Guy Orcutt and others, *Microanalysis of Socio-Economic Systems,* Harper, New York, 1960.

11. Leonard Salter, *A Critical Review of Research in Land Economics,* University of Wisconsin Press, Madison, Wisconsin (Reprinted) 1967.

Chapter II

THE DESIGN OF SURVEYS

Three Requirements

Designing anything means ensuring that the parts will fit together. One cannot focus on one aspect alone. And this fitting together of a gestalt, or pattern, occurs at two stages. The first stage is the selection of a topic that

will produce some important benefits,
can be studied at a reasonable cost,
has some chance of being financed.

This requires familiarity with:

the state of knowledge in the substantive field,
the state of technology in survey research,
the state of mind of the fund-granting sources.

Since most surveys involve substantial costs, particularly as compared with other more individualistic forms of research, the comparison of the benefits and costs of a proposed survey must be made somewhere, explicitly or implicitly. There are important topics which cannot be studied at costs reasonably consonant with their importance. There are things easy to study which are not worth it—readers of the results may fairly ask, "so what?"

A thorough grasp of the state of knowledge in economics, including *both* theory and fact, is not easy to come by, since theoretical and empirical developments tend to go their own separate ways, and bibliographic resources are unusually poor, particularly for quantitative research. Previous surveys may have been done, but published in obscure places and are not usually reviewed in the professional journals.

Knowledge of the possibilities of survey research comes largely through experience, but it is hoped that this book may assemble some of the relevant ideas. Since people usually do not advertise their failures or mistakes, the limitations of the survey method in particular need to be spelled out. Indeed, the second stage of design, to which we return below, spells out a consistent set of design decisions about the survey itself, decisions that fit together.

What can one say about the benefits of a proposed piece of survey research? Seldom will the result lead immediately to improved decisions that will
save money outright. More often, a general case can be made that better knowledge of human behavior helps avoid futile, disruptive, or wasteful policies of government or business. If, for example, extended family financial responsibilities are
dysfunctional and reduce people's incentives to earn and accumulate, then policy
about public responsibility for the indigent can be better shaped to meet the future. If we know what pleases or displeases people about their housing and neighborhood, we can allocate funds and make better design decisions about our cities.

In this enthusiasm for the research he wants to do, the proposer may well
exaggerate its benefits. What is less forgivable is for him to suggest benefits without spelling out what they are. *Why* is the topic of great national importance?
What decisions are being made which may involve costly mistakes if information
is poor? Will anyone do anything different on the basis of the results of the
study? Will the results contribute to a systematic and growing body of knowledge, the end results of which may have some benefit?

Proof that the research team knows the substantive area also requires at
least some search of the literature and summary of the state of knowledge.
There is sometimes an unwarranted demand for excessive bibliographic work,
but it is also true that sometimes research projects are started with inadequate
knowledge of what has already been done.

It is common to suggest that there should be an advisory group of experts
in the subject matter to advise on the survey. It might be suggested that this advisory group should also contain some experts in survey methodology since the
whole process of research design requires that the substantive needs and the scientific possibilities of surveys be merged.

The second question, whether the topic can be studied at a reasonable
cost, is really not independent of the first, since a cost is reasonable only in comparison with the benefits it produces. Cost must first be related to the volume
and precision of the information that will be produced. A common error in designing research is to design a study too large and expensive for the purpose.
Sometimes the sample is larger than necessary for the precision required. More
likely, the amount and variety of data to be collected are far beyond what is
necessary to study the main topics, and often beyond the point where the
respondent can be expected to provide good information. The tell-tale sign of
someone insufficiently informed about the technology of survey research is the
appearance of an excessively long questionnaire in advance of a carefully worked
out statement of detailed objectives.

Indeed, an important question is whether there should not be several alternative designs, ranging from an inexpensive study to scout the field, narrow
the focus, and check the feasibility of a larger study, to a full-blown definitive
design that leaves no reasonable hypotheses unchecked.

When we come to the interlaced set of decisions that must be made about any one design, however, it is a substantial task to work out one or two alternative designs, with cost estimates and some consideration of feasibility.

It is sometimes stated that a survey design should specify a formal theoretical structure that is to be tested. We maintain, on the contrary, that in the present state of knowledge in economics we are necessarily selecting among competing, alternative hypotheses. A good research design, then, must encompass a variety of alternative hypotheses or theoretical structures, and attempt to provide the critical information necessary to choose among them. The task is made more difficult by the loose connection between the theoretical constructs on the one hand, and the things that can actually be measured, on the other. The notion that it is efficient to test a single hypothesis has long since been obsolete in the field of experimental design, owing largely to the contributions of R. A. Fisher and others. And procedures for statistical analysis have been affected by the Bayesians who insist that any data analysis must implicitly or explicitly start with some *a priori* probabilities about what the world is like.

So, a good research design starts with a broad view of the various possible theoretical models that might explain. Some of these models will involve more complex structures than a single dependent variable (a state or a behavior), introducing chains of causation or a hierarchy of explanatory variables. Indeed, it is sometimes important to have a model where some of the variables are *dependent* variables in part of the analysis, and *explanatory* variables in another part. Studies of adoption of innovation characteristically use background factors and the input of persuasion to explain changes in information and understanding, and those in turn, to explain changes in attitudes, intentions and belief. They may then use changes in attitudes, etc. to help explain changes in actual behavior.

The third consideration in undertaking a survey topic was the availability of funds to support the research. Information about the state of mind of the foundations and the various government agencies with research funds is not easy to get, particularly since any given research team only engages in this exercise at scattered intervals. Funding procedures vary, and some agencies provide informal advice in order to avoid many formal refusals.

Given the substantial staff turnover, changes in structural divisions, and changes in stated policies in most grant-giving organizations, the researcher may have a difficult time knowing where to submit his proposal. Hopefully, however, a good proposal can somehow be made to fit in somewhere. In fact, the very variety of the funding sources gives new ideas a better chance than they would have at the hands of one monolithic source for all social science research funding.

An added difficulty, of course, is that survey research competes with other kinds of research which cost less per printed page of output. In between the very expensive detailed data collections of government, and the seemingly cheap small-scale individual research projects, small-sample survey research finds its uneasy place.

In these days of focus on "power," it is common to ask who decides on research design, the sponsors or the researchers. It is also common to assume that research focused on the immediate public problems of the moment is "problem oriented" not "basic" and will contribute little to the permanent body of knowledge. Less commonly heard in academic circles, but also widely believed, is a charge that social researchers left to their own devices, tend to study unimportant and esoteric problems of interest only to little "in-groups."

Our own experience of what actually happens is that it is usually a process of adjustment. Sometimes the process starts with a proposal being prepared by a researcher and then being refined and altered until it seems to meet some purpose seen as appropriate by some funding source, or by the experts consulted by that source. Sometimes a source of research funds specifies an area of research or a set of problems, and the researchers then design studies which attempt to focus on those problems while still contributing some basic knowledge of lasting value. The source of initiation is less important than the process of negotiation and fitting. It is our view that researchers need to justify their research in terms of some social benefits, but that it is possible to study real problems and still be contributing to basic scientific knowledge and to the development of improved methods.

Both extremes can lead to waste. There are examples of bad research, conducted under pressure of current issues or problems, often focused on some popular hypotheses, where the researcher seems to become the handmaiden of the particular views of the sponsor. There are also examples of research where the findings are of little relevance, either because the problem does not have any importance, or because the design tests some very particular theory while ignoring other possibilities.

As researchers, the authors have the feeling that too often administrators without much expertise in the design and conduct of research attempt to go beyond their legitimate concerns about importance and relevance of the research, and interfere with technical decisions about how the research should be conducted. On the other hand we have seen ourselves and others restrained from waste of resources by fund limitations or the demands of funding agencies for the justification of a broad design and its budget. One of the most common sins of survey researchers is to collect more information than they need, because "it would be interesting to know." This not only wastes resources but imposes a burden on respondents who are often annoyed by the obvious irrelevance to the main topic of many of the questions asked.

It is only fair to add that until very recently it was extremely difficult to get research funds to study racial problems. It is still difficult to get funds to study human attitudes and behavior in areas of international conflict, world peace, and arms control. Funds for developing and testing methods of measuring both economic and non-economic variables from theory have also been extremely difficult to get.

Some Questions to Answer

One way to look at overall design decisions is to frame a sequence of questions:

A. Is the goal or purpose clearly stated, with some potential benefits that would justify the expenditures involved?

While it is difficult to measure the economic value of information, it is still a useful exercise. Sometimes major policy decisions will depend on the answers, and the costs of error in those decisions can be assessed. Much information, however, is a public good, whose value depends on how many people use it. Some focus on why the information is needed will at least get away from studies which are done because "it would be interesting to know." Curiosity may be a good thing, but it is not enough to justify large expenditures.

B. Does the design fit the goals or purposes of the study?

The information needed must be at least potentially available from the respondents. The total scope of the objectives must be sufficiently bounded so that it can be handled in a single study, but not so narrow that some of the respondents' potential time is not used. We shall see later some examples where important objectives were not capable of adequate study with surveys.

C. Is there at least a rough working theoretical structure to guide the detailed design?

Is the level of analysis proper individual, family, or group? Are all the basic kinds of explanatory variables included: background factors, constraints, current outside forces, and motives of the respondents? Are the "intervening variables" also included in the design? For instance, background and recent events may affect people's attitudes, which in turn affect their behavior patterns, which then affect their incomes. To relate background or recent events to changes in income and omit the intervening variables is to fail to take the opportunity to study the whole process.

D. Is a survey really necessary rather than just an experiment?

A whole range of possibilities exists between a survey of a representative sample at the one extreme and a controlled laboratory experiment on the other. One might select extremes on a dependent variable for the sample in order to accentuate the possibility of explaining differences. One might manage to hold some things constant, by sample selection or manipulation. One might vary some things systematically, either for some group, or for a random subsample of a group. When a series of things are varied systematically with randomly selected subgroups, and other things are held constant for everyone, we are at the experimental-design end of the continuum. Semi-controlled experiments have a checkered history, but some fruitful ones may still be possible. Laboratory experiments may seem unreal, or expensive per person, but allow (a) a focus on crucial variables, (b) variation of things which may not move much or for very many at once in real life situations, and (c) an isolation of the effects of interest from the "noise" and confounding that otherwise cause difficulties.

E. Will a single survey suffice, or is it necessary to revisit and reinterview?

Economists need dynamic data, people's responses to changes in incomes, wage rates, prices, etc. At a minimum this requires data on the relation between an event or a situation and subsequent behavior. Given the limits of people's memories, this may well require panel studies. Yet panels raise difficult problems of shifting units, extensive costs, and require explicit justification and attention to detailed design problems.

F. Is the general allocation of resources an efficient one?

Is the allocation of time and money among the procedural steps optimum, that is, between design, sampling, data collection, processing, analysis, and writing and presentation? There is a tendency to short-change design and planning in order to get into the field, and to short-change writing and clarity of presentation in order to get the findings out and get on with the next piece of research.

Is the allocation of interviewing time optimal, (a) between measuring the dependent variables and the explanatory variables, (b) between more dependent variables and more precision in measuring each one—which usually takes more time and questions, and (c) between more variety and more precision in measuring the explanatory variables?

Finally, is the total magnitude of the study, including sample size, within a reasonable range of optimality? One can think of a "total benefits" curve which rises rapidly as one devotes enough resources to the study to make it efficient, then rises more slowly as the additional funds go largely to increased sample size, reducing uncertainty only by the square root of the increase, and increasing the problems of quality control. In the figure, total budgets less than OA might be cause to cancel the study as not worth the expenditure, while budgets larger than OC might be considered extravagant.

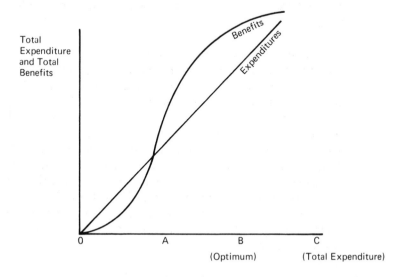

G. Are the basic outlines of the operational details proper, that is, the sample, kind of interview, designated respondent, and analysis plans?

These are taken up in more detail shortly, and again in subsequent chapters, but in the basic design of a study, they need to be considered sufficiently to be sure that they all fit together into an effective and operational pattern.

If we think of the basic design as the decisions made before a study is funded, in the process of writing the proposal, and the implementation as what is done after the funds are available, it turns out that a great many decisions must be postponed, and that the funds must be granted on the basis of a rather general outline of a design, often without proof that the procedures will work, or that respondents have the information or will reveal it. It is often suggested that a pilot study be conducted to check feasibility. The difficulty is that so much work must go into a properly designed pilot study that the proper economic decision about whether to go ahead may be altered in favor, while the sponsoring agency may well feel they have "the answer" from the pilot study and not want to do more. Furthermore, it is difficult to convince researchers to devote time and energy to something which may never come to fruition, particularly when after some past experience, they feel reasonably sure that a fruitful study is possible.

It is easy to state whether the margin of sampling errors on the dependent variables will be within some prescribed limits, but once the sample gets beyond the smallest sizes, the issue of response errors and non-response errors predominates, and is much more difficult to specify.

H. What are the basic limitations of the study?

Some things do not vary in a cross-section, such as prices, so that studies of price-elasticity of demand usually require some other design. Sometimes, particularly in special samples, an explanatory variable of interest is badly confounded (highly correlated with) some other variable or variables, so that one would never be able to decide which variable was really causal. Sometimes basically wrong assumptions are made, about who can report something, about whether people have ever thought about a subject and can talk intelligently about it, etc.

One way to think about basic design is that it attempts to avoid conceptual errors, whereas the more specific design decisions made in implementing the study attempt to avoid operational errors, or even mechanical errors.

I. Is some possible source of funds available?

Some of us like to try for the best, testing whether we can find funds for what we think is *most* important. But we may settle for second or third best. And the need for good survey research on economic behavior is so vast, compared with what has been done, that the third best may still be well worth doing.

It is often tempting to design a study around some enticing captive audience, or available sample frame, or other special circumstance. This frequently turns out to be a mistake—a smaller representative sample would have provided more appropriate information.

We might also distinguish studies according to whether they are intended to improve the design of a product or a public policy, or to figure out how to make an existing one more salable. It is our opinion that the former are not only ethically superior, but more creative and more productive. It is one thing to try to figure out how to sell the idea of supersonic transport to people in the path of the 100 mile wide sonic booms the planes trail behind them, and quite another to assess the relative importance of the various benefits and disadvantages of this transport to different groups in society, so that elected representatives can make intelligent decisions, or design the best options on which to let people vote.

Assembling the Elements of a Survey Design

The second stage of design, where many things have to fit together, is what is generally thought of as survey design, and much of it may have to be worked out before funds are assured, in order to convince some funding agency that the study is feasible. Consistent and appropriate decisions must be made simultaneously about:

the unit of analysis,
the dependent variables and their measurement,
the kinds of explanatory variables,
the sample size and design,
the data collection procedures (mail, phone, or personal interviews; reinterviews; other outside data also?),
required staff, resources, and advisory committee,
kind of analysis (will it select among competing hypotheses?).

However difficult it is to discuss these one at a time, we shall try. The reader should also remember that many of them are only specified broadly at the design stage, the implementation requiring many more detailed decisions that will be discussed in later chapters.

The Unit of Analysis

Since it is economic behavior we are likely to be studying, a crucial problem is the locus of decision making. Immediately at the end of World War II there were many married couples living with their in-laws, keeping separate finances, planning to move out as soon as they could find or afford housing, and making many of their own decisions about a car, insurance, savings, etc. The concept of a "spending unit" or nuclear family made sense, and required taking more than one interview in households with secondary units, a difficult thing to do. There were also complications, when the secondary unit paid rent to the primary, for instance. On the other hand, today a hippie commune, if it is a genuine commune, might be considered a single economic unit making unified decisions.

But if one is studying unions, or cooperatives, or rural villages, why not think of the whole organization as a unit? Are the variables that explain union militancy, or cooperative efficiency, or acceptance of innovation all measurable at the organizational rather than the individual level? Actually, we tend to doubt it, and shall argue below that one can use both group and individual variables if the analysis is at the individual level, but not if it is at the group level.

At the other extreme, if one is analyzing purchases of durables, or vacation trips, it may be the particular incident that is the unit of analysis, even
though some families account for none, and some for several. And to take only
one incident per family where there are several would produce a biased sample
of the incidents.

These decisions about the unit of analysis may affect the sample design,
and will certainly affect the interviewing, editing, coding, and even sampling.

Dependent Variables and Their Measurement

Adequate measurement of the states or behaviors to be studied is of crucial
importance. Random errors may cause no bias in the estimated relationship, but
they may result in no significant findings either; and one cannot be sure they are
random. In the case of economic behavior, the time dimension is a problem. Behavior over very short periods may be easier to remember, but is subject to more
random variance as well as to errors and problems in specifying the time boundaries, such as including acts which actually took place before the reference period
started.

The connection between things about which people make decisions and
act on the one hand, and the concepts of economics on the other, is not always
good. Economists may be interested in saving, or in spending (which is not the
same as income minus saving), but the family may make decisions about some
discretionary spending, and about some discretionary saving, which are easier to
isolate, study, and even predict.

Good research is often organized around the *dependent* variables, the
things to be explained. It is not functionally efficient to organize research around
"age" or "race" or "the city." Some explanatory variables, or places, may be
more interesting or more important to policy than others, but in order to study
how age, or race, affect behavior, one must study everything that affects that behavior, in order to make sure the effects of age or race are not spurious. While
the large city may be the focus of many problems, each of those problems may
best be studied explicitly. It is not the city that is being studied, but human behavior, or human situations in the city.

Kinds of Explanatory Variables

A good design must include consideration of the kinds of variables necessary to evaluate the various competing hypotheses. This includes measures not
only of the crucial variables involved, but also of other variables necessary to remove "noise," or to eliminate those who could not possibly respond to some
theoretically interesting variable, or to allow for interactions that alter the effect

of some other variable. In the early design stages, it is more important to list variables by type, rather than spell out all the details. The broad coverage, and the procedures for selecting among competing ones, are more important than details of how each is to be measured. At most, measurement errors may make us unable to see a relationship that exists, or distort our evaluation of the relative strength of different forces. They are unlikely to lead us to positive inferences that are wrong.

A major problem for economists is how to deal with the "non-economic" explanatory variables. Cooperation with other social scientists helps, but in fact the state of measurement of many psychological and sociological variables is not good. Even where some intensive development and testing of measures of some concept has taken place, it is often with captive audiences, or in studies where extensive blocks of time could be devoted to a single measure. The researcher may well find himself forced to alter some existing measure substantially, truncating the number of questions, eliminating irritating ones, etc. Or he may find himself inventing a new measure, and trying to test it before his main study starts. It is our belief that it is better to make some attempt to measure these other variables than to ignore them. And clearly a study design should consider them, even if attempts to measure them fail.

Sample Size and Design

We discuss sampling in more detail in Chapter 3, but the basic elements must be fixed, appropriate to the particular study. One must decide on the *unit* to be sampled, whatever the unit to be interviewed, or the unit to be analyzed. But where one is *analyzing* accidents, or purchases, or some other behavior, it may prove possible to *sample* the same kind of unit. On the other hand, one must always ask whether in sampling something, one has left out the other side of the picture, the control group, the sample of those who decided *not* to do something.

One may want to sample dollars rather than people, or employees when studying firms. This can be considered changing the unit of sampling, or varying the sampling fractions. One might, for instance, want to sample farms in proportion to their output of some crop, and this affects the presentation of the results, which are then in the form: "Farmers representing ____% of the aggregate wheat output, said that . . . . !"

In any case, the sample size is a critical decision. It affects costs and precision of data. One may prefer to spend the money on a smaller sample interviewed more than once. Or the choice might be a larger sample with a briefer questionnaire, using several forms so that some questions are answered only by subsamples. The sample size may be affected by existing facilities, the number of primary sampling areas with trained interviewers already present in them, plus the knowledge that it is inefficient for an interviewer to take fewer than 15-20 interviews on a single study.

Anyone proposing to depart from a single representative sample should openly answer the question about the groups oversampled: "Why is this particular group important out of all proportion to its numbers in the population?" One should also ask whether there are other purposes of the study for which this disproportionate sampling will produce a reduction in the amount of information per interview.

Design Decisions about Data Collection Procedures

Whatever the unit of analysis or of sampling, there may be a different unit for interviewing. For instance, one may want to analyze every individual in the family but only collect the data by talking to one person. There needs to be a decision about who is to be interviewed and the range of information to be asked of this person. There should also be decisions about reinterviews, about how much memory information is to be asked, and about the extent to which ancillary information is to be assembled about the area in which the man lives, or whether information is to be collected from records about him. There need to be decisions about the extent to which money should be invested in callbacks and other attempts to make the response rate as high as possible. Here again a decision must be made about whether some of the features are so novel as to require special pretesting in advance to be sure that they are practical. There needs to be some pretesting of the research instrument in any case. It is important to decide just how extensive this pretesting should be and the amount of time the pretesting process should spend on the field pretest itself, or on validating the information by some outside source. A very important design decision about data collection has to do with the length of the interview and the amount of material to be included in it. There are resource-allocation decisions about how many different dependent variables can fit into one interview and the number of explanatory variables to be used. Any particular construct can be measured with one question or five or ten or twenty, the added questions usually giving better precision on that particular variable. Clearly if one has ten or fifteen possible explanatory variables, the choice must be made whether to take all fifteen and use fewer questions on each one, or to take fewer explanatory variables and try to measure them more fully.

It is tempting to translate research objectives immediately into questions. But these questions are almost never appropriate when asked of the respondent.

How well does X understand what is expected of him in his job?

Does this retailer engage in the best approved business practices?

How much of his income did he save last year?

How much actual cooperation is there in this cooperative?

The process of getting to actual questions requires determining what reasonably exact and hopefully quantifiable information can be elicited by questions that bear on the research question. It may bear only indirectly. We may try to get at mutual understanding by looking at the extent of the communication.

The process can be thought of as a search for something *quantitative*. Cooperation in a cooperative village can be translated into the proportion of the land that is farmed cooperatively, or the proportion of people's working time they devote to the cooperative endeavors, or the fraction of the proceeds from selling the output that is not distributed among the members right away.

And in many studies of social change, the quantification can be either in terms of the inputs or the outputs, that is, one can measure the various programs designed to change things: time and money spent, the number of cattle-dips built, the amount of hybrid seed distributed, or one can try to measure the resulting outputs: increase in crop yields, healthier cattle, etc.

Even crude "quantification," categorizing people into groups, is better than nothing.

We go into data collection procedures and problems more fully in Chapter IV.

Required Staff, Resources and Advisory Committee

It is sensible of fund-granting agencies to require some evidence that those proposing a survey have access to the facilities needed to get the work done. The actual time commitments of the top staff must be presented, plus some statement of where the specialized skills and facilities are to be found. This makes life difficult for an individual who has an idea and wants to do a study. There are not always idle survey research stations ready to service his needs. Indeed, the requirements for team-work in survey research and for each specialist to understand enough about the other specialties to work with them, usually make it necessary for the subject matter specialist to find a survey methods specialist to work with. And since substantial funds are involved, some research advisory committee is usually required.

External Economies in Design

A major advantage of having a permanent organization, conducting whole sequences of surveys is that there are huge economies. The usual economies of scale are obvious—spreading the cost of a sample, of hiring and training interviewers, of getting a whole working organization together, over many surveys instead of one. But there are other kinds of economies. Topics which do not need a full interview, can share the costs of locating respondents and eliciting the background variables. Or a study with the same dependent variables (states, behaviors) may allow explanation in terms of the variables and interests of several disciplines.

A sample from one study can be revisited for a second, avoiding the need to ask the background information again, and allowing subselection to focus on or emphasize certain more interesting subgroups of the population. Previous studies in a sample using the same sub-areas until the addresses are exhausted, could be pooled to provide information about the area, as a kind of environmental variable richer than could be obtained from Census tract data.

Another kind of design makes two sets of data more useful by eliciting them from matched samples. One may have a sample of foremen and a sample of the workers they supervise, or a sample of politicians and of their electorates. It is often very useful to have information about how different groups look at the same situation.

Sometimes economies are possible because some list exists of a group of special interest, preferably with some additional information about them. This is particularly true where governments have form-filing requirements, but are interested in knowing more about the individual respondents from a small sample more intensively interviewed.

The technique of eliciting from a sample the names of those who form another relevant sample, is sometimes useful. It has its dangers, however, for when asked to name friends, people tend to name those a little better off than they are (their "best" friends). One study of tax compliance in Wisconsin asked a sample of tenants what rent they paid, and then checked the tax returns of the landlords to see if the rent was properly reported as income!

Where sequential processes, or sub-sampling do not work, and a special group needs to be sampled, it is frequently necessary to look for some bottleneck through which they all must pass, and try to find a method of sampling the flow. Tourist statistics, for instance, may be collected in the international departure lounges of a country's airports, or even in the planes themselves.

Analysis Design

It would be an ambitious researcher who thought he could specify in advance exactly how he was going to analyze the data. However, his design specifications require some statement about the kinds of constructs he is going to develop, the kinds of hypotheses he wants to choose between, and the kind of analysis that may allow him to decide that one or the other alternative

TABLE I

SUMMARY OF POINTS ABOUT WHICH CHOICES ARE MADE
IN THE DESIGN OF TYPICAL ECONOMIC SURVEYS

Specification of Objectives
(Overall objectives and second level objectives)

Planning
a. Selection of research staff
   (types of training and experience represented)
b. Selection of methods for bringing relevant knowledge to the attention of the research staff
   (literature search, consultation, advisory group)
c. Dependent and explanatory variables and how created from replies to questions
d. Unit of analysis and unit covered by each respondent
e. Preliminary investigations, if any
   (to estimate costs, to try out sampling procedures, to develop and test methods of measurement or analysis)

Sample Selection
a. Type of sample
   (cross-section sample, experimental design, unit of sampling)
b. Universe to be sampled and sampling frame
c. Use of repeated interviews, reinterviews, or screening interviews
d. Use of constant or variable sampling fraction
e. Size of sample
f. Procedure to select exact individuals to be interviewed
g. Method of estimating sampling errors

Field Work
a. Method of data collection
   (personal interviews, telephone interviews, mail questionnaires) (more than one per family?)
b. Mix of types of questions
   (fixed alternative, free answer, use of observations by interviewers, use of non-interview data, use of complex systems of measurement)
c. Length of interview
d. Procedures for selection or special training of interviewers
e. Number of callbacks and procedures for problem cases.

Analysis
a. Method of selection among competing hypotheses
b. Tests for universality of measured parameters or relationships

interpretations of data is the proper one. For instance, in a study of medical insurance and utilization of medical services there are two alternative hypotheses: one, that insurance leads to over-use and abuse of hospital facilities; and the other, that lack of insurance leads to inadequate medical care. Hence, the design needs to specify some procedure by which one can say which of these is more likely to be true. This might require either some outside assessment of the adequacy of the care, or some information from the individual about the extent of unmet needs or untreated symptoms. Sometimes lip service is paid to the notion that survey design starts out with one or two or three hypotheses which are then to be tested. This is not really what happens in practice. The hypotheses that exist are not specific, but general, having to do with the *kinds* of variables that affect the behavior in question, and most analysis discards a number of alternative hypotheses in the process. What is really required is the strategy of analysis and the specification of the kind of sequence of operations that may be used. Even if a main purpose is only to measure relationships (income elasticities, for instance) the analysis may have to check for different relations in different parts of the population.

It is useful to have a check-list of things about which decisions must be made in designing a study.

Privacy

One additional consideration needs to come into study design, particularly in view of the concern about privacy in behavioral research, and that is the specification of how the confidentiality of the data is to be preserved and the rights of the respondents to be respected. Actually, there are two issues here. One is the confidentiality of the data the respondent gives to a survey interviewer, and procedures need to be worked out for this purpose. Generally, this consists of separating the pages containing identifying information about the individual from the questionnaire material as soon as they arrive at the central office so that the processing of the data can proceed without any further identification of the individuals involved. The identifying information is, of course, necessary for checking out the sample and making sure that everyone has been contacted. An allied issue is whether the respondent's willingness to be interviewed was based on "informed consent," i.e. on reasonably clear information about the content and purposes of the survey. The second issue, however, is one not so fully discussed these days and has to do with the extent to which the findings of the research project are to be made generally available. It is undoubtedly quite dangerous for individuals to have information about them available only to one group in society. Potential use of such information for manipulation of people is fairly obvious. Therefore, one basic part of a study design should be some procedure for making the data generally available to the profession and, if possible, in summary form to the respondents themselves. Indeed the latter is often a very good way of inducing cooperation since many respondents would like to know what other people said about the same questions.

It is sometimes charged that survey research is too conservative, that it never really comes out with any exciting or dramatic conclusions. In a sense this is true. Quantitative facts about representative samples of the population usually turn out to be less dramatic than most of the hypotheses that have been advanced. There is a more meaningful sense in which this may also be true. Some social problems involve serious difficulties with very small groups of people and a sample of a representative population does not really provide adequate evidence. For instance, this is likely to be the case with problems such as frauds, extreme poverty, or extreme cases of mental illness.

Theoretical Constructs vs. Measurable Variables

It is a great temptation for an economist to want to collect all the components of some global construct, like total expenditures, or savings. Doing so puts such a burden on the respondent that it allows little time for any other explanatory or related variables. Furthermore, some components of the total may be very difficult for the respondent to remember. The design question, then, is whether some components which are accessible can be used as proxies for a more complete concept, and whether a focus on some aspects of behavior, with more attention to explanation, might not be more productive, than forcing the analysis into the formal mode of economic theory. Indeed, it seems likely that many of the concepts of economic theory, such as saving, may have little motivational meaning since they are the result of several different kinds of decisions which the consumer may not even see as related, and which may be differently motivated. The decision to buy a car, for instance, may be seen as an investment, but the decision to take a longer vacation as consumption, even luxury.

The collection of information about total expenditures or total consumption is very difficult. There is a common belief that in order to get it all, one must ask a great many detailed questions, and there is some evidence that asking more questions does get larger total amounts. What is not clear is whether these larger totals are more accurate, particularly in light of recent evidence on people's tendency to "telescope" expenditures forward into the period asked about (thus exaggerating them). Various devices have been suggested to take some of the burden off the respondent, but most of them exact a price—either collecting some expenditures from some sub-samples and the rest from others, restricting the period with the attendant problems, or going to the expense of reinterviews and even diaries. The question remains whether the basic problem that led to an interest in expenditure detail cannot be attacked better with other data, using house value or rent and size of dwelling as proxies for housing expense, miles driven and age of car as proxies for transportation costs, etc.

Advantages and Problems of Panel Designs

It is currently fashionable to argue that the dynamic data needs of economists call for panel (reinterview) studies. A summary of some of their advantages and disadvantages seems in order:

The main advantages of the panel study are a reduction in problems of recall, the ability to get data on changes in attitudes, expectations, and cash balances, and other things the respondent may forget over a period of time.

Improved rapport from revisits is also believed to lead to better data, in addition to the cumulative accrual of data and possible cross-checks for consistency and accuracy.

Validity studies are also possible by repeating questions to which the answers should not change. Triple measures on variables allow some tests for instability (measurement error).[1] Stable personality items which differ widely between people can be eliminated by relating changes to changes (using first differences), though with qualitative measures this is not so easy as it seems.

Most important, one may be able to uncover dynamic sequences: Did attitudes change before or after behavior changed? What was the time lag between an event and its influence?

Finally, there are some economies in locating people on revisits, and in the use of official records, etc.

What about the disadvantages? Cost is the main one. Reinterviews are expensive, requiring several interviews for information on one unit. The revisits often require extra travel because people have moved out of the geographic clusters in which they were originally sampled. Losses cumulate, since most panels cannot use cases where any one of the interviews is missing.

Changes in the composition of the units cause problems. What is the same unit, in cases of divorce, marriage, etc.? How does one replace the units which die, leave the country, or enter institutions? A partial solution is to treat the individuals of the original sample as the sample frame, and interview any family containing any of those individuals from then on. (Of course this soon becomes a non-representative sample of *families* overrepresenting those containing unstable individuals). And those same changes usually occur *during* the year, not on January 1, so measures of flows like income and expenditures require special editing adjustments, and must be related to family size, also adjusted in some way.

The cumulative improvement of information is itself a problem, since measures of real change are confounded with improved data, and multiple consistency checks may be required. Where inconsistencies occur and the truth is unknown, complex editing decisions are necessary.

Finally, there are even mechanical problems of handling the vast mass of information assembled for each individual (or family), and new computer procedures are still being developed to handle the problem. Unless one is willing to generate numerical indexes, the data on change in a set of five attitudinal questions can be a problem to analyze or to use in the analysis of other changes.

Perhaps the main reason why there have not been many panel studies is a more general problem for survey research, the lack of funding sources willing to commit funds for more than a year or two at a time. Panels need to be planned as panels, including informing the respondents and collecting information on how to find them if they should move. There needs to be enough agreement on the content so that major design decisions are not re-worked every year, leaving time for some analysis of one year's data before the press of the next wave of interviews is on the research staff.

But if panels require both substantial amounts of money, and long term commitments, then their justification and careful original design is even more important than with single surveys. Chopping out unnecessary or peripheral objectives becomes more important, too, since the cooperation of the respondents hinges on keeping the demands on them within reason.

Some Design Problems

We shall try now to put a little meat on these bare bones by giving some examples of actual or potential survey designs—good and bad—in an attempt to illustrate some of the principles. The difficulty, of course, is that it is much easier to illustrate examples of good or bad sample design or analysis design than it is to illustrate a good or bad case of specification of objectives or questionnaire design. Let us first give some examples of mistakes made in design, or designs that were not as good as they might have been, then go on to give some examples of design problems and ways they might be handled.

Suppose one took a sample of graduate students of a particular year and found them "x" years later, studied their incomes and the relationship between their field of study and how far they went in graduate school. This was actually done. The difficulty here is that there is an inevitable confounding between the amount of graduate education the man got and the number of years of experience on his job, so that there is no way really of sorting out these two influences. (Those who left school sooner have more job experience.) It would have been much better to take several cohorts of graduate students so that one could untangle these two influences.

Another example is a sample of personal bankruptcies. People who go into bankruptcy have to file a statement of their assets and their last three years' income. Researchers have taken samples of these statements and, in some cases, have also gone back and talked to the people. The difficulty here, of course, is that there is no way of comparing these people with others in equally bad circumstances who paid off their bills and did not go bankrupt.

The third example is a design that seeks to achieve minimum memory problems asking only about last week's expenditures. The only difficulty is that you cannot, from last week's expenditures, get *distributions* of monthly or annual expenditures. You can only get unbiased estimates of aggregates or means.

Another example is a study of farm housing which took the master sample of agriculture, sampled the segments and took three farms per segment. The problem here, of course, is that a segment with thirty small farms had only one farm in ten represented, whereas a segment with three large farms had them all represented. The result is a biased set of estimates which could have been corrected by weighting the data if someone had thought in advance about the problem.

Another study design problem involved getting information about the occupations and educations of respondents and their fathers in order to study the intergenerational transmission of education (or occupation). If one considers this as a Markov process, a set of transition probabilities which remain constant, one can extrapolate many generations into the future. The difficulty is, of course, that a sample of children (respondents) is not a representative sample of families (fathers), because the more children, the more respondents available to fall into the sample. What is worse, the transition probabilities (proportion of cases where father went to 6th grade and the son went to 8th, for instance) are probably affected by family size, the speed of upgrading being greater where there were fewer children for the family to support. One could weight inversely according to the number of brothers and sisters the respondent had, or do the analysis separately for different family sizes, or ask respondents about the completed education of their *children*. The latter raises other difficulties, since not all respondents have children who have completed their education, (and other parents are already deceased).

There was a study which inspected deed transfers to get a sample of home buyers. The difficulty was that not all transfers involved residential properties, and some real transfers were not recorded by deed transfers until years later. (They may have been transfers in the family, or conditional sales as with land contracts.)

In a study of industrial location, sampling fractions were varied from industry to industry to make sure that each of several industries was represented and could be discussed separately. It turned out that there were no appreciable differences between the industries, consequently the sample was quite inefficient.

Another study started out to be a panel, but in the initial interview respondents were asked to take part in the panel before any facts about them were ascertained which could have allowed an assessment of the bias from noncooperation. Since a substantial proportion refused, the bias could well have been substantial.

One study on farm housing, used an extremely long interview with a large number of questions about whether the respondent would like to have this or that housing feature. Without the discipline of a choice of alternatives, people could say they wanted many things. The reader of the report would have no way of knowing how poor the information was, nor how many interviewers quit in the middle of the project.

In a study of farm management, one objective was to study how farmers made decisions, but the implementation of this objective was a question fourteen lines long which really asked the farmers whether they used inductive or deductive reasoning. This was followed by a series of questions pushing the matter further. The polite farmers answered the questions but there is some doubt about the realism of the answers. It might have been better to have asked for details of some actual recent decisions, and then attempted in a central office to interpret the process.

Another study went to great lengths to get a sample of high income people, but was so concerned with getting accurate detail about their incomes and assets that this took up the whole questionnaire, and no questions were asked that could have thrown light on *why* people chose the portfolios they had. A similar study used a different design, asking about recent changes in portfolio and the reasons for them, purposes people had in investing their savings, their plans for the future, and their sources of information. This allowed more inferences about why people did what they did, even though the information on their actual incomes and assets was less precise.

A major study of poverty, revisiting addresses to measure changes in poverty, was revised after two waves, to introduce more questions about people's attitudes, plans, and actual behavior, so that it would be possible to say more about *why* some people stayed poor, and others improved their situations.

There have been a number of attempts in the past to start national studies of auto accident victims or work-injury victims. In both cases there are problems: auto accidents are reported locally, some not reported at all, and the reports are sometimes kept locally, or sometimes sent to the state offices. And in each state, Workmen's Compensation is a regime unto itself, each with its own system for filing work accident reports, and with varying levels of concern to see that all accidents are reported. A major analytical problem is whether the differences in state laws and state administration leads to differences in results, but the variety is such that a very large number of states would have to be investigated. It is possible that these problems could be solved by taking a national sample of hospitals, selecting a sample of their discharges, interviewing them about their experiences, costs, compensation, and whether they were in the hospital because of an auto accident, work injury, or something else. One would then have *three* representative samples, proper for studying three problems, at least as efficiently and economically as one could have studied one.

An elaborate study to assess the effects in several different areas of programs to educate farmers, concluded that while there were effects they differed from one place to the next. And it was difficult to tell whether this resulted from differences in the places, or differences in the quality of the local educational programs. In other words, in studies of "impact," it is essential to have some measurement of the *quality* of the inputs into programs designed to change things.

Another common problem is circularity, or uncertainty as to causal directions. Time sequences do not always solve the problem. For instance, if farmers who have had extensive visits from extension agents adopt a new practice more than other farmers, it is still possible that the extension agents visited them because they thought they were more likely to adopt the practice. In other words, the farmer's modernism led to the visits, rather than resulting from them. It may be possible to find out which is more likely, if the interviews with farmers and agents are designed with the problem in mind. Similar problems exist with studies of the effects of education, or geographic mobility.

The advantages of interviews should not blind the designer to the possibilities of other information. In a study of retail stores, for instance, a sample of observations at points of time, can provide quantitative data as to how much of the time there are too many clerks or too few, or as to how often displays are changed, etc. Samples of the cars in the parking lot may give indications of the kind of customers, etc.

It is much easier to give good or bad examples than to establish general principles. It is true that the respondent must have available in his memory the information we want, and that there should be some variation in the population that can be "explained." Information far in the past, not salient to the respondent, and not easy for the respondent to find in a record somewhere, is not a good candidate for survey research. Beyond this it is difficult to generalize. We turn now to a series of more detailed examples of research designs, first, some illustrations of things that have been done, and then a few which have not been carried out.

Detailed Examples of Research Designs

It is not possible in any brief review of the subject to include examples of research design that will cover anything like the full range of topics of inquiry, populations, and techniques of investigation in the field of economic surveys. The diversity of the field is extraordinary, and new investigations are continually being undertaken all over the world. What will be attempted here is simply to describe briefly the design of a few selected projects.

1950 and 1951 Surveys of Consumer Finances· Surveys of Consumer Finances have been undertaken annually by the Survey Research Center of the University of Michigan since 1947. They were developed from financial surveys inaugurated during the war years. Over the years there have been changes in the objectives and methods of these projects. The surveys of 1950 to 1951 are of special interest to economists because of the objectives pursued, the techniques employed, and what was subsequently learned about the techniques used at that time in special methodological projects.[2] This account, therefore, will be concerned with the surveys of that period.

The immediate objectives of these surveys were descriptive. The intention was to measure, for a national sample of households, the following: the income of each household, including considerable detail as to the components of total income and an estimate of federal income tax; the major assets, liabilities, and net worth of the household, with detail about the principal components both of assets and of liabilities; the annual saving of the household, also with detail as to the changes in its balance sheet; the principal outlays of the household, and the purchase of durable goods; and the attitudes, plans, and expectations of the household, especially those likely to influence or to reveal its propensity to consume in the immediate future. Given each of these items of information for each of a sample of households, together with measures of the demographic characteristics of the household, there were extensive possibilities both of descriptive tabulation and of analysis intended to explain or to predict consumer behavior. These possibilities, however, were not made explicit in a formal statement of objectives at the time each of these projects was planned. What was planned, however, was implied in part by reports of previous surveys in the *Federal Reserve Bulletin.*

The selection of research staff presents a less difficult problem on a continuing project than on a new survey. The staffs involved both at the Survey Research Center and at the Federal Reserve Board, which sponsored those surveys, had had the experience of work on earlier surveys in the series. No special efforts were made to bring relevant knowledge to the attention of the staff at this stage in the series. No preliminary investigations were undertaken, though there were pretests of each questionnaire. (There had been a pilot study some years before, prior to the first national survey.)

The sample was a cross-section of all households (spending units) living in private dwellings in the United States. (A precise definition of the empirical equivalent of the theorist's household will be considered in later chapters.) The dwelling units were chosen by methods based on the selection of small geographic areas for inclusion in the sample. In order to improve the accuracy of estimates of such statistics as mean income and mean assets, a variable sampling fraction was used. The method involved dividing the sample into three strata based on preliminary estimates of the economic level of each dwelling (estimated rent or house value). A higher sampling fraction was used in the "high" stratum than in the "medium" or "low" stratum. Another way of stating what was done was that half the medium dwellings in a sample were thrown out, and three quarters of the "low" economic level dwellings. (This technique, and the accompanying use of weights to prevent bias in the tabulated results, is discussed in Chapter III.) The total sample was about 3,000-3,500 households per year. Within households, the designated respondent was the head of each spending unit. Estimates of sampling error of means and percentages were made which allowed for the complexity of the sample design but stopped short of providing specific estimates of error for each statistic.

The field work relied on personal interviews using a questionnaire containing a mixture of open-ended and fixed alternative questions. Interviews averaged about one hour, and were conducted by the national staff of interviewers employed by the Survey Research Center. An interview was taken with the head of each economic unit (spending unit) in the household, covering the members of that unit. At that time there were still a considerable number of secondary spending units, usually children or parents of the main family head, who had their own income and kept their finances separate.

Analysis involved "editing" each questionnaire, a process which included calculation of a series of summary measures, prior to "coding," in which each answer was summarized by a numerical code on a transfer sheet. Processing then involved key-punching the data from coded sheets and the preparation of tables using punched cards and the I.B.M. machinery then available. Publication was initially in the form of a series of articles in the *Federal Reserve Bulletin,* with later special analyses published elsewhere.

Evaluation of the success of these surveys requires assessment of the usefulness and accuracy of the measurements made. While criticisms have been made of the choice of topics covered and definitions adopted, there has been little question of the usefulness of these surveys viewed as a whole. There have been serious questions raised, however, about the accuracy of some parts of the data. A considerable effort has been made to evaluate the accuracy, with complex results. A detailed discussion of this type of research is dealt with in Chapter IV. In brief, it is now possible to prepare a rough ranking of types of results according to the accuracy of the estimates in these surveys. Income was estimated with comparatively high accuracy, consumer debt with medium accuracy, and change in liquid assets (and, hence, saving) with comparatively low accuracy. Such findings have led to refinement in some measures and to de-emphasis or abandonment of others in subsequent surveys. Meanwhile, some of the major findings have been widely accepted.

Urban Income and Saving in India: A series of studies of income and saving in India was begun in 1958 by the National Council of Applied Economic Research, located in New Delhi. The starting point of this research was recognition of the importance of saving in a developing country. The program included work in compiling data from institutional sources and sample surveys. Both an urban and a rural sample survey were undertaken, but, for simplicity, only the urban survey is considered here.[3]

The broad purpose of the survey was to contribute to the overall goal of obtaining "a clear insight into the volume, composition, and motivation of saving." The topics of investigation included the demographic and socioeconomic characteristics of the population and income, as well as saving. Thus, the initial purposes of the survey were descriptive in the same sense as those of the Surveys of Consumer Finances. The general strategy of the project was also similar, except for the closer integration in India of the survey approach with the institutional approach to the study of saving.

The staff for the Indian project included a substantial investment in foreign consultants in addition to the Indian economists, and in this way foreign experience was directly brought to bear at every stage in the project. The investigators undertook a pilot study in Delhi in 1959, including interviews with 600 households, and its results were published.[4]

The national survey of urban India was intended to represent the population of India living in cities and towns of 10,000 or more population. As in the Surveys of Consumer Finances, the sampling procedure was based on the selection of small geographic areas, and a variable sampling fraction was used to oversample high income households. About 4,650 interviews were taken in addition to the 600 in Delhi. At the time of publication of the monograph, sampling error calculations which took into account the complexity of the design were in progress, but only limited results were available.

Data collection was based on personal interviews. The mix of questions included both fixed alternative and open answer questions. At the analysis stage extensive use was made of data from institutional sources, but these data referred to aggregates, not to individual households. Interviewers were trained as a group in the central office prior to the start of the survey, in contrast to American practice, in which training is done in or near the communities where the interviewers live. The questionnaires were prepared and printed in English and translated by each interviewer during the interview.

The analysis of the data involved editing, coding, key-punching, and the preparation of tables using punch card equipment. Publication was in the form of a series of monographs. No multivariate analysis procedures were reported in the monograph on *Urban Income and Saving.*

This survey achieved one of its objectives by making available many statistics which previously were unknown for urban India. Its success in providing information about saving which could be combined with the data from institutional sources was limited by conceptual differences and reporting biases. These two sources of discrepancy were separated in the report, but only on the basis of rough approximations. Essentially, the survey estimates were taken to be good approximations of gross investment in physical assets, but poor approximations of saving in the form of financial assets. (The survey estimate of the latter is 126.9 crores of rupees; the adjusted estimate, 340.5.) The estimates of income were believed to be reasonably accurate on the basis of what checks with non-survey aggregates could be made, and the demographic information also seemed reasonably accurate. In brief, on the basis of the published monograph, the survey seems to have been moderately successful as an instrument for obtaining new descriptive data on income and saving. Whether the total project, of which the survey is a part, will lead to the desired insights into saving and, hence, to more enlightened and effective economic policy is inherently more difficult to judge.

A Study of Capital Expenditures by Large Corporations: A study based on intensive interviews with business executives was published by Robert Eisner in 1956.[5] This project is of continuing interest because of the economic importance of knowing the determinants of capital expenditure. The work was a part of a larger study of "expectations and business fluctuations." To some degree, the objectives of the interviews were influenced by other parts of the larger study. The published statement of objectives of the specific project is as follows:

> In regard to capital expenditures, the interviewer was hunting in general for determinants of the level of expenditure.[6]

The entire project was under the direction of Franco Modigliani. This specific study was the work of Robert Eisner, who personally conducted the interviews, analyzed them, and wrote the resulting monograph. Some preliminary interviewing, "of a pilot nature," had been done by Modigliani and others in the spring of 1950.

The sample included fourteen large manufacturing corporations in six different industries. There was no attempt to select a random sample, but the firms were chosen to represent producers of both consumer and capital goods. Geographic convenience of accessibility to the interviewer was also a consideration. Several interviews were taken in most corporations, and in some cases reinterviews were undertaken in 1954-1955. The selection of respondents within the corporations was not systematic. Interviews generally commenced with a top executive and continued with subordinates. No sampling errors were calculated. Indeed, the report contains no tabulations.

The data collection began with a personal letter sent from the Dean of the College of Commerce at the University of Illinois. Further correspondence was undertaken by Eisner himself. No formal questionnaire was used. On the basis of the unstructured personal interviews, a "terminal letter" was sent to each corporation asking summary questions. Drafts of much of the final report, including case reports on the individual firms, were submitted for comment.

Analysis consisted in the preparation of a verbal summary based on Eisner's interpretation of the case studies. In addition fourteen reports on the individual firms were published. The latter vary considerably in length, occupying from two to twelve pages in the published report.

The conclusion which receives the most stress in the report is methodological. Eisner argues vigorously that what is important to individual firms may not be what is important in the aggregate. Changes in sales may influence many firms, but, conceivably, in ways which cancel in the aggregate. A factor such as an increase in the interest rate may be crucial only "at the margin" i.e. for a few firms where other forces are indecisive. Yet, those firms will be influenced in the *same* direction by a general increase in the rate. A "majority vote" is meaningless viewed from the standpoint of a theorist concerned with *marginal* considerations. This point is an important one, and will be further considered in Chapter VI, "Analysis."

Eisner is extremely cautious in what he says about substantive issues concerning the determinants of capital expenditures. Perhaps his most interesting findings concern "calculations," that is, various formal costs and earnings criteria. He found the methods used crude, frequently internally inconsistent, and subject to systematic bias. Fortunately, not all the biases operate in the same direction. These results are especially intriguing in view of the great interest, since Eisner's report, in "systems analysis" and "operations research." These areas involve the application of sophisticated methods of analysis to problems such as those with which he was concerned. If we take this view of his results, we must conclude that Eisner found something for which he was not looking, and underestimated its importance. He experiences considerable difficulty, however, in coming to definite conclusions about the topics he set out to investigate.

A Study of Job-Seeking Behavior: In late August to early October of 1964 a sample of unemployed workers in Erie, Pennsylvania, were interviewed in a project undertaken by Harold L. Sheppard and A. Harvey Belitsky of the W. E. Upjohn Institute for Employment Research. A monograph based on these interviews and ancillary data collection was published in 1966.[7]

The overall objective of the project was stated as follows:

> . . . to spell out in greater detail the widely accepted findings about the job-seeking behavior of unemployed workers and, in particular,

to explore the relationship of social-psychological and other factors, hitherto neglected in manpower studies, to job-seeking behavior.[8]

The study was intended more specifically to ascertain the social-psychological variables that affect "the nature and intensity of an unemployed worker's search for re-employment" and his chances of success. It was not intended to argue the primacy of social-psychological factors. Whether a worker *finds* a job will be "heavily influenced by basic economic processes." But job-*seeking* is open to explanation by social-psychological tendencies.

Three social-psychological measures were investigated—"achievement motivation," "achievement values," and "job-interview anxiety." The effect of each was sought on such measures of job-seeking behavior as how soon a worker starts looking for a new job, and the total number of job-seeking techniques that he uses.

While the above objectives were regarded as central by the investigators, there were a number of secondary objectives which are not easy to summarize concisely. It is fair to say that they amount to an attempt to describe the labor market in one urban area, with emphasis on the market for services of blue-collar male workers. In effect, the explanatory study using the social-psychological predictors was imbedded in a descriptive study.

The monograph is not explicit as to the training and experience represented by the research team, but it is clear that the effort was interdisciplinary and involved personnel with psychological training. They were able to supervise the administration and coding of picture protocols to obtain scores on need for achievement. The project itself, as noted above, was regarded as exploratory, and no preliminary investigations seem to have been undertaken.

The basic sample was a cross-section of workers unemployed at some time during a fifteen-month period, January 1, 1963 to March 31, 1964, in Erie, Pennsylvania. The sampling frame was the file of blue-collar workers who applied for jobs in the Erie office of the Pennsylvania Employment Service. From a cross-section sample drawn from this file certain marginal groups of workers were omitted (those with serious physical handicaps, recent entrants into the labor force, seasonal workers, those living at a distance). The sample designated for interview was a cross-section of the remainder whose names had been selected from the file. There was one round of interviewing, which produced 473 interviews. No attempt was made to follow those who had moved. Since the sample was essentially a simple random sample, no special calculations of sampling errors were needed.

Field work was undertaken by interviewers employed by National Analysts, Inc., of Philadelphia, who visited the workers in their homes. The questionnaire was unusual in that it included measures of the three social-psychological variables noted. Of these, the measures of achievement motivation and achievement values were taken from earlier work by David McClelland and Bernard Rosen. The measure of job-interview anxiety was adopted from measures developed by G. Mandler and S. B. Sarason in studies of the anxiety of students concerning the taking of tests. The questionnaire included some 156 questions including the four pictures and associated questions. No account of special training for the interviewers appears in the monograph.

The analysis consisted essentially in the preparation of tables of percentages without the use of formal multivariate procedures. As predicted, evidence was found of systematic association between achievement motivation and several of the measures of job-seeking behavior. The investigators seem to have expected to find that, since those who have high need for achievement search more diligently, they would be more likely to have found jobs. On this point the evidence for the hypothesis is marginal. Results for the second predictor, achievement values, are broadly similar, but the relationships seem somewhat weaker and are presented in less detail. Job interview anxiety seems to have had limited effects on job-seeking patterns but did have some effect, for example, in slowing the start of the search, and, for young people, in producing greater reliance on the Employment Service. In summary, the attempt to deduce differences in job-seeking behavior from social-psychological theory was reasonably successful.

The results of the descriptive portions of the study are not easily summarized. They included results of 48 interviews with industrial leaders, union officials, and community leaders, as well as results of small studies of Negro males and white-collar women. A considerable quantity of factual information is presented. The authors themselves refer in the final chapter to "the tree-like profusion of facts and statistics that comprise the preceding chapters,"[9] from which they emerge "at last." The difficulty is a common one: it is not easy to develop a description of something as complex as a local labor market in such a manner that the parts of the description form a whole which is well articulated and comprehensible.

A related difficulty is that the policy recommendations are not closely related to solid empirical results. For example, the first recommendation is for an extension of techniques used by McClelland and associates aimed at increasing achievement motivation and values among businessmen in other countries, and of programs of managerial technical assistance in areas of economic retardation in the United States. A similar recommendation is made for improving the job-seeking behavior of workers. Without prejudice to the merits of these policies, it must be said that the reasoning leading up to such recommendations is not carefully developed in this monograph. There is a considerable jump between a finding that need achievement relates to behavior in searching for jobs and the feasibility of a policy of increasing need achievement among workers—and, indeed, the monograph recommends experimental projects. The successful attempt at explanation of job-seeking behavior does not lead automatically to successful predictions or to a well-considered evaluation of probable consequences even if the proposed efforts to induce psychological changes were to succeed.

We turn now to some additional examples where only the unusual or crucial decisions are discussed, not the total design.

Effects of Lump-Sum Settlements on Insured Workers: The initial purpose of this study was to determine the effects of lump sum compensation settlements on the rehabilitation of injured workers.[10] Behind this were two conflicting hypotheses. One was that if an injured worker settles his claim against his employer and cannot count on any more weekly payments or medical care payments, he is more likely to get back to work. The competing hypothesis was that the worker is usually genuinely disabled and has a difficult time living on a weekly payment, so that if he settles for a lump sum settlement, he will merely pay off his back debts with the money, lose his right to decent rehabilitative medical care, and end up on the welfare rolls. An obvious way to discriminate between these two hypotheses is to take a sample of workers who have accepted lump sum settlements and see what happens to them. Workmen's compensation is administered differently in each of fifty states, and fifty separate samples would be impossible. Even in one state, like Michigan, there are several different files: A file of accident reports, a file of people currently being paid weekly benefits, and a file of actual redemption settlements. Clearly a sample of the file of current payments would not do. In the first place it is not a representative sample of accidents because the longer a man stays on weekly payments the more chance he has of being drawn in a sample.

If one samples accident reports one gets a very large number of accidents where very few weekly payments were made, and few where any settlement was ever made. So we took a sample of the actual redemption settlements, and then tried to find some kind of reasonably matched sample of people who stayed on actual weekly payments. Of course, it turns out to be impossible to do this matching cleanly because the kinds of accidents and kinds of people who stay on the weekly payment are different from the ones who settle.

How far back in time should one go to take a sample of settlements? This involves a substantive issue as to how long is required for the event to resolve itself. It would seem that it ought to be a year or so. But the longer one waits, the harder it is to find people, and the less they remember about what happened. We finally selected a sample of settlements about 1-1/2 years prior to interview date. In this particular study, it turned out that people who accepted these settlements were mostly not back to work a year and a half later, not even most of the "bad back" cases. The implication was that the settlements were being secured by people who were desperate for money to pay their bills, whose lawyers wanted to be paid, and where the insurance company was glad to get off the hook of an open-ended commitment. The settlements did not lead to rehabilitation and re-entry into the work force. Unfortunately, the practical results of this study were that the Workmen's Compensation Department simply made it more and more difficult for anybody to get a settlement. But the workers could hardly survive on the weekly payments at the level where they were fixed. It was not until a number of years later that the legislature finally raised the weekly payments so that people could survive on them.

A Study of Medical Insurance and Utilization of Medical Services: What is the effect of medical insurance on the utilization of medical services?[11] Here again there are two opposite hypotheses. One, that without insurance people will get inadequate medical care, and the other, that with insurance, they are over-cared for and stay in the hospital too long and use services they don't really need. Sometimes the hypothesis is that the doctor, knowing the insurance status, prescribes things unnecessarily. Others argue that the patient himself, being conscious of the economics of the matter, has some say about what goes on. Now, how should one design such a study? A major problem is that a very large number of people have little or no medical expense during the year, so that if one started with a simple cross-section sample, a lot of interviews would contribute little or nothing to the variance to be examined. How about a sample of hospital patients? Should one sample admissions, people currently in the hospital, or discharges? If we sample admissions, we have to go back in the past. Some of the people may still be in the hospital and some may be dead. If we sample people (patients) in the hospital, the sampling probabilities are in proportion to how long people stay in the hospital. But suppose we do take a sample of discharges? We still have the problem of the other people who were sick but did not go to the hospital. Furthermore, it is a rather complicated procedure. One would first have to take a sample of hospitals, secure their cooperation, sample their discharges, then look up the addresses and go interview the people. We certainly could not get the detailed hospital information about their illness or the amount of the bill. On the other hand, if we went to the individuals first, we could have them sign a release, and then go to the hospital and get the detailed billing information, provided we want to spend that much time and trouble to get detailed dollar figures from some source other than the respondent.

What was done to make the field interview more efficient was to take a large sample but then go to the door and ask some screening questions. Where the people had very little to report, we took only half or a quarter of those households. Two questions were asked. The first was whether there was anyone over 65 in the house, and the second was whether anyone in the household had been in the hospital in the last year. There is plenty of evidence that the incidence of the need for medical care skyrockets dramatically as people get older, so that people over 65 could be expected to have more to report, more choices to make, and perhaps more variance in their utilization of medical service, part of which might be explained by insurance coverage.

There were some problems with screening about actual hospitalization, however. In the part of the sample where we did no screening, but asked about hospitalization in the middle of a long interview, substantially more hospitalizations got reported than when we used an initial, screening, question. Of course, with any screening or subsampling it was necessary to weight the final data to maintain representativeness. Weights were adjusted so that they also took account of this "over-screening."

To test the hypothesis that the uninsured are using medical services less because they just cannot afford them and are undercared for, we asked people about treatments suggested by doctors they had done nothing about, and about untreated symptoms. (Things that might require going to a doctor but about which people had done nothing.) Of course other variables affect utilization of medical service too, such as differences in need and differences in attitude, so we also had to ask age and sex and whether people thought it was a good idea to go to the hospital or the doctor at the first sign of illness. Even taking into account age, sex, and attitudes, there was a relationship between lack of insurance coverage and reporting of unmet needs or untreated symptoms. Hence, the correlation between insurance and utilization was at least in part the result of inadequate care of the uninsured.

In this particular study we could not trust people's knowledge about what their insurance covered so we asked them the name of the company and the number of the policy. We were able to check a large number of these and make an estimate as to what fraction of a standard package of medical needs would be covered by these particular policies. This allowed us to use a scale variable of how well the person was insured, rather than a dichotomy; insured or not. We also checked some hospital records to see whether people were exaggerating their medical expenses and, of course, some of them were. This kind of validity study is one-sided, because we could only get expenses that people reported, and the hospital did not confirm the bills from doctors, other hospitals, or other hospital visits, which respondents failed to report. There is no way to find out where to look for such information.

Air Travel: How can the predictions of demand for air travel be improved? One approach is to find out why some people travel and some do not. What problems does this approach pose? First, many people *never* travel by air. Hence, in a probability sample of the population, we will have more non-travelers than needed to find out why some people do not fly and not enough of the people who do use air travel. On the other hand, suppose we take a sample of people in airplanes? Then we could get *only* the people who do travel by air, and the probability of selection would be proportional to the *amount* of travel. This is not necessarily bad if we weight the data appropriately. We may want more of the people who do a lot of traveling, particularly if we want to estimate the total demand for air travel, not merely the change in the proportion that do any traveling at all. Two samples could be spliced together: a cross-section sample and a sample of air travelers can be combined and the weights lowered for the people from both groups who do travel by air. The criterion for combining the samples and weighting them may be open to question, of course, because there may be response errors in people's reports.

Now suppose we have drawn some kind of sample. What might be a major reason why some people do not travel by air? Fear? How can we get people to admit they are afraid of flying? Some of them will admit it and maybe a few even exaggerate it, but the real problem is that at least some people will refuse to admit it. Studies designed by Lansing asked: "What might keep some people from traveling by plane?" More people mentioned fear in that situation than would admit they were afraid themselves.[12] There are dangers in these projection techniques, of course. Some people may really be saying literally that they think *other* people are afraid but that they are not. However, many psychologists argue that there is a lot of projection, and that if a man brings up fear in this kind of discussion, the chances are it has at least some relevance to his own situation.

Now, what else could we find out? We could ask some memory questions about when people first started to travel, and why. And we would have to separate pleasure from business travel. We could also find out some things about *where* people have some reason to travel, for example, where their relatives live. We can ask about car ownership, the size of the family, where they live in relation to airports, and the value of their time based on the husband's hourly earnings.

Then we can do some kind of economic analysis of what the actual cost of travel by various modes would be for such a family. We can determine whether some of the differences in travel are based on reasonable economic choices in each situation. We can also find out whether people know certain relevant facts. For instance, do they know what it costs to go by air, what it costs to get to the airport? It is difficult to believe that they are making careful economic calculations if they do not have the facts, or that they would even respond to changed air fares if they do not know what they are.

On the other hand, one must be careful with interpretation of the effects of ignorance because if and when air fares got to the point where they were really competitive, the news might travel very quickly.

A Study of the Decision When to Retire: A study of why people retire when they do has obvious importance in the future supply of labor. A representative cross-section sample contains many people too young to have thought much about retiring. Furthermore, it contains very few of those benefiting from private pension plans (few have qualified yet) or special supplemental early retirement benefits such as those available to auto workers.

A study designed to deal with these problems has been done.[13] It involved two samples: a cross-section sample, and a sample of workers in the automobile and agricultural implement industry 58-61 years old who were eligible for some special supplemental early retirement benefits.

The cross-section sample was in two waves, so that the retirement questions would be combined with other objectives, and those under 30 would not have to be asked about retirement. Those not retired were asked about their plans, how much retirement income they would have, etc. The retired were asked about their past decision to retire, whether they retired early or not, and whether the retirement was unexpected (precipitated by illness, unemployability, etc.). Interesting comparisons were possible between the plans of the first group and the retrospective reports of the second group on what they actually did. For example, the workers expected to do more community work when they retired, but the retired did not report doing more than before retirement.

The sample of UAW workers provided information about a group in a narrow age range and in rather special circumstances. It turned out that their working wages covered a very narrow range, but that the amount they were entitled to if they retired early (and even whether they were entitled to anything) varied widely, depending on how long they had worked for the company.

A screening questionnaire was sent out by mail to the UAW workers, allowing some analysis of who had already retired early, and provided a sample selection for personal interviews later. These interviews focused somewhat more on those who had retired early or planned to.

Later on, a check of the records revealed who had indeed retired early (after the interview), so that an analysis could be made parallel with that of planned early retirement, using actual early retirement as the dependent variable.

The design calls for an additional follow-up, perhaps by telephone, both to secure more data on the actual retirement decision, and to test a hypothesis that the joy of the early retirees will diminish as time goes on, inflation continues, and they reach 65, when, in some cases, their total retirement income will diminish. (The study has, however, already shown that the workers are quite well informed about the system, and about the change in income at 65.) Economic variables proved to dominate in the retirement decision, but perhaps more interesting was the appearance of a nonlinearity, a threshold retirement income (about $4000 a year) below which few planned to retire early (or even voluntarily). The implications for the aggregate labor supply are clear—only when private pensions push people's retirement income up *substantially,* will they cause any large volume of early retirement. It is the number pushed beyond the threshold, not the aggregate, that matters.

Two Study Designs Still on the Drawing Boards

Philanthropy: The following is a design for a study of philanthropy, a study which has not yet been done. Its purpose is to study people's contributions of time *and* money to worthy causes. Do some people contribute time, others money? Will the growth of government welfare systems cause private charity to decline? Does this seem like the kind of subject that could keep a respondent interested for 50 minutes? If someone is giving neither time nor money to anything, he will not have much to report and the interview might be relatively short. On the other hand, the attitudinal material and the background material need to be collected for these people too. Fortunately, a substantial number of people in this country give at least some time and money, if not to organized charity, at least to helping friends and relatives. This study is proposed to build on previous studies which have already collected partial data, one study on contributions of *money* to church, charity, and individuals. The other on *time* devoted to helping others.[14]

Suppose one wanted to define a single dependent variable for this study. First, how would one decide whether it was feasible to combine time and money gifts into a single dependent variable called philanthropic activity? One might want to find out whether the same explanatory variables were operating in roughly the same way to explain contributions of time, and contributions of money. The federal income tax law is neutral in respect to the choice of giving time or money, so long as a man has a possibility of earning more money by working more. He can either work longer, give the money away, and deduct the contribution from his income, for tax purposes, or he can devote the time directly to charity instead of to earning income. If we discovered that the effects of explanatory variables like income on the two kinds of contributions are roughly similar, we could then combine the two kinds of philanthropy into one dependent variable. How would we combine the different units? One is in hours and the other is in dollars. If we believe in marginalism, and if we think that the individual has some choice as to whether he works hard and earns more money on the one hand, or spends more time on charitable work on the other, we could argue that his wage rate measures his marginal time value. If he spends so many hours on charity he must think that the time he spent was worth that much in terms of his contribution. Now this theory does not work if he is under some kind of restraint, e.g., if he can work only 40 hours a week, or if he really does not want to do any more work. On the other hand, you cannot argue that people merely like variety, because this can be specified in the diminishing curve of the marginal utility of leisure, the increasing curve of the marginal disutility of work. One can also argue that the producers' surpluses are ignored by this marginal calculation, but they are ignored in evaluating people's work effort and their paid work too. So we would have, at least, some rough way of converting everything into dollars. What about a housewife? We do not have a dollar value for her time on any simple basis, but we could estimate what women of the same age and education make in the labor market. We can assume that most housewives could work for money (or at least that their skill levels are such that if they did not have children at home to take care of, they could make that much working at a job).

Finally, there is an analysis problem: We may explain philanthropy on the basis of current income, attitudes, and religious identification, of course. But we might want to find how a man's current attitudes depend on some past history, like his parent's beliefs, or religious activity, or philanthropy, his early church experience, and the gradual development of his interest in doing things for other people.

A Study of People's Preferences about Housing and Community: Finally let us look at another, more complex design, which also has not been carried out, but may well be if the concern about urban problems is implemented with research funds.

The purpose of such a study would be to find out, or infer, what people really want in their homes, neighborhoods, and communities. The results would not be used to make policy directly, but would be combined with information from engineers and urban economists, in order to help the elected representatives decide what ought to be done.

How should one go about such a study? We could ask people what they like or do not like about their neighborhood. This runs into a difficulty that is illustrated by the fact that there is a correlation between whether a man likes his neighborhood and whether he likes his wife. Some people just like everything and other people dislike most things. We could ask people who moved recently how they compare the neighborhood they moved to with the one they left, their reasons for moving, and why they were willing to spend more or less for the new place. This is subject to a second difficulty, namely, rationalization and memory error in remembering what the other neighborhood was like. This error can operate in both directions. Some people are nostalgic about an old neighborhood, and have difficulty getting used to a new one. On the other hand, most people tend to justify a decision they have made by remembering all the good things about the place to which they have moved and the bad things about the place they left.

If we remove the restriction of a single survey, we may try to set up a more elaborate design where we (a) interview people about their past and present neighborhoods, and the detailed things they like and do not like about each neighborhood, (b) then return several years later to the same dwelling and talk to the people who live there, (c) if the people have moved, we would also follow those people and interview them in their new dwelling.[15]

This allows several kinds of triangulation on the problem. For those who have not moved but whose neighborhoods have changed, we can find out how they currently see their neighborhood before and after the change, and also how they think back in the second interview on the changes that have taken place. Those who have moved are even more interesting because they can now describe the new neighborhood they are in, and we can compare those ratings with the concurrent ratings made of the old neighborhood. Most of the personality differences between people will thus be neutralized. We can also ask movers to think back about the neighborhood they used to live in as a check on what they told us earlier, and as part of the explanation of why they moved, and as a general methodological check on the kinds of biases one gets in using retrospective data about previous neighborhoods. Other people will have moved into the houses that the first people left, and they can be asked these same retrospective questions about the previous neighborhoods since we now have another group from which we tell what kind of biases exist. Finally, we also have, in the original houses to which new people have moved, both their attitudes about this neighborhood and the attitudes expressed earlier by another set of families who previously lived there. In this way we can develop some information particularly in unchanging neighborhoods about the variety of responses of different people with the same situation.

It might, of course be useful in a study like this to oversample areas where something is likely to happen, or oversample people who are likely to move, because the more neighborhoods change, the more information we would get from the revisits, and the more people move, the more they can tell us about actual decision-making processes and considerations. Scientifically, however, it must be remembered that we may want to compare those who move with those who did not move, since a critical dimension of action is moving or not moving, and it is very dangerous to look only at those who have made a decision one way, namely, to move, ignoring those who made the other decision, namely, not to move.

We may also want to cluster the sample somewhat more heavily, so that we can make better use of the averages of several people's responses in the same neighborhood. The average income, age, mobility, and evaluation of the neighborhood of a small sample of people in a neighborhood provides a set of variables of interest to sociologists as well as economists, and has less variance than the individual data, even though they would be used to help explain individual behavior and attitudes.

Design of Consumer Expenditure Surveys

We have not said much about the design of consumer expenditure surveys, which attempt to secure details about a great array of expenditures. Those who are interested can find a recent summary of the experiments and some suggestions in a monography by Robert Pearl.[16]

Much attention has been given to improving expenditure information by repeated visits, diary-keeping, allocation of part of the items only to subsamples, etc. Revisits at short intervals are proposed to improve the accuracy and get "bounded estimates" that do not bring two Saturdays into one week. Reinterviews at longer intervals are proposed to get better trend data.

Strangely enough, little attention has been given to reducing the respondent's task by doing the classification of expenditures in the central office, asking the respondent only to list how much he spent and on what. It is possible that the classification of expenditures could then be done by computer, the vast cost of getting an interpretative dictionary into the computer being amortized over the repeated expenditure surveys, and justified by the possibility of classifying expenditures in several ways. For instance, expenditure studies currently do not distinguish consumption expenditure from investment expenditure, e.g. the gasoline from the purchase of a car. Both are classified by general purpose, such as transportation, housing, food, etc. One might even want to allocate parts of some expenditures to different purposes, for instance part of the car to transportation and part to recreation. This seems like one of the few places where computer interpretation of words might be functional and economic.

Summary

We have tried in this chapter to say some general things about the designing of studies, and then to make these principles more realistic through a series of examples, some of specific problems and some of whole designs. It is easier to see what is wrong with a study, particularly after completion, than to state in general what good design is. Perhaps the one most important principle of all is that every aspect of a study, and every question asked, should have a clear justification and relation to the purpose of the study. The single most common design mistake is to become too diffuse, trying to cover too much ground and asking too many unnecessary questions. This leads to each topic being inadequately handled. Scientific judgement requires comparison, which means a control group for every behavior studied, and an alternative (opportunity cost) for every preference. The question one must keep asking is "compared with what?"

Finally, since the essence of science is quantification and measurement, the design should allow for some kind of quantification. This may range from the crudest use of dichotomies (dummy variables) through arbitrary scaling and the creation of indexes to elaborate calculation of factor weights. But it makes a difference in designing questions whether one has clearly in mind the necessity for quantified measurement of the theoretical concepts.

Footnotes to Chapter II

1. James Coleman, "The Mathematical Study of Change" in H. M. Blalock, Jr. and B. B. Blalock, *Methodology in Social Research,* McGraw Hill, New York, 1968.

2. See sundry issues of the *Federal Reserve Bulletin,* June 1950-Dec. 1951. See also "Methods of the Survey of Consumer Finances," *Federal Reserve Bulletin* and James N. Morgan," Repeated Surveys of Consumer Finances in the United States," in *Family Living Studies,* International Labour Office, Geneva, 1961, pp. 191-206.

3. *Urban Income and Saving,* National Council of Applied Economic Research, New Delhi, 1962. See also other publications of the N.C.A.E.R., e.g. *All India Rural Household Survey* (3 vols.) 1964; 1965, 1966.

4. *Delhi Saving Survey,* National Council of Applied Economic Research, New Delhi, 1960.

5. Robert Eisner, *Determinants of Capital Expenditure: An Interview Study,* University of Illinois Bulletin, Volume 53, Number 43; February, 1956. Published by the University of Illinois, Urbana.

6. *Ibid.,* p. 14.

7. Harold L. Sheppard and A. Harvey Belitsky, *The Job Hunt,* The John Hopkins Press, Baltimore, Maryland, 1966.

8. *Ibid.,* p. ix.

9. *Ibid.,* p. 211.

10. See J. Morgan, M. Snider, and M. Sobol, *Lump Sum Redemption Settlements and Rehabilitation: A Study of Workmen's Compensation in Michigan,* Survey Research Center, University of Michigan, Ann Arbor, 1954.

11. See Grover Wirick, Robin Barlow, and James Morgan, "Population Survey: Health Care and Its Financing," in McNerney, ed., *Hospital and Medical Economics,* 2 Vols., Hospital Research and Educational Trust, Chicago, 1962, Vol. 1, pp. 61-357.

12. John B. Lansing and Dwight M. Blood, *The Changing Travel Market,* Institute for Social Research, University of Michigan, Ann Arbor, 1964, pp. 83-87.

13. See Richard Barfield and James Morgan, *Early Retirement,* Survey Research Center, University of Michigan, Ann Arbor, 1969.

14. For money given, see J. Morgan, M. David, W. Cohen, and H. Brazer, *Income and Welfare in the U.S.,* McGraw Hill, 1962, and Helen H. Lamale and J. A. Clorety, "City Families As Givers," *Monthly Labor Review,* Dec. 1959, pp. 1303-1311. For time given, see J. Morgan, I. Sirageldin, and N. Baerwaldt,

Productive Americans, Survey Research Center, University of Michigan, Ann Arbor, 1966.

15. Panel designs are also useful when precise measurement of changes (in unemployment for instance) are desired, and then an overlapping panel may be best. For a sophisticated example see: U.S. Bureau of the Census, *The Current Population Survey, A Report on Methodology,* Technical Papers No. 7, U.S. Department of Commerce, Bureau of the Census, Washington, D.C., 1963.

16. Robert B. Pearl, *Methodology of Consumer Expenditure Surveys,* Working Paper 27, U.S. Department of Commerce, Bureau of the Census, Washington, D.C., March, 1968; see also W. F. F. Kemsley and J. L. Nicholson, "Some Experiments in Methods of Conducting Consumer Expenditure Surveys," *Journal of the Royal Statistical Society,* Series A, Vol. 123 (1960), pp. 307-328.

Chapter III

SAMPLING PROBLEMS IN ECONOMIC SURVEYS

There is a well-developed literature on survey sampling. The economist interested in sample surveys can turn to such books as Leslie Kish's *Survey Sampling* for an extensive account of the subject, or to any one of a number of excellent introductory accounts such as that in chapters V-VII of C. A. Moser, *Survey Methods in Social Investigation* or the U.S. Census' *Sampling Lectures.*[1] This chapter is focused, therefore, on certain limited aspects of the sampling problems of special concern to economists. Special attention will be paid to the choices of strategy in designing a survey. In giving formulas we focus on making clear the issues, not on such niceties as small sample corrections or how one estimates population values of variances or frequencies.

Choice of Type of Sampling Procedure

The types of sampling procedure in common use may be grouped into three broad categories: cross-section sample using probability sampling; experimental designs; and non-probability samples using methods of selection based on judgment, quota sampling procedures, and the like. In any proposed study, there is a basic choice to be made among the three.

Cross-section surveys using probability samples: The standard procedure in economic surveys is probability sampling. The crucial characteristic of probability sampling is that it is based on a method of selection designed so that every member of a specified population has a known non-zero chance of falling into the sample. The theory is simple, but in practice, dealing with real sampling problems in an efficient way requires great skill.

In probability sampling one does not usually select elements directly but makes use of a sampling frame, that is, a list of the elements in the population to be studied. The practical problems involved in the selection and use of a sampling frame will be considered below.

The population specified may be broad, e.g., all families in a nation; or it may be narrow, e.g., all families in a certain city who purchased a house in a specified period, or all establishments in a certain type of manufacturing industry employing over a minimum number of persons.

The unit or element sampled may be dwellings, families, transactions, automobiles, etc., and it is crucial that attention be paid to the relation between this unit and the unit of analysis. If one samples car purchases, one can analyze families purchasing cars, but must remember that some families may have to be counted more than once if they bought more than one car. If one samples dwellings and then selects only one adult in each dwelling, the result is only a representative sample of *adults* if one weights each respondent by the inverse of the number of adults in his dwelling to allow for differences in the final probability of selection.

The surveys discussed in Chapter II are all cross-section surveys using probability sampling except for the pilot study by Eisner and the UAW part of the retirement study. We return to the details of probability sampling later. The remainder of the chapter is concerned with ways of developing and using this type of sample design.

For projects whose basic purpose is unbiased estimates of facts or relationships, the usefulness of probability cross-section sampling does not need elaboration. A sample from a given population with suitable data collection procedures will provide a miniature representation of the population, which can be manipulated to provide a great variety of information about the whole population.

When the purpose of a project is explanation, limitations of cross-section samples may become more important. Isolation of the effects of variables may prove difficult. Either independent variables or dependent variables may be distributed in a way that is not optimal for analysis. Experimental designs deserve consideration here.

Experimental Designs: An "experimental design" for a survey involves a sampling procedure which does not represent the full population. Such designs fall into two broad groups, truncated cross-sections and experiments with randomized treatments.

Truncated Cross-Sections: A cross-section sample is selected as a first step; in a second step, a probability of zero is assigned to certain elements in the sample. These sampling procedures may be classified according to the basis on which elements are excluded. Information may be available from the sampling frame either concerning the dependent variable in a study, or concerning an explanatory variable, or both. The truncation can also be done in the field, using screening equations at the time of the interview.

Experiments with Randomized Treatments: An experiment may consist in the assignment of "treatments" to members of a specified population or subpopulation, the "treatments" being assigned to individuals by a method which involves randomization. There are a limited number of possibilities for the use of these methods in economics. It may be noted that it is sometimes possible to apply randomized treatments to individuals selected from a cross-section; such projects will be considered along with others involving randomised treatments.

In some cases, the knowledge of the values of the principal *dependent* variable in a project is available for individuals in advance, and is used to exclude part of the population from the sample. An example of such a situation arose when a study of long-distance telephone calls was undertaken for a telephone company. The records of the telephone company included information on the frequency and cost of the trunk calls made by each subscriber in a certain period. This information was used in the selection of the sample. The distribution of all telephone subscribers by expenditure for long-distance calls is J-shaped. Many subscribers make no such calls in a period of a few months. A considerable number of subscribers make a few calls.

The procedure adopted was to interview only the extreme groups. Equal numbers were selected of frequent users, that is those whose spending was K or more, and non-users. The analysis consisted essentially in the comparison of these groups. In effect, the study was designed to answer the question, what variables distinguish frequent users from non-users?

This type of design has advantages. A simple random sample would have yielded very few frequent callers. The design used solved this problem by minimizing the sampling error of comparisons between the selected groups for a given number of interviews by making the groups equal in size.[2] This method selects groups which are known to be very different in behavior, and, hence, makes it probable that large differences will be found in the values of the explanatory variables between the groups. The sensitivity of the design is much greater than it would be if the groups were more similar in purchasing behavior.

This type of procedure also has limitations. Nothing can be said about the intermediate group except by inference from what is learned about the extreme groups. Also, behavior in a limited time period may not be typical. The underlying situation *may* be one in which certain people are persistently at the extremes of the distribution. Then the stable characteristics of those people which drive them to the extremes can be examined. But the true situation may be one in which every individual is as likely as any other individual to be found at any given place on the continuum. Events may lead anyone to make several long-distance calls. That is, people may do their long-distance calling in "spurts," say, when a young couple has its first child. Then the search for stable characteristics of people which predict their behavior will fail, and research can at best reveal the circumstances which produce frequent calling. If both models operate, each for part of the population, the length of the time period considered will be a matter of importance in distinguishing the two types of callers.

The importance of the length of the period may be illustrated by a hypothetical example. Suppose that it is desired to study the factors which lead some people to spend a great deal on cars and others to spend much less. A sample of those who bought new cars in any given month would include some people who buy new cars frequently and some for whom buying a new car is a rare event.

Only the former might be of interest for the project. A dramatic example from another field was a study of marriage announcements in the *New York Times.* The authors selected the month of June, and took that month each year for ten years. Finding disproportionately few Jewish names in the announcements, they concluded that the Times was anti-semitic or else Jews had low social status.[3] A critic pointed out that June comes between two important religious holidays in the Jewish calendar and that few orthodox Jews would consider getting married in June. Spreading the sample over ten years had not helped at all.[4]

The second type of situation is one in which a measure of one or more *independent* variables is available in advance. For example, a measure of family income may be available. It may be advantageous to use this information in selecting the sample by varying the probability of selection of individuals at different income levels. Variable sampling fractions are considered below. An extreme type of objective is to set aside the study of a cross-section of the population and consider only the objective of measuring the effect of income on some dependent variable (or variables).

Gains in statistical efficiency will result from selecting individuals who differ widely in their score on the predictor provided that the relation between the predictor and the predicted variable is monotonically increasing or decreasing. Consider the case of a linear relationship. The more widely separated the scores on the predictor, the smaller the sample that will be required to establish the existence of a relationship.

Suppose, however, that the problem is to estimate the *shape* of the relationship between the predictor in question and a dependent variable, and that nothing can be assumed about the relationship. The best procedure then would be to specify the range of the independent variable and select the sample so as to provide observations which are evenly spaced over that range. For example, there might be K interviews in each thousand dollar interval of income up to some level of income. (It would also be necessary to specify such a maximum level of income owing to the small number of families in the population at very high income levels and their inaccessibility to interviewers.) The range of greatest interest might well be above the range where most observations would be found in a straight cross-section. Incomes are rising in most parts of the world, and there is interest in studying the economic behavior of those now at the income levels which will contain the bulk of the population in the future.

This procedure, however, would be optimal only if the investigators were satisfied that the predictor as measured, e.g. income, was the variable of crucial concern, and that the effect of this variable could be considered without regard to the effects of other dependent variables or to the proportion of the population represented in each interval. In practice, the contrary is often the case.

A theoretically optimal design for some purposes is known as factorial design. Here, several predictors are taken into account, with equal numbers of observations for subgroups specified in several dimensions. For example, one would like to have an equal number of interviews from each of these populations, and within each of them an even distribution over the range of incomes. Practical considerations of the lack of availability of information prior to sample selection have tended to inhibit the development of designs of this type. Even where such prior information seems to be available, it frequently turns out to be of low quality, or to cover only *part* of the population. However, the possibility should not be ruled out. For example, when a two-stage inquiry is undertaken, it may be possible to use the first stage to select for the second stage subgroups defined on almost any desired basis. Such data form a kind of pseudo-factorial design which can be analyzed as such, provided there is not some other variable influencing which subgroup the individual is in.

There is a special class of independent variables which can be defined in geographic terms. That is, it may be possible to identify locations across which the variables of interest vary systematically. These situations lend themselves easily to experimental designs. For example, if one is interested in the effects of climate, he can select areas to represent the range of climates which are important to him. Or, there may be interest in the location of homes within a metropolitan area as a predictor, say, of the use of certain recreation facilities. Samples of homes at different distances from a facility could be used to study the effect of distance on use.

There is an interesting class of truncated cross-section designs in which information is available both about a dependent variable and one or more predictors. The information might come, for example, from a preliminary sample survey conducted on a large scale but with a limited number of questions. Then it may be possible to carry out a preliminary analysis of the relation between one or more predictors and the dependent variable. For example, in the study of long-distance telephone calls, if data had been available, a curve might have been fitted to estimate the relationship between family income and frequency of calling. Then the two groups selected for special study might have been those who made either a very large number of calls or a very small number *for their income group.* Those in the lowest income groups might even have been excluded from the study altogether. In principle, the method of selection could be based on a highly multivariate analysis, not just one predictor. All that is required is that the analysis yield a predicted score for each individual which can be compared with an actual observation on some dependent variable, making possible the selection of individuals with large positive and large negative deviations from predicted scores.

This hybrid design avoids a basic limitation of designs based only on the dependent variable. In a great many studies in economics one or two independent variables are obviously important. Income is a crucial variable in practically all studies of consumer behavior. An investigator is likely to find himself solemnly concluding that the major difference between those who spend a great deal on commodity X and those who spend very little is that the former have more income than the latter. Of course, the effect of income can be taken into account statistically in the analysis, but it would be more efficient if this effect could be taken into account in the design. In general, one would like to consider in the experimental design what is known about the effects of the predictors already studied.

A third type of experimental design is one which conforms to more familiar ideas about what constitutes an experiment. The essence is assignment of "treatments" to members of the population on a random basis. It is this type of experiment which is the subject, for example, of R. A. Fisher's classic, *The Design of Experiments*.[5] Experiments with randomized application of treatments are unusual in economic surveys but they are by no means unknown. The greatest number of examples of their use is in methodological studies. For example, a sample may be selected, and different methods of data collection may be used on a random basis. It can then be observed whether the results differ. Methodological studies of data collection will be considered in Chapter IV.

Experimental manipulations to investigate the effects of altering variables are sometimes undertaken, especially by business enterprises. The most interesting experiments are those concerned with the effects of variations in price. Two types of situations may be distinguished, those in which the commodity to be priced is new, and those in which it is already on the market.

If the commodity is new, the seller has the advantage that he has complete control over the supply. He may then introduce it at different prices in different markets, and observe the difference in his total revenue. The problem of designing the experiment becomes one of selecting areas of similar market potential, and weighing the extra information to be gained against the extra cost of including more areas and extending the study over a longer period. It is entirely possible, for example, that price is more important in repeat sales than for initial sales.

For a commodity already on the market, the problems are different. The effect of a change in its price on total spending for a given commodity may be thought of as a problem in estimating the substitution which will take place as the price is varied. Some substitutions may take place during an experimental manipulation, however, which would not occur if an actual price change occurred. The experiment will succeed in its purpose only if the manipulation can be prevented from producing such effects.

Substitution among competing firms will take place if one firm varies its price experimentally while its competitors do not. It may be expected that an actual price change would be met by changes in competitors' prices. In studying the effect of changing the price of a *commodity,* some method must be found of varying the price charged across the entire market. Perhaps all sellers will cooperate. Perhaps a market can be found in which one seller has a monopoly. In any case, a survey to find out what the customers are thinking would provide useful auxiliary information.

If the experimental manipulation is believed by the customers to be temporary, they may shift their purchases over time. A large cut in price, for example, may lead people to buy in advance of needs. It may be necessary to maintain the experimental price for some time in order to estimate more normal, long-run sales at the lower price.

How long a time is a difficult question. It is entirely possible that the response to a major price change may be slow. It may take time, for example, for people to increase consumption of a food when its price falls secularly. (Housewives may have to learn new recipes and/or convert conservative husbands.) There may be a "ratchet" effect on consumption. In the market for air travel there is evidence that, once people begin to fly, they are likely to continue. It may take time before such effects take place with any commodity.

There remains the special problem of how a change in price is to be brought to the attention of the customers. With a price increase, the information will be passed on more or less automatically at the point of sale. With a price cut, it is not clear how the new price may be brought to the attention of potential buyers. If an entire geographic area is to be involved, the advertising media may be used. If only a selected group of people are to be offered the reduced prices, special procedures may be needed. It will be important to design those procedures so as to convey the information without confounding the experiment by adding unusual selling procedures. For example, a personal visit to a potential customer may sell a commodity even without a price cut. If visits seem needed, perhaps a control group of customers can be used who receive a visit but are not offered a price reduction. This allows a measurement of the effects of price reductions, but not of the effects of visits.

Such experimental manipulations may be accompanied by special sample surveys with limited objectives. This is discussed in Chapter IV, "Surveys as Part of an Experimental Design." A probable objective is to study the processes of substitution among commodities in detail. For example, a fare cut may be followed by a survey of the customers of a transit company to determine if any increase in travel comes from people who used to drive themselves, from people who were members of car pools, or from people who formerly walked to work, and how much from an increase in total travel. It might also be desired to compare the income level of the users before and after the fare cut. What is the economic level of the new users? If a cut in fare leads to losses for a publicly owned or subsidized company, the economic level of both the new and old customers would be matters of interest.

Such factorial designs allow an elegant statistical analysis which tests not only for main effects of each of the classifying variables but also for each of the interaction effects. For instance, X1 may alter the effect of X2 on Y. With more than two classifying characteristics, one gets higher order interaction effects. The tendency of economists to focus on multiple regression for its efficiency and economy has tended to make us eager to assume additivity of the separate effects (no interaction effects), or at least a specific few that could be introduced explicitly. In fact, the real world seems to be full of interaction effects. The classic illustration of this is, of course, the search for the best unbiased estimate of the marginal propensity to consume, a foolish quest if there are indeed several different income elasticities depending on the values of other variables.

There remains an important problem with factorial designs. They give equal importance to each subgroup (possible combination of the explanatory classes), even though they may have widely differing size and importance in the population. Indeed, one rapidly comes to combinations which should not exist except for errors.

Furthermore, while statistical convenience might dictate equal-sized groups, economic considerations may not. In the case of experiments with the "negative income tax," the high cost of the experimental income subsidies led the analysts to decide that the control group should be much larger than the experimental groups, since it provided so much more information per dollar.

Finally, experimental designs focus on hypothesis testing, on significance, rather than importance. If one is primarily concerned with what will account for the real world variations in some behavior, or other dependent variable, then the only reason for disproportionate representation of any subgroup would be that it reflects forces which do not affect cross-section differences so much as aggregate changes over time (because the changes in that variable tend to be in the same direction for many people, and do not cancel out).

The considerations which may be involved in the decision whether to use an experimental design, then, include the following:

(1) The distribution of population on the dependent variable. (Is it J-shaped?)
(2) The distributions of the population on the independent variables.
(3) Measurement problems (for all variables).
(4) The variation over time of values of the dependent variable for any individual.
(5) The same, for independent variables.
(6) The problem of taking into account known relationships.
(7) The availability of sample frames allowing such selection for the experiment.

(8) The likelihood of uncontrollable events that would confound the whole experiment.

(9) Confidence that the manipulated variables are the ones that matter, i.e., tend to produce aggregate changes, by affecting many people in the same way.

(10) The need to manipulate in order to assure that x varies, or varies in a manner uncorrelated with other factors affecting y.

Judgment Samples and Quota Samples: There are many methods for selecting samples based on judgment or quota sampling procedures. It is easiest to define these methods negatively: they are *not* based on mechanical selection from a frame. Elements of personal choice, usually the choice of the interviewer, enter the process of selection. It is rarely claimed that these methods of selection lead to superior quality in terms of information per interview taken. They do seem to yield more information per dollar spent on data collection. As a result of the element of personal choice in the selection procedure, there is an inherent tendency to ambiguity and uncertainty as to exactly what is done.[6] Hence, there is uncertainty as to the merits of the claim of more information per dollar. It would take a good deal of trouble and expense to prove the claim to be false in a specific situation, and the job must be repeated for other specific procedures and specific objectives.

The usual procedure in quota sampling is to estimate, primarily from census data, the number of individuals in each of a set of subclasses of the population. These subgroups may be specified using such controls as geographic area, age, sex, race, and economic level. Interviewers are then assigned to quotas of interviews designed to produce a total sample which will match the population with regard to the control variables. One might think of discarding interviews afterward, or weighting to achieve quota distributions, but this would increase costs per unit of information and eliminate most of the economies.

Only those variables which are manageable from the interviewers' point of view are usable as controls. It must be possible for an interviewer to assign people quickly and with reasonable accuracy to the categories specified. Classification of potential respondents by economic level presents greater problems to an interviewer than classification by age, sex, race, or geographic area.

There are three difficulties with procedures of this type, which may be indicated briefly. First, the method may be biased. The quotas themselves may be wrong, and within quotas the interviewer is free to select the respondents. There is a tendency to select those most easily available, and they may differ systematically from those who are harder to locate. For the probable nature of the bias, see the comparison in Chapter IV of interviews taken on first call with those taken on second and higher order calls on probability samples. Second, the method may lead to an underestimate of the variability in the population.

Interviewers tend to select, within quotas, people who are similar to each other. For example, the number in the "low" economic status group may be correct, but there may be too few people with very low economic status. Excessive clustering may lead to larger variance between clusters and, hence, to a lower effective sample size. Third, it may be difficult to estimate correctly the variance of the sample estimates. It is possible, however; Moser and Stuart did so and concluded that one could not count on higher precision, even per dollar.[7] Such estimates are not usually made because procedures of this general type are often used in very small and informal studies, especially in pretests. When no statistical presentation is planned and it is desired only to try out a procedure, it may be useful to make a systematic effort to cover a broad range of situations with a few interviews. The pilot study by Eisner involved such a sample, with the 14 studies of companies distributed by industry. Also, in trying out a questionnaire, a special effort may be made to locate people of very different characteristics with different experiences to make sure that the questions fit the full range of situations. As will be discussed in Chapter IV, a common error in questionnaire design is to develop question sequences which fit most people—but not everybody.

When it is the purpose of a study to estimate such statistics as measures of central tendency and percentages which apply to a population, there is a presumption against methods of sample selection which may be seriously biased. A more difficult question, for the economist, is whether to analyze data already collected from a study which used quota sampling. Essentially the same question arises when an investigator must decide whether to take seriously results reported by others based on such a sample.

Bias in a selection procedure does not necessarily lead to bias in the estimation of a relationship. Suppose, for example, that a selection procedure is biased in such a way that the samples contain too few peoples at the top and too few at the bottom of the income distribution. It may still be possible to use the data to estimate the relation between income and, say, expenditure on commodities. The relative lack of data at the extremes will not in itself distort the estimated relationship in the range where the number of observations is adequate.

It may be that the relation between income and owning commodity X varies depending on the value of some third variable, Z. With Z present, the slope may be steep; with Z absent, it may be flat. The line fitted may be an average relationship. Then the estimated equation will vary depending on the distribution of Z in the sample. For example, the relation between income and travel for married couples aged 20-24 may be different depending on whether they have young children. Those without children may travel frequently or not depending on their income. Those with children may make one trip a year to visit the grandparents regardless of income.

It is possible for the sample estimate of the average income effect to be biased if there is a tendency to underrepresent those for whom Z = 1. For example, in the extreme, the interviewers might fill their quota for young couples entirely from those with children, for whom Z = 1. The average amount spent on X, however, might be estimated correctly. *In general there will be a bias in the estimate of the relationship between a predictor and a predicted variable if (1) there is an interaction between the predictor's influence and a conditioning variable, and (2) the sampling procedure is biased with regard to the conditioning variable.*

To demonstrate that there is a *risk* of bias is by no means the same as to demonstrate that there is in *fact* a bias in the estimate of relationship. In any particular problem it may be possible to test for a suspected bias. What is required is that all relevant variables be measured—in our example, income, X, and Z—and that a search for interactions be made. In the absence of measures of Z, it may be possible to test for bias by repeating the analysis for interviews obtained on different calls, for example, on first and second call—assuming at least two calls were made. If the relation estimated is not the same, the conclusions which can be drawn about the population must be carefully considered.

It should be noted that the above discussion concerns only the possibility of bias in the estimate of relationships. There is little doubt that the sampling errors of complex statistics will be much larger when the statistics are based on a sample of this type than the sampling errors of estimates based on a well-designed probability sample with an equal number of interviews. This statement seems justified even though to the best of the authors' knowledge no estimates have ever been made of the sampling errors of complex statistics based on quota samples using methods which take into account the actual nature of the sample design. The greater variance per element found by Moser and Stuart may be expected to lead to this result.

There is one final use of judgment or quota samples which deserves mention. There may be in existence no feasible method of sampling some special populations. Frequently an ingenious investigator can devise a scheme for selecting a probability sample. Yet, if he cannot, he may be better advised to use a judgment sample than to leave out the sub-groups entirely. The judgment sample may at least permit a preliminary assessment of the magnitude of the bias resulting from omitting the subgroup. For example, area probability samples ordinarily omit those with no permanent dwelling, such as migrant workers in the United States or sidewalk dwellers in India. In a study of extreme poverty, a poor sample of such groups might be better than no sample at all.

Summary of Quota Samples

Quota samples can mean anything from almost no instruction to interviewers to very highly structured directions that can get almost to the point where they are as good as probability samples, except that then they may cost more. The basic element is that they allow the interviewer some freedom in selecting the respondent. The more freedom the interviewer has, the more likely she might be able to cut costs, but the more likely also she is to introduce a bias and even higher variability. The difficulty in comparing quota samples and probability samples, is of course that there is no easy method of estimating the precision of a quota sample. The Moser-Stuart study compared paired interviewers and discovered that the between-interviewer variance was so high for quota samples that it cast doubt on the existence of any savings from the quota samples in terms of information per dollar. Quota samples are not the same thing as screening. One can take a probability sample, eliminate by some screening device those of less interest, and produce a probability sample of the selected subpopulation. It will have all the good characteristics of any other probability sample, so long as the screening operation works.

There may be times when it pays to take a little bit of sampling bias rather than very high costs, but this should be a conscious decision. If one decides not to take some cases because of their high cost, it is still important to a few of them to find out how much bias there is, even though it is costly and gives only an estimate of the bias with a fairly small number of degrees of freedom. For instance, one might eliminate ten interviews in scattered rural places. But, if one actually spent the money to go out and interview these people, one would have an estimate of bias based on ten cases.

If the quotas do not come out right, or there are other controls that cannot be used in the field, it is always possible to discard some interviews to improve the balance (reduce the bias). Even more efficient, one can weight the interviews. This assumes, of course, that the people who are interviewed, say at the ends of the income distribution are like (representative of) those high- and low-income families who were not interviewed. A difficulty from the reader's point of view is that if a quota sample is weighted properly, the overall distributions on most of the main explanatory variables will look correct, even though substantial biases may exist.

The use of weights allows a quota sample user to relax the rules for interviewers, since if they do not get exactly the right combinations, the weighting "makes up for it." But of course the efficiency per dollar spent falls if the interviewers get many interviews with the easy middle class groups, interviews which have to be weighted down, and hence add less to the precision of the final estimate.

Partly Probability Samples

It is tempting to compromise—to select a basic sample by probability methods, but leave some discretion in the field. This is usually a mistake; biases in the field selection undo all the good of the original sample.

It is not often that the biases become apparent. One dramatic case occurred in a rural development survey in an East African country. A probability sample of small rural areas was drawn, and interviewers instructed to interview the farmer on every second farm in each area. Three years later, another set of interviewers was sent back with the same instructions, so that data would reflect changes over the three years. Casual reports from the second interviewers indicated that about two-thirds of the interviews were reinterviews. (Half should have been by pure chance.) There were both "experimental areas" and "control areas," but in both, dramatic "changes" appeared:

	Experimental Areas		Control Areas	
	1965	1968	1965	1968
Percent who:				
Were 45 or older	51	40	69	49
Had 2 or more wives	44	26	42	28
Were literate	39	55	47	54
Utilized mass media (5 or more on a scale)	21	42	22	48
Had fields at least partly divided	47	68	43	63

While the peasants might have divided their fields in the three-year period, and even started utilizing mass media, it is doubtful that they would become literate, drop their extra wives, or get younger.

When it was learned that the 1965 interviews were taken by civil servants, and the 1968 interviews by university students on vacation, the possibility that each group of interviewers selected respondents closer to their own age and degree of modernity seems likely. The biased selection might have been of the farms, or of whom to talk to on each farm selected. The report does not state whether the students knew which were the experimental areas where changes were supposed to have taken place. However, problems of bias in the substantive findings would also arise even if one merely compared the changes in experimental areas with those in control areas, hoping that the respondent-selection bias would operate evenly everywhere.

The obvious way of avoiding the sampling difficulty would have been to take smaller grids, and instruct the interviewers to interview the senior farmer on *every* farm, defining senior in some way, such as closest to age 60.

Clearly there is no point in elaborate sampling unless it carries through to the final unit, and a substantial proportion of those units are interviewed.

Avoiding biases when interviewers know which is the experimental group is much more difficult. Even if they are not told, and if groups fall into geographic areas, the clever interviewers will soon figure out which area is which. Or they may even find out from the early replies in the interview. Here the best one can hope for is that interviewers ask questions as they are written and write down answers as they are given. An experimental researcher might want to mislead subsets of the interviewers in opposite directions as to the hypotheses to see what biases would creep in! This would require randomizing the assignment of respondents to interviewers, always a difficult and expensive process. Or one might want to put the interviewers' notions into the analysis as part of the set of explanatory variables, hoping to remove the unwanted variation arising from that source.

Ratio Estimates

Estimates of means, aggregates, or proportions from a sample, whether a strict probability sample or not, can always be improved (given smaller sampling variance) by using subgroup estimates of the variable in question, weighted by outside estimates of the proportion of the population represented by that subgroup. Sample variability in the second of these is thus eliminated. There are various methods available to estimate aggregate income. These range all the way from multiplying the sample average income per family times the census estimate of the number of families (plus unrelated individuals in their terminology), to the use of many small sub-groups defined on several variables, weighted by outside estimates of their importance in the population. Of course, as one goes from simple to complex, it becomes more difficult to find outside estimates of population proportions, and they may be less reliable or less up-to-date. As a result, the sampling stability of the subgroup estimates from the survey also falls. There is a long debate in the literature about "ratio estimating bias" which seems to have ended with the discovery that there may actually be such a bias but that it will usually be so small that it may be ignored.

Sampling Frames and the Coverage Problem in Economic Surveys

Since the process of selection of a probability sample requires the use of a sampling frame, the characteristics of the frame and the methods adopted to remedy any deficiencies in it are matters of fundamental importance. The subject is especially important because weaknesses in a frame may pass unnoticed unless an explicit effort is made to locate and correct them.

There are two general types of sampling frames. The first type consists of actual lists of the elements to be sampled. For example: in Great Britain the adult population is listed in an electoral register; in Michigan the office of the Secretary of State maintains a file of vehicles registered in the state; a trade association will have a list of its members. The second type of frame does not involve a list of the elements to be selected but provides a systematic description of some intervening set of elements so that it is possible to associate the elements in the population to be sampled with the elements in the intervening set. The most important example is population sampling for which the frame is a set of locations on maps.

A perfect sampling frame of the first type would comprise a complete list of all elements in the population to be sampled. Each element would appear on the list once and only once. Nothing else would be included in the list. In addition, a sampling frame may include information directly useful in analysis about the characteristics of each of the elements, or it may include information useful for purposes of stratification but not for analysis. For example, the list of members of a trade association may include information on the total number of employees of each member. Or, a list of cars registered in a state may give make and year model, weight, and even the amount of any lien on the car.

A perfect sampling frame of the second type would be so constructed that the identification of elements from the intervening set with elements in the population under study was exact. Each element in the population would be identified with one and only one of the intervening elements. Each intervening element would be identified with one and only one of the elements in the population. None of the elements of the intervening set would be identified with anything else.

By preference, the task of associating elements in the two sets would be one which could be carried out easily and economically (by preference at zero cost) and without error. For example, it would be ideal to proceed from a set of selections based on maps to a set of families to be interviewed without ambiguity or risk of human error. The real world is not ideal, and investigators must concern themselves with how to locate weaknesses in sampling frames and with methods of remedying weaknesses and controlling errors in procedures.

Lists and Files as Sample Frames: There are three basic types of problems with list samples, each of which will be considered briefly.

(1) *Missing elements:* To check on whether there is a problem of missing elements, it may be necessary to investigate carefully the nature of a list and to ask, how do people get on the list? Under what circumstances might someone be

left off the list? How is the list kept up-to-date? The essential question is, does the list in fact represent all elements in the population which is to be studied?

Auto accident reports may be missing, and particularly so in areas where police are known to give a ticket to one or both drivers (for not having their car under control), or particularly at night when the police are busy on other things like catching thieves. Or those under litigation or prosecution may be temporarily out of the files.

If so, it will be necessary to judge whether the missing elements are numerous and whether they have special properties of such importance that a special supplemental sample should be selected. Some lists, of course, are obviously incomplete; for example, the list of telephone subscribers in any city will not be a list of all families. The usefulness of an incomplete list depends on the degree of incompleteness and on what methods can be devised to sample the population not included in the list.

(2) *Foreign elements:* There is usually no problem in identifying foreign elements selected from a list if the survey is one which uses personal interviews. For example, the interviewer can tell well enough that the address to which she has been sent is that of a dwelling recently destroyed by fire. There will be some marginal cases—is this building a seasonal residence now closed for the winter or will the people be back in a few hours? But usually she can tell. The difficulty is the trouble and expense involved in making the check. When the data collection does not involve personal interviews there may be some margin of uncertainty as to who replied, whether there were other units at the same address, and whether some of the non-response was really non-sample.

The correct procedure to allow for foreign elements is to select a large enough initial sample so that the foreign elements can be rejected and the desired number of interviews still obtained. It sometimes happens that inexperienced investigators substitute the next valid item on a list for the foreign element. This procedure will produce a bias and should never be used. To understand why there is a bias, consider what this procedure would do to the chances of selection of the one year-round dwelling in a group of summer cottages if all the cottages appeared on the list just ahead of the year-round dwelling. The next valid entry would be the year-round dwelling if *any* of the cottages were selected.

(3) *Duplicate listings:* A list may be so constituted that the same element appears more than once. For example, it may be desired to select a sample of auto owners from a file in which each owner appears once for each car that he owns. This type of duplication usually is obvious from the way the file was constructed.

There are two possible treatments. First, it may be possible to correct the file. A new file might be prepared based on the "first" car only. Similarly if "first" cars are somehow designated in the file, it may be possible to proceed as if the file had been corrected without physically correcting it. Second, it may be possible to select from the uncorrected file, but compensate for the unequal probability of selection by using the inverse of that probability as a weight. Those who own two cars will be given a weight of .5 in the final tabulations while those with one car are given a weight of 1.0. There would be twice as many two-car owners selected as there "should" be, compared to one-car owners, but the weight would lead to a correct estimate of such statistics as the proportion of two-car owners in the population. Facing this problem in advance would remind the investigator to ask respondents how many cars they owned.

An example of an ingenious system for solving a massive problem of multiple listings was one developed for a study of owners of record of common stock. The same person, of course, may own shares in many companies or be listed more than once on the company's lists. Yet, it was desired to develop a sample of owners of stock. The "Alph-Seg" method of detecting duplication was based on defining narrow ranges of letters of the alphabet and selecting people from each list with names in the ranges. Within ranges the problem of checking for duplication was manageable. This example illustrates a general technique: in correcting or checking a frame it may not be necessary to work with the complete frame. It may be feasible to develop a procedure for selecting part of the frame to be checked or corrected. If the frame to be checked is very large or if the process of correction is expensive, in cost per element checked, the economy of effort from this approach may be important.

Projects based on samples from lists or files may rely on the data in the files for purposes of analysis, as noted above. The completeness and accuracy of the data in the file then become matters of vital concern. It is not unusual for analysts to be disappointed in this respect. The people responsible for the creation and maintenance of a set of files are the usual sources of information about the files. They may be expected to have a natural tendency to think well of their files. It is also possible that the files are well adapted to their purposes but less well adapted to the purposes of an investigator. A methodological study by Ferber involving use of the files of a local credit bureau may illustrate how a set of files can fall somewhat short of expectations.[9]

A second type of problem concerns, not the data in the file, but the manner in which individuals are selected for inclusion in the file. It may appear that a file is reasonably representative of a broad population, but it may turn out that a hidden process of selection is at work. This problem may be illustrated by a methodological study of car debt in Chicago. It was thought that the people with evidence of debt listed in the file of chattel mortgages in Cook County would be reasonably representative of the larger population who buy cars on credit. It developed that the file contained primarily people who had bought on credit and later refinanced their debt, a highly selected sub-population.[10] The list was accurate enough, but much less satisfactory for the purposes of the project than had at first appeared. The limitation could have been foreseen only if the preliminary work on the project had included a more careful check on the nature of the population represented in the file.

Geographic Areas as Frames: Maps of geographic areas as a frame is a widely used approach to probability sampling in the absence of lists of the elements in the population to be sampled. If, as is usual, the sample is selected in two or more stages, the selection of the first stage may proceed without maps if a list of the elements is available for that stage. For example, one can select counties in the U.S. from a list of counties, or, in an underdeveloped country, there may be a list of villages or districts. After completion of the first stage (or stages) of selection it may be possible and not prohibitively expensive to obtain detailed maps or aerial photographs of the selected areas. Thus, detailed maps will be required of the selected counties, not of all counties. This approach to the development of a frame may be attractive compared to any available alternative. Indeed, there may be no practicable alternative.

The most serious potential departure from the ideal described above for this type of frame is that coverage may be incomplete. That is, the practical method of proceeding from the selections on maps to the individual elements in the sample may be such that some elements properly in the sample are missed. For example, if it is a sample of dwelling units, some dwelling units may be missed. It is also possible, if a dwelling unit contains two or more families, for one of them to be missed.

The fact that some dwelling units are missed is not a cause for great concern if the missed units closely resemble the units that are not missed. Unfortunately, the contrary is virtually certain. For example, an interviewer may be sent to a block in a city and instructed to prepare a list of all dwelling units in the block. She can hardly miss single family homes located on large lots which are complete at the time she prepares the list. She may miss small apartments tucked away in unlikely places, in the basement or attic of an old home, or the second floor of a commercial structure. There are likely to be systematic differences in the economic status between people living in the missed dwellings and people living in dwellings which are counted.

A serious problem of this type existed in the Survey of Consumer Finances for several years.[11] A procedure which was theoretically quite correct and should have worked still ended with fewer dwellings than would have been expected. The product of the inverse of the fraction of the areas taken (sampling fraction) and the number of dwellings found in the sample was less than the census estimates of the number of occupied dwellings. By adding some further procedures, largely involving the use of city directories and other listings in a seemingly duplicate operation, the end result was a substantial closing of the gap. One difficulty was that a theoretically adequate procedure of checking to the right of each address for any new construction between it and the next listed sample address— the half-open-interval technique—was not always correctly executed in practice.

The lesson is that some redundancy may be useful, particularly where procedures have to be carried out by many people far from the central office.

In view of the possibility of serious bias from imperfect coverage, it is important to check for this problem especially in any survey based on a geographic frame. There are two methods of checking. First, it may be possible to expand the sample using the inverse of the sampling fraction, as reported by Kish and Hess. The product of the number of dwelling units located and the inverse of the sampling fraction may be compared with the best available estimate of the number of dwelling units in the universe. This procedure is subject to a margin of error resulting from differences in definitions of universe and of sampling elements. It is good practice, therefore, to use in a sample survey definitions which match as closely as possible those used in other compilations, especially in censuses. For example, a "dwelling unit" should be defined in the same way. Adjustments of counts to the same date may also be troublesome. The Census Bureau modified their definition of occupied dwelling unit to a "housing unit" in the 1960 census, counting as a separate unit any room or set of rooms with a separate entrance *or* cooking facilities. This slightly increased the total number of units as some light housekeeping rooms became separate housing units. Needless to say, borderline cases are possible.

The second method of checking is to send at least two or more investigators independently to the same areas armed with the same instructions and compare the results.

Any disagreements in the resulting lists should be reconciled. There is the possibility, of course, that the two will repeat the same mistakes. It may be feasible, however, to minimize this risk by making intensive checks in a limited number of areas. This type of check can lead to a description of the errors made, which may then prove manageable.

The same three general types of problems arise with area sampling frames as with other frames:

(1) *Missing elements.* There may be some members of the population who have no dwelling unit. For example, in the Delhi Savings Survey sidewalk dwellers were omitted from the frame.[12] In the United States those omitted include migrant laborers, persons living in institutions, on military bases, abroad, and the like. New construction may be missing. The resulting bias may or may not be serious depending on the objectives of the project. The risks are particularly great in studies of extreme poverty and studies of highly mobile people.

(2) *Blanks or Foreign elements:* Addresses which are not dwellings may appear on a list. Ordinarily they can be excluded, if selected as noted above.

(3) *Duplicate listings:* There is a growing problem of seasonal residences. Each family should be identified with a single dwelling only. There may be uncertainty as to whether to treat college students as resident with their parents or at college. Similar questions arise when any individual is absent from his "permanent address" for an extended period.

One solution is to determine where the eligible respondent spent most of the time during some specified period, e.g., the interviewing period. He then belongs in the sample if during most of the interviewing period he was living in a dwelling unit selected in the sample, or at least was not living in some other dwelling where he could have been sampled. But if he was out of the country, in jail, or living in another home not in the sample during most of the interviewing period, then he does not belong in the sample, and the sample dwelling becomes "house vacant," a non-sample dwelling, not part of the non-response. Ambiguous cases occur when the man was in hotels the whole time. Does one consider them institutions, or quasi households, and say the man was not in the population living in private households? And of course, in many cases where the respondent is away during the whole interviewing period, there is no way to find out where he was, and he is conservatively treated as in the sample but part of the non-response.

The Basic Elements of Complex Designs: Clustering, Multi-Stage Samples, Stratification and Controlled Selection

In the development of sample designs there is a presumption in favor of simplicity. Before deciding to use a complex design it is appropriate to consider whether a simple design may not be satisfactory or even preferable.

In some situations it may be possible to avoid sampling altogether and include the entire population in the survey. For example, Donald T. Brash undertook a study of *American Investment in Australian Industry*.[13] He was concerned with companies which were American-owned and engaged in manufacturing in Australia as of June 30, 1962. The first stage of his project consisted in developing a list of such companies—he located 208 which met his criteria. He included all 208 in his survey. Problems of incomplete or unsatisfactory response remained to be solved, but at least he eliminated sampling error. Whenever a sample is an appreciable fraction, f, of the population, the sampling error is reduced by a factor = (1-f).

When it is unreasonable to include the entire population, it may be appropriate to take a simple random sample. There are two advantages to this procedure. First, most of the estimates of sampling errors in common use are based explicitly or implicitly on simple random samples. If the techniques of statistical analysis to be used will be interpreted as if they had been applied to simple random samples, why not make the procedure match the interpretation? Second, when complex sample designs are developed and executed by people who are inexperienced in this type of activity, there is a risk that they will make mistakes, and pay a penalty in inefficiency or bias, or both. Experience shows that this risk is not negligible. It may be prudent to rely on a scheme based on simple random sampling and spend one's energies in making certain that the scheme is correctly conceived and executed.

The randomness in the selection of elements from a frame may be achieved by a lottery of some sort developed *ad hoc*. An investigator working with a list might number the entries on his list, prepare a set of strips of paper with matching numbers, place them in a hat, stir well, and instruct his research assistant to draw the required number. It is better practice, however, to rely on published lists of random numbers which have been painstakingly developed with precautions taken to ensure that they are, in fact, random.

It is common practice when a list is being sampled to determine the sampling interval, say, k, needed to select a sample of the required size and begin by selecting at random a number between 1 and k. Thereafter every k^{th} entry will be included. (If the first selection is a, where $1 < a < k$, the second selection is $a + k$; the third selection is $a + 2k$; etc.). This procedure may be as satisfactory as the repeated use of a table of random numbers for each selection provided there is no periodicity or trend in the list. But suppose, for example, that a list of business enterprises engaged in manufacturing is the frame, every 200th is to be selected, and that the list is arranged in order by total sales starting at the top. Then it will make a difference in the sample estimate of mean sales per enterprise whether firms 1, 201, 401, 601, etc., are selected, or firms 200, 400, 600, 800, etc.[14] It would be appropriate to consider a more complex design.

There may be compelling reasons not to use simple random sampling. There may be possibilities of substantial reductions in sampling error at little or no extra cost. And it may be difficult to impossible to develop a frame which could be the basis of simple random selection. The basic features of complex designs are clustering, multi-stage selection, stratification, and controlled selection.

Clustering: Clustering is usually a necessary evil. It is undertaken only to reduce data collection costs per interview; it cannot reduce the sampling error of estimates for a given number of interviews. It is obviously not efficient to scatter interviews with no geographic clustering, say, 1000 personal interviews representing the population of the U.S. Development of sampling materials and travel time per interview would be prohibitively expensive. Clustering reduces the dollar cost per unit of information, and it produces *no bias.*

The effect of clustering on sampling error is usually indicated by comparing the standard error of the mean under simple random sampling with the standard error of the mean in a cluster sample when each cluster is fully enumerated*

$$(1) \quad \text{var } \bar{y}_0 = \frac{S^2}{n} \quad \text{(S.R.S.)}$$

---

*We ignore here and elsewhere the finite population correction, which is trivial for the type of problem with which we are concerned. We also assume equal-sized clusters.

where $\bar{y}_0$ = mean of some variate y estimated from a simple random sample

S^2 = variance of the variate y

n = number of interviews in the sample

var = variance

(2) $\text{var } \bar{y} = \dfrac{S_a^2}{a}$ (clustered sample with enumeration of cluster)

a = number of clusters

(3) $\dfrac{\text{var } \bar{y}}{\text{var } \bar{y}_0} = \dfrac{S_a^2/n}{S^2/n} = D = [1 + \text{roh } (B\text{-}1)]$

D = design effect

B = number of elements per cluster

roh = coefficient of intraclass correlation

Alternatively, we may write:

(3a) $\text{var } \bar{y} = [S^2/n] \ [1 + \text{roh} \ (B\text{-}1)]$

$= \text{var } \bar{y}_0 \ [1 + \text{roh} \ (B\text{-}1)]$

Note that we multiply the variability of a simple random sample mean (var $\bar{y}_0$) by a factor which is 1 plus a term which depends on, (a) the size of the cluster—the larger the adjustment—, and (b) the homogeneity of the cluster. If roh = 0, there would be no loss from clustering. If it were 1, the variability of a single random sample, [var $\bar{y}_0$], would be multiplied by B, the number of elements per cluster. From consideration of this formula it is apparent why sampling statisticians are concerned with the determinants of roh, and especially the relation between roh and B.[15] For an intuitive feel, consider clusters of addresses on the same street if the purpose is to estimate the proportion of non-whites. Given segregation, roh could be as high as 1 (either the whole cluster is white, or it is non-white) in which case the variance is a multiple of simple random sampling equal to the number in the cluster (because you have only one bit of information on race per cluster, the additional interviews told you nothing more). Roh is a large-sample modification of Rho omitting some minor adjustments for small samples and small numbers of clusters. Roh is equal to

$1 - \dfrac{\text{within-cluster variance}}{\text{total variance}}$, so it varies from 1, (when all the variance is between-clusters, none within clusters and the second term becomes zero), to 0, (when all the variance is within clusters and the cluster means are all the same).

In practice, it is not common for all elements in a cluster to be enumerated when there is only one stage in selection.

Multi-stage sampling: Multi-stage sample designs are those in which the clusters are subsampled. For example, in a sample of the population of the United States, the first stage may be the selection of counties, and the counties in turn may be subsampled. The effect of subsampling is to add another component to the standard error or variance of the estimate of any statistic in addition to the variance resulting from sampling at the first stage. Thus, the formula for the variance of the estimate of the mean is:*

$$(4) \quad \text{var } \bar{y} = \frac{S_b^2}{m} + \frac{S_w^2}{mn}$$

S_b^2 = variance of Y between clusters

m = no. of clusters selected at stage one

S_w^2 = variance of y within clusters

n = no. of interviews within each cluster

There is no limit in theory to the number of stages of selection which may be introduced. In practice, attempts are made to limit the number of stages in the interests of simplicity. Each stage of selection presents a new problem in sampling, an additional set of complications in every part of the work from the development of the frame to the estimation of sampling errors. Each additional stage also implies additional clustering of the sample, and, hence, at least a risk of an increase in the sampling error. Gains from stratification are, however, possible at each stage (see below). Most designs are limited to three or four stages. We may note that the number of stages need not be the same in all strata in the sample. For example, in a sample of the U.S., New York and other very large cities may be selected with certainty while rural counties will be sampled.

The sample may still be self-weighting, since different probabilities of selection at one stage can be offset by reversed differences at a later stage. What

---

*Again we ignore the finite population corrections and assume the same number of units are selected in each cluster. If the cluster n_i's vary, terms must be added for variance in the n_i's and for covariance between the cluster mean and the cluster size.

matters is that the product of all the probabilities (from each stage) for any individual be the same as for all other individuals.

Thus, a part of the development of a complex sample design is the specification of the number of stages of selection and the size of the clusters at each stage in each of the major strata of the sample. There are, in theory, an indefinitely large number of ways to select a probability sample of a given total number of interviews from a given population. While some of the theoretical possibilities can be ruled out quickly, there remain difficult problems involving: (1) the number of stages of selection, (2) the definition of the elements to be sampled at each stage, and (3) the number of elements to be selected at each stage.

In theory, it is a simple problem of maximizing the amount of information per dollar, or minimizing the cost of a body of information. The difficulty is that the facts are frequently not known precisely, and there may be a variety of kinds of information wanted, differentially affected by the choices made in sampling design. For instance, very local clustering may do damage to estimates of race, but clustering at county or state level may affect things which vary by government jurisdiction (treatment of people on welfare, for instance).

Stratification: Some use of stratification is made in all but the simplest sample designs. A major attraction of stratification is that it makes possible a reduction of the variance of the estimates, and often the gains may be realized at little or no additional cost. Stratification may also be used to divide the population into groups within which different procedures are employed. No bias is introduced, but the amount of gain in efficiency may depend on the wisdom of the stratification used.

The procedure is to arrange the population into subpopulations or strata and *then* select a random sample of each. For example, a list may be arranged in order and *then* every k^{th} individual may be selected from the list. The object is to arrange the population into strata which differ as widely as possible from each other but are as homogeneous as possible within each stratum.

The variance of the estimate of a mean within a stratum when simple random sampling is used is the same as if that stratum were a complete sample (See equation (1) above.)

$$(5) \quad var\,(\bar{y}\,h) = \frac{S_h^2}{n_h}$$

The subscript h refers to stratum h.

Then the variance of the mean for the entire sample can be computed from the means for all strata:

$$(6) \quad \text{var}(\bar{y}) = \Sigma W_h^2 \frac{S_h^2}{n_h}$$

W_h is a weight assigned to stratum h, and $\Sigma W_h = 1$.

Note that only the variation within strata enters the sampling error. The gain from stratification can be seen more easily from the following expression:

| Variance of $\bar{y}$ with proportionate stratified sampling | = | Variance of $\bar{y}$ with simple random sampling (var $\bar{y}_0$) | − | Weighted variance of stratum means $\dfrac{\Sigma N_h (\bar{y}_h - \bar{y})^2}{\Sigma N_h} /n$ |

Consequently, the gains from stratification are greatest when the strata means differ greatly, but not by finding very small strata. Unequal N's reduce the potential size of the last term, other things being equal.

It is important to understand the implications of errors or inefficiencies in the development of strata. Suppose, for example, that it is desired to stratify households by income but no actual measure of income is available. All that the investigator has at hand is estimates of economic level made by interviewers who have looked at the outside of the homes of the subpopulation being considered. Frequently, the interviewers will make mistakes. Yet, so long as their ratings have *some* correlation with actual incomes, it will be better to use them to stratify the population than not to stratify at all. The question is one of whether variability estimated from (6) is appreciably lower than variability estimated from (1), i.e. are the strata based on the interviewers' ratings more homogeneous inside than random subgroups of that size? The question of using such ratings in practice is not whether they are better than no stratification at all but whether they lead to sufficient improvement compared to other possible methods of stratification to justify the cost of preparing them. No bias is involved, only differences in efficiency. Whether to use such ratings as a basis for varying the sampling fraction is a different question—see below.

Note that at every stage in a multistage sample, stratification is possible. Moreover, the principles of stratification need not be the same across the entire sample at any stage. For example, if counties are to be selected in the first stage of a population sample of the United States, the list of all counties may first be stratified by region. Within the South, the further stratification may be based on different variables than those used elsewhere, e.g., percent of total agricultural land planted to cotton.

It is almost always advisable to stratify a sample. In sophisticated designs, stratification may be carried to the point where there is only one element selected per stratum.

It is practically impossible for stratification to increase the sampling variance, or to produce any bias. It seems likely that the substantial gains from even relatively simple stratification apply to a wide range of variables and study purposes, so that multi-purpose samples save more in spreading of sampling costs over many studies than they lose by not tailoring the stratification to the needs of each study individually.

Controlled Selection: Controlled selection is an ingenious solution to the problem of how to retain randomness of selection and yet exercise a greater degree of control over the selection than is possible through simple stratification alone. The essential principle may be illustrated for a Latin Square design. (See Table Y.) Suppose stratification has been carried to the limit of one selection per stratum for each of the three strata. It may still be desirable to take into account an additional variable. If no controls were introduced, there would be a total of 3 x 3 x 3—twenty-seven possible patterns of selection of three cells. Of the twenty-seven, three would be particularly undesirable, in that the selections for the three strata would all come from control class 1, or 2, or 3. But there are six especially desirable patterns because there is one selection from each control class. These patterns are indicated by the letters A through F in Table Y. A random number from one to six may select one of the six desirable patterns. The twenty-one less desirable patterns will be given zero chance of selection. (Pattern A selects a C1 from Stratum I, a C2 from Stratum II, and a C3 from Stratum III.)

TABLE Y: LATIN SQUARE DESIGN

Control Classes Based on X_1

Strata	1	2	3
I	AD	BE	CF
II	CE	AF	BD
III	BF	CD	AE

This method can be carried farther. An additional principle of control X_2, may be introduced. Instead of a 3 x 3 square we may have a cube, 3 x 3 x 3. (We are still assuming equal cell sizes.) Then there will be a new set of preferred patterns such that three elements will represent each stratum once, each control class on X1 once, and each control class on X2 once.

In practice controlled selection must take into account the inequality of stratum sizes[17] and a good deal of judgement is involved in deciding what the various controls should be. It is a matter of how *large* the gains in efficiency will be.

Economists who are not specialists in sample selection are unlikely to make use of controlled selection in drawing samples. They may well encounter data based on surveys which have been taken using this procedure, however. They should recognize that its use imposes limitations on the analysis of the resulting data. The extreme case is one in which an investigator wishes to examine the nature of the relationship among variables related to the characteristics used in the controlled selection without realizing what he is doing. For example, he might wish to see whether being in stratum I had an effect on whether an individual fell in 1, 2, or 3 on X-1. He would find that all those in I were in *one* of the three categories on X-1. He might further find that all those in I were in category C on variable X-2, which he might argue was unlikely to have arisen by chance. With sufficient diligence he might be able to reproduce exactly the pattern of controlled selection actually chosen—but he would have found nothing about the population.

This type of difficulty has arisen in practice when tabulations have been made for finer geographic breakdowns than were intended. For example, the sample might be so designed that three cities fall in strata I, II, and III, and X-1 might be income level of suburbs. Then the sample might include a high income suburb of city I, a medium income suburb of city II, and a low income suburb of city III. It might represent the three cities combined quite adequately, but it would be a poor sample of any one of the three in isolation. If the sample had been intended to represent each of the cities individually, it would have been selected in an entirely different way.

One need not understand the detail of Latin Squares or Graeco-Latin Squares; it is the principle that is important. That is, it is always possible to do better than simple random or even stratified random sampling if you are willing to forego inclusion of all possible combinations of strata in the sample. The limitation of this kind of procedure is, for example, that you may not have a genuinely representative sample of each of twelve metropolitan areas, although you may have a representative sample of the central city of each area.

Sampling Dwelling Units: Households and Quasi-Households: In the United States we have no sampling frame that lists all the families or adult individuals so dwelling units are used. The reason we exclude the institutional population and those in quasi-households is that they are difficult to interview, very badly clustered and represent only a very small fraction of the population. A decennial census counts everybody including the institutional population. Institutional populations as largely people in places where they cannot get out easily, like hospitals, mental institutions, jails, and the like, but there are also quasi-households such as flophouses, communes, residential hotels and some old peoples' homes, with a lot of people in one structure without separate entrances, or separate cooking facilities.

The Census changed its unit from a dwelling unit in 1950 to a housing unit in 1960, the housing unit being defined as having *either* a separate entrance *or* separate cooking facilities. Consequently an old hotel where people have cooking facilities in their rooms might now be considered several hundred housing units, rather than being a quasi-household. Quasi-households are included in the Census Current Population Survey, but not the institutional population. The Survey Research Center samples generally exclude the quasi-households as well as the institutional population. Other dwellings may, however, have roomers and boarders in them who are included and treated as separate families. Alaska and Hawaii are also generally excluded from most small samples.

When the interviewers actually go out to interview at the addresses selected to form a sample, they sometimes meet with surprises. The original field work in listing addresses and selecting the sample may have been correct, but in the meantime, dwellings may have been torn down, subdivided, converted to institutions, or newly built in large numbers. When the result is fewer dwellings than expected, some efficiency is lost, but there are no great problems. But when the buildings or the areas included in the sample suddenly have large unexpected clusters of dwellings (all of which belong in the sample), an alarming problem arises. If they are left out one has a large non-response, and a bias. If they are all taken, it is extremely costly and difficult, yet each interview adds little to the total information. The usual procedure is to take a fraction of the interviews and weight them up to represent the rest. The inefficiency remains, but at least the field costs have not been blown up, nor delays in completing the study encountered.

The Unit of Analysis: Families may also include members who are quasi-independent. The early Surveys of Consumer Finances used a "spending" unit in which even related people who kept separate finances and had an income of their own, were treated as separate units and interviewed separately.

After World War II there were a substantial number of people who lived doubled-up waiting for the housing shortage to ease, often with quite separate finances, quite separate purchase plans, and quite separate expectations about the future. As the proportion of these related secondary units dropped to less than ten percent, and they became more and more restricted to very old or very young people, it became less important to talk about them separately. Now the interviewing is done on a family basis, although in the SCF each year some tabulations are done on a spending unit basis by separating income between spending units within a family and asking who owns the cars so that one can prepare tables about what kind of cars people own, by income, on a spending unit basis. Of course there are also unrelated people in one or two percent of dwellings, who are separate families, and are usually interviewed separately.

In a national poverty study we became concerned about doubled-up families even when the people who were being housed by their relatives had no income of their own.[16] So, although we interviewed on a spending unit basis, and combined the data to create family information for some purposes, we also took families apart into what we called "adult" units. An adult unit consisted of a single adult or a married couple and their children. This required dividing the income and making some estimates of the extent to which aged relatives or adult sons or daughters were receiving free housing and free food from their children or parents with whom they lived. We wanted to include this as part of their real income. There is a very large amount of potential poverty hidden by doubling up in this country. As a result, anyone who wanted to establish a guaranteed income as a matter of right, with no relatives' responsibility requirements, would be faced with a much larger problem than he might think if he looked only at family income distribution.

Problems of Sample Selection of Special Concern to Economists

Self-weighting Samples: In the design of samples for economic surveys, there is an initial presumption in favor of equal probability of selection of the elements, which implies that the resulting sample will be self-weighting. That is, each interview will be given the same weight in analysis as any other interview. For the analyst it is convenient not to have to use weights in calculating statistics based on the sample, nor to have to shift from weights to number of interviews in getting degrees of freedom for significance tests. This consideration may be of minor importance, however, if the data are to be analyzed on a computer using programs which will accept weighted data. The presumption in favor of equal probability of selection rests more fundamentally on the proposition that interviews in each stratum are expected to cost about the same and that for the important statistics under study, estimates from different strata will have similar variance. It also assumes that units are important in proportion to their frequency in the population. If in some stratum interviews are known to be cheap, or the variance of important statistics is known to be large, or the people important for some policy reasons, oversampling in that stratum should be considered. In the absence of these conditions equal probability is preferable.

We may contrast this approach with one in which the design is planned by specifying a certain number of strata and taking an equal number of selections per stratum. For example, one might specify three strata of counties, those with high, medium and low income per capita, and select 10 counties per stratum. If there are unequal numbers of counties in the three strata, the result will be unequal probabilities of selection of families and of family units. If the same procedure is followed at each stage in a multi-stage sample, the final probabilities of selection may be extremely unequal.

Equal probability of selection can be achieved, however, by assigning to each element a probability of selection proportional to size, i.e. the number of basic units in it (housing units). One of the possible methods of achieving this result is to consider a list of elements $x_1 \ldots, x_n$ from which a sample is to be selected. For each element there is a measure of size. For example, we might have a list of 1000 city blocks, with an estimate of the population of each, the total being 30,000. Then the data may be arranged in the following format:

(1)	(2)	(3)
Block Number	Population per Block	Cumulative Population
1	572	1-572
2	409	573-981
3	51	982-1032
....	...	...
1000	207	- 30,000

If ten blocks are to be selected, we use an interval of 30,000/10, or 3000. Then we apply an interval of 3000 to column 3, and with a random start select a sample of ten blocks. If the random start (a random number between 0 and 3,000) is 313, then one selects blocks which include the numbers 313, 3313, 6313, 9313, etc. The probability of selection of any block will be proportional to its population. *There is no need to assign equal probabilities of selection to the blocks.*

Use of Variable Sampling Fractions: It is sometimes efficient to use a sampling fraction which varies from stratum to stratum in a sample. It is useful to consider the formula for optimum allocation, and its implication. The optimum allocation requires that sampling rates within strata be directly proportional to the standard deviations within strata of the variable being studied and inversely proportional to the square root of the cost per element within strata:[18]

$$(7) \qquad f_h = \frac{n_h}{N_h} = K \frac{S_h}{\sqrt{J_h}}$$

where f_h = sampling fraction in stratum h

n_h = number of elements selected in stratum h

N_h = number of elements in the population in stratum h

K = a constant of proportionality

S_h = standard deviation (of a variate to be investigated) in stratum h

J_h = cost per interview in stratum h

This formula refers to the standard deviation of a single variable. Actual surveys involve the estimation of measures of many variables, often several hundred. For a practical decision to be taken with full information, some estimate would be needed of the optimum value of f_h in each stratum for each variable. The optimum may well differ from variable to variable. A low level of precision may be acceptable for some variables, and some judgments or perhaps some rough system of weighting, may guide the choice of sampling fractions to be used for the strata in the survey.

Gross differences in cost per interview (J_h) from stratum to stratum occur where a different method of data collection is used. For example, in one stratum it may be possible to collect data by telephone while in another personal visits must be made. There may also be geographic strata in which interviewing is very expensive because of the physical isolation of an area. In such cases an adjustment in the sampling fraction may be needed. Note that even a substantial adjustment will not destroy the representativeness of the sample, as would a decision to omit the expensive stratum entirely.

Differences in standard deviation per element from stratum to stratum (S_h) are ordinarily of more concern in the design of economic surveys than difference in cost. In general, for the estimation of percentages the gain from the use of variable sampling fractions is small, while for the estimation of the mean of a distribution, the gain may be substantial.

The gain in estimating percentages is small because the variance of a proportion is p(1-p). Within a stratum the standard deviation will be $\sqrt{P_h (1-P_h)}$.[19] For values of P_h from 0.10 to 0.90, $\sqrt{P_h (1-P_h)}$ ranges only from 0.3 to 0.5. It does not often happen that strata can be defined in which P_h will vary so widely.

For the estimation of means, however, the situation may be very different. In some situations it may be efficient to include in a sample *all* elements in a stratum. For example, in a sample of business enterprises in a certain industry, all enterprises in the largest category when ranked on a specific characteristic might be included, with sampling of the enterprises only in other strata.

A method of variable sampling fractions based on field ratings used for some years in the Survey of Consumer Finance illustrates the uses and limitations of variable sampling fractions. Interviewers listed the dwellings in a sample of blocks and estimated the income of the family in each dwelling by observation from the outside. Dwellings were divided into three groups, "low," "medium" and "high" (L, M, H). The following tabulation from Kish, p 414, summarizes the results of a study of the usefulness of this procedure:

TABLE 1

Variances at Three Economic Levels,

and Optimum Sampling Fractions

Variable	Mean			Standard Deviation			Optimum Loading			Efficiency of Optimum Compared to Proportionate
	L	M	H	L	M	H	L	M	H	
Mean income	$2800	$4200	$8000	$1700	$2800	$8100	1	1.6	4.7	1.36
Mean liquid assets	700	1800	5800	1700	3400	10,100	1	2.0	5.9	1.45
Percentage with income over 10,000	0.4	5	31	6.4	21	46	1	3.3	7.2	1.43
Percentage below median income	70	44	32	46	50	47	1	1.1	1.0	1.00

For mean income, the optimum sampling fraction for the High stratum is 4.7 times the fraction for the Low stratum, since the standard deviations are in the ratio 8100 to 1700 or 4.7 to 1. The ratio of the *mean* income in the High stratum to that in the Low, 8000 to 2800, is smaller. Yet the table shows there is a tendency for the standard deviation to increase as the mean increases.

Note that the potential gains in efficiency from optimal loading are substantial for the means, and also for the percentage with income over $10,000. Note too, that the optimal loadings vary, and that the optimum loading for estimating the percentage with income below the median is not loading, but a constant sampling fraction. Most items estimated in this survey were of the latter type.

This type of investigation has been carried much farther for single descriptive statistics (such as the mean of a distribution for the sample as a whole) than it has for complex statistics (such as regression coefficients from multiple regression equations). It is clear that the device of using variable sampling fractions may be extremely useful in studies intended to estimate the mean or aggregate of some financial quantity for the population of a geographic area. On the other hand, the more variances differ, the more likely the variable is skewed and not effectively estimated by a survey. And the gains in complex statistics are likely to be smaller, just as the clustering losses are smaller.

Of course, in designing a sample one often does not know the variances to be expected within strata. He may use estimated differences in strata means, assuming that the variances are proportional to the means, but even the means may not be known. High precision is not required, but unless the range among the variances is substantial (four to one or more) the gains are probably not worth the complications.

A special type of varying sampling fractions arises when they vary across sampling units because one wants the sample to represent something other than families, for instance, dollars of income. One might, given a list of people with their incomes, sample dollars of income—a sample which would contain many high-income people, and only a small fraction of the numerous low-income people. Without weighting, then, one could give results in terms of dollars of income represented. "People representing x% of the income say they like to invest in common stock."[20] Similarly, a sample of firms proportional to number of employees allows one to talk about employers representing some fraction of the employees in the state. If one sampled transactions, proportionately to their size, again it might make sense to report the information or intentions or backgrounds of people according to the volume of transactions they accounted for. This would be a self-weighting sample, but of dollars spent, not of people. Again it is important to remember that the unit of sampling, of interviewing, and of analysis need not be the same.

Point Sampling: Sometimes the desire to sample something other than people or dwellings leads to the necessity to sample some continuous stream, like time, or some continuous surface like area. One may want to determine in what fraction of time something happens, or what fraction of a land area is covered with a particular crop. In these cases, it is frequently simpler and more efficient to use pin-point sampling; that is, to take a large sample of points in time or space. If 50% of the points satisfy the criterion (the man was working, etc.) then 50% of the continuum does also. This procedure was probably first publicly suggested by an Australian agronomist who put a point on the tip of his boot and took a random walk around the pasture to estimate the proportion of the area covered by each of several grasses.[21] One recent study asked researchers to carry a random alarm mechanism, and report what they were doing every time it sounded.

Screening Interviews: It is not unusual in economic survey work for problems to arise which can be studied only by interviewing a narrowly defined population. One might be interested, for example, in interviewing people who had moved within a year from one county to another, in order to study the cost of such moves. Or one might wish to study the cost of college by interviewing the parents of undergraduates. While it sometimes happens that a list will be available which can serve as a sampling frame, often there is no such list. In this situation screening interviews may be useful.

This method of developing a sample will be successful if three criteria are met. First, the screening interviews must be cheap. One way to hold down the cost is to include the screening questions in an on-going survey with other purposes and content. Or it may be possible to screen a large number of families economically in some other way, perhaps a brief doorstep interview with questions which even neighbors can answer.

Second, the screening question must yield accurate information. Clearly the doorstep screening questions cannot involve sensitive information like income, assets, family planning, or some forms of disability or medical care. In a study of hospital utilization, doorstep screening for occupants 65 or older worked well, but for people who had been in the hospital in the last year it under-selected. Data from a parallel representative sample allowed weighting to reduce biases.[22] It is crucial that the number who are erroneously classified as *unsuitable for inclusion* in the sample be small. If some are erroneously *included,* the error could be detected in the subsequent intensive interviews and those cases eliminated.

Third, the original sample must be satisfactory (both in design and execution). Any loss from non-response in the screening interviews implies a corresponding loss in the sample for the intensive interviews. It may be that the probability of non-response on the screening interviews varies systematically and that the probability of non-response is somehow related to the probability that a unit will be eligible for the intensive interviews. (See the discussion of non-response in Chapter IV.)

When the three criteria are met, however, screening procedures can be extremely useful. The criterion used in screening need not be a simple demographic characteristic. An analyst, for example, might carry out a complex statistical procedure from which he emerged with a predicted score and an actual score for every member of a cross-section sample, as discussed above. He might then select for reinterview every individual for whom the discrepancy between these scores exceeded some absolute amount. This strategy is, in effect, a special type of reinterview.

Reinterviews and the Estimation of Changes over Time: For efficiency in sample design, reinterviews are especially useful for surveys intended to measure changes over time. The Current Population Survey, for example, is intended to measure changes in the unemployment rate over time with a high level of precision.

The problem may be regarded as one of estimating the difference between two means:[23]

$$d = \bar{x} - \bar{y} = \frac{\Sigma x}{n_x} - \frac{\Sigma y}{n_y}$$

where d = difference between two means

$\bar{x}$ = mean from the first sample

$\bar{y}$ = mean from a second sample

n_x = no. of interviews in x

n_y = no. of interviews in y

If n_x and n_y are taken as given, the variance of the difference becomes:

$$\text{var (d)} = \frac{\text{var}(x)}{n_x^2} \times \frac{\text{var}(y)}{n_y^2} - \frac{2 \, \text{cov}(x,y)}{n_x \, n_y}$$

Thus, the variance of the difference is reduced by a factor which depends on the covariance of x and y. For many variables of economic importance, the covariance will be substantial with reinterviews. Labor force status, for example, does not change for most people over a one-year period. Hence, there will be gains from the use of reinterviews. However, repeated samples using the same sampling areas (down to small subareas) also have substantial covariances.

These gains must be weighed against the tendency of a sample to become unrepresentative over time because of problems of non-response, moving, and the appearance of new units in the population or changing of the units (divorce, for instance). These problems are treated at length in Chapter IV. There is the additional possibility that repeated interviewing of the same unit may in itself create a change in the behavior of the unit or in the completeness and accuracy of the report given. Any change in quality of report, even a change toward greater accuracy, may cause a bias in the estimate of the change taking place in the population. Continuing projects, therefore, use designs involving partial overlaps, with systematic periodic addition of new sub-samples and retirement of old ones. A sophisticated scheme of this type is used in the Current Population Surveys of the Bureau of the Census. Reinterviews are particularly useful where analysis of change is desired and where nuisance variables (such as stable personality characteristics which differ between individuals) need to be eliminated.

Highly Skewed Distributions: One way to check the validity of a study is by multiplying a mean by the inverse of the sampling fraction to estimate the aggregate and then comparing these aggregates with some national income statistics or other source of aggregate data. The items that seem to check out best are the ones that are not badly skewed, in other words, not concentrated in the hands of a few people. Also, they are something people are not terribly sensitive about, something regular like contractual payments, and things that are very likely to be *personal* assets, or debts, and not institutional or business accounts. Many of the aggregate statistics are assumed to be either individual or business, depending on their name or on some rough estimates from institutional reporters, when in fact we really don't know.

It would be very useful to do methodological studies which start out with a sample of the records on which the national income or other aggregate data are based, follow them back to their original source, and find out what the ownership, function, and purpose of that particular amount really was. This would help us to better understand the aggregate statistics and would also improve our notion of the comparisons with survey data.

In general surveys are not good to estimate aggregates of skewed distributions. It is not true, as intimated in many books on statistics, that the distribution of a sample of sample means is normal even though the basic distribution of the numbers is skewed. If the sample is badly skewed, even the distribution of sample means is skewed so that more than half of the samples would produce estimates below the true average. It is not hard to see how this would be true if you had samples of 1,000, and one man in 1,000 has an income of $1,000,000 and everybody else has an income of $6,000. You might take many samples before you found one with a millionaire in it and he would produce a sample with a very high estimate. The chances are that in dealing with skewed distributions, any estimates of means or aggregates should be done with an arbitrary cut-off point and stated to be estimates of the amounts excluding the extremes, e.g., those with incomes over $100,000 or assets over 1/2 million. These boundaries should be determined before reporting survey results, not after.

Effects of Non-Optimal Sampling on Analysis: A problem which sometimes presents itself to an economic analyst is whether or not to use an existing unrepresentative sample for analysis. For example, two well-known econometricians, H. S. Houthakker and John Haldi, carried out an extensive analysis of the demand for automobiles using data from a panel operated by J. W. Thompson on a commercial basis.[24] The panel was set up and replacements were made to it in such a way that the panel did not comprise a representative sample. Two elaborate studies have been based on very special samples of (a) subscribers to *Consumers Reports* (highly educated for the most part), (b) who sent in their ballot and annual mail questionnaire (still more select), and then (c) were willing to participate in further inquiries.[25]

The proposition that the representativeness of a sample can be ignored for analytic work has interesting implications. A good deal of money might be saved, for example, if unrepresentative samples could be used for analysis. There are two questions which must be raised about results based on such samples.

First, is it possible to measure accurately the variance of the estimates based on such a sample? It is certainly not justified to assume that the individual families were selected independently; clustering is virtually certain. Hence, the variance per element is likely to be substantially higher than with a simple random sample, and this variance will not be known unless there were special efforts made to design the study so that it could be estimated. For the ordinary non-probability sample no adequate basis for estimating sampling errors exists.

Second, will the estimates themselves be biased? For example, will the estimate of the relation between income and purchases be correct? There is no reason to suppose that the estimates will be biased *provided* there are no *interactions* between the variables whose predicting power is being investigated and the variables related to the probability of inclusion in the sample. How seriously this proviso must be taken cannot be considered in general; it will depend on the type of analysis being undertaken and the particular methods of selection actually used. It is certainly quite possible that people who are willing to participate in a panel—that is, willing to keep fairly detailed financial records and make periodic reports—may differ in the way they handle their money from those who are not willing to do so. There is consequently a possibility that, say, income elasticities of demand for some commodities will be different for panel members and non-members.

It does not follow that unrepresentative samples should never be used. They should be used with caution and efforts must be made to deal with the problems just described. A theory of panel selection would be especially useful—that is, a theory which specified the characteristics of panel members, including any variables likely to be related to subtle differences in their tastes and attitudes as well as their gross economic and demographic characteristics.

Sampling Errors for Complex Samples

In estimating the sampling errors of statistics based on complex samples it is necessary to consider the effects of the method used. There will be gains in efficiency from stratification and controlled selection, which ordinarily are more than offset by losses due to clustering. As mentioned above, it is useful to define a summary statistic called the "design effect":

$$D = \frac{S_c^2}{S_{srs}^2}$$

where S_c^2 = variance (for a given statistic) for a complex sample

S_{srs}^2 = variance for a simple random sample of equal n.

Use is often made of $\sqrt{D}$, sometimes written $\sqrt{deff}$, which is the ratio of the actual standard error to the standard error for a simple random sample of equal n. If an investigator knows $\sqrt{deff}$, he knows by how much to increase estimates of error computed using formulas appropriate for simple random samples.

The design effect need not be the same for all estimates. The system of stratification used may well produce larger gains for estimates of one variable than another. The system of clustering may also have different effects. But if it is reasonably similar, general purpose tables of sampling errors are possible without computing them individually.

The details of direct calculation of sampling errors for complex probability samples will not be given here. They are only possible for simple statistics such as means and proportions, not for complex statistics such as regression coefficients or proportions of variance explained by one variable or another. The procedure requires assembling strata in pairs (using random halves of the strata selected with certainty) and estimating components of variances associated with differences between the two items of each pair.

It would be expensive to compute sampling errors specifically for every statistic in a published report, and the publication of the sampling errors would multiply the complexity of the tables. In principle each table showing a column of percentages could be accompanied by another table showing the sampling error of each percentage in the main table, as well as tables showing the sampling errors of the differences between all possible pairs of percentages. This would take more space than the data themselves. Some simplification is necessary, but there is no substitute for the calculation and presentation of specific sampling errors when a high order of precision is important.

A common simplification for sampling errors of percentages is to present a table of general-purpose sampling errors showing an estimated range within which the sampling error may be expected to lie for a given 'n' and a given range of estimated percentages. (The sampling error of a percentage varies with the size of the subgroup for which it is calculated, as one can tell from the simple random sampling formula $\sqrt{P(1-P)/n}$.) But, since most users want to compare two percentages, a table showing the range of sampling errors of *differences* between two percentages for different levels of the two percentages, and different n's of the two subgroups, is even better. The width of the range (the amount of possible design effect) is greater, the *larger* the subgroup sizes, because the full impact of clustering is felt with the full sample. Subgroups often contain only one representative or none from each of the final clusters, and fewer in each of the larger clusters, so the main impact of clustering is felt with the items based on the largest fractions of the sample, where the larger number of cases reduces the sampling error to offset some of the clustering effect.

Such general purpose tables of sampling errors of percentages take care of these two effects (a) the subgroup size (more precision and more design effect), and, (b) the general level of the percentages (how close to 50% where sampling errors are largest), leaving the analyst to use his judgment about whether a particular item for particular subgroups is larger or smaller than average losses in efficiency from the sample design. Geographically clustered variables like home ownership, for subgroups which do not cut through clusters (like city size) are likely to have serious design effects, and high sampling errors.

For averages of numerical variables, which can have widely different variances, one can still provide the reader with some approximate notions of sampling errors by calculating and developing estimates of the design effects. The reader can then use the variance of a variable in the sample, the number of cases the mean is based on, and a range of design effects from none to x%, to put lower and upper limits on the sampling errors. $2 \sqrt{\dfrac{VAR\ x}{N}} \times DEFF = $ Sampling error.

The usual way of interpreting such two-level sampling errors in a simple random sample is to say that anything below the lower level is clearly not significant, anything larger than the upper level is clearly significant, and that in between one should withhold judgement.

Beyond proportions and means, there are no formulas for calculating sampling errors from complex samples. Even for the median, one estimates the sampling error of the proportion below the median level and infers the sampling error of the median from that. In the case of regression, there are computer programs which produce sampling errors, based on the assumption of simple random sampling, which is not the case.

However, there are ways of estimating sampling errors for complex statistics, such as multiple regression coefficients, indexes, etc. The leading candidate among a number of similar methods is what Kish calls balanced repeated replication.[26] It requires arranging the sample strata in similar pairs as much as possible. Where there was only one primary selection per stratum, one can still pair the adjoining strata for the small ones, or develop pairs within the strata for the very large ones selected with certainty (the twelve largest metropolitan areas, for instance, in the Survey Research Center sample).

If there are k pairs of strata, there are 2^{k-1} possible ways of selecting one of each pair to form a proper half-sample that takes into account the sampling design. But almost all the information is contained in k + 1 half samples, selected by balanced controlled selection procedures. The squared differences of these half-sample estimates from the full sample estimate provide an estimate of the sampling variance of the estimate in question, although the variance of the squared differences is *not* an estimate of the variance of the variance estimates. Since each split-half provides an estimate of the sampling error with only one degree of freedom, however, we know that it is not a stable estimate, and a substantial number of half samples, say a dozen or more, are required for stability. A variant of this procedure involves dividing the sample into many replications and comparing an estimate based on each replication with one based on *all* the other replications. This is called "jackknifing," from the analogy of slicing a wedge out of an apple.

When the balanced repeated replication procedure is used to estimate sampling errors of multiple regression coefficients from the Survey Research Center's national sample, an average design effect of about 1.12 (standard errors 6% higher than simple random sampling) was found. This still means that using computer-supplied SRS sampling errors or t-ratios is dangerous and non-conservative, but it is a smaller design loss than people had feared, and smaller than for means or simple percentages. Perhaps the use of several predictors, cutting across the sample design in different ways, reduces the clustering effects somewhat.

A special possibility for simpler estimation of the sampling errors of regression coefficients of dichotomous (dummy) variables arises because they can be thought of as subgroup means (means of the dependent variable for the subgroup non-zero on that predictor) adjusted for intercorrelations (for the fact that that subgroup is not distributed like the population on the other predicting variables or characteristics). We return to this in Chapter VI.

Estimating Required Sample Size

One of the basic decisions in developing plans for a sample survey is the selection of the size of the sample. The penalty for too large a sample is economic—too much money will be spent on field work and data processing. The penalty for too small a sample is that the results of the project may be inconclusive.

Two examples may indicate the type of difficulties which arise when an analyst finds himself with too small a sample for his purposes. Sheppard and Belitsky conducted a study of job-seeking behavior of unemployed workers in Erie, Pa., in 1963-64.[27] Their basic sample of 450 blue collar workers was selected from the files of the State Employment Service. For most of their purposes the size of sample was sufficient. But they found themselves writing a chapter on the "Re-employment Status and Job-Seeking Behavior of Negro Blue-Collar Workers" essentially on the basis of thirty-one interviews with Negro males. Attempts to supplement this sample by non-random methods yielded an additional ten cases. Sampling errors of percentages based on thirty-one (or even forty-one) observations are so large that only very limited conclusions are possible concerning differences between whites and Negroes.

Lansing and Mueller conducted a study of the geographical mobility of labor.[28] A large part of the analysis consisted in the study of variables measured in a first interview which were believed to be possible predictors of whether or not a family moved between labor market areas during the interval between the first interview and a reinterview. About 948 families with the head in the labor force were covered by the reinterview. The importance of some variables as predictors of mobility was readily confirmed. There were other variables of analytical importance, however, whose importance could not be definitely confirmed nor rejected. For example, does home ownership inhibit mobility, other things being equal? In a regression equation in which the dependent variable was whether or not the family moved between interviews the coefficient for home ownership had a value of -.03 with a standard error of .02 and a T-ratio of 1.75. The estimate of the standard error should be increased by about 10 percent to allow for the design effect. The desired T-ratio was the conventional 1.96. Thus, data are inconclusive on the question of whether home ownership inhibits mobility. A larger number of reinterviews, which would have yielded a smaller error, would have contributed substantially to the analysis. This study, like that by Sheppard and Belitsky, is typical in that the sample was adequate for many purposes but not for all purposes which the analysts considered important enough to discuss in print.

The problem of estimating in advance the required sample size is somewhat different for simple and complex statistics and the discussion which follows treats only the former.

Required Sample Size for Simple Statistics: The problem of determining required sample size has been well developed for simple statistics such as percentages which are so widely used in descriptive surveys. For a simple percentage based on the sample as a whole, all that is required is a table of sampling errors such as Table 2. Note that the errors shown should be estimated taking into account the design effect. The analyst then need only know the approximate level of the percentage in which he is interested and the sampling error which he can tolerate in order to consult the table and select the required sample size. More often, he knows how big a sample he can afford and wants to state in advance how much precision can be expected from it.

Where the percentage to be estimated is from only a part of the sample, then the desired number for the base of the percentages has to be multiplied by the inverse of the proportion of the sample that is relevant for the calculation. For instance, if one wanted to estimate the proportion of women who were Republicans, within six percent, this would require interviews with 500 women, hence a sample of 1000, assuming half the respondents are women.

In most surveys no single statistic is of overriding importance. A common rule-of-thumb approach to the problem in cross-section surveys is what we may call the *crucial subgroup method.* The analyst may conclude that he needs enough observations to obtain reasonably accurate estimates for a crucial subgroup, say, those with incomes over $K; or, the top ten percent of families ranked by income; or, people who moved last year. In effect, he may make a

TABLE 2

Sampling Error of Percentages

	Number of Interviews					
Level of Percentage	2000	1000	700	500	300	100
50	3	4	5	6	8	14
30 or 70	3	4	5	6	7	13
20 or 80	2	4	4	5	6	11
5 or 95	1	2	2	3	4	

Source: Kish, p. 576.   Sampling errors are twice the
          estimated standard error of a percentage.   Based
          on calculations on the Surveys of Consumer Finances.

judgment that if there are enough interviews in that subgroup, in the cross-section survey, there will also be enough in any other important subgroups. For example, he may decide that the sampling errors associated with a subgroup of one hundred are tolerable.

A slightly different and more appropriate analytical approach is to focus attention on the sampling error of the difference between two percentages. A set of estimates of sampling errors is required which should incorporate the design effect. Table 3 shows such information. This table has been constructed assuming a certain design effect, that of the Survey Research Center's national sample. For example, if the difference between two groups in an important percentage is expected to be about six percent, the percentage is around fifty percent, and the two groups are each about thirty percent of the sample, then for the difference to be significant one would need about 700 in each group, or a sample of 700 x 100/30 = 2300.

An analyst may have in mind a more powerful statistical procedure than the comparison of two percentages. Yet, he may find it useful to carry out the simple type of calculation of Table 3 to help him make a rough estimate of the sample size which he will need.

Once desired sample size has been estimated, it remains to establish a sampling fraction. (See the Kish-Hess article on the Survey Research Center's National Sample of Dwellings[14]). The sampling fraction is given by dividing the desired number of interviews by a product of several items: the total number of occupied dwelling units, an estimated response rate, an estimated

Table 3

APPROXIMATE SAMPLING ERRORS[a] OF DIFFERENCES

(In percentages)

Size of Group	Size of group						
	3,000	2,000	1,400	1,000	700	500	200
For percentages from 35 percent to 65 percent							
3,000	3.5	3.7	4.0	4.4	4.9	5.5	7.9
2,000		3.9	4.2	4.6	5.0	5.6	8.0
1,400			4.5	4.8	5.3	5.8	8.1
1,000				5.1	5.5	6.1	8.3
700					5.9	6.4	8.6
500						6.9	8.9
200							11.0
For percentages around 20 percent and 80 percent							
3,000	2.8	3.0	3.2	3.5	3.9	4.4	6.3
2,000		3.2	3.4	3.7	4.0	4.5	6.4
1,400			3.6	3.8	4.2	4.7	6.5
1,000				4.1	4.4	4.9	6.7
700					4.8	5.2	6.9
500						5.5	7.2
200							8.5

(Table 3 continued on page 94.)

---

[a]The values shown are the differences required for a significance (two standard errors) in comparisons of percentages derived from two different subgroups of a survey.

Table 3

(continued)

Size of group	Size of group						
	3,000	2,000	1,400	1,000	700	500	200
For percentages around 10 percent and 90 percent							
3,000	2.1	2.2	2.4	2.6	2.9	3.3	4.7
2,000		2.4	2.5	2.7	3.0	3.4	4.8
1,400			2.7	2.9	3.2	3.5	4.9
1,000				3.1	3.3	3.6	5.0
700					3.6	3.9	5.2
500						4.1	5.4
200							6.4
For percentages around 5 percent and 95 percent							
3,000	1.6	1.7	1.8	2.0	2.2	2.5	3.6
2,000		1.8	1.9	2.0	2.3	2.5	3.6
1,400			2.0	2.2	2.4	2.6	3.7
1,000				2.3	2.5	2.7	3.8
700					2.7	2.9	3.9
500						3.1	4.0
200							4.8

Source: 1968 Survey of Consumer Finances, S.R.C., Ann Arbor, Michigan, 1969.

coverage rate, and an estimate of the number of eligible respondents per dwelling. Estimates of the number of occupied dwellings in the continental United States are usually secured from the Census Bureau. But if one took dwelling units instead of occupied dwellings one would have to multiply this by an estimate of the occupancy rate as well. Response rates can be estimated on the basis of previous surveys, how difficult this one is, and how much money one is going to spend on call-backs. The coverage rate is an estimate based on the fact that in previous sample surveys the number of occupied dwelling units as discovered, was fewer than the number one would expect. By multiplying the inverse of the sampling fraction by the number of interviews, one should get an independent estimate of the number of occupied dwelling units. In other words, Census enumerators do a better job of finding every doorbell than interviewers concentrating on the subject matter of some substantive study. Therefore, it is necessary to take a larger sampling fraction than you might think in order to make sure you find enough dwellings. Finally, even if you are interviewing only primaries, secondaries are also to be interviewed, there may be more than one respondent per dwelling unit.

Summary

A great many problems may seem to call for a non-representative sample, focused on some special group. It is always wise in these cases to ask why some groups are important out of all proportion to their frequency in the population, or why it is not important to know something about the group that did not do something or is not in something, as a kind of "control group." Any fancy sampling intended to improve precision for one purpose may well make the sample substantially less efficient for many other purposes.

Scientific analysis and generalization calls for probability sampling. But this does not mean random sampling. Even the simplest type of stratification can do better than random sampling, with no bias. And if the stratification was for one purpose, it will usually leave the sample at least as good as a random sample for other different purposes. Where the sample is multi-stage, stratification can be imposed at each stage, using whatever information is available at each.

Economy, not increased precision per interview, is the reason for clustering. But in some situations, good control over field operations may require taking smaller or fewer clusters, and taking everyone in each cluster. This is particularly important where a series of surveys may be taken over time to assess changes, but where identifying individuals, or individual houses, is difficult or where assuring careful field work in locating all eligible respondents is difficult. (Migrant workers camps?)

It may seem that when a sample gets so complex (and efficient) that sampling errors can be computed only with difficulty and only for simple statistics by exact methods, it is not worth it. Our position is that efficiency and unbiasedness in the sample are more important than ease and precision in estimating sampling errors. Experience shows that design effects can be estimated, and approximate sampling errors used. Experience also seems to show that for the more complex multivariate statistics, the design losses become smaller, and the dummy variable regression coefficients are so dominated by differences in the sizes of the subgroups (not-zero on that dimension), that approximating the variance is not much of a compromise. There remains a question of the sampling error of subgroups isolated by more complex searching procedures like the Automatic Interaction Detector (See Chapter VI). So many things have been tried that there are clearly no degrees of freedom left. On the other hand, a subgroup defined in many dimensions, may cut across the clusters in such a way that the sampling error of its mean in a series of samples, might be close to that estimated by simple random sampling (overall standard deviation divided by the square root of the number of cases). The standard deviation within the group would clearly underestimate the sampling error of its mean, since the group was "found" by the program in such a way as to make it different from others, and homogeneous (low variance) inside the group.

We suggest, then, focusing on efficiency in sampling rather than on ease in estimating sampling errors, and on approximations rather than a heavy investment in computing or estimating sampling errors. The balanced-repeated-replication method provides a method of estimating sampling errors, and we need more experience in using it to see whether design effects are reasonably constant. But the purpose of most analysis is finding what matters, what helps explain something, and explanatory *power* is what counts. Almost anything that substantially reduces the unexplained variance in some dependent variable will be significant, or would be if the sample were a little larger. Indeed, what we are really interested in is the sampling stability of our estimates of the fraction of variance accounted for by an explanatory variable, or the stability of our ranking of a number of explanatory variables according to their importance (power in reducing the unexplained variance).

The preceding discussion of sampling has assumed that economists who are concerned with sample surveys will find themselves in one of two situations. They may undertake on their own projects which require only fairly simple sample designs or they may be involved in the design or the analysis of large-scale and expensive projects, involving specialists in sampling.

The merits of simplicity in sample design have been stressed for those in the first situation. In a great many situations it is possible to use simple random sampling, or simple random sampling modified only by the introduction of stratification. Especially for small scale or pilot studies there is a presumption in favour of self-weighting samples with equal probabilities of selection of the final elements in the sample. It should be kept in mind that many refinements have been developed in order to improve the *efficiency* with which simple descriptive statistics can be estimated. Such statistics may or may not be important in a given project. This presumption in favor of simplicity, however, does not extend to situations in which there are large potential gains from such techniques as the use of controlled selection or variable sampling fractions.

For economists concerned with the design or analysis of large scale sample surveys, it is important to understand the nature of the sampling procedures used to develop them. Such techniques as controlled selection impose limits on the possibilities of analysis which are not obvious to someone without knowledge of sampling. The use of complex designs complicates estimates of the variance of sample statistics and, hence, estimates of the sampling errors of estimates. The execution of sample designs is a potential source of bias, which is insidious because it is concealed. There is an initial problem of the specification of the basic type of sampling procedure to be used. Anyone concerned with the design of sample surveys should have a grasp of the full range of possibilities.

Footnotes to Chapter III

1. Leslie Kish, *Survey Sampling,* John Wiley, New York, 1965. C. A. Moser, Survey Methods in Social Investigation, Heinemann, London, 1958. For an excellent introduction, see *Sampling Lectures* (Supplemental courses for case studies in surveys and censuses), I.S.P. Supplemental Course Series No. 1, U.S. Department of Commerce, Bureau of the Census, Washington, D.C., 1968. ($1.00).

2. See any text on the design of experiments for the proof of the optimality of equal-sized groups, and for the efficiency of excluding the middle third of a distribution, e.g., W. G. Cochran and G. M. Cox, *Experimental Designs* (second edition) John Wiley and Sons, New York, 1957.

3. D. L. Hatch and M. A. Hatch, "Criteria of Social Status as Derived from Marriage Announcements in the *New York Times,"* American Sociological *Review* 12 (Aug., 1947) 396-403.

4. Cahnman, "Comment," *American Sociological Review* 13 (Feb., 1948) 96-97.

5. See R. A. Fisher, *The Design of Experiments,* 6th edition, Oliver and Boyd, London, 1953.

   and R. A. Fisher, *Statistical Methods for Research Workers,* 12th edition, Oliver and Boyd, Edinburgh, 1954, and the reference in note 2.

   For a neat design, see Bernard Berelson and Ronald Freedman, "A Study in Fertility Control," *Scientific American* 210 (May, 1964) 29-37.

6. See Kish, *op. cit.*, pp. 562-566.

7. C. A. Moser and A. Stuart, "An Experimental Study of Quota Sampling," *Journal of the Royal Statistical Society*, Series A, 116 (1953), 349-405.

8. The discussion follows Kish, *op. cit.*

9. Robert Ferber, *The Reliability of Consumer Reports of Financial Assets and Debts*, Bureau of Economic and Business Research, University of Illinois, Urbana, Ill., 1966.

10. John B. Lansing, Gerald Ginsburg, and Kaisa Braaten, *An Investigation of Response Error*, Bureau of Business and Economic Research, University of Illinois, Urbana, Illinois, 1961.

11. Leslie Kish and Irene Hess, "On Noncoverage of Sample Dwellings," *Journal of the American Statistical Association* 53 (June, 1958), 509-524.

12. National Council of Applied Economic Research, *Urban Income and Saving*, N.C.A.E.R., New Delhi, India, 1962.

13. Donald T. Brash, *American Investment in Australian Industry*, Australian National University Press, 1966.

14. Kish, *op. cit.* pp. 29 ff. For a full description of the Survey Research Center sample, see L. Kish and I. Hess, *Survey Research Center's National Sample of Dwellings*, Survey Research Center, University of Michigan, Ann Arbor, 1965.

    Moser, *op. cit.*, Chapter 6.

15. Kish, *op. cit.* p. 164 ff. See also U.S. Bureau of the Census: *Supplemental Courses for Case Studies in Surveys and Censuses*, Sampling Lectures I.S.P. Supplemental Course Series No. 1, Washington, D.C., 1968, pp. 52 ff.

16. James Morgan, Martin David, Wilbur Cohen, and Harvey Brazer, *Income and Welfare in the United States*, McGraw-Hill, New York, 1962.

17. For a method of treating this problem, see Kish, *op. cit.*, p. 493.

18. Moser, *op. cit.*, pp. 84-88.

19. Kish, *op. cit.*, p. 95.

20. See Robin Barlow, Harvey Brazer, and James Morgan *The Economic Behavior of the Affluent*, The Brookings Institution, Washington, D.C., 1966.

21. H. F. Huddleston, "Point Sampling Surveys for Potato Acreage in Colorado's San Luis Valley," *Agricultural Economics Research* 20 (Jan., 1968), pp. 1-4.

22. Grover C. Wirick, James N. Morgan, and Robin Barlow, "Population Survey: Health Care and Its Financing," in Walter J. McNerney, ed., *Hospital and Medical Economics*, Hospital Research and Educational Trust, Chicago, Illinois, 1962 (2 vols.), Vol. 1, pp. 61-357.

23. Kish, *op. cit.,* pp. 457 ff. See also U.S. Bureau of the Census, *The Current Population Survey: A Report on Methodology,* Technical Paper No. 7, Washington, D.C., 1963.

24. H. S. Hauthakker and John Haldi, "Household Investment in Automobiles: an Intertemporal Cross-Section Analysis," in Irwin Friend and Robert Jones, eds., *Consumption and Savings* (2 vols.), University of Pennsylvania Press, Philadelphia, 1960, Vol. 1, pp. 174-224.

25. F. Thomas Juster, *Anticipations and Purchases—An Analysis of Consumer Behavior* (National Bureau of Economic Research General Series No. 79), Princeton University Press, Princeton, 1964;

    Philip Cagan, *The Effect of Pension Plans on Aggregate Saving* (Evidence from a sample survey), Occasional Paper 95, National Bureau of Economic Research Columbia University Press, New York, 1965.

26. Kish, *op. cit.,* pp. 582-587; see also Philip J. McCarthy, *Replication: An Approach to the Analysis of Data for Complex Surveys,* National Center for Health Statistics, U.S. Public Health Service, U.S. Department of Health, Education and Welfare, Washington, D.C., April, 1966; and Leslie Kish and Martin Frankel, "Balanced Repeated Replications for Standard Errors," *Journal of the American Statistical Association,* 65 (Sept., 1970) 1071-1094.

    See also Walt R. Simmons and James T. Baird, Jr. "Pseudo-Replication in the NCHS Health Examination Survey," *Proceedings of the Social Statistics Section,* American Statistical Association, 1968, 19-30. They find larger design effects, presumably because their data come from more heavily clustered samples.

27. Harold L. Sheppard and A. Harvey Belitsky, *The Job Hunt,* W. E. Upjohn Institute for Employment Research, Johns Hopkins Press, Baltimore, 1966.

28. John B. Lansing and Eva Mueller, *The Geographic Mobility of Labor,* Survey Research Center, University of Michigan, Ann Arbor, Michigan, 1967.

29. See Kish, *op. cit.,* pp. 600, and T. Dalenius, *Sampling in Sweden,* Almquist and Wicksell, Stockholm, Sweden, 1957.

Chapter IV

METHODS OF DATA COLLECTION

Introduction

It is in data collection that economists who undertake sample surveys are most likely to find themselves in difficulties. In economics there is no well-developed tradition of methodology in data collection at the microeconomic level. The existing methodological literature on surveys has been written for the most part by non-economists, typically by sociologists, social psychologists, or statisticians. Often it is oriented toward problems which have little substantive importance to economists. Another difficulty is that there may be no neat answer to the question of how to handle a specific problem. Yet, it is possible to be wrong—and it is sometimes possible to prove that a particular method led to wrong results. Variables as measured may be poor approximations to the variables which an investigator meant to measure. In the extreme case, they may be so poor as to be useless.

We may contrast problems of data collection with those of sampling and analysis. Sampling is a specialized branch of statistics, but there is an extensive literature, and an economist with a good background in mathematical statistics is likely to find that he can learn what he needs to know about it without too much difficulty. In analysis he is likely to feel that he is on home ground. It is here that the work done by economists is often technically more sophisticated than that done by people from other disciplines. In data collection, however, this chapter will start from the beginning, assuming no special background of knowledge, and treat the subject in detail.

The Measurement of Economic Concepts: Introductory Remarks

The tension between economic theory and variables as measured in economic surveys becomes apparent when we recognize that economic theory for the most part is highly abstract. In the theory of the household, for example, one assumes initially the existence of a household. This household is conceived to have an income, and a set of preferences. It also will have a set of assets and liabilities and is thought of in any given period as dividing its income between

101

saving and spending, allocating the expenditure among a set of goods and services. It will have expectations (subjective probabilities) about the world and the
future. There is a tendency to think of the empirical referents of these concepts
as falling into two categories: "factual" and "psychological." The "factual"
variables would include income, prices, expenditures, assets and liabilities, while
the "psychological" variables are the preferences and the subjective probabilities.

This dichotomy is a useful starting point, but it has a tendency to break
down. It is not the objective magnitude, but what is perceived by the household
which often turns out to be theoretically relevant and useful for prediction. The
leading example of a construct now approached in this manner by economic
theorists is income: it is income taking into account income expectations, "permanent" income, or some such concept, which is now commonly used in the
theoretical literature, rather than a "factual" measure of income received in the
past. But even with last year's income, issues of non-money income, capital
gains, payroll withholding, or direct employer contributions to pensions, are
problems.

Factual concepts may be defined by economists in a highly sophisticated
manner. One thinks, for example, of the questions that must be resolved to determine the exact income of the owner of an unincorporated business. Or, of the
complications introduced by the concept of a flow of services given off by each
durable good owned by a family. The concept of "preferences" is highly abstract.
It incorporates the whole of the psychology of each of the several members of a
household, not to mention the psychology of their interaction with each other.

As a consequence, it is often difficult to define the empirical counterpart
of a theoretical construct. It is common to use in analysis variables which are at
best "proxies" for the theoretically relevant variables. For example, house value
has been used as a proxy for permanent income. Obviously, the two are not
identical, and it becomes a matter of judgment whether the one is a useful proxy
for the other in the context of a particular analysis.

There are two sides to the problem. Starting from a theoretical construct,
it may be difficult to find a satisfactory empirical counterpart. Starting from an
empirical variable as measured, it may be difficult to find a satisfactory theoretical counterpart. The problem is to develop methods of data collection that bring
the two as close together as possible. Of course, the gap may also be reduced by
the elaboration of appropriate theory.

While the above examples are drawn from the household sector, the same
type of problems also arise in studies of business enterprises. Problems of definitions for a business firm are particularly acute with such concepts as "research
and development" costs. Comparisons of a 1956 Bureau of Labor Statistics
study with a 1957 Census Bureau survey showed such large differences, that the
Census Bureau visited some of the firms to study the basis on which the figures
were reported.[1] In both areas it is important that an investigator have a thorough

knowledge of the problems with which he is concerned, preferably both theoretical and empirical knowledge.

Many economic concepts have been measured to a satisfactory level of accuracy using the survey method. A leading example is the measurement of the size of the labor force and the level of unemployment through the *Current Population Surveys.* It took years of development, under pressure from representatives from industry and labor who challenged the figures, for the present state to be reached, and problems still exist.[2]

A special set of problems arise in the collection of economic data because some are stocks or situational variables at some point in time and others are flows over a period of time. Theoretically one might like to use rates of flow at the same point in time, but in practice that is impossible with some flows which vary and need to be summed (averaged) over a period. In practice then, one may have data on a man's income for the previous year 1970 and his rate of payments on current installment debts as of February 1971. To compare one with the other and ask how many are paying more than twenty percent of their income on installment debt raises difficulties with people whose current rate of income differs from its average over the previous year, or whose debt payments will not continue for a whole year. Relating his current outstanding debt to his debt payments will at least tell one how many payments he is away from being out of debt, unless he has some complex mixture of debts, or balloon notes.

Similar problems arise with family composition, which may have changed during the year. If secondary earners have left the household, one is unlikely to have their earnings included in the family income reports for the previous year, but neither will they be counted as part of the family. If new income-earning members join the family, there is danger of getting their income only for the time they were with the family, but counting them as though they were in the family the whole year. Such problems are particularly difficult with budget studies, where elaborate editing may require putting in "partial people" as well as part of their annual incomes.

And if one is interested in an individual's total contribution to the flow of credit, it would be necessary to inquire about debts incurred during the previous year and already paid.

In general a problem may arise whether to measure a flow by asking for a flow, or by getting change in stocks. If there are many transactions, as with a savings account, one may want to ask the balance at beginning and end of the year, but with stocks or houses it may be better to ask about purchases and sales, unless one wants to include unrealized capital gains. Estimates of saving have traditionally been built out of a combination, some components being changes in stocks and some flows of saving (into retirement pensions, or mortgage repayments, or life insurance).

Other problems arise with unincorporated businesses and farms where it is difficult to distinguish the business from the private household. Even if one wanted to include the whole thing, problems of business accounting still intrude, since household accounts are largely on a receipts-expenditures basis, not appropriate for dealing with capital transactions and depreciation. In practice, we tend to ask about profits taken out of the business, and profits left in, as two components of family income. But poor accounting creeps in, when the respondent says there was no profit in the business because he had to pay for two new machines.

Ideally one could allocate the family income into such components as: contractual saving, discretionary saving in liquid form, other discretionary saving (stock purchases, etc.), investment in future consumption (in durables and house), regular "necessary" consumption, and discretionary consumption (vacations, etc.). But one could also measure everything in real—not monetary terms— taking into account of income in kind, irregular cash receipts, realized and even unrealized capital gains, etc. Attempts to get precise measures that fit the analysts' definitions may make the interviewing dull, difficult, and even irritating, sometimes out of proportion to the gains in accuracy.

An Overview of the Problem of Choice of Methods of Data Collection

There has been a proliferation of methods of data collection in the period since World War II and an increase in the sophistication with which methods are evaluated. It may be useful to review the range of choices and the criteria for selection of methods before considering details.

Basic Methods of Data Collection: There are three basic types of data collection: personal interviews, telephone interviews, and self-enumeration. Personal interviews are by far the most expensive method. Costs depend on a variety of characteristics, especially on the dispersion of the sample. Personal interviews are generally used where the material in the interview is complex or extensive, and where the sampling frame is such that personal visits are required to locate or select respondents. It is sometimes assumed that the quality of data from personal interviews is best, but this assumption is not always justified, especially when anonymity may be important.

Telephone interviews are much more economical than personal interviews. They have a basic limitation from a sampling point of view because some people have no phone, but the importance of this limitation is slowly declining, especially in the United States. Telephone interviews are advantageous when a sample is geographically dispersed.

Self-enumeration may be used with the questionnaire delivered to the respondent either by mail or in person by an interviewer. Mail questionnaires are *even* cheaper than telephone interviews but there is a major problem of non-response—people do not automatically return mail questionnaires. People may return partially filled-in replies. The wrong person may fill out the questionnaire and return it. The quality of the replies is also a matter of interest, but the most important limitations concern the length and complexity of the questionnaire.

The most satisfactory choice of technique may be a combination. For example, personal interviews may be followed up with telephone reinterviews. Again, a sample selected from a list may be approached by mail, with a follow-up in two stages of those who do not respond, the first follow-up on the telephone, and the second, in person. (Though telephone calls in advance have been known to *increase* refusal rates.)

Another possibility is to combine survey data with non-survey data about the individual in the sample. Sampling may be from a list which contains information in addition to the identification of the elements. It may be possible to find out more about the individuals interviewed, for example, by locating their homes on maps and reading information from the maps. Respondents may be asked for permission to release data in various records, such as social security.

Types of Questions: Questions may be classified according to the form of the stimuli presented to the respondent or according to the type of response desired. The stimulus is usually a fixed question intended to be asked or read precisely as written. It may be a form to be filled in accompanied by instructions rather than questions. It may be presented orally, or printed on a card which is shown to a respondent during a personal interview. Studies of attitudes make use of a variety of other stimuli: single words (in word association tests), pictures, incomplete sentences, and the like. The choice among stimuli depends primarily on what is to be measured, but, for a given objective, there may be a choice between a more or a less direct approach. It may be a little easier for a person to tell an interviewer that his income falls in the "G" range than to say, "It's about $9,000." Pointing to that range on a card may be still easier.

The response may be open or closed, that is, the respondent may be asked to answer in his own words, or to select from categories specified for him. It is cheaper and easier to process closed questions, but the risk of persistent misinterpretation of meaning is greater with closed questions. Closed questions may take many forms, including simple dichotomies (agree-disagree), multiple choice, numerical rankings, and scores indicated by the position of a mark, such as the position of a check mark along a line.

The problem of varying interpretation of the meaning of fixed alternatives is most serious where personal interviews are used and the interviewer does not read off the possible alternatives but tries to fit the respondent's answers into one of the categories. Not only is the variability of the interviewer's coding likely, but it may be persistent for each interviewer, leading to errors clustered geographically, and hence correlated with other variables.

Scales or indices may be constructed combining answers to several questions. For example, answers to a series of dichotomies may be combined in some way to place a respondent on a scale. There is an extensive psychological literature concerned with the methods of construction, interpretation, and validation of such scales. There is also much material in literature concerned with interviewing and questionnaire construction.

Use of Pretests and Pilot Studies: It is standard procedure in surveys to conduct a pretest of a questionnaire before it is used. Inexperienced investigators sometimes fail to realize the risks of error in using instruments which have not been adequately pretested. The difficulties which may be detected at this stage are legion, including ambiguities in questions, failure of questions to be understandable to respondents, and failure of questions to "fit" all respondents given their situations as they perceive them. How extensive a pretest is necessary, however, must be a matter of judgment. It is also a matter of judgment whether to carry an extensive pretest through the stages of tabulation, analysis, and the writing of a preliminary report.

A useful procedure in pretesting is to use many more questions in each area than will be retained in the final version, starting each area with the ones that may be used and adding a series of supplementary questions and probes in order to see whether the introductory question was getting the right information.

Criteria in Data Collection: The first criterion for a method of data collection is whether it can reasonably be expected to produce measures of the variables required for the objectives of a project. There may be only one method with any chance of success. For example, in surveys of illiterate peasants in underdeveloped countries there is no question of mail or telephone surveys. Some types of stimuli must be presented visually. Again, sheer length and complexity of an instrument may dictate the choice of personal interviews.

When there is a choice, two considerations apply, cost and quality of data. By data of good quality are meant data that will lead to correct conclusions concerning questions raised in the project.

Two broad classes of errors may arise, errors arising from non-response, and errors arising from inaccurate response. The relevant concepts have been developed most clearly for simple statistics such as the arithmetic mean. Consider, first, response accuracy. Suppose that there is conceptually for every element in a population a true score on some variable. Then there will also exist a true value for the arithmetic mean (and other parameters) for the population. We prefer methods of measurement such that, given a large enough sample, the mean for the sample would coincide with the population mean, i.e., no bias. We seek to avoid methods of measurement which would lead to understatements (or overstatements) even if we had very large samples. We *also* prefer methods which are accurate for each individual as well as accurate on the average for a large number of individuals, i.e. minimal random response variability. For a given sample we seek to minimize the sum of the squared discrepancies between true score and measured score.

The costs of the two types of "error" are different. If there is response variability but no particular bias, then we may fail to prove a relationship from the data when one really exists. On the other hand, if there is a persistent response bias it is always possible for it to lead to positive conclusions that are wrong, either about a measurement or, if the bias is correlated with some other variables, about a relationship. For instance, if people tend to understate their assets, particularly old people for whom they are a major source of security, then the survey will both underestimate consumer assets and also underestimate the correlation of asset accumulations with age.

Even if the methods of measurement were precise, the estimate of the true value for the population might be in error as a result of non-response. We may fail to obtain data from some elements in the sample, and these elements may differ in some systematic way from those we do enumerate.

What we seek to minimize is the discrepancy between our estimates of the statistics in which we are interested and the true values of those statistics (the parameters) in the population. We also need to know the probable magnitude of the discrepancies between the statistics we estimate and the corresponding parameter. There is a tendency to think of sources of error one at a time—response error, error of nonresponse, and sampling error. This tendency is natural, even necessary. But it should not distract us from our central concern, are conclusions we reach about the population correct?

Field Procedures

While all the decisions about a survey fit together into a pattern which must be consistent and appropriate, we cannot talk about everything at once, and have chosen to organize the discussion roughly according to the temporal order in which things happen. Regardless of the kind of instrument used, there are a set of field procedures which have to be worked out and designed. Getting a survey done is like organizing a major construction project or getting a banquet on the table while it is hot. Any little mistake may delay, or ruin, the whole process. There may be a limited time on the calendar when the field work can be done. Delays in completing the interviewing may hold up all subsequent steps and, since much of the cost of a survey is the salaries of the research and ancillary staff, delay means increased cost.

Assuming that some sample has been drawn, there is a considerable amount of work in getting procedures set up for checking out each sample address or identification. This is necessary first, to be sure that every address has been assigned to some interviewer; second, to monitor the field work and provide help where interviewers are falling behind; and third, to check out the sample and make sure some data are assembled on the nonresponse and nonsample addresses to allow an analysis of these problems. Where respondents are paid, or reinterviews are involved, even more elaborate records must be kept.

Procedures must be worked out to assure the privacy of respondent's replies. This means that the identifying information about the respondents should be capable of physical separation from the substantive replies, so that the latter can be processed without continual guarding. The general procedure is to have a separable cover sheet (often a double sheet) containing sample information, field experience reports, and whatever information the interviewer can be expected to report about nonsample cases. For instance, if the interviewer can estimate the rent level of dwellings where no interview was taken, the analyst can check whether the non-response come from more or less expensive dwellings than the response, i.e. whether there is that kind of non-response bias.

Some of the sampling information needs to be part of the analysis: city size, region, etc., which requires transfer of some information from the cover sheet to the questionnaire before they are separated. And for control purposes and later checks, it is usually essential to have a number identifying the location of the record in the sample books (and on the cover sheets), also on the questionnaire, and even coded as part of the information. This means that it would still be physically possible to isolate one record in the data file, go back to the sample books and identify the address (and even name if names were used). Such identifiability is impossible to avoid in reinterview surveys where the next wave's data must be connected case by case with that from the first wave. In single surveys once the sample has been checked the basic sample books can be locked up for a period, then destroyed. It is particularly important to do this if the information is such that someone might want to subpoena it later.

It is conceivable that one might still be able to identify individuals from the basic data in the data file by complex sorting, particularly if the local area information is quite detailed, but in most small sample surveys where the probability of selection is one in thirty thousand or so it is most unlikely.

There is also a problem when surveys are done for others because lawyers sometimes write into contracts that the basic data belong to the sponsor. It is essential to make clear in these cases that the phrase "basic data" does not include the information in the sample books. Indeed, there is another issue here, since survey data about individuals retained for the exclusive use of one group or agency (including the government) allows the use of that information to manipulate or exploit individuals. It is probably against good public policy for any surveys to be done and the data not made publicly available, at least after a brief period, not just for their utility in scientific analysis but to prevent their exclusive use by one group possibly to the detriment of another group. It is for that reason that survey organizations, like the Survey Research Center of The

University of Michigan, have charter provisions prohibiting them from conducting surveys unless the data will be made freely available.

Preparation of the basic sampling materials includes not only sample books and cover sheets (one for each address in the sample), but also control lists for the field supervisors, address labels for sending advance letters to respondents announcing the study and justifying it, and other materials for the interviews. Since it is often impossible to have extensive training sessions on each survey, the interviewers' instruction book for each study must contain material on the purposes of the study, and any special problems it may involve. The sheer magnitude of the problem of mailing out materials to interviewers (or sending out mail questionnaires) necessitates planning and organization if everything is to start on time. And it has to start on time if it is to end on time.

Whenever new *procedures* are involved, it may pay to pretest them, as well as the questionnaire itself. But in any case, pretests of the basic instrument, using regular interviewers and in a variety of circumstances, are essential. Given the natural propensity to keep changing and improving things, it is only too easy to have a questionnaire which has been changed considerably since the last pretest. It is a matter of judgment whether the changes require further testing, but the time schedule should allow it.

Mail questionnaires and other self-enumerated forms frequently show evidence of inadequate pretesting. A well-trained interviewer can sometimes get information even when the questionnaire is inadequate, but the main result in self-enumeration is either nonresponse or nonsense response.

If the interviewer's motivation is so important—as we shall see later that it is—how is it to be increased? Quick feedback as to good and bad interviewing is certainly important, whether from the field supervisor or from the analysis staff which looks over the interviews as they come in. Some sense of what happens to the interviews, both mechanically and scientifically, also helps the interviewer. Direct contact with both the central office administration and the research staff of each project is difficult when interviewers are scattered all over the country. Hence, the quality of the written material is crucial. It should have a personal touch, since interviewers, just as respondents, react as much to the desire to please *someone* as to a vague sense of scientific importance.

There is usually an interviewers' manual containing general instructions on procedures, preliminary sampling work, time and cost reporting procedures, etc. With each study there is also an interviewer's instruction book, giving procedural details, a general statement of purpose and how it is to be achieved, and question-by-question instructions. The latter often tend to become wordy and redundant, while failing to give instructions on how to handle difficult cases. Some also attempt to make up for an inadequate questionnaire by instructing the interviewer to "be sure to find out" without telling her how she is to do it. It is hard fact that if you want an answer, you have to ask the question. If you want to know whether the respondent is including in his reported food expenses the cost of milk delivered to the door, you have to ask him. It does no good to tell the interviewer to find out; she would only have to violate her general instructions by asking several questions not in the questionnaire.

There is one acceptable thing to tell interviewers to do when the questionnaire becomes inadequate, as the best of them do in such cases, and that is to find out a little more detail by asking a probe like "Tell me more about that" and writing down a story which the editor in the home office can then interpret.

Continuous monitoring during the course of a survey is very important. If flaws show up, interviewers can be warned about them or changes made. If individual interviewers are making errors—skipping sequences of questions, accepting inadequate answers, etc.—they can be told before they make the same errors on the rest of their cases. Extensive use of the long distance phone is often necessary, though the better the materials, and the better the interviewers' training, the less monitoring should be necessary.

In many studies it is essential that the preparation include securing the informed consent of various important interest groups. The local police and newspapers should know about the study, and the local bank or business community if it involves consumer finances. Often the local interviewer can do this but press releases help. Where the study involves some professional group or interest group, lawyers, doctors, labor unions, etc., problems are even more delicate. In one study of auto accident compensation, the state *Bar Journal* issued a statement before the study was even designed, asserting that no good could come from such a study. One study aborted completely because the medical association became hostile to one of the potential directors because he was associated with the field of public health, though he was a doctor. The usual objection of specialists is that the researchers do not really know the field and hence cannot do the study properly. Since studies often involve many specialties, even in a single study, the only solution seems to be research advisory committees and extensive efforts to consult with the "experts."

Decisions also have to be made about such field problems as call-backs and follow-up procedures. Standards of response rate levels are often used, but some rules about how many calls to make at any one place and what to count as a call (passing by and noticing no lights in the house?) are needed. This is the implementation of an economic decision, whether to get more interviews by taking a larger initial sample and restricting call-backs (with potential greater non-response bias) or whether to spend the money trying to get high response rates. We shall see later that there is some reason to believe that the reliability of the data from people difficult to find and interview is lower, so that the higher response rate may provide less non-response bias at the expense of some greater response bias.

Field procedures also involve preparations for feed-back to interviewers and respondents about the outcome of the study. Interviewers are usually interested in how their respondents compared with others and like materials so that they can talk intelligently with reluctant respondents about what happens to survey findings. Respondents, even if they are not to be reinterviewed, deserve to know the findings if only as a gesture of appreciation for their cooperation. The promise of such a report seems to be useful in inducing them to cooperate in the first place. In the case of reinterviews the mailing of a report between waves also serves as a check on the validity of mailing addresses and a way of finding who has moved in time to locate the new addresses.

The researcher's preoccupation with his study objectives may make it difficult for him to prepare a summary of results that would interest either interviewers or respondents. What is interesting to respondents may be such simple things as what kinds of people use seat belts or how long it takes other people to get to work, not elaborate interpretations of complex concepts.

A final problem is that while some respondents may want to secure a copy of the full report, it cannot be offered free on most budgets, and offering to sell it may irritate.

There is some doubt whether it is advisable to set up rules about procedures where interviewers may have to use their judgment, such as scheduling of interviews, when to call, etc. Sometimes, however, choices must be made which depend on the policy one seeks to implement. For instance, one study discovered that in interviewing employed persons there were ten to fifteen percent fewer not-at-homes if one called on week-day evenings, but also five to seven percent more refusals at those times.[3] The author's conclusion that the week-day evenings were better, is true only if one wanted to minimize costs, not if one wanted to maximize response rates.

Specific Methods of Data Collection

Personal Interviews and Telephone Interviews: There has been considerable interest in recent years in the use of interviews taken by telephone to replace or to supplement personal interviews. As previously noted, costs are much lower for telephone interviews. And the proportion of families who have a telephone is high and rising. How, then, do telephone and personal interviews compare?

The logical starting point of analysis is the lack of the personal presence of an interviewer in a telephone interview. Social motivation arising out of the presence of an interviewer is important in gaining the cooperation of respondents. In a telephone situation, since the interviewer physically is not present, one would expect the social motivation to communicate to be somewhat reduced. It is easier to say "no" over the phone. And the interviewer lacks the visual cues by which she may change her approach. In some degree, however, the social motivation should be found over the telephone.

It is also possible that the personal presence of an interviewer helps to communicate a sense of the importance of the research. It is more trouble to visit someone than to call by phone and respondents who accept the idea that a survey is important should be more likely to take trouble to answer carefully.

Another obvious limitation of telephone interviews is that visual stimuli cannot be used. The interviewer's credentials cannot be examined. Respondents cannot look at cards or place check marks and the like. For some purposes this limitation may be important, but most questions in personal interviews are presented orally. The lack of visual stimuli will also tend to reduce some of the subtler forms of communication that take place when two people meet face-to-face. Facial expressions, body movements, eye contact—all may play some part in the interpretation of what is said and of pauses in the verbal interchange. This loss no doubt would be serious for some types of interviewing, say, for a clinical diagnostic interview. It may be a small problem for routinized mass interviewing. There may even be some gain in standardization of interviewer behavior resulting from the elimination of visual contact.

There may also be some gains in how comfortable respondents feel.[4] There is a greater anonymity in a telephone interview, and a greater degree of control in the hands of the respondents, who knows he has the option of putting down the instrument. He may assume the interview will be brief.

The preceding observations are primarily deductions from what is known in general about interviewing, and should be checked by further research. There has not been as much research into the quality of data obtained by telephone as into the response rates by telephone which are comparable to those by personal interview.

There has been one extensive comparison by Jay Schmiedeskamp of data obtained by telephone reinterviews with data from a comparable sample of personal interviews taken at the same time with the same questionnaire.[5] The comparison was made as part of the Survey Research Center's regular quarterly survey of consumer intentions. Results from the telephone reinterview in general were similar to those from the personal interview. There were some differences, however, especially in the direction of less differentiated responses over the phone. This finding is consistent with the somewhat lower degree of motivation in telephone interviews suggested above.

There are a variety of ways in which telephone interviews can be used: entire studies can be conducted by telephone; preliminary interviews may be by phone; follow-up interviews may be by phone; and the phone may be used as part of a multi-stage approach, as in the study by Donald reported above. Follow-up interviews have been especially successful.[6] But preliminary telephone contacts have in at least one case *reduced* response rates substantially.[7]

There are two kinds of validity questions we deal with when we reinterview people by mail or telephone. One is the question of non-response bias and the other is the question of whether mail or telephone is getting different answers from what personal interviews would get. In the Schmiedeskamp data there is a third problem because reinterviews have two kinds of non-response: one because some people do not have telephones, and another because some people do not give the reinterview. In fact, there was an eighty-five percent response rate originally; then seventy-six percent of the people had telephones, ninety-one percent of them gave their numbers, and eighty-five percent of them agreed to an interview later when phoned. This gives a total non-response rate of fifty percent, starting from the initial sample frame. So when Schmiedeskamp compares the telephone reinterview with a new cross-section, he is combining various kinds of response biases from using the telephone with some non-response biases. But he does find that people tend to make more non-committal answers and are more likely to refuse to give sensitive financial information on the phone.

Mail Interviews, Self-Enumeration, and the Problem of Anonymity: The third general category of methods of data collection is characterized by the lack of participation by an interviewer in the process of recording answers to questions. Self-enumeration may take place after delivery of the questionnaire by mail or by an interviewer in person. Return of the questionnaire may be by mail, or an interviewer may call to collect it. If the interviewer calls, she may or may not check over the answers. In one variant the respondent places his response in a sealed envelope and the interviewer simply walks to the nearest postal box with the respondent and they mail the envelope together. A basic question concerning these techniques is the effect on the data of the partial or complete removal of the interviewer.

The most obvious loss is the reduction or elimination of social motivation to respond. As discussed earlier, low response rates often characterize mail questionnaires. Yet, as noted above, response rates vary widely depending upon three types of consideration: the nature of the inquiry and its auspices, the population being studied, and the techniques used. There are many situations in which reasonably good response rates can be obtained with self-enumeration procedures.

What, then, can be said about the quality of the resulting data? The removal of the interviewer from the communication process has one major consequence for the design of the questionnaire. Interviewers can be trained to make their way through contingencies. These contingencies may be important in a complex questionnaire for the purpose of adapting the questions to the respondent's situation. Whole blocks of questions may be meaningless for some people but not for others. Which sequence fits best may depend on answers not just to a single question but to two or more questions. "If A or B to Q.1 or Q.2 ask Q.3." An interviewer's job is like operating a set of switches to keep the interview on the right track. Respondents seeing a form for the first (and only) time cannot be expected to do this job as well.

It is also true that some respondents are illiterate and cannot handle a printed questionnaire at all. The difficulties of the semiliterate, however, may be exaggerated. Cannell and Fowler found in their study of accuracy of report of hospitalization that, contrary to expectation, level of education was more highly correlated with accuracy of report in personal interviews than in self-enumeration.[8] They suggest that people of low education may find it difficult to reply quickly to the sequence of questions in a personal interview. With a self-administered form at least they can take their time. The topic would bear further investigation.

Cannell and Fowler also suggest that the interviewer contributes to the quality of the data by evaluating the adequacy of responses. An interviewer can be trained to judge what constitutes a reply. She can wait for it and not proceed to the next item until she has it. (And she can at least try to cut off a flow of irrelevant material.) Cannell and Fowler do produce some evidence to support this contention, but, in their data, the differences are small. In reporting type of surgery in the personal interviews seventy-five percent reported replies which were coded in the same category as the report from the hospital records. The comparable percentage for the self-enumeration proceedings is sixty-nine percent.

Another difficulty is that one is not sure just who filled out the questionnaire. This is particularly bothersome with mail questionnaires to business establishments and with questionnaires dealing with plans, attitudes, expectations, or other matters likely to vary from person to person among those who might be replying.

The use of self-enumeration procedures, on the other hand, may lead to improvements in quality of data in some situations. First, a personal interview is ordinarily restricted to a limited time at one place. It may be advantageous to allow people time to check with other members of their families or to consult records. There were gains in the self-enumeration procedure in percentage of episodes reported by proxy respondents in Cannell and Fowler's project. Housewives could ask their husbands after the men came home from work. This advantage would be irrelevant, of course, if people responded only for themselves. In financial surveys, however, even if people speak for themselves they may not have all their records at hand when an interviewer calls.

Self-administered forms are sometimes used in the collection of data on household expenditures as a means of controlling the problem of memory error. Small outlays can easily be forgotten or recalled inaccurately. People may be asked, therefore, to keep a record book of some kind. This procedure is used by the Social Survey in Great Britain.[9] Interviewers re-visit the households periodically to supervise the record keeping.

There has been considerable interest in another potential advantage of self-administration, the possible gain in people's willingness to reveal information about their finances if they do not have to give the information to an interviewer.

There has been some research on the importance of anonymity in inquiries on a variety of subjects. Hyman summarized some of the findings in his monograph on interviewing.[10] Anonymity is clearly a matter of degree, and it is not obvious what constitutes anonymity as it is perceived by a respondent. The limiting case would be one in which a respondent was certain that the replies he gave could not be traced to him. He cannot be given this absolute assurance as long as he states his answers to an interviewer, who obviously associates the answers with the man who gives them. Yet there is some degree of anonymity in talking to an interviewer whom one has never seen before and never expects to see again. It may well make a difference whether or not the interviewer knows the respondent's name. If no interviewer is present, it may matter whether or not the name of the respondent is entered on the report form. Unsigned questionnaires administered to groups of people seem to meet the criterion of psychological anonymity, and there has been research on the difference between signed and unsigned questionnaires administered to groups. The subject matter of the studies, however, has not been economic.

The signature does make a difference in studies in the personality field. Unsigned instruments are more likely to elicit feelings associated with instability and physical symptoms with neurotic implications.[11] In studies among soldiers about attitudes toward military service those who signed their questionnaires gave more favorable attitudes toward officers and expressed more job satisfaction. In a study by Festinger of the voting behavior of Jewish and Catholic college girls in electing officers to an artificially created club, results were complex. Catholic girls always preferred Catholic officers. Jewish girls expressed preference for Jewish officers only when the girls were not identified by name and religion.[12]

Cannell and Fowler report no difference between personal interviews and *signed* self-reports in the completeness of report of "threatening" diagnoses. That is, there was no difference in the reporting of malignancies, venereal diseases, mental disorders, and the like. They infer that it was the signature which made the difference—unsigned self-administered forms might have been different. Of course it is difficult to do validity studies if there is *real* anonymity.

In a study of accuracy of reporting loans Lansing, Ginsburg, and Braaten experimented with use of a sealed envelope technique.[13] Results were inconclusive. There was some tendency toward greater reliability with the sealed envelope technique, but the difference was so small that it might have been the result of chance.

It is difficult to come to firm conclusions as to the importance of anonymity in financial surveys on the basis of the available evidence. There is convincing evidence that some types of economic information are underreported because people are not willing to reveal the answers. The worst biases are for bank accounts and other financial assets, and for income from property. People who are asked for such information are being asked for information which is not normally discussed. We may ask why they should persist in concealing this information and whether some degree of anonymity could overcome their reluctance.

It is possible that people withhold information for fear that it will come into the hands of the Internal Revenue Service. There is evidence that income tax is not paid on all income that is taxable. Recent improvements in enforcement procedures, such as the use of information returns from banks, should reduce evasion, and it will be interesting to see if survey reports improve correspondingly. To the extent that people evade taxes, the only chance of getting them to report the income in a survey would seem to be to provide absolute guarantees of anonymity. People cannot be expected to risk fines or imprisonment to help somebody's research project.

A second type of fear may be that financial information will somehow be used by people with opposing economic interests. The extreme case is a respondent who hesitates to admit he has large amounts of currency for fear the interviewer will steal it. It may be more common to be vaguely nervous about the interview—are those credentials forged? Is the interviewer really going to try to sell something after all? The suspicions aroused may be ill-defined, but they may lead people to be cautious. This type of difficulty should be soluble by procedures such as the sealed envelope technique and other devices for developing a solid identification of the research with an organization of impeccable reputation.

It may be that what is involved is a general sense of personal privacy, a feeling that certain things are nobody else's business. "Nobody else" may include the research organization. For people who take this view, anonymity may be a necessary but not a sufficient condition for accurate reporting.

Hyman has pointed out one additional consideration. Suppose that anonymity does tend to remove inhibitions about reporting. The removal of inhibitions may lead some people to report, not their actual situation, but the situation they would like to be in. Wishes and fantasies may lead to distortions. The desire to impress an audience may play a part, and the interviewer may provide the audience. This mechanism has been alleged to be at work in interviews on sexual behavior under Kinsey's auspices. We can only speculate about the psychological analogies between money and sex.

In the case of mail questionnaires, the gains from promised anonymity may be lost if one requires identification in order to check out the sample and to follow up those who have not responded. One way out of this is to ask the respondents to send in an anonymous questionnaire and, separately, a postcard with identification indicating that the questionnaire has been sent in.

A comprehensive analysis of research done on mail surveys, including comparisons with personal interviews, and with a bibliography of well over one hundred items, concluded:

"Despite the large amount of research reported on stimulation of response, the follow-up is the only technique which has been consistently found to raise response by a substantial amount—say over 20 percent. The evidence on the reliability and validity of mail survey response is meagre in quantity and poor in quality."[14]

The meager results of varying methods, even with elaborate factorial designs, was in spite of response rates which varied from less than twenty to more than ninety percent. Of course the quality of the instruments used varied and was not measured. The author, Christopher Scott, summarized the advantages and disadvantages of mail surveys admirably:

Advantages:
  Low cost
  No clustering in the sample
  No interviewer bias
  Respondent can consult others for information and take his time to
    consider his answers.

Disadvantages:
  Inadequate control over identity of respondent
  Inadequate control over whom he consults
  Inadequate control over date of response
  Inadequate control over order of questions (respondent can look ahead
    to see where you were going—you cannot funnel questions)
  Cannot use complex questions or complex instructions (skip sequences)
  Cannot secure spontaneous, first reactions
  Questionnaire design and coding are more troublesome
  Cannot be *sure* of an adequate response rate—they vary too much
  Cannot have the benefit of interviewers observations (race, neatness of
    house, type of neighborhood)

He might have added that it is difficult to separate non-response from bad addresses in mail studies, and that it is impossible to control the order in which the questions are actually answered.

Panels and Reinterviews: The choice of whether or not to use a research design involving reinterviews may depend upon the need to control response error and the cost of data collection as well as upon problems of non-response, discussed later in this chapter. There are also considerations related to analysis, which will be treated more fully in Chapter VI. (We may anticipate that discussion by noting that in the analysis of causal sequences it is an advantage to have observations for the same individuals at different points in time.)

There are advantages in the use of reinterviews from a sampling point of view. The cost of the preparation of a sample is less on a per interview basis when the same sample is interviewed more than once.[15] There are gains in statistical efficiency in estimating changes by the use of panels. Variation between successive samples does not enter the calculations. Thus, it is efficient for the Current Population Survey to use a rotating panel to estimate changes in labor force participation rates and unemployment rates. Each address is included in the sample a total of eight times.[16] Reference has been made earlier to reinterviews based on screening questions to select samples with special characteristics.

There is a corresponding disadvantage to the use of reinterviews which should be obvious but is sometimes overlooked. Repeated surveys can be combined to assemble large total samples for analysis which does not depend on the exact date of the interview. But an analyst may be better off with a total sample, say, 5000 interviews rather than five interviews with each of 1000 individuals. His sample of people in the top ten percent of the income distribution will be 500 people, not 100, and his opportunities for analysis of that group will be greatly increased.

There are economies in interviewing the same people repeatedly. The number of calls necessary to find people at home can be reduced. It may not be necessary to repeat all the questions asked in the first interview. For example, some of the background data of the family will not change. It may be possible to use cheaper methods of interviewing, especially the telephone, for interviews after the first.

There are important uses of reinterviews to control response error. First, in order to compare measurements of two dates, it is an advantage to reduce memory error by making the measurements close to the dates in question. Withey has shown the importance of this point for change in liquid assets and change in income over a period of twelve months.[17]

Second, it is possible only through reinterviews to use the important technique of "bounding" to prevent people from shifting events to points in time closer to the date of interview than the dates when they actually took place. This technique has been developed by the Census Bureau.[18] It consists of obtaining a detailed description of a particular event, such as a particular expenditure, in the initial interview. In the second interview reference is made to this information. It is not possible for the respondent to assign to the expenditure a date subsequent to the first interview. Some degree of control may also be gained over shifts in time in the opposite direction, to dates earlier than the first interview. If the event had already taken place, the interviewer may say, "you did not tell me about it in the first interview." In general any overlapping measurements offer possibilities of asking for reconciliation of differences.

Third, there may be some increase in accuracy of report associated with the longer experience of the respondent with the interview situation. This gain is more speculative, but the respondent may be better satisfied as to the good faith of the interviewer, and may have developed a more positive feeling toward the various aspects of the interview situation. This advantage did not prove to be important, however, in a validity study of savings account balances.[19]

There is a possible disadvantage to be set against these reductions in response error. There may be negative "conditioning" effects on the panel members. In the Current Population Survey, for example, conditioning is a problem. Families interviewed for the first time show a higher rate of unemployment, a score of 107.3, if the average for all groups is taken as 100.[20]

This reason for this phenomenon is not known. It could be that interviewers are more careful on the initial interview, or that new respondents report more fully. Or respondents may find it harder to maintain that they are looking for work when month after month they are still reporting no work. Conditioning may also influence the attitudes and behavior of respondents outside the interview situation. For example, people who are asked repeatedly for their opinions on some topic may develop opinions on that topic more fully than if they had not been interviewed about it.

There is also a potential non-response problem from the panel losses of people who move and there is, of course, an economic decision to make in a panel study of how far to follow movers. Since three-fourths of movers will move within the same county, it is easy to decide to follow some of them. On the other hand, if they move out of the county, following them becomes very expensive and you might prefer to trade a little bit of bias for a larger sample of the rest, and more precision.

We tend to lose from panels the young people, and we may also lose some people for whom the subject matter is basically completely unpleasant. Sobol reports losing more pessimists.[21] Pessimistic people are usually having financial difficulties or expect them, and it seems logical that they would not want to keep on granting financial interviews year after year if their financial situation were grim. In an extended panel study it is fairly clear that total losses can become substantial.

Another difficult problem with panels arises from changes in the composition and even identity of the unit (family, etc.). A sample of individuals can be followed, and the only sampling problem arises because older ones die and should be replaced with young ones coming in at the other end. If one starts with this in mind, however, it is possible to keep track of all those under eighteen in an original sample and bring them in as they become eighteen, to make up for those leaving the population. But if the unit of analysis is a nuclear family, or a regular family, or a household, then more serious problems arise. Suppose a couple gets divorced and each of them remarries. If one retains only the husband or the original wife in the sample, the panel develops a sex bias and some confusion as to whom to interview in later waves—the original person, or the new head of the family. If one decides to follow and interview *any* family containing *anyone* in the families originally interviewed, the sample gets larger, and biased in favor of larger unstable families, though it remains an unbiased sample of individuals.

To assess the extent of panel bias one can always compare what happens to a panel with an independent cross-section but, in a sense, a simpler, cheaper, and more advantageous procedure is to revisit the address of the original sample and interview people who moved in or were non-response of the previous year. This gives an independent cross-section sample, of which a very large fraction, say eighty percent, will be the same people as the members of the panel. The panel will include the people who did not move and were reinterviewed and also people who moved and were reinterviewed after they moved. The differences between these two overlapping samples, the interviews with all the people at the old addresses, and the reinterviews with people who did or did not move, consists in differences in the non-overlapping parts of the samples, and there is no simple sampling variation on the other part to "noise up" the estimates. The non-overlapping part of the new cross-section consists of some people who moved in and some people who were non-response last year but were willing to give an interview this year.

The non-overlapping part of the panel consists of people who moved and were followed and interviewed. What is missing in the panel, of course, are those who moved and could not be followed and the non-response of people who did not move. If we think carefully, there is one difficulty with this comparison. That is by going back to the old addresses there will be some non-response among people who did not move and were supposed to be interviewed, who may be slightly different from ordinary non-response in a brand new sample of addresses.

Selection of the Respondent

When information is to be collected about a unit consisting of more than one individual, there is a choice as to who will be designated as the respondent. There are four main possibilities in a general cross-section survey: (1) any responsible adult may reply; (2) there may be a random selection within the household or a random selection of husband or wife; (3) the head of the unit may be designated (i.e., the husband, if he is present); (4) each adult may be interviewed, either separately, or, possibly, together. The cost of data collection is probably lower when the interviewer can interview any adult. It is certainly more expensive to interview two or more adults per family. (It would be useful to know these exact cost differences.) On the other hand, the quality of data may vary according to who reports.

When information is to be collected involving people as individuals, there is clearly a risk of loss of accuracy when one person replies as a proxy for others.

In the validity study based on hospital records previously mentioned Cannell and Fowler found that the percentage of episodes not reported was twice as high when one adult was being interviewed about another as when the adult was reporting for himself.[22] It has been shown that the use of a self-enumeration procedure practically eliminated the difference, and it would be valuable to have comparable measures for other kinds of data.

When information is to be collected about the family as a unit, the selection of a respondent becomes essentially a question of whether husbands and wives give similar reports and, if they differ, which is more accurate. In a study by Haberman and Elinson of 645 marital pairs in New York it was found that the husbands do report higher total family income, $7377 versus $7179, and since income is commonly understated, there is a presumption that the husbands report somewhat more accurately.[23] The husbands in some families seem to have omitted or understated their wives' employment incomes. In the same study rent was asked in six class intervals. In 89.5 percent of the 612 families for which there were two reports, the reports were in the same category. As to the number of income earners, 90.1 percent agreed. With respect to these two variables, then, there is approximate agreement but by no means perfect consistency.

Wohlgast has reported a series of comparisons of data from husbands and wives.[24] Hers is the only study that finds out who actually predicts what happened. All the other studies are based on reports by husband or wife, or both, on who "usually decides" or who "has the most to say," or even who decides at each stage in the process. One gets a lot of role stereotypes in studies asking people who decides, but the Wohlgast study shows that in most cases, the wife is a somewhat better predictor than the husband, even for things like automobiles. The reason for this finding is not clear. Perhaps wives really and subtly dominate family decisions, or perhaps they are more realistic about what may happen, or perhaps they have a better sense of the desires of their husbands than husbands have of their wives' desires. It may be misleading to think of the husband-wife problem as one of power when it may be one of communication, consensus, and mutual understanding.

One small study throws some light on the possibility that wives may have better perception of the wants of husbands than the reverse.[25] Husband and wife were interviewed separately, hopefully simultaneously, and asked not only about their own attitudes, desires and plans, but their perception of how their spouse felt about each of these things. A whole series of comparisons is possible with such data.

There is a more general problem in that there is no theory about decision making in the family. Arrow's famous book shows that there *is no* set of criteria by which one can define the social optimum and maximize social welfare.[26] This is true for a family as well as for the whole society, so not only do we have very few descriptive findings about what happens in the family, we do not even have a deductive theory about what *should* happen. Psychologists have tried to develop something like an international trade theory of interpersonal relations. It assumes that people bring various goods and services and trade them for other goods and services, including affection.[27] However, there are problems with that theory if the different taste patterns are too disparate or, what is worse, if each party places a very high value on the other person's affection and doing what the other person would like. There is a funny passage in C. S. Lewis' *Screw-Tape Letters*[28] entitled "The Tea in the Garden Episode" where a family is being tricked by the devil's agent into sending themselves to Hell by getting very angry with each other. The whole process starts when each person sets out to try to do what the other person wants to do, and this "after you, Alphonse" process ends up with everybody angry.

A study by Sirken, Maynes, and Frechtling also contains data relevant to the evaluation of the accuracy of income reports from different respondents.[29] This project involved reinterviews by Census interviewers in August and September 1950 of about half the respondents from the Survey of Consumer Finances of January-February 1950. The project was part of the Census Quality Check (CQC). Identical, or virtually identical, sampling instructions were issued to the two sets of interviewers, and the resulting interviews were carefully matched so that it could be determined when the same families had been interviewed. In the SCF study "first quality respondents" were defined as heads of spending units. In seventy-six percent of the interviews the actual respondent was first quality. In the CQC a "first quality" respondent meant that all income recipients reported for themselves. In eighty-seven percent of the interviews the respondents were first quality. There was an initial expectation that reports of total income for a given family would agree more closely when first quality respondents were used in both surveys for that family. The reports did in fact agree more closely when first quality respondents were interviewed in both surveys. Under those conditions 62.6 percent of families reported incomes which fell in the same class interval. When other than first quality respondents were used in one survey or the other, 53.3 percent of the families reported incomes in the same class interval.

These results are consistent with those reported by Wohlgast and by Haberman and Elinson. In obtaining data on family income if a single individual is to report it is preferable to interview the husband. It is probably still better to interview each income receiver separately, if funds permit. Results for secondary earners were considerably improved in the later Surveys of Consumer Finances, however, on the basis of the study just mentioned without interviewing each person separately. A separate question was introduced in which the head was asked limited, specific supplemental questions about the income of his wife and other earners. In theory, that questionnaire had required that a long list of income questions be repeated for income receivers other than the head. The form was clear on the point—a column was provided for the answers—but it was less clear what the interviewer was supposed to do. The revised procedure, adopted in 1954, increased the percentages of spending units with more than one income receiver from 25.7 percent to 31.7 percent in one year. This experience illustrates a general point: it may be possible to reduce or even eliminate errors arising from the use of proxy respondents if the questionnaire is carefully designed with the problem in mind.

Problems of selecting respondents in business enterprises are not so easily reduced to precise rules. Different organizations have different internal divisions of labor and different systems of titles. It is especially difficult to apply the same rules to small firms as to very large ones. There may also be problems as to who is willing to respond. One cannot always go to the top. Instructions for selection of respondents, therefore, tend to be in more general terms, and to specify a function rather than a position—they specify the person concerned with and informed about a certain topic of inquiry. It may be useful to interview more than one person. On the other hand, where the respondent is extremely verbal and quick, it may be useful to have two interviewers or an interviewer and someone else to write it all down.[30]

What can one conclude about these joint decisions as to the mode of getting information and the selection of respondent? Those engaged in financial and economic surveys have concluded that even though the wife may have better overall view of the family's needs and desires, the husband is more likely to be able and willing to talk about financial matters. And in most families the degree of consensus on general goals (or at least mutual understanding on them) is sufficient so that the cost of interviewing more than one person has not seemed justified. On explicit purchase plans, however, some further attention to this problem may be required—the optimal outcome varying from attempts to interview the family together if possible, through random selection of head and wife, to separate interviews with each. Studies of details of family consumption (or expenditures) usually take any responsible adult (which means usually the housewife). Of course, for trend measurement, as distinct from analysis, there is little advantage of interviewing both over a random selection of husband or wife in a large sample. And for any intensive study, it seems clear that some personal contact from an interviewer is preferable. Extensive telephone interviews have been successfully done but usually with people previously interviewed in person.

Special Problems with Studies of Expenditure Details

While the calendar year is an excellent time period for studying income and saving and major expenditures, consumer expenditure studies which seek to secure detail on expenditures by categories or subcategories, face problems of deciding on the period of time for which to ask for each type of expenditure. If a very short time period, yesterday or last week, is used; then it is difficult to avoid double counting (telescoping, or bringing into the period things bought just before or just after), or omission of borderline or ambiguous items. If the period is too long, then memory errors are more likely. One expensive way out of this problem is to revisit a sample regularly and get reports of expenditures over a series of short periods covering the longer period (or to ask them to keep records over a series of short periods). An extensive discussion of these problems and of experiences in various countries with various methods, plus an extensive bibliography, was prepared by Robert Pearl as part of a proposed design for a continuous consumer expenditure survey (rotating panel) in the United States.[31]

Actually the experience is rather inconclusive, for one trades a smaller error variance (and perhaps less bias) with short period reporting for a larger sampling variance at least between families. Indeed, one cannot add up expenditure reports given for different periods and then look at the distribution of total expenditures, for although fifty-two times the average weekly expenditure is a good estimate of annual expenditure if one can eliminate seasonal bias, fifty-two times an individual's weekly expenditure is not a good estimate of his annual expenditure, nor is a distribution of such products a decent estimate of the distribution of annual expenditures. At least one major study did not consider this problem until the data were collected, probably because the objectives were not clearly spelled out and the focus had been on overall expenditure data for use in weighting cost of living indexes, rather than studies of interfamily differences.

The use of flows measured over short periods also exacerbates the problem of distinguishing between consumption, acquisition (purchase) and payment, and of trying to use one as an approximation for one of the others. The shorter the period, the more likely for the purchase to happen in one period, the acquisition (delivery) in another, the payment in a third, and perhaps the consumption in a fourth or over several periods.

In fact, it often turns out that diaries and records show less total expenditure than interview questions covering longer periods (and often more global groupings of expenditures). Most of the discussion is about telescoping, people getting tired of writing things down, etc., but it is entirely possible that some of the missing or shifted items were ambiguous as to just when they occurred, or as to which category they belonged to and, hence, were omitted.

One major technological possibility in this area, not used yet as we have pointed out in Chapter II, is to ease the load on the respondent and perhaps reduce the problem of his omitting items which do not fit the categories, by the machine coding of expenditures into categories. One expenditure study (Israel) let people put down just their expenditures in journal (list) form, but most of the others expect people to put them in categories, deciding whether telephone is utility or communication and transportation, and whether liquor for a company dinner is gifts, recreation, or consumption of liquor. Modern computers can store a very extensive English list of words with decisions as to the categories to which they belong. Only words missing from the machine dictionary would have to be hand-coded. Then the analysis of the data could be flexible as to where items were put. For instance, for trends one could put mortgage payments into expenditures, but for a more sophisticated analysis, the mortgage interest payments would go there, plus some fraction of the net equity in the house as imputed interest cost, while the rest of the mortgage payments would go into saving where they belong.

A major problem with expenditure surveys is the multiplicity of their purposes and the vast load they place on respondents. A reconsideration of the purposes might well lead to proposals for separate designs for each of several purposes, or at least some priority order among the various demands being put on the respondent.

If one were interested in getting short-run changes in consumption expenditures with details on categories, prices, and quantities, of secondary importance (or to be collected later after respondents get involved and motivated), then it might be useful to start with a sequence of topics which help the respondent understand the procedures. If one asked first only for cash receipts during a recent short period plus decrease (or increases treated as negative) of cash on hand, one could then explain that the sum represented what the family must have expended during the period. It would be an easy step then to ask about some expenditures which might have taken place which were not really expenses: money invested or loaned, use of expense account or gift money, investments in durables or home. After these corrections, the respondent should find it easy to remember fixed items like rent or installment payments or utilities, and large irregular items like trips, gifts, or repairs. Asking him to account for the rest presents him with a problem he has probably faced for himself and one which makes sense. Then, if he tries to build up from components the food, clothing, etc. expenses and they do not account for the total, he is motivated to search his memory for the missing items. But the expenditure total is reasonably accurate even if the allocation is not, and a repeated call for information on receipts since the last point in time, and change in cash, puts very little burden on the respondent.

If one then wanted to move toward saving estimates, one would have to ask about specific payroll withholdings, the value of the house and car (for depreciation estimates), and the details of any debt or insurance payments to separate insurance or interest costs or interest receipts from increases in equity (saving). And one would have to ask about financial investments—money put into or taken out of them and, if sales, whether there were capital gains.

The basic problem with the call for details of expenditures is that the ordinary person does not have all the information. As anyone knows who has tried to keep track of expenditures, they never add up to the correct total (receipts plus decrease in cash).

Surveys as Part of an Experimental Design

Whenever anything happens that may cause a change in people's attitudes or behaviors, the possibilities of securing revealing data from surveys are increased. Surveys before and after, particularly if they are with the same individuals, at least assure that one of the independent variables will change, whether it be the tax laws, the welfare laws, employment possibilities (if a plant shuts down, or opens), or some purposeful campaign by government or business designed to inform or convince people. Of course most such "experiments" are confounded, in the technical sense, both by other things which also just happen, and by the fact that most changes affect some people more than others (aside from their own responses). And being limited usually to one locality, such designs do not permit easy generalization.

There is also a possibility of designing such studies to cover a variety of areas where different things may happen.

As we pointed out in Chapter II, the situation is much better if the "treatments" or changes can be allocated to people or areas according to some experimental design, randomly, or better than randomly. There have been very few such experiments reported in the literature, though it seems likely that a certain amount of market research experimentation may never have been reported. One of the most intriguing such designs was in Taiwan where family planning educational and promotional programs were assigned, in varying intensity, to small districts, and the follow-up survey on the spread of information and acceptance covered the whole area, so it was possible not only to see what influence this program had locally but the spread of such influence to neighboring areas.[32]

One experiment allowed consumers to choose beef of various grades, all at the same price, and interviewed them later about how it tasted. They tended to select inferior grades because they had less fat, but their reports of taste correlated with the USDA quality ratings.[33]

There was one study of pricing and packaging of apples which used a very sophisticated Latin square design but no detailed data from the consumers. Another manipulated the price of milk.[34]

An elaborate attempt to compare those who moved into a housing project with those left behind, illustrated the difficulties: confounding in the selection of applicants, other events unevenly affecting people, etc.[35]

There is a great temptation to localize experimental studies in order to "control" over variables and reduce the variability of other forces. But such localization *increases* the possibility of some unique events particular to that area, spoiling the experiment and/or reducing its generalizability. It may well be better to take some probability sample of areas so that special local conditions are "randomized out," and indeed so that one can also study the effects of things that vary from area to area.

The design of experiments is a vast area of statistics which has gone through a great deal of development since R. A. Fisher's work, but the experience is frequently neglected or ignored when people first move from non-experimental designs to those which allow some manipulation. Or they make the other mistake of using such complex experimental designs that nothing about the results is firmly established. The subject is not simple and, since our concern is with the design of the surveys which accompany such designs rather than the designs themselves, we refer the reader to recent texts on experimental design.

The one thing that must always be kept in mind in experiments is that designing an experiment to test only one hypothesis is usually very inefficient and unnecessary. It may even be misleading if there are complex interaction effects present.

The focus of most "effects studies" has been more on the design of the programs whose effect was to be studied and their distribution over populations rather than on the surveys which determined the impact. A comprehensive investigation of the design of such studies in the communications industry reveals a good deal of poor design and also an overwhelming lack of significant effects, or impact of the media.[36]

The Use of Non-Survey Data about Individuals

Many successful research projects make use of non-survey as well as survey data for purposes of analysis. (All projects necessarily use non-survey data for purposes of sampling.) One basic reason for using non-survey data is that it may be useful for error control. The outside data may be more accurate than interview data. Where it is of equal accuracy it will still be valuable to have independent measurements of variables measured in the survey. It may be true that the outside data measure a construct which cannot be measured in a survey. The juxtaposition of the outside data and the survey data may be enlightening. It may be economical to add information from outside sources to the body of materials to be analyzed.

A study of attitudes toward government guarantees of employment found a correlation, other things considered, between support for such guarantees and the level of unemployment in the county several years earlier, even among those who had not experienced the unemployment themselves.[37]

From an analyst's point of view, there is nothing to be lost by increasing the information at his disposal. The only loss will be the trouble and expense of collecting the data. There are sometimes problems of confidentiality which limit access to non-survey data about individuals. Often, however, the real limitation is the lack of imagination and insight of the researchers. All that can be done here is to raise the subject, list some examples of possible sources of data, and suggest that on every project the question should be asked: Are there non-survey data which could be made available which would make a contribution to this research?

Examples of sources of such data include the following:

1. *Census data.* An area sample implies a sample of people located in a set of different areas which can be characterized using Census data for the block, tract, city, county, or other unit. It is a characteristic of an individual that he lives in areas with certain average income, racial composition, mix of types of housing, etc.

2. *Maps.* It will usually be possible to locate the place of residence of a person on a detailed map, and perhaps also to locate other places of importance to him. Measurements may be made, for example, of his journey to work.

3. *Observers.* The interviewer may observe characteristics of a location, or others may observe it. For example, professional appraisers may observe people's homes.

4. *Photographs.* The interviewer or other observer may photograph a dwelling and its surroundings, and the photograph may be used for analysis.

5. *Public records.* A variety of public records exist and may be consulted either for selecting a sample or for later collection of supplemental data. For example, there are records of real estate transactions, automobile registration, building permits.

6. *Special files.* Many files are kept by public and private organizations which may be made available for research under the proper conditions. They include police files of accidents, records of the Social Security Administration, records of sales, school records, records of people who have participated in some program or belong to some organization.

7. *Mail inquiries of those with access to records, or special knowledge about an area.* In a longitudinal study of income and income changes a simple mail form was sent to the directors of state unemployment compensation to be relayed to those in charge of unemployment compensation in selected counties (one for each selected county) asking for the unemployment rate, the hourly wage for casual unskilled labor, and the tightness of that casual labor market.

An important source of non-survey data is the interviewer herself. She saw the house and the neighborhood, even if she did not secure an interview, and having been interviewing in these areas for some time, is able to provide some rough data about the house values or rents in the neighborhood. She can report the kinds of structures, the size of the city, the distance to the nearest large city, etc. And where there is an interview, she can report such things as the race of the respondent (or his obvious color at least), the visual impact of the respondent and the interior of the dwelling, and who was present during the interview. In addition, she can provide a description of the situation and such other ancillary information that may help understand the answers to the structured questions. For instance, most surveys do not ask about emotional or physical disabilities but having a disabled or senile person in a household can affect a family's economic situation or make sense of otherwise unusual responses.

Design of Instruments and Interviewing Procedures

It may seem like putting the cart before the horse to discuss practice first, and the theory of interviewing second, but theory is built by testing it against reality in a series of revisions.[38] Following are some examples of the most obvious kinds of errors that are made in interviewing.

A common kind of mistake made in questionnaires is to ask "IFFY" questions. "If you had a million dollars, what would you do?" "If your taxes were cut ten percent, would you spend the money, and on what?" It is very tempting to do this because many study objectives are originally stated in this form, but it very seldom gets realistic responses, except in the rare cases where the phrase that comes after the "IF" is something a man has actually experienced in the past or expects to experience and can speak realistically about.

A second kind of bothersome question is the suggestive question. "Will you promise not to move your factory out of the state if we do not raise your property taxes?" People tend to give the answers that they are expected to give, particularly if they see some way in which it will benefit them.

In general, any question which asks the respondent to agree or disagree with something, tends to get more agreement than disagreement and, what is worse, the agreement comes from people of a particular sort—those who score high on scales of authoritarian personality and are less educated. It is necessary to balance questions. On the other hand, sometimes when people try to balance questions, they make them confusing. "Are you in favor of A or against A?" To this the respondent can reply, "Yes." Or, "Are you in favor of A or against B?"

There is a body of literature on response set, the most striking manifestation of which is the "acquiescence factor" just described, a tendency to agree with statements rather than disagree. This tendency is correlated with low education and high ratings on an authoritarian personality scale, so misinterpretations and substantial biases are possible.[39]

Then there is a type of questions known as "flabbergasters" which are long, complicated, and nonunderstandable. A classic example is a thirteen line question asking farm managers whether they used mostly inductive or deductive logic. It was actually used in a study of farm management and followed by a series of questions on which of these thinking methods was most natural, can you use one method without using the other, what proportion of your thinking is like the first method, what proportion of your thinking is like the second method, then could you give me an example of the first method, etc. The one thing that was done in this sequence that does make some sense is the check-up question asking a person for an example. It is often useful to ask for details, or for an example in order to be sure the general answer was meaningful. If a man says he reads a lot of magazines, he ought to be able to name a few of them. If he says he plans his vacations far in advance, he ought to be able to say something about his next vacation.

There is a general technique often used in questionnaires to determine both the salience and importance of the reason for doing something. It might be described as the "funnel technique." One starts with a series of very general questions about what is important or why in a certain area and gradually focuses on the thing one is really after. The final question might be, "Well, does the interest rate really have any effect on this?" If the respondent only mentions the interest rate at that point, you know it is not very salient, and you have doubts about its importance. On the other hand, it can be non-salient and still be important. He might say, "Oh yes, that's the most important thing of all. . . . I just didn't bother to mention it." Indeed, studies asking people what is necessary for a good diet finds people frequently failing to mention milk altogether because they spend all their time talking about leafy green vegetables and fresh fruit.

Then there are questions that threaten people, "Do you worry?" To which they often answer, "I'm not supposed to worry." And questions which have an indefinite comparison involved, "Is the world better?" Are you the kind of guy who worries?" "How is your wife?" All of which leave the respondent, if he is smart, with a feeling that he should reply: "Compared with what?"

The real problem with much questionnaire design, particularly mail questionnaires, is that people who designed them have never really tried them on a live victim and watched him squirm. Even with a mail questionnaire it is possible to let a man sit down and fill it out while you stand there listening to him complain, and noticing the questions where he has to hesitate for a long time.

Validity studies are extremely expensive and complex. They are really only worth doing if there are some fairly explicit hypotheses or real alternative procedures to be used. Methodological studies without validity data similarly are very complicated and often tell very little about "WHY" the particular results appeared. Consequently, one should think carefully about the kind of pretesting and pilot study work that goes on in a survey. It may be far more important to spend time developing the best instrument, than designing a fancy experiment to test various things without much evidence as to what might work and what might not, or any real willingness to shift the design depending on what happens. It is quite crucial for the researcher, himself, actually to take an interview or two, just to see how the process goes and discover how difficult it is to ask some questions. Sometimes a fairly small number of pretest interviews is enough to show that some attitude or event being examined is so rare in the population that it is hardly worthwhile asking about in a representative sample.

On the other hand, it is *not* possible in a pretest to *prove* that some questions are not good, because people will answer even when they do not have a real attitude or opinion. In political behavior studies, researchers are concerned with the possibility that they may get a substantial fraction of the sample for whom a question is either meaningless or uninteresting, the answers forming a random distribution. The rest of the people may be giving meaningful answers, which should correlate with other things and predict their behavior. But in analyzing the data, how does one distinguish the meaningful replies from the meaningless ones? Perhaps the best way is to collect additional information on people's information level and their interest level in the areas being talked about. Then one can analyze separately the informed, interested people.

Sometimes it is a question whether the respondent understands what the issue is. One could ask people whether they believed in the Mosaic Authorship of the Pentateuch. The fundamentalists would know exactly what was meant—you wanted to know whether they believed that Moses wrote the first five books of the Bible. On the other hand, you could ask perfectly understandable questions where some respondents really do not care, like, "What is your opinion of the XYZ corporation?" The person may not really have *any* opinion of the XYZ corporation, so he will give you a random response or his notion of what the interviewer wants.

A great deal can be learned in pretesting and development work. Hopefully one will end up with an instrument to which people respond, which they seem to understand and enjoy, and which does not take too long.

There is a kind of a natural time period for Americans—one hour. When an interview runs longer than that, the interviewer gets nervous, talks fast, and does not allow the respondent enough time to talk. Indeed, she may get a refusal at the doorstep, if she is unable, with confidence, to tell the man he is going to enjoy the interview and that it will not take very long. There are very few refusals once the interview is started, but that does not mean that length is not important, because length *is* correlated with refusals at the beginning. It takes pretesting to find out what the length really is, but pretests usually run faster than real interviews. When she does not dare take a chance of losing the interview, the interviewer has to spend a little more time on developing and maintaining rapport. Consequently, pretest interviews usually underestimate the length of time the real interviews will take. There are articles and books on interviewing, ranging from cook-book descriptions of details to theoretical discussions of the process.

In fact, a great deal of what is known about good techniques is not in the published reports. One can tell a great deal about the quality of an interview from the ease or difficulty in coding it, from interviewers' reports, and from the correlations which should exist among variables. Ambiguous questions are difficult to code, threatening questions usually result in no answer or an uncodable answer, double-barreled questions lead to dichotomous answers—some people answering one part, some the other. Questions forcing the respondent to accept the researcher's definitions of some complex concept of economic measure produce enough marginal interviewers notes, or replies inconsistent with other information in the interview, to raise doubts about what is really being answered. A major advantage of the fixed question-open answer technique is that the dropping jaw when a flabbergasting question is asked, can be reported by the interviewer.

Some other generalizations have come to be accepted by those with extensive experience in interviewing: People's views of themselves are subject to all kinds of distortions and distorted again by the impression they have of what the interviewer approves or expects. Furthermore, their statements about themselves in general terms do not agree with the impression derived by asking about explicit past behavior. For instance, questions about whether the respondent liked new products and bought them early or waited until others had tested them, and whether he thought most new products were good rather than just a way to get one's money, did not correlate with an index of reported actual use of new products.[40]

Questions need to be simple, brief, and focused. People have difficulty keeping long questions in their minds, particularly those which seek to redefine a concept to suit the investigator: "Do you have any debts—I mean debts to institutions on which you make regular payments that include interest or revolving accounts, but not debts to friends?" Faced with such a question, the respondent, who may think of installment credit as buying something bit by bit, not as a debt at all, may think only of the one hundred dollars he owes his uncle as a real debt, is asked to restructure his whole view and language. It may take longer, and require more questions, but it is ultimately easier on the respondent and provides better information, to ask a series of short explicit questions from which the concept can be built. Sometimes this requires asking a sequence of questions to determine in which category some set of payments belongs.

A concrete example, with both good and bad aspects, may help. The two pages reproduced here are from a panel study of changes in family well-being.

(ASK EVERYONE)

22. How much do you (FAMILY) spend on the food that you use <u>at home</u> in an average <u>week</u>?

                                              $_____ PER WEEK

23. Do you have any food delivered to the door which isn't included in that?

     [ ] YES ——▶ G24. How much do you spend on that food? $_____ per _____
     [ ] NO (GO TO G25)   (WEEK, MONTH)

25. How about alcoholic beverages -- how much do you (FAMILY) spend on that in an
     average <u>week</u>?
                    $_____ PER WEEK   [ ] NONE (GO TO G27)

     G26. Is that included in the food bill?   [ ] YES   [ ] NO

27. Do (any of) you smoke cigarettes?

     [ ] YES   [ ] NO (GO TO G30)

G28. About how many cigarettes do you (FAMILY) smoke in a day or week?

     _____ per _____
     (CIGARETTES, PACKS, OR CARTONS)   (DAY, WEEK)

G29. Is that included in the food bill?   [ ] YES   [ ] NO

---

30. Do you (or your family) get meals at work or at school?

     [ ] YES   [ ] NO (GO TO G34)

G31. About how much do all these meals cost you (FAMILY) in an average <u>week</u>?

            $_____ PER WEEK   [ ] NOTHING, FREE
                                                       (GO TO G33)
G32. Were any of these meals free, or at reduced cost?

     [ ] YES   [ ] NO (GO TO G34)

G33. About how much do you think these free meals saved you last year -- was it
      about $25, $50, $100, $200, or what?

     [ ] ABOUT $25   [ ] $50   [ ] $100   [ ] $200   [ ] OTHER _____
                                                              (SPECIFY APPROX. AMT.

---

34. About how much do you (FAMILY) spend in an average <u>week</u> eating out, <u>not counting</u> meals
     at work or at school?
                         $_____ PER WEEK

G35. Did you (FAMILY) raise any of your own food during 1968, or do any canning or freezing?
[ ] YES   [ ] NO (GO TO G37)

G36. About how much did that save you in 1968 -- was it about $25, $50, $100, $200,
      or what?
      [ ] ABOUT $25 [ ] $50   [ ] $100   [ ] $200   [ ] OTHER _____
                                                            (SPECIFY APPROX. AMT.)

G37. Did you (FAMILY) get any help buying your food with government food stamps
      (commodity stamps)?
[ ] YES   [ ] NO   [ ] NOT ASKED: FAMILY CLEARLY INELIGIBLE
                              (GO TO G41)

G38. How much would you say that saved you (FAMILY) in an average month?

                    $_____PER MONTH (GO TO G41)

      (IF   G39. Tell me how you use the stamps. _____
      DON'T
      KNOW)   _____

               _____

               G40. How much do you pay for the stamps?

                              $_____ per _____

G41. Did you (FAMILY) get any (other) free food during 1968?
[ ] YES   [ ] NO (GO TO G43)

G42. About how much would you say that was worth in 1968 -- was it about $25, $50,
      $100, $200, or what?
      [ ] ABOUT $25   [ ] $50   [ ] $100   [ ] $200   [ ] OTHER _____
                                                            (SPECIFY APPROX.
                                                            AMOUNT)

(ASK IF 2 OR MORE PEOPLE IN FU -- OTHERWISE TURN TO H1, PAGE 21)

G43. How many days a week does the family sit down and eat the main meal of the day together

The study design called for an estimate of family food consumption, but could devote only a few minutes to it:

G22 starts with what the respondent may know best—the weekly bill at the market, though it does force a definition (at home) on him and ask him for an average week, which may be biased.

But people may easily forget the milk bill, or other extras, so G23-24 asks about that, and whether it is included in the first figure given. Again G23 is not an easy question because it is double-barreled—the answer is yes only if two things are true: there is food delivered to the door, and it was not included.

And people may get their beer and cigarettes at the supermarket and forget that they are included in the weekly bill. Hence, the next series asks about them. We ask about number of cigarettes, and in editing we use data on cigarette taxes and prices to calculate dollars, differently in different states.

Again a strategy decision was made to exclude cigars and other tobacco products, because they are less common and less likely to be bought in food stores. And we also excluded cleaning supplies and other non-food items which may have been included because they would not vary much between families and would be difficult to separate anyway.

Then, people may pay for food at work or school, so the next sequence asks about that. But since we are after food consumption, not merely expenditures, a sequence asks about free or subsidized meals. To save the respondent from unnecessary work, the savings from such subsidies are asked in Question G33, which informs the respondent that we only want a rough estimate. After all, these items will be added to a much larger amount and need not be more precise than those other amounts.

When we come to eating out in restaurants it is necessary (G34) to make the respondent follow our definitions and not double-count by including the cost of meals at work or school again. Some such defining of terms is often unavoidable.

While only a few families grow their own food or get it free or with government food stamps, the amounts may be so substantial that we must ask about them, particularly in this study which oversampled the poor.

The question about raising food or preserving it (G35) again adds the phrase about canning or freezing so the respondent knows it is included, and it is followed by a question on amount which gives the respondent an easy selection, rather than the difficult job of estimating an exact amount.

In asking about amounts saved through the use of government food stamps (G37), we use a month rather than a week, knowing that the administrative procedures make this a more appropriate period. We could have asked how much the respondent paid for the stamps and how much food they got with them. We elected to use a single question for those who can say what the difference was, but ask the others for details. One reason for this procedure is that asking for amounts spent on stamps would have confused the respondent who had already included that in his food expenditures earlier, whereas the extra saving was not included.

Finally there was a general question on other free food, the interviewer using the "other" where appropriate. Such "mop-up" questions are common.

Similar problems of clearing up definitions arise with rent where it may be necessary to find out whether the utilities are included and, if not, how much they are. Or if you want rent exclusive of utilities, you would ask how much they were when they were included, so you could subtract them. And it might be necessary to ask whether the place was rented furnished or not.

The realism of people's replies can often be assessed by asking for details, or examples, or evidence of information or activity. If a man claims to be looking for work, questions about where he has applied may be useful, or questions about how much he expects to earn, or what kinds of jobs are available.

Evaluative questions are still more difficult. The respondent needs some standard of comparison: a question from the same panel study was:

Is there public transportation within walking distance of here?
[ ] YES   [ ] NO—go to Question _____
↓
Is it good enough so that a person could use it to get to work?

While vague, this sequence still provides an evaluation in the relevant framework, and perhaps more relevant than one would get by asking for actual frequency and directions and *assuming* which situations allowed people to ride public transportation to work. The open answer may pick up a number of unsuspected reasons why it is not good enough—though they should not be coded because this is volunteered information. If one suspected a variety of reasons and wanted quantification, it would be necessary to ask "WHY" to those who replied "NO" to the second question.

In asking respondents to rate themselves, some pairing, selected so that substantial numbers place themselves on each side, is helpful: "Are you the kind of person who plans his life ahead all the time, or do you live more from day to day?"

Sometimes it is useful in clearing up what is to be included to read off a reminder list, but, while this increases the chance of any item in the list being included, it may well lead to poorer reporting of items not explicitly on the list. A broader definition of the category, with a repeating of "Anything else?" until the reply is "NO," may do better, unless the list is limited and complete.

The wording of individual questions and the procedures used in the field are not all that matters. Certain general procedural suggestions follow: The sequence and structure of the interview matters. It is customary to start with easy, inoffensive and, hopefully, even interesting things, and work up to the more difficult or sensitive items. On the other hand, the early questions should suggest the general topic area for the interview, or else the later transitions will be difficult and seem like trickery. There should be some variety or change of pace. Respondents seem to like to be given something to hold, or to have some short-answer questions in between those which may take thought and require extensive answers. On the other hand, they resist things which seem to test them, questions to which there are right or wrong answers. Yet if tests of information or ability are to be given, it seems best to be frank as to what they are.

When there are transitions to a new aspect of the subject, or a new subject, some transition statement is often useful, but it cannot be very long. Remember that the interviewer is supposed to read everything word for word. It is very difficult to read more than a few lines to someone, and the respondent doesn't want a long justification anyway, just a warning that some different questions are coming.

As we shall see later, the motivation of the respondent is crucial. He will sense the interviewer's enthusiasms and dedication, and that helps; but the more the interviewer can provide emotional rewards, indications that the respondent is doing a good job, the better. There may be indirect rewards that motivate some sophisticated respondents with broad horizons, e.g., contribution to science, or the possibility of receiving a report about how others respond to the same questions, or assurance that people like him are being properly represented in the results, etc., but the pleased reaction of the interviewer and the sense that he is helping her do her job properly are probably more motivating for most people.

The archives of any survey center are full of stories about situations which no structured questionnaire could handle properly: unrelated missionary ladies living together in Christian communism sharing everything, hippy communes with rotating and uncertain occupancy, the man who spent more than his income on additions and repairs because the gasoline company bought his lot and moved his house for him providing him with a large capital gain, or the man with fifteen Cadillacs because he was going into the limousine rental business.

The number of objectives reflected in a questionnaire should be severely limited to those essential to the study design. The most common fault of anyone's first study is to include too much. No questions should be included because "it would be interesting to know." A good study design, with each question linked to some specific objective, will soon tell whether some variables are represented by too many different questions, and others by too few or none. The problem becomes particularly acute when one wants to measure attitudes or personality dispositions, and has available extensive scales developed and used with captive audiences of college students or paid subjects. In fact, there is usually some subset of items which correlates well with the total. It is also frequently necessary to select items that still have some face validity or appropriateness to a voluntary interview situation with a wide range of ages and education levels.

A general principle in questionnaire design is to postpone to later stages anything which can be postponed. For instance, if one is asking about components of income, so long as the questions are reasonably well designed to avoid double counting or omissions, there is little point in asking the interviewer to add total income and check the result with the respondent. Interviewers, focused on maintaining rapport with a respondent, frequently make mistakes in addition, and respondents, not knowing what the total should be anyway in many cases, will agree with the number the interviewer reports back, even if it is added up incorrectly.

Similarly, precoding, or arranging questionnaire format to make direct keypunching easy, or having the interviewer mark little boxes that can be read by a machine like a test-scoring machine, all increase the interviewer's work, lead to errors, and save relatively little cost. What is worse, if the interviewer marks the wrong box, there is no way to find it out, but direct coding and keypunching can be checked for reliability, and reforms instituted if needed. Paper is cheap, particularly when several thousand questionnaires are to be printed, and good open format with space for comments is likely to ensure that every question is read, comments noted, and skip-sequences properly used.

Redundancy is also helpful. Complex sequences where some respondents answer one set of questions, some another, are aided both by boxes and indentations, and by explicit instructions at the answer boxes of any question which may lead to a skip, telling the interviewer where to go. The interviewer should never have to read any long statement or instruction before deciding what to do next. If it is necessary for her to recall later whether the respondent is married, then one can instruct her to check one of two boxes (married, not married), each of which is followed by an instruction where to go.

In some cases, one group is asked one set of questions, another group a set which is partly different. In this case it is frequently best to print all questions in both sections. Again, paper is cheap, and a full sequence of questions in each section may be important.

A general issue which arises in many areas is how direct and blunt to be about things. If one wants to know whether people are thinking of spending a lot of money in the near future, one can focus on explicit purchase plans, or ask more indirectly about their expectations about their own and the country's economic future and whether the present seems like a good time to buy things. On the surface the more explicit questions may seem safer, but in practice the more open questions are often better (including more open questions about plans to spend in the next twelve months *or so,* rather than shorter-run intentions).[41] One reason is that the more explicit one gets the more some relevant things might be omitted because they were not asked about or did not fit neatly into any one category. The experience with detail varies. One case trying alternative methods secured larger total expenditure reports (presumed better) using more detailed questions.[42]

On the other hand, a very detailed set of questions about both sources and purposes of consumer debt secured less total debt than somewhat more condensed questions in surveys in a repeated series of national studies (Surveys of Consumer Finances).

A similar issue arises in attempting to measure people's basic predispositions (personality types) or goals. One can think of a continuum from very vague projective questions asking what others, or most people, etc. want or feel, at one extreme, to very explicit questions about actual behavior in relevant situations, at the other. In between are other alternatives: asking respondent for a self-assessment, asking for attitudes which may reveal his goals or motives, asking for more specific attitudes or reactions in situations calculated to be revealing. Experience and opinions vary. One major study concluded:

"Our own experience with projective methods as a means of getting richer data on opinions was anything but successful. . . . Rather, it was our experience that the best method of getting richer material about a man's opinion was by the rather naive and direct device of asking him to talk about those things that mattered most to him as far as the world was concerned and then to direct him from general values to the specific topic under discussion."[43]

It may seem that goals and attitudes should not be very important in economic surveys, but economists concerned with the real world are seeing the need:

"Decisions must relate to initial conditions and expectations of the future. And here is where the most intractable difficulties develop. It is very difficult to find a stable relation between expectations of the future and observable past variables or initial conditions. Changes in taxes, government expenditures, monetary policy, consumer demand, and income may all have quite different effects as they relate differently to expectations of the future. Analysis and prediction of business cycles will remain sharply limited in their power as long as this nexus from past to present to future is so incompletely specified.[44]

The choice of broader or more explicit questions and of questions more personally or more generally oriented involves, as usual, a trade-off. The more personal, the more likely the question is to arouse defenses or the need to preserve some self-image, or the desire to please the interviewers; while the more impersonal, the more likely the responses to be not the specific feelings of the respondent.

Similarly, the more general the reference, the less it may reveal about the respondent, but the more explicit the situation he is asked to talk about, the more likely that that situation is not relevant for *that* respondent. It is tempting to argue that a series of explicit reports on the respondent's own past behavior, in situations calculated to reveal his goals or personality or attitudes, is best, but each of the specific situations may be irrelevant for some respondents (never happened, etc.) or his behavior may have been dominated by some other constraint or consideration.

For example, take risk avoidance. One can ask individuals to characterize themselves as cautious or bold, but people may well have distorted images of themselves. What is worse, they are rating themselves against some unknown and probably variable norm. The attempts to devise scales that are "self-anchoring" may or may not succeed. Alternatively, one can ask some attitudinal questions about specific kinds of risks and what it is best to do. Or one can ask what the individual really does: Does he fasten his seat belts, carry medical insurance, lock his car, etc. But he may not have a car, or it may not have seat belts, or he may get free medical care as a veteran, or be unable to get medical insurance. One way out of these difficulties is to select a set of such behaviors and neutralize the scoring for those for whom that item was irrelevant or constrained, hoping that at least some will apply to any one respondent. Optimal neutralization requires assigning to the irrelevant cases the mean score among those for whom the item is relevant, but even rough procedures assigning some mid-value will go a long way. An index can then be created and if it works (helps explain other behavior), one can dissect it to see which components do the most good.

Some studies have tried both the attitudinal and the behavioral approach to assessing motives and goals. When the two scales do not correlate with one another, however, it still becomes necessary to select one, and the authors find themselves more comfortable with behavioral revelations of goals or attitudes than with self-evaluations.

The Logical Sequence of Steps in Questionnaire Development

There is a logical order of steps to be taken in the development of a questionnaire or any research instrument. These steps are the preparation of a series of written statements as follows:

1. General Objectives
2. Specific Objectives and Analysis Plan
3. Specifications of Data
4. Questionnaire

We will consider each in turn. The general objectives are part of the basic research design, which should set forth the purpose of the project and the means by which that purpose is to be achieved.

The specific objectives should flow directly from the general objectives, but they will be much more detailed. They should include an outline of the strategy which is to be followed in analysis. For example, it might be stated that major dependent variables in the analysis will include Y-1 and Y-2, and that the predictors will include especially X_1, X_2, etc.

The specifications of data represent a list of variables to be measured with an indication of any special requirements or problems in regard to each. For example, precise measurement of variable Y_1 might be of critical importance, while X_1 may be peripheral in terms of the objectives as developed, and a rough approximation may be adequate. When the questionnaire itself is developed, it should be possible to refer back to the Specifications of Data and the Specific Objectives for each question. Conversely, each Specific Objective and Specification of Data should have its counterpart in the questionnaire.

There is a tendency on the part of many investigators to go directly from a statement of objectives, even a statement of General Objectives, to a questionnaire. This tendency is natural because the investigator must always have in the back of his mind the thought that he is planning a survey, and, ultimately, a survey consists in asking people questions. What objectives are possible to achieve depends on what question can be asked. In effect, he keeps the intermediate considerations in his head.

There is no necessity, however, for the chronology of the development of a questionnaire to match the logical sequence from the general to the specific as outlined above. An investigator may do well to consider in detail what questions he can ask, and have satisfactorily answered, before he freezes his statement of specific objectives. Yet, there is often a good deal to be gained by working out the full logical sequence at *some* time before the questionnaire is complete. Errors of omission can be detected. Questions without objectives can be eliminated. Importance can be assessed, so that it does not turn out that major variables are measured in a casual way while peripheral topics fill the questionnaire. It may also be useful to set down on paper what is in the mind of the principal investigator, to permit its examination by others. Later on it may be useful to attempt to label the specific objectives of *each* question.

The reader should not get the idea that we know conclusively about the relative merits either of various modes of data collection or about the best methods of asking the questions. A great deal of the published findings have been on small special groups, with a wide variety of techniques, of interviewer training, *and* of subject matter. There is just enough disparity in the results that do exist to cast doubt on their generality. It seems likely that the quality of any data collection procedure depends on the whole mix of procedures, that *everything* must be right if the results are to be good, and that there are *combinations* that are right. For instance, a brief mail questionnaire using mostly check boxes, may work beautifully with simple and limited information easily accessible to the respondent. Telephone reinterviews, where the legitimacy of the study has been established by mail or personal visit, may be excellent for questions on what has changed, or on current expectations and attitudes.

It is our general impression that not enough time and energy goes into developing instruments in most studies, but the problem may be less in the level of investment than in its direction. For proper improvement, perhaps a better theory is more important than a lot of rules developed from experience.

The Theory of Interviewing

The central problem of data collection in surveys is how to obtain the information required by the objectives of the project from the individuals selected by the sampling procedures. A simple view of the problem is that all that is required to obtain information from people is to ask them whatever one wants to know. Experience has shown that this view may be too simple. Sometimes investigators obtain the data they require easily, but sometimes they find themselves in difficulties, either because they cannot obtain information, or because they mistrust the information obtained. The purpose of a theory of interviewing is to develop generalized knowledge of the interviewing process to guide the development of technique and to improve the quantity and quality of data.

Most of the relevant theory represents applications of theory developed in psychology, social psychology, or sociology. Most of the work in the field has been done by members of those disciplines. There are several ways to look at the interviewing process which have been emphasized by different investigators. These approaches are not mutually exclusive. In spite of the overlap, it may prove useful to look at the interview from each stance in turn.

Focus on the Interviewer: In much of the work on interviewing, especially the earlier work, the focus has been on the interviewer. This emphasis is understandable. The process of data collection by personal interview consists essentially in selecting and training a group of interviewers and sending them out to collect data. If they are carefully selected and well trained, and if they go about their work conscientiously, one might suppose they would do the job satisfactorily. If the results leave something to be desired, then one should re-examine interviewer selection and training, and devise checks to prevent sloppy work or cheating.

There have been a number of studies which have investigated whether the interviewers' own opinions influence their report. There are several such studies mentioned by Hyman[46] in his monograph on interviewing written in 1954. The evidence concerns such matters as accuracy in recording opinions. For example, Fisher found some evidence that interviewers tend to record more material which conforms with their own attitudes on controversial issues.[47] There is also evidence that interviewers vary in their probing habits. Those interviewers who probe fully may not be evenly distributed over the sample.[48] Hence, certain groups of respondents will be better reported. Hyman also reports a study of the effects of whether interviewers themselves held the majority opinion on how they pre-coded answers to opinion questions when the neutral category was omitted, so that respondents had to be classified as leaning either pro or con or as "don't know." Those interviewers holding the majority view pushed answers in that direction. Those holding the minority view pushed answers to "don't know.[49] Thus, there is evidence that interviewers' opinions can influence results, at least to some degree, even when there is no gross distortion.

Hyman was not overly impressed with the importance of these effects in well-conducted surveys, and argued that the beliefs of the interviewer *about the respondent* may be more important than what the interviewer herself thinks about matters of public controversy. The interviewer, he argues, may develop a stereotyped view of a particular respondent. This stereotype may make the interviewer insensitive to any aspects of the respondent's attitudes or behavior which do not fit the stereotype. Thus, the interviewer may make systematic errors of probing or of recording certain sorts of material which have nothing to do with his own personal opinions. Note that this type of error could apply to any kind of question. For example, an interviewer might decide (prematurely) that a respondent was a poor man, and neglect to ask him questions about his ownership of some kind of assets even though the questionnaire included such questions. Or she might decide that a widow with small children could not take a job, so not ask about whether the respondent was looking for work.

Hyman did not have great success, however, in demonstrating the practical importance of this mechanism. The most reasonable conclusion seems to be that it may operate in some situations, but is probably not serious. Methods of control would include training interviewers to ask questions conscientiously and asking interviewers to write down answers, not precode them into categories. In designing questionnaires to prevent the development of situations in which interviewers are forced to ask questions which obviously do not apply to some respondents, there should be reasonable rules for the omission of questions, rules which can be insisted upon.

In addition to their opinions and attitudes, interviewers are members of social groups. They may be characterized by sex, race, social status, and the like. There is evidence that *disparities* in group membership between interviewer and respondent may be important: they will be considered in the discussion of the interview as a social situation. But it is much less clear that *in general* members of certain social groups make better interviewers. Minimum standards of education, intelligence, and social skills seem to be what are required, as will be discussed under administration of field work. Efforts to discover measurable characteristics or combinations of characteristics which will predict success in interviewing in social surveys have not been successful.

The research on this subject has been handicapped by lack of satisfactory criterion variables. A leading study is that by Axelrod and Cannell.[50] They used three measures of effectiveness: ratings by field supervisors, by office administrative staff, and by coders. The latter rated individual interviews. From the ratings of a number of her interviews, ratings of each interviewer were constructed. Note that not one of these three groups was in possession of data on accuracy of response. They did have data on such matters as satisfactory completion of assignments and completeness of the reports submitted.

The predictors used in the project were standard socio-economic background variables and three well-known psychological tests: the Strong Vocational Interest Inventory, Kerr-Speroff Empathy Test, and Guifford-Zimmerman Temperament Survey. The population studied was interviewers employed by the Survey Research Center—that is, a group already presumably screened to remove obvious misfits. The analysis did reveal some differences in the measures of performance associated with difference in scores on the predictors, but the differences were small. It may well be that it is the *combination* of interviewer and respondent characteristics that matters.

Others concerned with the selection of interviewers have reported similar types of work. Sudman of the National Opinion Research Center has published a systematic scheme for rating interviewers, which indicated the type of evaluation which can be made.[51] His system is as follows:

Errors Forming Criteria for Rating of Interviewers

Error Weights	Type of Error
	1. Failure to probe initial response
5	a. Don't know
4	b. Vague answer
5	c. Irrelevant answer
5	d. Uncodeable
	2. Use of
1	a. Dangling probes
1	b. Unpreceded probes
	3. Improper probing
3	a. Accept partial answers
4	b. Use encouraging probe without using clarifying probes

Errors Forming Criteria for Rating of Interviewers—Continued

Error Weights	Type of Error
2	c. Accept first clear answer without probing for additional ideas.
5	d. Probe irrelevant answer instead of probing for a relevant answer, which results in irrelevant response.
5	e. Leading probes
1	4. Unexplained changes of code or answers (including erasures)
	5. Circling errors
5	a. Contradictions
1	b. Failure to code reply when codeable comment exists
5	c. Multiple coding
1	6. Answer recorded in wrong place
	7. Failure to complete
5-10	a. Omitting any part of classification. If race, sex, age, or marital status is omitted along with other omission, score in 10.
5	b. Enumeration and/or sampling table.
5	8. Evidence of paraphrasing (Always check other interviews. Give per interview, not per question.)
1	9. Unclear parenthetical notes
	10. Omission and superfluous notes
5	a. Omitting questions or portions of questions
1	b. Excess questions (or portions of questions)

This system of rating interviewers obviously rests on close scrutiny of completed interviews.

Another recent study of interviewer performance in studies of income and saving has been reported by Hauck and Steinkamp.[52] They attempted to relate characteristics of the interviewer to measures of performance in a series of panel surveys. Their results are of little interest for present purposes because of difficulties in obtaining a sufficient number of cases in which reported data could be checked for validity, but they propose methods of measuring performance which are of interest. They suggest that it is useful to distinguish four aspects of performance:

1. *Contact rate.* The contact rate measures the percentage of addresses in which the interviewer makes contact with a person eligible to be interviewed.
2. *Response rate.* The response rate they define as the ratio of the number of interviews to the number of contacts.
3. *Completeness rate.* The completeness rate for a given item under investigation is the percentage of interviews with respondents known to have the item (e.g. the percent known to own a particular asset) in which the item is reported.
4. *Accuracy rate.* The accuracy rate is measured for a given financial item for those interviews in which the item is reported. It measures the percentage of such interviews in which the reported magnitude is within some predetermined range from the true value, say, plus or minus ten percent.

Their proposed distinction between "contact rate" and "response rate" differs from conventional usage and will not be adopted here. As previously discussed, the distinctions among types of non-response are difficult to make and the most useful distinction is that between refusal and other forms of non-response. But the "completeness rate" and "accuracy rate" would be most useful measures. They amount to a method of breaking down total response error into two parts for purposes of analysis.

The U.S. Census Bureau has conducted extensive and well-designed studies of interviewer effects on the types of data collected in the Censuses of Population and Housing.[53]

Finally, the motivation of the interviewer, her belief in the importance of the study and the appropriateness of the instrument, must matter since there are large differences between studies in their refusal rates, and most refusals come before the respondent really knows what the study is about—certainly before he has heard the actual questions.

Focus on the Respondent: A second basic approach to the analysis of the interview is to focus attention on the respondent. One may seek to explain his response to the interviewing situation in terms of his perception of the situation and his motivations. In a sense this approach to the subject is indirect. The investigator cannot exert the degree of control over respondents that he can over interviewers. He must take his respondents as they are. Yet, he may hope to influence respondents through his control over those aspects of the interviewing situation which he *can* change.

For a respondent to participate in a survey at all, he must have some motivation to respond. In general, however, the motivation to respond is weak. A small pilot study reported by Cartwright and Tucker may illustrate the point.[54] They proposed to inverview sixty-three people from each of two parliamentary constituencies in London. A sample of names and addresses was drawn from the electoral register. Alternate respondents were sent a courteous note asking for their help in a study about people's health and the use of doctors and requesting that they return a form showing "which times you are most likely to be in and able to be interviewed." Only eleven percent replied giving suitable times to call, but fourteen percent wrote saying they did not wish to be interviewed. The pilot study was pushed through to completion, omitting those who had so requested, with a final response rate of eighty-two percent for those who had been sent no letter and only fifty-three percent for those to whom letters had been sent. The main study, when completed, had an eighty-six percent response rate. As this experience indicates, people's initial response to the idea of being interviewed is often unenthusiastic.

What, then, are the motives which may be aroused by an interview? It is usual to distinguish three broad groups of motives. People may respond to the content of the study or its stated purposes; they may respond to the sponsorship of the study; and they may respond to the social situation created by the presence of an interviewer. Their response may be positive or negative. Thus, the content of the study may interest them or may not be something they want to discuss; they may be sympathetic to the purposes of the study or they may be unsympathetic or suspicious; they may be positively disposed to the sponsor or research agency, or negatively disposed; they may respond positively or negatively to the social situation. In personal interviews, of course, the social situation involves the physical presence of an interviewer; in telephone interviews the interviewer is not physically present; and in self-administered procedures no interviewer is present and the social motives are altered or eliminated.

We note immediately that there is likely to be a dramatic contrast between the attitude of the respondent toward the topic of inquiry and the attitude of the investigators. The investigators are almost certain to be interested in the topic they are studying. Many respondents, however, may have paid little attention to the subject, and may be quite disinterested in it. They may even feel it is not appropriate to talk about.

The importance of variations in motivation toward a sponsor in explaining variations in willingness to respond may be illustrated by a study done for the League of Women Voters among its membership reported by Donald.[55] This study involved a questionnaire which covered nineteen pages, asked for 198 separate responses, and took an hour or more to fill out. It was, in a word, a formidable instrument. The procedure in data collection was sequential. First, a questionnaire was sent by mail to a sample of 2768 dues-paying members of the League. Second, a follow-up letter was sent to those who failed to reply. Third, a second letter and another copy of the questionnaire was sent. Fourth, personal telephone calls were made to those still not replying.

The response was as follows:

Responded to:	Percent of Sample	
First mailing	46.2	
Reminder letter	12.2	
Additional letter and questionnaire	8.8	77.3
Telephone call	10.1	
Non-response	22.7	
Total	100.0	

We may note, first, that a sixty-seven percent response rate was achieved entirely by mail, which is very high for so demanding a study. It appears that the average motivation to respond was high. Donald also made extensive comparison of the replies received at different stages. She found a strong tendency for those most involved with the organization to answer earlier. For example, officers of local chapters replied promptly. On the other hand a follow-up study showed that those who never turned in a questionnaire were often not involved at all, or barely involved. Half of the non-respondents were zero or marginal participators in the League.

Another example of a special group of respondents are the professionals, where both in Great Britain and in the United States, mail questionnaires have been used to secure information about their occupations and earnings, with high response rates (but declining if the survey is repeated several times).[56]

An extreme example of a situation in which people respond to sponsorship was reported by Boek and Lade.[57] They report a mail study undertaken for the Commissioner of Health of the State of New York among his own staff of 178 people. The commissioner was interested in what people said they would do in case of atomic attack. The staff had been given instructions about what to do—the study was directed to whether they accepted these instructions as practical guides to their personal planned behavior. The method of inquiry was to send to the staff members two items—a questionnaire, which was to be anonymous, and a postcard to be returned separately but at the same time as the questionnaire, which respondents were expected to sign, thus indicating that they had returned the questionnaire. The response rate was not quite one hundred percent—it seems the Commissioner did not fill out his own questionnaire, and somebody else was sick.

A mail questionnaire to Michigan deer hunters achieved a response rate in the nineties, perhaps because the hunters thought it might affect their chances of getting a special doe-hunting license, but also because they were interested in the subject. An intriguing study which mailed out a container into which respondents were to put their cigarette butts for a week before returning it, achieved a return rate above ninety percent.[58] Perhaps people liked the idea of having a portable ash tray.

Social Situation: There is evidence, however, that often it is the third type of motivation to respond which is most important, the motivation which arises out of the social situation created by the interviewer's presence. The experience of Cartwright and Tucker illustrates the point. As we have seen, when they wrote and asked for an appointment for a particular project, the response was often apathetic or negative. Yet, their main survey, with identical sponsorship and subject matter, reached a response rate of eighty-six percent. The personal presence of the interviewer made the difference. Similarly, Donald was able to obtain cooperation by telephone from people who had not responded to repeated approaches by mail.

Emphasis on the social aspects of interviews is also prominent in post mortem reports by respondents about the experience of being interviewed. This interpretation has been stressed by Cannell and Axelrod.[59] They sent a follow-up postcard to respondents on national sample surveys. Respondents were asked if they wanted a report, and a space was provided for comments. People's comments were primarily about the interviewer and their relation to the interviewer, not about the content of the study. Personal interviews in Detroit in which respondents were asked about their experience in the initial interview also led to comments about the interviewer, not the content. People almost always rated the interviewer as "friendly" in postcard follow-ups to personal interviews. In four such surveys, about eighty-five percent rated the interviewer as "very friendly."

Axelrod and Cannell also suggest that many people enjoy being interviewed. They interpret this reward to respondents as similar to the cathartic element in psychotherapeutic interviews. People often like to talk to someone who is friendly and supportive, interested in what they say, and who never criticizes them or disagrees with them. This sense of freedom to express one's self may be reinforced when the interviewer assures the respondent that his replies are anonymous.

The importance of the social aspect of the interview has been demonstrated indirectly by Gergen and Back. They start from a theory of aging, whose central theorem is that the transition from middle age to senescence is a process of progressive disengagement of the person from other members of society. Hence, they predict a lack of interest by older people in many topics and a lack of responsiveness to social pressure generally and social pressure from interviewers in particular.[60] They predicted specifically that older people would express fewer opinions and give more "no opinion" answers. Further, in expressing opinions they would avoid finer gradations and intermediate response categories and select undifferentiating or extreme answers. To test these ideas Gergen and Back analyzed an extensive body of material, primarily reports from a series of Gallup polls. The data supported the hypotheses for the most part. The one major exception was that among those with less than a high school education the tendency to express opinions rises rather than falls with age. (Perhaps, they suggest, because these people make up for low formal education as they age.) Measures of extremism and frequency of "no difference" replies do fit the hypotheses. The "no opinion" reply was more frequent for "old" than "middle aged" people for 38 of 46 items investigated, from four different surveys.

It is sometimes impossible to distinguish which motives operate in respondents, yet it may be possible to show that total motivation of respondents is important. Cannell and Fowler conducted a validity study in which they worked with a sample of hospital discharges and enjoyed access to the hospital records.[61] A subsample of respondents were asked to fill in a form left by the interviewer and mail it to the regional office of the Census Bureau. If the form was not returned in seven days, there was a mail follow-up. If that failed, a telephone call was made as a reminder, or a personal visit if the respondent had no phone. Cannell and Fowler argue that motivation of respondents must fall as one compares those who sent in the form on their own with those who required a mail reminder and with those who required a telephone or personal visit. They compare for these three groups the percent of known episodes not reported. The differences were substantial:

| | How the Reply Was Obtained | | | |
	First Mail Form	Second Mail Form	Telephone or Personal Visit	All
Percent of episodes not reported	13	15	22	16
Percent of hospital stays in which length of stay was correct	60	53	33	57
Number of hospital records	394	75	77	546

Focus on the Interaction Between Interviewer and Respondent: There is a substantial body of evidence that what happens in an interview may be influenced by major discrepancies between the group membership of interviewer and respondent. Within the United States the evidence is especially clear that racial differences are important, at least for some topics of investigation. There also seem to be differences in response attributable to discrepancies in social status, age, and sex. The importance of these discrepancies, however, seems to depend upon the topic of inquiry.

In his monograph on interviewing published in 1954 Hyman reviewed a series of studies on disparities in group memberships between interviewer and respondents.[62] The results were especially clear with regard to race. During World War II it was found by Stouffer that there were substantial differences in responses of Negro troops to Negro versus white interviewers. In 1952 the National Opinion Research Center conducted 1000 interviews with Negroes in Memphis, Tennessee. Half were interviewed by white, and half by Negro interviewers. There were large differences in response. The white interviewers tended to be given "acceptable" answers.[63]

Status differences can also be important. A study by Katz in a low-income area in Pittsburgh found differences in radicalism of response depending on whether the interviewer was middle class or working class.[64]

These projects were concerned with subject matter of little intrinsic relevance to economics. The importance of the relative status of interviewer and respondent was emphasized, however, by Hund in a study of business executives.[65] Hund personally conducted interviews at three levels of business executives in connection with two research projects. He reports a sharp difference in relative status of himself and his respondent which influenced the conduct of his interviews. At the highest level, the men were asked, not directed, to take part in the project. They did not submit passively to being interviewed. Hund was placed in an inferior position. One of the devices used seems to have been an insistence by respondents on maximum eye contact. He found it difficult to record the interview as it progressed. In thinking about this situation, it should be kept in mind that it is not easy to get cooperation at all at this level. At the middle level Hund felt he had rough equality of status, and at the third level, superiority, and he felt much more in control of the situation.

Ehrlich and Riesman have shown that the age and authority of the interviewer do influence the responses of adolescent girls.[66] They conducted a secondary analysis of data obtained in 1956 by Elizabeth Douvan in a study of girls undertaken for the Girl Scouts. On this project only female interviewers were used. The data analyzed concerned willingness to give "unacceptable" responses to projective questions concerning behavior of girls in relation to their parents and their evening social activities. The age of the interviewer did make a difference: older women (aged fifty-three or above) reported fewer unacceptable responses. More psychological measures of interviewer characteristics were available. "Ascendance" and "objectivity" of the interviewers also seemed to influence response. The highest percentages of unacceptable responses were obtained by women interviewers under fifty-two years of age with low scores on "ascendance" and "objectivity."

These findings do not apply directly to surveys on economic topics. They do suggest, however, that similar phenomena may be found there. It may be that the closest similarity will be to economic surveys in underdeveloped countries, which are discussed below.

Note the consistency between the above argument that people respond to the social aspects of the interview situation and the findings that the group memberships of interviewers sometimes influence responses.

Finally, while there is no solid evidence, there is reason to believe that respondents are interested in the results of some surveys and would like to know what others say to the same questions. Hence letters announcing that an interviewer will call often promise that a summary of findings will be sent to respondents. When offered an option, *many* ask for reports.

Another useful way of looking at the interview is to think in terms of interviewer and respondent as both having socially defined roles. The interviewer, according to this view, has a role into which she can be trained. The ideal, from the point of view of comparability on a project using several interviewers, is to develop a standardized pattern of behavior for interviewers so that each interviewer will obtain similar responses. The interviewer becomes a scientific measuring instrument. The more tightly the role of the interviewer is defined, the less reason will remain for variations in response among interviewers. If the respondent is precisely selected in advance, the questions are exactly specified, and probing is standardized, differences among interviewers are less probable.

Note that there is a conflict between an approach which emphasizes standardization of roles among interviewers and one which emphasizes the more subtle interviewing skills. The tendency in recent years has been toward standardization, at least in large-scale data collection. Role theory suggests the usefulness of role playing as a training device for interviewers. This technique is widely used.

Role theory also raises questions or role overload. There seem to be definite limits to the number of functions which interviewers can carry out successfully. The practical difficulties experienced by the Survey Research Center in getting interviewers to use the "half-open interval" technique to check for missing dwellings illustrate the point. (See Chapter III)

Respondents as well as interviewers have a role, and it is sometimes suggested that one of the most important jobs of the interviewer is to train respondents in that role. It is the general experience of survey organizations that once respondents start an interview they almost always carry through to the end of the interview. Experience on panel surveys is that people who are going to refuse to participate usually do so either before the first interview or before the second interview. Once the second interview is safely started, the chances are good for continuation for more interviews.

There are some people for whom the role of respondent is difficult or even impossible, but they are more likely to be found in underdeveloped countries.

Some may also consider an interview as a process of communication. From this viewpoint the central question is, what are the conditions under which effective communication will occur? It is not difficult to specify the logical requirements: (1) The respondent must understand correctly the questions which are being put to him. (2) The respondent must, himself, possess the information required. (3) The respondent must be able and willing to communicate the information. (4) The system of receiving and recording the information must function correctly. That is, in a personal interview the interviewer must hear correctly and write down correctly the answer as given: in a self-administered procedure the respondent must do the job correctly himself. Any one of these requirements may not be met.

(1) It is not easy to state questions precisely, and it is not sufficient for a question to be precisely stated for it to be precisely understood. Economists venturing into the conduct of surveys often underestimate the importance of this difficulty. Changes in a research procedure which do not change the logical content of questions may yet change the comprehension of the questions by respondents.

For example, Bauer and Meissner report the results of a mail survey of business enterprises in Germany.[67] They asked three questions only. These questions concerned changes in "basic" orders, changes in "re-orders," and changes in "total" orders, this month versus last month. Three answers were allowed for each: increase, no change, or decrease. Note that, since all orders must be basic orders of re-orders some combinations of answers are logical impossibilities. It is not possible, for example, for each of the *types* of orders to increase while the total decreases. From July to December 1952 Bauer and Meissner used a format in which the three questions were printed on one page. They found 1.5 percent nonsense answers (of 198 replies). In 1953-1954 they printed the same question on two pages. They found 5.0 percent nonsense replies (of 765 replies). The inference seems reasonably safe that respondents had a better grasp of the meaning of the questions when they were printed on a single page.

Haberman and Elinson report a study in which separate personal interviews with husband and wife were taken with each of 645 marital pairs in New York City.[68] The study concerned "The Public Image of Mental Health Services," but it included a question on family income. Each respondent was shown a "flash card" which had printed on it sixteen income intervals identified with letters. Both weekly and equivalent yearly ranges defined each interval.

The question states:

The figures refer to the total income of the entire family living here before any deductions, as for taxes or social security. Include income from all sources—wages and salaries of all family members, rents, pensions, etc.

Only 59.6 percent gave reports in the same interval, but on the average the reports were fairly close, with the median reported by the husbands $7377 and by
the wives, $7179, or about $200 less. One aspect of the findings is of special interest in the present context: wives on the average reported *higher* total family
income than husbands in those families in which the wife was working. The
comparison of the two reports of income varies depending on the wives' working
status as follows:

Comparison of Reports of Income for the Same Family	Wives' Working Status	
	Housewife	Some Occupation
Spouses the same	60.6%	57.9%
Husband's report higher than wife's	27.7	19.6
Wife's report higher than husband's	11.7	22.4
Total	100.0	99.9
Number of interviews	386	214

Thus, the wives' reports are higher than the husbands' in 22.4 percent of the
families where the wife is employed compared to 11.7 percent where she is a
housewife.

The question asked was perfectly explicit and even repetitive. It calls for
income of the "entire family" and the wages and salaries of "all family members." Yet it seems highly probable that some husbands neglected to include
their wives' incomes. It illustrates one of the problems of forcing a definition on
the respondents, rather than asking the pieces and developing one's own
measure.

Experience in asking income at the Survey Research Center has been similar. The remedy adopted has been to ask a separate additional question such as:
"Does that include the income of everyone in the family?" Often enough, people
then remember that there was an omission.

We repeat, it is difficult to communicate complex definitions all in one
question. It may be more effective to start with a concept which comes easily to
the respondent, and then correct or adjust it, step by step.

(2) Respondents may not have the required information, or they may be
able to produce it only with some degree of difficulty. There are several possible
reasons: (a) The information may be known to one family member but not to
all. (b) The information may not be easily accessible to the respondent because
he finds it related to something painful to think about—he has repressed it. This

possibility is more obvious for psychological inquiries in depth than for economic studies, but it may arise. (c) The information may not be easily accessible because it refers to something which the respondent has forgotten because it is remote in time, or because it is trivial to him.

To illustrate the importance of memory error we cite recent work done at the United States Census and reported by Barbara A. Powell.[69] She was concerned with reinterviews as a means of investigating the correctness of responses from initial interviews, an approach which has been developed extensively by the Census. She reports that a lag of three months between interview and reinterview is preferable to six months for reports of income and mobility, but that there is no difference for reports of ages, number of children, or children in school.

(3) The respondent must be able and willing to communicate the data. An interesting example of the difficulty which can arise in persuading respondents to communicate has been described by Jung.[70] He has been concerned with the problem of collecting reliable price data on goods and services for which the market price is different from the posted price, such as new automobiles. His basic method is to send out shoppers who, to be successful, must succeed in convincing salesmen that they are definitely in the market and will buy if the price is acceptable. The salesman is undoubtedly well informed about the price—the problem is to get him to state it. Jung has developed a complex standardized procedure which his shoppers follow. They pose as sophisticated shoppers. The routine involved includes: asking for a specific popular model with a standardized list of accessories; always rejecting the salesman's initial price as more than the customer had planned to pay and suggesting in reply a price approximately equal to the dealer's invoice; listening sympathetically to the complaint that this price was impossible; and then taking the next offer by the salesman as the market price. This system, Jung stresses, works only if the salesman is convinced the shopper will buy if the price is right; otherwise he may quote a "lowball" price which is lower than that at which he actually will sell.

There have been several investigations of the quality of interviewers' work in recording what takes place in an interview. The usual technique of investigation is to "plant" respondents, who are not known to the interviewers to be "stooges." Hyman has reported such a study done by the American Jewish Congress in cooperation with N.O.R.C.[71] For this study fifteen interviewers were hired, mostly with no experience. Each interviewed one to four "planted" respondents as well as actual respondents. There were fifty questions per interview, and an interviewer could make several errors per question. The study concerned race relations. At least one of the planted respondents, the "hostile bigot," was extremely difficult to interview. Under pressure, these inexperienced interviewers made mistakes. They averaged eight recording errors per schedule. They also made errors in asking questions—omitting questions or changing wording—averaging thirteen errors per schedule. And they committed thirteen probing errors, failures to probe when appropriate, or use of "bad" probes.

(4) Recording errors may be expected to increase in proportion to the difficulty of the interviewer's task. Verbatim recording of lengthy answers to open questions is more prone to error than the mere marking of answers to questions with fixed alternatives.

Focus on the Instrument and Clarity of Questions: There has probably been more work done, and less said, about the problem of the questionnaire itself, than the other issues. Yet when one looks at surveys with low response rates, and other problems, one has the impression in many cases that they were using a crude and confusing set of questions. There is very little which can be said in a general way except to note that pretesting is usually inadequate, and that changes are often incorporated after the last pretest. The mere fact that changing the questions produces different answers does not tell us which is correct, although we tend to assume that more assets or expenditure or debts reported is usually better (more nearly correct).[72] The discussion earlier in this chapter on response set (acquiescence factor or social desirability) is also relevant in designing an instrument. If it is impossible to remove biases from attitudinal questions, one can at least do a better job of interpreting them if there are ancillary questions determining the respondent's information level, his understanding of the necessary insights, his level of interest, and how strongly he says he feels about something.

Conclusions: The accumulating body of evidence, inadequate as it is, seems to focus on the interviewer as crucial. Little can be done about the respondent, and once well-pretested protocols have been developed, there is little evidence that further manipulation of procedures or wording will pay off. But there has been recent evidence not just that interviewer's motivation and behavior matters, but that purposeful changes in interviewer behavior can affect the results. This is more exciting than merely finding interviewer differences, since one might not be able to do anything about such differences except attempt to randomize interviewer assignments (at great expense) and reduce the scope of interviewer judgment (no interviewer selection of the proper response category).

In general, these recent studies seem to show that purposeful procedures by the interviewer to "reward" the respondent for working at his task, lead the respondent to work harder. This is not a matter of looking the respondent in the eye, but in actual expressions, "Good, that's the kind of information we are after," and the like.[73]

In the process of development of such techniques, the problem arose of measuring what went on. Techniques are now being developed not only to measure the interviewer's behavior, but also to assess quantitatively the quality of the interaction, by counting the number of times questions have to be repeated, probes have to be used, etc. Such measures may allow an assessment of the quality of questions, too. A question commonly followed by long pauses, requests that the question be repeated, inquiries as to its meaning, need for additional probes ("Tell me more about that" "How is that?") to secure an adequate answer, is clearly either a bad question, or searching for something difficult to elicit or both.

There is reason to believe that the best interviewers already engage in a great deal of the emotional-reward-giving behavior we have described. They may be very ingenious at tailoring it to the particular respondent, so that training interviewers to do better may require much more than giving them a few tricks. It probably requires giving them a real understanding of the needs of respondents, and the character of the interaction. One additional casual bit of information in this matter is that whenever professionals in some substantive field have tried to do interviewing, they have generally done much worse than professional interviewers even when the latter do not understand the subject matter. The reason is at least in part, that the "experts" are focusing on the subject matter, not on the respondent. Indeed, they have great troubles even getting interviews.

The Problem of Non-Response

In view of the importance of minimizing errors in data collection, we shall consider systematically the problems of non-response and response error. A final section of the chapter will consider the special problems of data collection in developing countries.

A Statement of the Problem of Non-Response: We may define non-response as failure to obtain a usable report from an individual who properly falls into the sample on a survey. There may be a margin of doubt as to what should be classified as a "usable" reply. If many items are missing from a questionnaire, or if a few crucial items are missing, it may lead to better results to reject the report than to retain it for analysis. For example, in the Surveys of Consumer Finances in the 1950's schedules which contained neither income nor liquid assets were rejected, but those with one of the two were accepted. The underlying criterion is whether the report in question contains enough useful information so that the estimates will be better if it is included.

There is also room for uncertainty as to whether an element is properly in the sample. For example, on a personal interview survey based on a sample of occupied dwelling units, a vacant dwelling should not be considered a non-response: it should be classified as a non-sample address. But a dwelling with nobody at home (after repeated calls) should be classified as non-response. Interviewers, however, may not be able to distinguish between the two with precision. On a mail survey the distinction between a non-response and an incorrect entry on the list may present problems. The investigator may never know which forms actually were delivered. There may be a tendency not to bother with the distinction. From the point of view of what can be done to improve the survey, however, a failure to respond is obviously different from a faulty address. Comparisons in response rate across mail surveys also are more satisfactory if isolated from differences in the quality of the lists used. The same is true with telephone surveys.

From the point of view of the cause of the failure to obtain a useful report we may distinguish the following categories:

Type of Non-report	Examples from Samples of Dwelling Units
I. Non-sample elements Includes any element selected in the sample which is found not properly to be in the sample.	Address is not a dwelling, address has been destroyed, address is vacant.
II. Non-response	
A. Refusal	R Refuses altogether,
B. Not-at-home	Nobody at home, Somebody at home but not the designated R.
C. Other	Address inaccessible (because of weather), Report lost (in the mail or the office), R unable to cooperate (because of serious illness, inability to speak any language known to interviewer).

The response rate (or non-response rate) should be calculated after subtracting from the original number of elements in the sample those elements found not to be properly in the sample, and adding any additional element found to belong in the sample not separately counted on the original list of elements. For example, in a sample of families based on a list of addresses if a sample address contains not one family but two, both should be included in the adjusted count of families who should be interviewed. The percentage of non-response should be computed using as a base the corrected count of the number of elements properly in the sample, even if the latter must be estimated.

The "not-at-home" rate can be reduced by persistent efforts by interviewers. There will be some point at which the extra interviews will not be worth the extra expense and delay in completion of the field work. One possible rule is to tell interviewers to keep calling until their response rate reaches a specific level. Another is to set a maximum number of calls. Efforts to push the not-at-home rate to zero are likely to approach this result in part by converting some "not-at-homes" to refusals. For example, there is a rather fine distinction between a respondent who breaks an appointment, i.e. who is not at home even though he made an appointment with the interviewer, and a respondent who refuses. If the interviewer keeps trying, it may turn out that the respondent was accidentally away from home or that he did not wish to be interviewed. Even after making some allowance for the presence of concealed refusals among the not-at-homes, we return to the point that the "true" not-at-home rate can be reduced by persistent calling. It is sometimes useful to distinguish between an address with nobody at home and one with somebody other than the respondent. In the latter situation the interviewer often can obtain useful information. For example, she may be able to remove any doubt as to whether the address is properly in the sample.

The refusal rate is another matter. It may be possible by persistent effort to reduce the number of refusals on a study. A second interviewer may succeed where the first failed. Added letters of persuasion may help. Success is likely to be the result of sensitive adaptation of the approach to the respondent. It is not simply a question of repeated calls.

The other forms of non-response are less common in cross-sections in the United States. The remedies which can be applied vary according to the problem —they range from improving handling techniques to prevent the loss of completed schedules in the office, to hiring Spanish-speaking interviewers to talk to recent immigrants from Puerto Rico. (A memo showing the details of the calculation of response rates for a Survey of Consumer Finances appears as an appendix to Chapter V.)

Non-Response Rates under Varying Conditions: The range of non-response rates in surveys is very wide. For the Current Population Surveys it is about five percent.[74] For personal interview surveys of the general population conducted by the Survey Research Center it is in the range of ten to twenty-five percent. For mail surveys losses may be anything up to ninety percent. For telephone surveys non-response rates are roughly comparable with those for personal interviews. In a follow-up primarily by telephone of a sample of married women in the Detroit area, the non-response rate was held to about two percent of those originally interviewed.[75]

It is obvious that the risk of bias in the findings resulting from non-response is serious in surveys where the losses are enormous, and small or even trivial where the losses are only a few percent. It is also obvious that a high loss rate will present problems to the analyst only if those who are not interviewed are systematically different from the respondents. We shall consider the determinants of response rate, and then the problem of bias.

First, the large variations in response rate seem to be attributable to differences in the willingness of people to respond. Accordingly, we may classify survey situations according to the types of motivation which operate. The usual starting place is the type of data collection:

Method of Data Collection	Motivation of R
Personal interview	Social motives present
Telephone interview	Social motives absent or weaker
Mail interview	No social motives

We have noted the importance of social motivation for many respondents; these motives are absent in mail surveys. Experience has shown that there is a difference between initial interview and reinterview in response rate. An initial personal interview seems to make for high returns from later mail or telephone interviews. A more complete classification, then, would be as follows:

Method of Data Collection

Initial interviews:
  Personal
  Telephone
  Mail

Reinterviews following personal initial interviews:
  Personal reinterview
  Telephone reinterview
  Mail reinterview
Supplementary forms to be completed after a personal interview
  (drop-offs)

Various combinations of methods became possible; the above classification is by no means exhaustive.

A second basic principle of classification is according to the intrinsic interest of the content of the survey for the population being interviewed. As we have seen already, people are more ready to respond to questions about something in which they are interested. Since some topics are interesting but people do not like to talk about them because they are too personal, perhaps we should speak of people's readiness to discuss topics as varying. This principle of classification is clearly independent of the first—readiness to discuss certain topics relates to the state of mind of the people being surveyed, while the choice of method of data collection is in the hands of the investigator.

A third dimension of the problem concerns variations in the details of the techniques used, basic type of data collection being held constant. There is a considerable literature on this subject, especially for mail surveys, where experimentation is comparatively easy. Some specific techniques seem to be useful, while others are of secondary importance. For example, Jeanne E. and John T.

Gullahorn experimented with different techniques in a mail survey of former Fulbright and Smith-Mundt grantees.[76] They had a response rate of about fifty percent. They found that when they used a standard return envelope rather than a business reply form the response rate was fifty-two percent rather than forty-eight percent. There is a difference but it is trivial.

We have offered at least some insight into the reasons for variations in response rate by type of data collection and content of the survey in terms of the motivation of the prospective respondents. Why should detailed variations in technique make a difference? Partly they may operate through getting people's attention. Partly it may be through leading people to distinguish between the data collection and other situations, e.g., advertising and selling efforts. Partly it may be through conveying to the potential respondent a sense of the importance of the project and its relevance to some goal which he has or some organization which he values. Unfortunately, most of the literature concerns what techniques work, not why.

There is, of course, a difference among interviewers in response rates, as well as in the quality of the responses they secure. Experienced interviewers often get lower response rates but tend to get biased samples (they do not lose respondents at random).[77] It is difficult to document this because it is generally difficult and costly to assign interviewers randomly to respondents.

Non-Response and Number of Calls: One standard method of examining the effects of increasing the number of calls made (or the number of mailings) is to compare results from successive calls. This method is most satisfactory when enough calls have been made to reduce non-response to a small percentage. One can then consider what the result would have been if the field work had been cut off after the first call, second call, or at any other specific point.

In economic surveys of the population of the United States people interviewed on different calls differ substantially. In one survey in 1963 conducted by the Survey Research Center with sixteen percent non-response rate the median income of those interviewed at different calls was as follows:[78]

Number of Call at Which Interviewed	Median Income	Number of Interviews
First	$4188	427
Second	5880	391
Third	6010	232
Fourth	6200	123
Fifth	6010	77
Sixth or higher	7443	59
All	$5598	1309

A survey with no call-back (i.e. one call only) using similar methods would have resulted in an estimate of $4188 for median family income compared with

$5598. The difference between people reached on first and later calls, in other words, is far from trivial.

Deciding how many calls should be made is a problem in economics, the only difficulty being that all the cost and benefit functions are not known. For instance, call-backs are somewhat more likely to produce an interview than original calls because interviewers have learned things about when the people are not home, and sometimes have even made appointments. But as one gets to respondents who were not only not home but reluctant, the probability of a call resulting in an interview drops. The expected quality of the information may also drop. So much for the cost side, but the benefit side requires the application of marginalism too, since the higher the response rate, the less additional responses will change estimates based on an incomplete sample, so the smaller the reduction in bias. And of course the smaller the increase in precision, since it goes up with the square root of the number of cases.

What the investigator needs to know is the extent to which the later calls will produce data which differ from early calls, how the cost per interview secured increases, and how the benefit of the information per added interview decreases. Our investigations leave the impression that after four or five calls, and a response rate in the eighties, the remaining non-response are widely scattered rather than systematically biased, costly or impossible to get, and likely to produce inadequate or incomplete information. But this may well depend on the content of the questionnaire.

The Reinterview Approach to the Study of Non-Response: A second basic method of studying the non-response problem is to seek to reinterview people about whom a good deal is known from an initial interview. One can then analyze the losses subsequent to the first interview. This type of inquiry is a necessary part of the most panel studies. Losses tend to cumulate, and it may be vital to know whether the individuals who remain in a panel are still reasonably representative of the population for purposes of the particular inquiry.

An example of such a check on a panel was reported by Sobol.[79] The study involved five waves over three years, 1954-1957, and the cumulative losses were substantial, as the following tabulation shows:

	Panel Mortality		Interviews Taken as a Percent of:	
	Interviews Taken	Lost	Addresses	Interviews in Wave I
Addresses sent out	(1358)		100%	
Wave I June 1954	1153	205	85	100%
Wave II Dec. 1954	958	195	71	83
Wave III June 1955	856	102	63	74
Wave IV Dec. 1955	819	37	60	71
Wave V Mar. 1957	707	112	52	61

Thus, in Wave V interviews were taken at only fifty-two percent of the addresses originally sent out. The original response rate on Wave I, however, had been eighty-five percent.
Sobol provides a breakdown of the losses which is as follows:

	Movers Not Followed		Refused		Unavailable	
Wave	Number	Percent	Number	Percent	Number	Percent
I	-	-	95	7	110	8
II	68	5	97	7	30	2
III	41	3	40	3	21	1
IV	12	1	13	1	12	1
V	41	3	35	2	36	3
Total	162		280		209	

Note that in this panel movers were not followed unless they moved to an address which was readily accessible to an interviewer. Note also that refusals were especially numerous in Waves I and II.
Converse has reported loss rates on a political panel study involving five waves also conducted by the Survey Research Center. They are remarkably similar to Sobol's in spite of the fact that the political panel extended over a longer period, 1956-1960:

Wave	Percent Response
I	100%
II	91
III	70
IV	63
V	61

Both projects ended with sixty-one percent of respondents in Wave I still in the panel for Wave V.[80]
Sobol compared those remaining in the panel with panel losses on a variety of socio-economic characteristics (degree of urbanization, age of family head, education, occupation, home ownership, income, sex of family head). She found some differences. For example, movers tend to be young. Home owners are less likely to move than renters. In general, however, considering the extent of the losses, the bias was remarkably small. Her results on family income were as follows:

1954 Family Income of Panel Members and Panel Losses

Income	Wave I	All Panel Members	All	Panel Losses Movers Not Followed	Refused	Un- available
Under $2000	12%	10	14	20	11	14
$2000-4999	43	44	43	47	37	47
$5000-7499	25	27	22	21	25	17
$7500+	15	16	12	8	15	13
Not ascertained	5	3	9	4	12	9
Total	100%	100	100	100	100	100
Number of families	1153	707	446	162	190	104

Note that twelve percent of those who eventually refused had not disclosed their income in Wave I, while only three percent of the panel members who stayed for all five waves had income "not ascertained" in Wave I.

Another aspect of Sobol's results is of interest for the light it sheds on non-response. This project concerned people's economic attitudes. She found that those who said they did not follow business news in Wave I had a tendency to drop out. Thirty-three percent of losses fell in this group compared to twenty-six percent of persistent panel members. People differed in their willingness to remain in the panel, evidently, because of differences in interest in the topic.

Converse reports much the same thing. By 1960, he found, the political panel was overrepresenting people who had described themselves as politically involved in 1956. Converse was also concerned about the effect of panel membership on those who remained—"contamination" or "conditioning," as it is called. After 1960 he found he had five percent more people saying they had voted than in a new sample. The cumulative effect of five interviews, he felt, might have been to sensitize people to politics. Conditioning effects have also been found in panel studies of home repairs, as will be discussed later.

A study of refusals under special circumstances has been published by Robins.[81] He followed up thirty years later a group of 524 patients in a child guidance clinic plus 100 matched normal control subjects. He found some tendency for people to refuse more often if they were in routine white collar occupations, had low education, or came from foreign born parents. His most interesting finding is that those who had moved away to another city were much more likely to respond. Robins suggests that these respondents may have felt the interview was more important—they were told in advance that an interviewer was traveling to see them. The importance of the visit may have seemed greater also to the interviewer. And the distance may have lent anonymity.

In summary, the analysis of panel losses shows them to be not so bad as one might think. When one compares, on the basis of what was found in the original interview, those who got lost with those who did not in the succeeding waves, the differences seem to be small. Note, however, that this does not prove that there may not be substantial biases. Suppose, for example, that the people whose incomes fell since the first interview do not like to be reinterviewed. None of the analysis of the non-response would show this. Only comparing a panel sample with a total cross-section later, and asking about changes in income, would uncover this even in a rough way. On the other hand, spending a lot of time, energy, and money trying to locate the panel losses may turn out to be wasteful. For one thing, the easiest ones of the non-response to find are the ones the most likely to be like the response and the least like the rest of them. For another thing, even if one find some subset of the non-response, what does one do with this information?

There is a choice between adding them to the original panel, with very large weights so that they represent the rest of the non-response, or using them as an independent estimate of the size of the bias, but not putting them in. Or one might compromise and put them in as part of the original sample without weighting them up, claiming that they do not really represent the rest of the non-response anyway. If one puts them in and weights them, they may have such large weights that they increase the sampling variance, causing more troubles than the small reduction in bias is worth. If one puts them in unweighted, they will not change things much and may delay analysis and create a lot of confusion. If one leaves them out, then the estimate of biases is based on a very small sample and may not be a true estimate of the bias anyway. It must be kept in mind that a total bias is essentially the difference between two weighted estimates and that weighted estimates are relatively insensitive to fairly substantial variation in weights.

The Frame as a Source of Data about Non-Response: The third basic method of investigating non-response is to use data available from the sampling frame itself. Mayer and Pratt were able to use the frame in this manner in a study of individuals listed on personal injury auto accident reports.[82] They had considerable information about the accident as well as the age, sex, race, and occupation of the people listed on the report in the police files. Their methods of data collection and the resulting response rates were as follows:

Method	Percent of Sample Responding
1. Mailed questionnaire with cover letter	23.5%
2. Second mailing	23.2
3. Telephone	27.7
Total	74.4%

They found approximate similarity in many characteristics among those responding at each of the three stages and the non-respondents. There were differences in social status—those in low-status occupations and Negroes were considerably underrepresented on the first wave. They found a tendency for the refusal rate to be higher for drivers than passengers. The reason, they suggest, is that drivers might fear that they would be found at fault—with unpleasant consequences. Passengers could respond since they were merely spectators who could not be blamed for the accident. This interpretation, of course, is consistent with the emphasis in this discussion on the importance of the degree of readiness people have to respond to questions about the topic being studied.

Unfortunately, the amount that is known about non-response simply by knowing the geographic location of their residences, is relatively small. In general it appears to be both ends of the income distribution, families where all members are working (and hence seldom home), and people in congested areas (less trusting?) who are non-responses.[83]

The early Surveys of Consumer Finances were weighted to offset differences in response rates (as well as sampling rates), but it turned out that with response rates in the eighties, no appreciable difference was made in the results (hence no appreciable gain). This may, of course, have reflected only the lack of information about the non-response.

Other Methods of Reducing Non-Response: Two other methods have been used to "reduce" non-response, one illegitimate and the other legitimate. They both attempt to substitute someone like the original non-response. The illegitimate way to do this is to substitute someone next door. The Gallup organization did this during World War II and came up with a very high estimate of the proportion of families with victory gardens. When the Division of Program Surveys of the Department of Agriculture, using a probability sample and making callbacks, came out with a much lower estimate, they looked at their data according to the number of calls required, and of course, the more calls it took (the less the man was home) the less likely he was to have a victory garden. There was a characteristic, on which people differed, which might be called the "tendency to be at home," and it was highly associated with having a garden.

A more appropriate technique is to focus directly on the matter of not-at-homeness. The technique is a replacement technique which is possible if one has done previous surveys recently. *If* one can assume that those not-at-home in a previous survey, who can be interviewed in this survey, share with the not-at-homes in the current survey, the characteristic of not-being-home-much, *then* they can be treated as substitutes for the current not-at-homes. There is a chance of introducing bias this way, but also a chance of reducing bias. They are expensive interviews, usually taking more calls even the second time, and there are usually not enough of them to test the initial hypothesis that justified their use. They should clearly not be weighted up to substitute for all the not-at-homes.

Methods of Dealing with Non-Response in Analysis: The simplest procedure is to "do nothing" and prepare tabulations on the basis of the completed reports. In effect, to do nothing amounts to assuming that the non-respondents are like the rest of the population. The second possibility is to assume that the non-respondents resemble, not the whole population, but some specified subpopulation. For this purpose one needs to know how many of the non-respondents (and of the respondents) belong to that subgroup. Such information may be available, say, from the sampling frame. One may know, for example, the distribution of the population by size of place of residence. For example, non-response tends to be higher in urban areas than in the rural parts of the United States, and income is higher in urban than in rural areas. The assumption that non-respondents resemble the entire population with regard to location is less reasonable than the assumption that they resemble the other residents of places of similar population.

The analyst, therefore, may decide to assign unequal weights to interviews from different strata in the sample. He may estimate the fraction of the total population which should be represented by stratum K, and assign a corresponding total weight to stratum K. It may be convenient to let the total weight of all interviews in all strata equal 10,000 or to make the weights run only up to 9 or to 99. Then the total weight for stratum K will be Wk, where $0 < Wk < 1$. The weight for each interview in stratum K will be Wk/Nk, where Nk is the number of interviews actually completed in the stratum. With modern data processing equipment there should be no special problems in using the weighted data in tabulation instead of simple counts of responses, except in tests of significance.

In analytic surveys the problem is somewhat different. The issue is not whether means, medians, or percentages based on the full sample are biased, but whether measures of relationship such as regression coefficients are biased. The answer depends on whether there is an *interaction* between the variables in the relationship and some factor systematically associated with non-response.

Suchman has published an example of a survey in which such an interaction exists.[84] He was working with a panel study of a presidential campaign. Low-education people tended to have a low interest in politics and to drop out of the panel. He found that the relation between reading and looking at TV varied between panel members and those who dropped out as follows:

	Percentage Looking at TV Often			
Reading	Respondents to Both Waves		Non-respondents to the Second Wave	
Often	37	(907)	56	(461)
Sometimes	40	(303)	57	(221)
Hardly ever	59	(79)	59	(128)

Thus, among the non-respondents to the second wave (who were low-education people) there is not much substitution between reading and looking at TV often. Among respondents to both waves, there was such a substitution.

How can one search for such interactions? What is required is to consider, first, what are the factors associated with non-response on a project? Then one can check specifically to see whether the relationships in which one is interested are any different for those with different scores on the variables associated with non-response. Mayer and Pratt, for example, might have checked for differences in relationships within the two groups, passengers and drivers. Since respondents and non-respondents may differ in attitudes and motives relevant to the topic being studied, such searches may well be rewarded.

One difficulty is that we know very little about the non-response in most surveys. If and when good data become available in several dimensions on what the national population is like, it should be possible to devise weights not on the basis of evidence from a small study, but from a large sample survey with high response rates like the C.P.S. One would then divide the small sample into sub-groups, say by age, education, sex of head, race, and city size jointly, and assign weights to the members of each subgroup so that their sum was appropriate for the proportion of the population represented by that group. What this requires is the basic population estimates, which must be in several dimensions, recent, use identical measurement of the variables, and use a selection of variables appropriate for the maximum reduction in bias.

Assuming that weighting may be needed, the problem is how to select the groups on which to compute the response rates to be used for weighting. One criterion, of course, is groups that differ as much as possible in terms of response rates. But another criterion equally important, is that the groups should differ on things you are trying to measure. You might find substantial differences in response rates between those who live in vertically stacked duplexes and those who live in horizontally connected duplexes, but this may well not make any substantial difference in the variables of the survey, and may be neglected. On the other hand, if there are different response rates according to family size, income, or home ownership, one might very well want to weight on these bases. Clearly by defining groups in several dimensions, you can find small groups that are substantially different from one another both as to response rates and as to their responses.

The question then is, how small should you make these groups? The smaller you make them, the more they differ from one another and the more you eliminate bias. But the smaller you make them, the more unstable the estimates of the groups and the larger the weights and you introduce potentially large sampling variance. In a group that is fairly small, there may turn out to be *no* response, so the theoretical weights would be infinite. But even if you take a group that had one hundred in the beginning, and you had only five responses, then you would have to assign weights of twenty to each of those five. Any idiosyncrasies in those five would be vastly exacerbated in the final results. So there is a optimization problem here, a strategy problem in making the groups big enough to be stable and not have too much difference in weights but small enough and well enough defined to be quite different so that you do as good a job as you can in reducing potential non-response bias.

There have been some other less adequate methods suggested for adjusting for non-response. One is to look for trends according to the number of calls it took to secure each interview, and extrapolate, assuming that the non-response is different in the same direction, only more. This can only be one item at a time, and it makes an unlikely assumption. The chances are that the final non-response are at least half refusals, who may be quite different from the people who were busy or not home much and required many calls to get.

Another scheme, associated with the Politz organization, is to ask the respondents who are interviewed whether they were at home at specified other times, and weight up those who were not home much, as a kind of replacement for others who were presumably not home and were not interviewed. One then cuts the number of call-backs. This is only really legitimate if you can randomize the time of the first call, if the reports people give on when they are home are accurate, and if you assume that not-at-homeness is a major source of bias, not refusals. Furthermore, the weights tend to be widely different and to increase variance while reducing bias. Finally, it costs time and money to tabulate the information and design the weights.

Item Non-Response: A special form of non-response is lack of response to particular items on a questionnaire. The omission may be the result of an oversight on the part of the interviewer or, in a self-administered procedure, an oversight by the respondent. One of the goals of questionnaire design is to minimize these inadvertent lapses. Omissions may also be deliberate. Respondents may be unwilling to respond to certain sensitive questions, or they may be unwilling to take the trouble to fill out all of a long, complex form.

Ferber has analyzed the number of omissions in a survey of the membership of Consumers Union.[85] This survey had an overall non-response rate of thirty-six percent. It involved a four-page leaflet with some seventy-one questions—an unusually lengthy form for a mail questionnaire. The omission rates were as follows:

Number of Omissions	Percent of Respondents
0	37.5
1	24.8
2-5	21.0
6-10	6.8
11-15	3.7
16-25	4.5
26 +	1.7
Total	100.0

While comparable data are scarce, it seems probable that the omission rate on this study is unusually high. There may well have been a marginal group of people who were fairly willing to respond, yet found seventy-one questions tedious.

Ferber conducted an elaborate analysis of the omissions. His main finding is that the omission rate is much higher for aged respondents, a result which is consistent with the findings of Gergen and Back. Low-education respondents omit more items—the task may well be more difficult for them. It is less obvious why women were found to omit more items than men.

Treatment of omitted items in analysis may be a considerable nuisance. As with non-response the simplest procedure may be to "do nothing," either showing "not ascertained" as a category in tables, or recomputing tables on the basis of those for whom data are available. The assumption that those who omit items are similar to the rest of the population, however, is dubious. As just shown, it is definitely false for the Consumers Union survey. It may be useful, therefore, to assume instead that those who omit items should have responded in the same way as others of similar socio-economic characteristics. A possible procedure is to "assign" for each omission a value equal to the mean for respondents with similar characteristics. More elaborate procedures may be worth the trouble in some situations. For example, one might base the assignment of family income on a multiple regression with income as dependent variable. Or, one might use a procedure which assigned the mean plus a random component so that the assigned values would be reasonably distributed instead of clustered at a limited number of incomes. Such procedures have two purposes: to remove bias from sample estimates and to simplify tabulating procedures for later work. These gains are purchased at the price of some delay in processing the data plus the cost of developing the assignment procedure. With a continuing program of surveys, a previous survey can provide the data for assignments. In case of variables which are zero for substantial numbers (expenditures on durables) the procedure may be first to assign whether any expenditure was made (on the basis of variables like age and income) and then if the first assignment is "Yes," to assign the amount on the basis of past expenditures of those who spent something, within income, etc. groups. This two-stage procedure is particularly useful when some cases are known to have spent something and only the amount has to be assigned. We return to this topic in Chapter V.

The Problem of Response Error

Even with a completed interview schedule in hand, we cannot proceed to analysis without some concern for the quality of the information. It is not easy to answer questions about response error, for if the data were easily available elsewhere, there would be no need for a survey. Evidence as to quality of data comes from several sources: The schedule itself may have evidence of respondent confusion, internal inconsistencies, substantial item non-response, or the need for substantial probling by the interviewers to build up an answer.

But the most startling and disturbing evidence of problems of response error in economic surveys comes from comparisons with aggregate data. Many economic magnitudes are estimated in the aggregate from published records, but a survey may be required to secure information on distributions, and on relationships at the micro-level with other magnitudes. We can estimate aggregate personal incomes, or savings accounts, but we may want to know how concentrated they are, and whether the low-income people also have little or no savings to fall back on. If a survey produces an estimate of the mean per family, one can multiply by an inside or outside estimate of the aggregate number of families to get an estimate of the aggregate amount.

There are of course various conceptual and coverage problems which require adjustments: the institutional population, non-personal incomes or assets belonging to unincorporated businesses or non-profit foundations, or universities, etc. But some general impressions remain from such aggregate comparisons: Asset holdings seem to be underreported by the widest margin. Consumer debt is better, particularly installment debt which is usually connected with purchases and involves regular payments easy to remember. Income is still better, particularly if enough time and attention is given to it in the interview.

Such comparisons leave one in the dark, of course, about the distribution of response errors—are they all concentrated in a few large amounts not reported, or held by those who were non-response in the survey, or widely distributed? In practice, such aggregate discrepancies, without any real evidence as to how damaging they were to distributions or correlational analyses, have led to the discontinuance of financial surveys, and to uncertainty as to the validity of analysis based on them. Yet, forgetting the few with very large amounts, survey analysis would only be badly biased if the errors were concentrated in a way correlated with one or more of the explanatory variables used. If every tenth person was just unwilling to admit he had a savings account, the result is noise and lower correlations, but not positive findings that are erroneous.

Hence, we are in serious need of better assessment of response error. The difficulty is, as we shall see, that this is expensive. When we turn to less quantitative measures—attitudes, expectations, plans, or classifications like occupation, the very concept of response error gets more complex.

Preliminary Statement of the Problem: It is useful to postulate the existence, for any individual respondent in a survey, of a "true value" representing the correct score for that individual on some characteristic measured in the survey. For example, the "true value" might be the actual amount of wages paid to an individual by his employer in a calendar year. Then the response error for that individual for that characteristic may be defined as the difference between the reported value and the "true value." It would be possible to think of the "reported" value as the value as entered on the interview report form. The term will be used here, however, to mean the value as used in the tabulating of the results of the survey. Response error, thus, is equivalent to total measurement error, including both collection and processing errors.

The assumption that there is a "true value" is not the same as assuming that the "true value" is measurable. Whether or not it is possible to measure something reasonably close to a "true value" varies according to the nature of the variable. For simple factual variables, the estimation of a "true value" is often possible. In economic surveys it is reasonably easy to define an acceptable true value for assets and debts with fixed money values and for financial flows. There exist, as a rule, institutional records where these amounts are recorded. For example, employers record the wages paid.

As one moves away from items of fixed monetary magnitude, problems of valuation and imputation become increasingly serious. The "true value" of the income of the owner of an unincorporated business is an elusive concept. It depends, of course, on such matters as how one estimates the annual depreciation of the assets of the business and how one values any income in kind the owner may have received. An investigator must adopt some set of definitions; for example, he may speak of income as defined for tax purposes by the Bureau of Internal Revenue. Even families which have no entrepreneurial income are very likely to own houses or at least durable goods which last beyond the period in which they are purchased. Economists may wish to take into account the flow of services received, say, by a home owner from his place of residence. The "true value" of that flow is a sophisticated concept, nowhere recorded in a set of reliable records. We may think of methods, however, for estimating the accuracy of reports of magnitudes which will enter into estimates of the imputed flow—we can seek to assess the accuracy of reports of house value, for example.[86]

It is when we turn to psychological variables that the measurement of a "true value" becomes most elusive and even the concept of such a value presents difficulties. There is, however, a literature on the subject of the validity of psychological constructs, especially of scores on psychological tests.[87] Cronback distinguishes four types of validation:

1) *Predictive* validity. Do the scores on a certain variable, as measured, predict future performance? In economic surveys one may investigate whether scores on some measure taken in one interview predict behavior at a later date as measured in a second interview. For example, one may investigate whether plans to buy cars are fulfilled.

2) *Concurrent* validity. Do the scores on a certain variable, as measured, correlate with performance measured at the same time? In economic surveys one may investigate whether scores on some measure taken in

one interview are associated with behavior as measured in the same interview. For example, one may investigate whether plans to send children to college are accompanied by saving money for the purpose.

3) *Content* validity. Do the items which enter into a measurement bear a reasonable relationship to the content to be measured? This requirement is for a logical study of the items in relation to the concept.

4) *Construct* validity. How can the scores on a measure be explained in terms of psychological theory? The test consists in setting up hypotheses and checking them by any suitable empirical procedure. For example, reasoning from the fundamental nature of a construct, one may deduce that people who have certain scores on this measure should have certain scores on related measures of their attitudes or behavior.

Cronback states that the validation of a test involves a long-continued interplay between observation, reasoning, and imagination. Imagination plays its part in suggesting what construct might account for test scores. Or, we may add, might be accounted for by such scores. Reasoning enters in deriving testable hypotheses from the theory surrounding the construct. And empirical work enters to test the hypotheses.

We may think of the "true" score of an individual on some psychological dimension, then, as the score which we would assign to him if we could apply a test, or a process of measurement, which had been validated as a result of careful, painstaking work of the type just described.

There is an unfortunate tendency for economists who work with constructs which are essentially psychological to be satisfied with elementary efforts at validation. For example, they may be satisfied to measure income expectations with a question which simply asks whether people expect their income to go up, stay the same, or decline. One may simply look at the content of such a question, note that on its face it has to do with what economists mean by income expectations, and proceed with the analysis. And the results may well be meaningful. But a sophisticated validation of the measure would require much more.

Methodological Studies: While it is possible to assemble an impressively long bibliography of reports on methodological studies of data gathering processes, a careful perusal shows that very little good-quality, reasonably conclusive work has been done. The best work has been on relatively simple variables where there was great concern with accurate estimates: morbidity, housing, unemployment, and population counts.

It is useful to distinguish various kinds of methodological studies:

1) One kind is studies of interviewer differences, that is, of apparent effects of the attitudes or social class of the interviewer, on the responses she reports. In many such studies, interviewers are not randomly

assigned to respondents, so that the effects are confounded with real differences between respondents, differences which can only crudely be controlled statistically.

Where there has been an experimental design, some interviewer effects have been found, mostly on attitudinal questions, of course. It is not clear what one does with the results, except to try to minimize the opportunities for interviewers to affect the results, by carefully training them to read the questions as written and write down the answers as closely to verbatim as possible. Or, if a limited set of choices is allowed, to have the interviewer read off the choices and let the respondent repeat one, rather than attempting to code a reply into some category in the field. And in view of differences in the number of responses given (e.g. reasons), some control over the probes is called for, such as repeating the phrase "anything else" until the answer "no" is reached.

2) Studies of differences depending on who is the respondent are much rarer. Most of these are, of course, husband-wife studies, and some are as concerned with who makes the decisions as with who is the best respondent—the two may not be the same.[88] Indeed, there is some reason to believe that wives may be better *predictors* of future family decisions, even in areas where both of them agree that the husband makes the decision.[89]

3) There are studies of differences between the findings of different surveys, or between survey data and outside aggregates, or studies based on demographic checks. These studies are generally inconclusive sometimes as to which is the correct figure, and generally as to why the errors exist. Over the years, various changes were made in the schedule and procedures of the Surveys of Consumer Finances sometimes in split half samples, and sometimes from year to year since the distributions were not expected to change much. In general the differences were small and, occasionally in an unexpected direction. We have already mentioned the case where a much more elaborate and detailed schedule of questions elicited less aggregated debt than the simpler procedures used the previous and the following years.

4) Studies of non-response bias should be included in this catalogue of methodological studies, even though they do not study response error. Indeed, by working to increase the response rate, one may be trading less non-response error for more response error, from those unwilling and uncooperative respondents.

5) There are somewhat more elaborate designs, allocating different procedures to separate samples or part samples, including varying the data collection between mail, telephone, and personal interview. Again differences may appear, though they have often been small, without

evidence as to where the truth lies, and little clue as to why there were differences. With reinterviews it is possible to study reliability by asking again for information that should not change, such as when the respondent was born, or his education. Or one can reconcile information by tracking back reported car transactions to see whether one can get back to the car reported the year before.

Reinterviews also allow elaborate designs to check on the reports of transactions where dating may be a problem, as with additions and repairs to homes. Questions in several waves may cover the same time period, and by identifying the particular transaction, one can see whether it was dated consistently. The most impressively elaborate such study was done at the United States Census Bureau and reported by Neter and Waksberg.[90]

Neter and Waksberg studied the accuracy of household expenditures for additions and repairs. They found that reported expenditures during a period of one month as given in a single interview seriously overstated actual expenditures, probably by about fifty-five percent, largely because of telescoping in time the dating of these expenditures, where the exact timing is often ambiguous. This error could be reduced if not eliminated, they found, by a procedure using two interviews, one at the start as well as one at the end of the period.

They used an unusually sophisticated design, and the study is a classic of careful analysis. However, it is unlikely that the results can be generalized to other consumer expenditures. The study dealt with a kind of consumer expenditure that is difficult to assign to one date. Often a long time span passes from the time someone first calls someone to do something around the house, or starts buying the materials, to the time that the job is commissioned or started, to the time when it is almost finished or a bill is rendered, or a bill is paid. It is doubtful that the amount of telescoping or shifting of time would be as large as most other consumer activities as it is in this one. Notice, however, that their problem was to estimate aggregates as accurately as possible, on a quarterly basis preferably, and not necessarily to provide for a detailed cross-section of information, which could be used to explain differences between people or over time, in people's behavior. It is quite possible that if one wanted to do the latter, one would insist on asking about annual expenditures, do the best job one could of getting it reasonably accurately, follow a panel over time to get changes from one year to the next, and mostly be concerned that the year-to-year changes in individual's reported expenditures were reasonably good.

In discussing needs for future research, the authors do *not* talk about experimenting with different specifications. Which date is relevant for these expenditures? They might very well ask the date that the first piece of work was actually started. It would be the easiest thing to remember, and yet this would cause problems if you wanted expenditure data, because people might have all kinds of things started in one period but paid for in another.

6) Finally there are genuine validity studies which check an individual item from an interview against some outside source, usually some record assumed to be correct.[91] Such checking is expensive, and in any case cannot cover more than a few items. It is not easy to secure access to records anyway.

An additional difficulty is that most validity checks are directional, that is they start with a list of people known to have been in the hospital or used a library, or had a bank account, and see whether they report it in an interview. Or they secure reports from an interview, and check a source to see if they also exist in the records. Such validity tests are biased in the sense that they mostly pick up one type of error and not the other. Starting with record information, one mostly picks up underreporting. If the respondent also reported an account in another bank, he might be over-reporting but that would not be discovered.

Similarly, if one starts with respondent reports, then it is only possible to find some that do not exist in records, presumably over-reports.

But a worse problem is that one is often not sure whether the amount is in error, or the name of the bank or hospital, or the date of the illness.

Finally, validity studies still do not go far toward providing notions as to why the errors exist. One can infer a little from the types of people who report well or badly, including their attitudes. In some of the best studies, validity checks have been combined with experimental variations in procedures, so that one at least knew which procedure was best, not just that they produced different results.

Mismatches in validity checks are always a possibility, and unfortunately they systematically distort estimates of error.[92]

In order to reduce mismatches, it may be necessary to ask for additional information in the interview, such as the name of the bank and in whose names the account is held, and the exact date for the amount given. Then the respondent may have to give permission for release of the records and in many cases, it is a complex task to get the right information out of the records. In the case of checking accounts, for instance, some adjustment must be made for the float of uncleared checks, already deducted in the owner's check book, but not yet subtracted from his account at the bank.

What is worse, having to rely on cooperation of both individual and institution, one may have a biased sample of both, so the results may not generalize, and the very detail asked to allow the check means that one does not have a validity test of the kind of procedure that would be used in a major study without a validity check.

One unpublished study in Detroit asked about property taxes, and using the address, checked the tax rolls. Most respondents were precise in reporting their taxes, but there were a few very large errors, mostly two-family houses where it was not clear whether the taxes were supposed to refer to the whole house or half of it, or people who gave their city taxes only rather than city, county, and school taxes.

An attempt to assess the coverage of individuals' health insurance policies by asking the name of the company and the policy number revealed problems of identifying companies when several had similar-sounding names and the fact that some people counted their auto insurance medical payments clause as medical insurance.[93] The same study compared people's reports of their medical costs after an accident with hospital records, finding as might have been expected, somewhat more overreports than underreports.

Given all these difficulties it is easy to see why people look for some cheaper or easier method to assess the validity of their data, or ignore the problem altogether. When one considers that a fifty-minute interview may contain some 400 items of information, each one of which may be potentially capable of some comparison with other information, or even verification, the magnitude of the problem is staggering. And when one considers that the other sources of information, even ignoring the conceptual and matching difficulties, may themselves be subject to error, and the final fact that there is not much use merely measuring error if one does not know why it arose or what to do about it, it may seem more profitable to invest the time and energy in better pretesting, reinterviews, investigation of consistency of people's reports, etc., rather than experimental validity studies.

Mathematical Models of Response Error: A substantial body of work has been done on the development of models of response error, primarily by statisticians who have approached the subject with a background in sampling. A center of work on the subject has been the United States Bureau of the Census. The purposes of the work of the Bureau evidently have been to assist in the formulation of policy in data collection and to provide information concerning the accuracy of Census' statistics for the guidance of users of the results. The focus of interest, therefore, has been on the accuracy of total counts and of estimated means and percentages. It has not been on the accuracy of estimates of analytical statistics, such as correlation coefficients and regression coefficients. This latter topic, which is of concern to economists who work with sample surveys, will be considered in Chapter VI.

The nature of the work done at the Census may be indicated by a brief treatment of a model of response error developed there. A more extended discussion will be found in publications by Census staff.[94]

Measurement error is defined by Hansen, Hurwitz, and Bershad to include both collection and processing errors. They consider surveys, including censuses, as conceptually repeatable. The particular results in one survey are the results of one trial. The value observed even for a particular measurement on a particular individual is only one of a universe of many values which might have been obtained if the same measuring process had been repeated many times for the same individual.

Consider the problem of estimating a proportion. For a member of a population under study, say, the jth individual, it would be possible ideally to measure without error whether or not he falls in some category. We may say that $U_j = 1$ if he falls in the category, and $U_j = 0$, if he does not. Then it is possible to define the "true value" of the proportion for the population:

$$(1) \qquad U = \frac{1}{N} \sum_{j=1}^{N} U_j$$

For example, if ten percent of the population fall in a certain income group, then for those individuals U_j will be 1, and for all others, zero. The average value of U, or $\bar{U}$, will be .10. It is this hypothetical "true value" that we seek to estimate.

The data that we actually have will be observations for individuals, say, individual j is typical; for a particular trial, say, a certain survey, survey t; taken under certain (uncontrollable) conditions according to certain specified procedures, say, conditions and procedures G. Thus our observations may be said to be of the form X_{jtg}.

Our estimate of $\bar{U}$, then, will be:

$$(2) \qquad P_{tg} = \frac{1}{n} \sum_{j=1}^{n} X_{jtg}$$

That is, we will estimate the mean of the values of X which we observe for the n individuals in the particular sample, t, taken under the particular conditions, g. (For a census, n = N.)

The expected value of P_{tg} over many repeated surveys (under conditions and procedures G) may be defined as follows:

(3) $\quad P_G = E_{PtG}$

It is not necessarily true that P_G will *equal* $\bar{U}$. There may well be some bias in the procedure which will persist regardless of the number of repetitions of the survey or census. This bias may be defined:

(4) $\quad B_G = P_G - \bar{U}$

The bias carries the subscript G since it will depend upon the conditions and procedures used.

The total variance of the estimate, P_{tG}, will depend upon the distribution of the values of P_{tG} around their expected value, P_G:

(5) $\quad \sigma^2 P_{tG} = E (P_{tG} - P_G)^2$

The mean square error of the estimate takes into account the bias in the estimate of P_{tG} as well as the variance in the estimate. It is, therefore, the basic measure of the accuracy of P_{tG}:

(6) $\quad MSE_G = E (P_{tG} - \bar{U})^2 = \sigma^2_{PtG} + B^2_G$

The mean square error, or its square root, is conceptually the best measure of the accuracy of any estimate. Of course, in practice the mean square error is unlikely to be known. Useful approximations, however, are possible.

For one individual, individual j, over many trials, there will be an expected value:

(7) $\quad E_j X_{jt} = P_j$

This expectation should be understood to assume that the conditions and procedures, G, are constant over all the trials.

There will be, then, a difference between the observed and expected value for unit j on trial t:

(8) $\quad d_{jt} = X_{jt} - P_j$

Estimates of this difference, the response deviation, play an important part in practical work on response error. Note that the response deviation is measured from the expected value for the individual in question.

It is possible that the expected value for individual j should be thought of as depending not only on conditions and procedures G but also on the other particular individuals who happen to be selected in the sample. The presence of these other individuals may influence the interviewer's approach to individual j. She may develop expectations about respondents as a result of her experience with these individuals. Hence, it may be necessary to think of an expected value for individual j over many repeated surveys with an identical sample:

$$(9) \quad E_{js} X_{jt} = P_{js}$$

If it turns out that the effect on the estimate for j of the composition of the sample is close to zero, equation (7) will be all that is required.

The total variance of a survey will include contributions from response deviation and from sampling deviation as well as, possibly, from the covariance of the two. It may be stated:

$$(10) \quad \sigma_{p_t}^2 = E (p_t - P)^2 = E [(p_t - p) + (p - P)]^2$$

$$= E (p_t - p)^2 + 2 E (p_t - p) (p - P) + E (p - P)^2$$

where (11) $p = \dfrac{1}{n} \sum\limits_{j=1}^{n} p_j$.

Since P_j is the expected value for one individual (see equation (7)), p is the average for n individuals over many trials.

The first component is the average of the response deviations for the sample:

$$(12) \quad \sigma^2 d_t = E (Pt - P)^2 = E (\frac{1}{n} \sum\limits^{n} d_{jt}) = E (\bar{d}_t)^2$$

The third term represents the sampling variance of P_t:

$$(13) \quad \sigma^2_p = E (p - P)^2 = E [\frac{1}{n} \sum\limits_{j=1}^{n} (pj - P)]^2$$

In a census there is no sampling variance; this term will have a value of zero.

This model has been developed in work on a number of problems. Topics considered include the effects of correlations among response deviations on a survey and methods of estimating interviewer variability (in 1950) and the effects of interviewer, supervisor, and processing variability (in 1960). Findings concerning the magnitude of individual response deviation for proportions (σ_d^2) are presented in the form of ratios to PQ, i.e. ratios to the variance of a proportion of the observed magnitude assuming the magnitude had been found in simple random sampling without response deviations. It turns out that the estimates of σ_d^2 are of the order of three to ten percent of PQ for items such as age which are regarded as measured with high reliability, but on the order of fifty percent of PQ for items measured with low reliability such as condition of housing in a census of housing, or unemployment in a census of population. In the Current Population Survey the estimates of σ_d^2/PQ are on the order of half the value in the decennial census.

Estimates of the bias in the 1950 Census have been made using the Current Population Survey as a standard. For some items, for example, the percent of persons who are classed as farmers or farm managers, the estimates of bias are on the order of magnitude of seven percent of the estimate from the Current Population Surveys. Such findings have led the Census Bureau to reconsider the allocation of resources between complete enumeration and sample surveys using more refined methods of data collection.

Kish has developed a model for the analysis of response error in a situation in which two estimates of a quantity are available for every individual in a sample and there is reason to consider one of the estimates to be preferable, but neither can be accepted as a close approximation of the "true value."[95] The data consisted in estimates of the market value of each of a sample of owner-occupied homes made by the owner and by a professional appraiser. The model considers the relationships among the variances and covariances of these estimates and the (unknown) "true value." In contrast to the previous model, only one estimate is considered for each respondent and each appraiser.

Let: r_i = response by the resident owner of home i
        a_i = estimate by the appraiser for home i
        y_i = "true value" for home i

We may estimate the mean of each:

(1) $\bar{R} = E(r);\ \bar{A} = E(a);\ \bar{Y} = E(y)$

We may also define the variances:

(2) $V(r) = E(r - \bar{R})^2;\ V(a) = E(a - \bar{A})^2;\ V(y) = E(y - \bar{Y})^2$

We may also define the difference between the estimates:

(3) $d_i = (r_i - y_i) - (a_i - y_i) = (r_i - a_i)$

Then $(\bar{R} - \bar{Y})$ will be the response bias, and $(\bar{A} - \bar{Y})$ will be the appraisers' bias. These are unknown, but we can estimate:

(4) $\bar{D} = (\bar{R} - \bar{A}) = (\bar{R} - \bar{Y}) - (\bar{A} - \bar{Y})$

We can also estimate the mean-square difference of the measurements:

(5)   M.S. $(d) = E(d^2) = E(r - a)^2$

Finally we may write an expression for the covariance between the difference in measurements and the appraisers' values:

(6)   Cov. $(da) - E(d - \bar{D}) (a - \bar{A})$

The basic equation of the model is the following:

(7) $V(r) + \bar{D}^2 = V(a) + M.S. (d) + 2 \, Cov \, (da)$

Or in terms of expected values:

$$E (r - a)^2 = E (r - y)^2 + E (a - y)^2 - 2E (r - y) (a - y)$$

The first term (left side of the equation) is available, and is larger than the next term (the true response error) by an amount composed of two other items: the third term which is the mean square error of the appraisers' estimates, and the four covariance term which is likely to be small. So the model tells us that the variance of the discrepancies between the two reports exaggerates the response error unless the check-source, here appraisers, is totally free of error. Hence a big improvement would be a double appraisal to provide evidence in the appraisers' errors.

The terms in the equation could be estimated in different situations in order to obtain further insight into the errors of estimation. For example, where the respondent had purchased the home recently his estimate of market value might be assumed to be better informed and the mean square difference should be smaller.

Ferber has developed a method of estimating the importance of contributions from different sources, including response error, to the bias in survey estimates of means. This procedure is descriptive.[96] He applied the method to the small sample of results from a study of farmers for whom data for validation of demand deposits was available, names having been selected from a list. The method consists essentially in estimating the proportion of the sample in each of four groups: (1) non-respondents (including all those not interviewed who should have been interviewed); (2) respondents who failed to report the existence of the deposit; (3) respondents who reported the existence of the account but refused to estimate the balance, and (4) respondents who reported a balance. For each group an estimate of the "true value" could be made and compared with the estimate that would have been made from the survey without the validation procedure to yield an estimated bias. The bias for the sample as a whole becomes an average of the biases for the four groups, weighted by the number of sample members in each group.

In Ferber's notation:

$$E = P_s(A_s - X_s) + P_o A_o + P_1 (A_1 - X_2) + P_2 (A_2 - X_2)$$

where:

P_i is the proportion of sample members in the ith category;
A_i is the average actual balance of sample members in category i;
X_i is the average recorded balance for category i.

Subscripts have the following meanings:

S non-respondents
0 respondents, account not reported
1 respondents, account reported but balance refused
2 respondents, account reported and balance given

Ferber also develops estimates of the effect of non-sampling errors on estimates of the reliability of the mean. His expressions for the mean square and sample variance, respectively, are as follows:

$$MSE_{\bar{y}} = (1 + k^2 p) \, \sigma \frac{2}{\bar{y}}$$

$$(?) \qquad \sigma \frac{2}{\bar{y}} = \sigma \frac{2}{\bar{x}} + \sigma \frac{2}{\bar{e}} + \sigma \frac{2}{\bar{y}} \, \bar{x} \, \sigma \bar{e}$$

where:

x_i is the true size of account i
y_i is the reported size
bars denote means
$\bar{e} = \bar{y} - \bar{x}$
r = correlation between x and e

In the example based on the farm study, results were as follows:

k .78
r -.67
apparent standard errors of mean $(x_{\bar{y}})$ $317
true standard error of mean (MSE) $403
response-error-free standard error of the mean $413

Problem of Data Collection in Underdeveloped Countries

There has been a very considerable amount of effort devoted to survey research in underdeveloped countries since World War II, and there has begun to
accumulate a literature describing the experiences of those who have undertaken
these projects. In a sense nothing new has emerged from these reports—the problems encountered all have their analogues in the United States and other developed countries. Yet some problems which are easily handled or even trivial in developed countries are very much more serious in other parts of the world, so serious as to suggest that the limitations as to what can be done with sample surveys
are quite different. It will require a further accumulation of knowledge before
there is a reasonable degree of consensus as to what methods are optimal, what
projects are and are not feasible. But it certainly is proving true that the possibilities and limitations of sample surveys are very different in different countries.

The Need for Data: There is reason to believe that data of the types obtain-
able from sample surveys in developed countries would be useful for many problems in underdeveloped countries. Freedman has published a list of conditions
which make surveys related to family planning especially helpful in developing
countries where there is a problem of high fertility.[97] His conditions also may
have broader applicability:

1) In the context of a desire for massive social change there is little information about how much change has already occurred.
2) There is likely to be a gap of understanding between the leadership and
the masses which is much greater than in developed countries. The mass
media all communicate in one direction, to the masses, and feedback is
poor.
3) Traditional ideology exists about family planning. The ideology may
not fit the facts.
4) There may be many people in favor of a program who do not realize
that others are too.
5) There is a need for surveys to check on the effectiveness of the programs.

One might find that a similar set of conditions applied, say, to the introduction of improved agriculture methods.

Controversy Over the Usefulness of Survey Methods: There have been attacks on the usefulness of survey from an anthropological standpoint. Such an attack by Thomas Rhys Williams was published in the *Public Opinion Quarterly* in 1959.[98]

Williams objected to two assumptions which he attributed to survey research. First, he objected to the assumption of the validity of a survey response as a social datum. There may be institutionalized patterns of saying one thing and doing another. People may describe their actions as they ought to have been, not as they actually were. Williams, in a word, is highly sceptical of what people say. He urges detailed empirical observation of social behavior.[99]

Second, Williams objects to the assumption of dynamic equivalence among survey responses as well as to equivalence between such responses and actual social behavior. Responses may be far from equivalent in different contexts. They should be interpreted in the context of the behavior of a specific social group. Presumably, while Williams might object to any comparisons across social groups, the more diverse the groups, the greater the force of the objection.

Surely, it would be going too far to urge that people *never* report their actions and their attitudes correctly or that responses are *never* comparable across social groups. It is entirely proper to raise questions on these points, however. Skepticism on these matters is a better general approach than a simple faith in the validity and comparability of responses to any and all questions.

Problems in Sampling: The problems of developing a satisfactory sample frame in underdeveloped countries were reviewed briefly by Wilson in 1958.[100] There may be a lack of census data. Existing statistics may be unreliable. There may be a lack of estimates of size at the local level, for example, of city blocks. There may not be adequate maps. Listing may be difficult because of makeshift housing arrangements. Random selection within households may clash with custom—it may be difficult to interview anyone but the accepted spokesman for the household.

These difficulties are not necessarily permanent. Frey, for example, reports that a study in rural Turkey was greatly facilitated by a 1960 census, which provided data on all 35,000 villages in the country, including especially measures of size, so that it was possible to select villages with probability proportional to size. Frey also found that it was possible to develop lists of villagers on the spot, relying on several sources of names, including lists of eligible voters and the fact that in small villages the leaders know every adult personally.[101]

It has been argued that the unit of opinion is not the individual in places such as rural Madras in India. The unit, it is argued, is communal, an extended family, sub-caste, or village.[102] This argument, however, need not imply a change in sampling. Presumably, the importance of an opinion can be gauged by

how many people hold it, regardless of its origin. It is also argued that it is difficult to interview people in isolation. Groups gather automatically. The arrival of
a visitor is a great event in some villages. The person selected may feel it is not
his role to respond—that is the responsibility of the leader, who is the one who
has opinions. It is not easy to insist on following through with a random sample
of individuals. Carried to its logical conclusion this argument would imply that
the population sampled should not consist of individuals or families but of some
larger units. There may be situations in which such an approach should be considered, perhaps in combination with a more standard procedure. In Turkey,
Frey reports that on his project the sample in each village included the political
leader and his wife and the religious leader and his wife, as well as a random sample of other villagers.

Roe Goodman has suggested that problems of sampling and interviewing
overlap, that if one wants to make sure the interviewer interviews each person in
the sample, it may be better to go so far as to take fewer villages and include
everyone in the village, so that the interviewer and the villagers both know that
everyone is to be included. This also avoids the necessity for explaining principles
of sampling so people will know why not everyone was interviewed.[103] It may
also reduce field problems where roads and overnight accommodations are primitive or absent.

Problems in Interviewing: There is always a need for social acceptance of a
project involving interviewing. In underdeveloped countries this acceptance is
not necessarily automatic. It may be essential to obtain political support at levels
which seem unreasonably high to an American. For example, Carlson found that
in order to carry through a survey of mass media and communication behavior
for Columbia University in Jordan he had to talk personally to the King.[104] The
King responded favorably, and the project was successfully completed. In Turkey
Frey reports it was essential to have top level political support, which was provided by the Turkish State Planning Organization. In India the National Council
of Applied Economic Research, which carried out the project described in Chapter I, had the benefit of being an established Indian organization with close ties
to the Planning Commission, which was one of the most powerful agencies of
government. Working from the top down it becomes possible to obtain the necessary political support at the local level. Questions raised by local officials as to
the legitimacy of an inquiry can be answered. Of course they may have to be
educated in the process. In a number of countries *any* research project requires
approval by the relevant government official.

An excessive display of political support can be disastrous, however. Frey
reports a pilot study in Turkey (on another survey) in which interviewers dressed
like officials and behaved like officials, summoning certain peasants to be brought
before them. The peasants came, and lied in the manner demanded by the occasion. It seems likely that the social status and perceived role of the interviewer

may cause trouble in many underdeveloped countries. Law enforcement may be lax, so that many people have something to hide. If they are squatters on the land, they may want to hide their very existence. If they have income too high to justify staying in a subsidized housing project, or are illegally converting part of a housing subsidy into cash by renting out some of the space, they are not likely to report income or household composition accurately. They may well distrust the government, or respect the higher social status of the interviewer, and hence give socially acceptable answers, or answers which agree with anything the question suggests, or that they think the interviewer would approve. Particularly where adopting new ways is promoted by the government as not only economically superior, but a patriotic duty to one's country, reports on adoption of, or the experience with, some new practice are likely to be biased.

The problems of communication in underdeveloped countries often begin with problems of language. Some countries, like Korea, are fortunate enough to have a common language.[105] In others there may be more than one language, and there may be dialects within main languages. A common reliance is on bilingual interviewers. This method was necessarily used in Turkey to reach people who speak Kurdish, a language which is unwritten. The standardization of questions becomes hard to enforce in such circumstances. When languages are written, it is possible to translate questionnaires, and check on accuracy by independent re-translation back into the original language. In the United States subtle differences in questions do make a difference in replies even concerning factual information, as was shown earlier in this chapter. (See the discussion of questions about income.) There is no reason to suppose that this problem is peculiar to the United States.

There may be difficult problems of finding generally understood equivalents for particular words, even when, as in Turkey, a single language is widely spoken. Frey reports difficulties with "problem," "prestige," and "loyalty." The choice is between synonyms, which may not have identical connotations, and explanations, which may introduce bias or become elaborate and formidable.

Even if we stick to "factual" material, there may well be problems with the definitions of terms. "Sorghum" may mean a grain meal or a molasses. Questions about ownership of livestock may cause trouble where cattle are commually owned, or frequently rented, so that possession and ownership do not jibe. The concept of depreciation may or may not exist, nor the notion of distinguishing current expenses from investments in capital improvements. Patterns of interfamily transfers may differ, particularly as to whether they incur obligations like loans or are genuine transfers. And the whole notion of careful definitions of boundaries or exact measurement or enumeration may be foreign to the culture and even regarded as improper or dangerous. In short, the appraisal of what one can expect to secure with reasonable accuracy in an interview requires an intimate knowledge of the culture as well as a good theoretical grasp of the concepts that would need to be measured for a particular study.

A different related problem of communication arises out of social divisions and factionalism. Extreme difficulties of this type were found by Hanna and Hanna in Nigeria and Uganda.[106] They spent three months in 1963 in each of two small urban centered communities, one in each of these countries. They interviewed probability samples of one hundred adults in each. In the community in Nigeria the population was almost all from the Ibo people, but they were divided into five clans with marked differences in dialect and feelings of social distance. In the Uganda community the population was split into two districts, one further divided into six distinct ethnic groups and the other with three clans. To these splits were added the problems in the town of an Asian minority comprising a third of the urban population but split into three religious groups, Hindus, Muslims, and Catholic Goans. In addition there was another category of "stranger" Bagandi families. And age and sex differences were much greater in both Nigeria and Uganda than in the United States. Interviewing had to be done by natives who knew the dialects, and each interviewer could reach only a few people. The Hannas calculated they should have had at least eighteen assistants in Uganda and fourteen in Nigeria so that each respondent could be approached by someone with whom he would communicate freely. We can compare these problems with the problems found to exist in the United States in interviews with Negroes and, on some subjects, in interviews with people of much lower socioeconomic status than the interviewer or wide disparity in age.

A familiar set of problems in the United States concern response variability and response set. There is evidence from a study by Landsberger and Saavedra that these problems are serious among lower-status, less-educated people in Chile, much more than among the better educated in that country.[107] They were especially concerned with acquiescence set—that is, with the number of "Yea-sayers." They argue that, in general, response set is greater the greater the ambiguity of an item. Hence, individuals to whom a given item appears more ambiguous will have more response set.

The experiment concerned a well-known psychological measure, the California F scale. The method consisted essentially in reversing the content of the items, as in the following examples:

Form A

1. Human nature being what it is, there will always be war and conflict.
2. The most important thing to teach a child is to obey his parents.

Form B

1. The existence of war and conflict is not due to man's nature.
2. In a child's education, it is least important that he learn to obey his parents.

There were two types of respondents: (1) university students (N = 230); (2) working class groups, including (a) mothers attending discussions in community centers in a purely working class area (N - 140), and (b) housemaids attending adult-education classes in their trade-union center (N = 144).

The experiment involved two observations on each subject. All four possible sequences of forms were used: A form twice, B form twice, A then B, and B then A. Length of time between measurements was also varied.

For the students when the same form was repeated the scores were correlated in the range r = .72 to r = .93. When the forms were reversed the scores (corrected for the reversal) were still positively correlated r = .19 to r = .88. For both working class groups a reversal of forms actually led to negative correlations between scores: for the mothers, r = -.19; for the housemaids, r = -.33 to r = -.56. When the same form was repeated scores for the mothers were positively correlated at about the same level as for the students, r = .73. For the housemaids even when the same form was repeated the scores were correlated only r = .23 to r = .31. Landsberger and Saavedra are not quite so blunt, but we may go so far as to say that for the housemaids the form was worthless. The California F scale is of little intrinsic interest to economists, but acquiescence set can be a problem with any type of subject matter.

There is an assumption in survey research that when people reply to questions they will tell the truth. Errors are often regarded as the result of ambiguity, misunderstanding, inappropriateness of the questions, and the like. It is assumed that people will tell the truth, unless, perhaps, there is some special reason for them to conceal it, say, because the question concerns illegal or immoral activity. In some cultures, however, untruth may be tolerated much more than in others. Gastil has asserted that among the "modern middle class" in Iran in many circumstances telling the truth is regarded as foolish and stupid.[108] Gastil, who speaks Parsi, spent eleven months in Shiraz and wrote a dissertation on *Iranian General Belief Modes as Found in Middle Class Shiraz* (Harvard 1958). He regards this tolerance for untruth as associated with a general tendency for members of the "modern middle class" to distrust those around them. The evidence he cites in the article referred to above is essentially impressionistic, but it does grow out of personal experience of the society in some depth. We must agree that at least it raises a question of potential importance in economic surveys: who will tell the truth concerning economic matters in different situations in different societies?

A final comment about interviewing in underdeveloped countries is that unconventional methods of data collection may be developed which will prove helpful. For example, Stanton, Back, and Litwak report successful use of role-playing techniques in interviews in Puerto Rico.[109] Respondents entered into the role-playing readily in spite of the use of tape recorders. Such methods may be useful for some types of data as an intermediate method between conventional interviews with random samples and direct observation of behavior as it occurs naturally as proposed by such writers as Williams.

Problems of Research Design: As the preceding section suggests, there is an increasing body of experience about data collection in underdeveloped countries. The problems are identified, if not solved. There is little very written on the subject of research design. Yet we may at least point out the critical importance of the question, what research designs can be carried through to successful completion and what designs are unlikely to lead to useful results? There is reason to think the choice of projects will be particularly difficult. Investigators arriving from developed countries will be unable to rely on their own personal observations and prior experience to the degree to which they can do so in their own cultures. They will be tempted to apply directly the procedures which have worked elsewhere. For adaptation of these procedures to the society in which they are working they will tend to rely on the local intelligentsia, the people with whom they will have the most personal contact. There is reason to be cautious about excessive reliance on these people, however. They may be only too ready to adopt the "symbols and ceremonials" of research without adequate grasp of its essential character.[110] They are likely to come from the top strata of their own society, and, as previously discussed, the social distance between them and other members of the society may be much greater than in countries like the United States.

The danger is that projects will be undertaken which appear to be better designed than they really are because they do not adequately take into account the situation as it exists in the society where they will be conducted—either the situation in terms of the potential usefulness of the research or in terms of what research can be completed successfully. In view of these uncertainties and risks, perhaps the best policy is one of caution, with unusual emphasis on simplicity and limited objectives in the basic design, and on preliminary pilot investigations.

A knowledgeable anthropologist sensitive to economic matters can be very useful in survey design if social incentives, or social constraints are important in affecting people's behavior. Some paths to economic goals may be closed by cultural or institutional barriers.[111]

APPENDIX A

A List of Some Reports of Economic Surveys in Other Countries
(including broadly economic items like family planning and economic
attitudes but not strictly methodological discussions)

Accra, Office of the Government Statistician, *Surveys of Household Budgets in Accra, Akuse, Sekondi and Kumasi.*

Ione Acqua, *Accra Survey: A Social Survey of the Capital of Ghana, Formerly Called the Gold Coast, Undertaken for the West African Institute of Social and Economic Research 1953-56,* University of London Press, London, 1958.

Peter Russell Andersen, *Discretionary and Contractual Saving in Canada, a Cross-Sectional Study,* Harvard University Ph.D. Thesis, Cambridge, Mass., 1967 (based on Canadian Dominion Bureau of Statistics 1959 family expenditure survey of 3,031 families in urban areas of 15,000 or more).

Joseph R. Ascroft, Niels G. Roling, Graham B. Kerr and Gerald D. Hursh, *Patterns of Diffusion in Rural Eastern Nigeria,* Diffusions of Innovations Research Report II, Department of Communication, Michigan State University, East Lansing, Michigan, Feb. 1969.

A. Asimakopulos, "Analysis of Canadian Consumer Expenditure Surveys," *Canadian Journal of Economics and Political Science,* 31 (May 1965), 222-241.

Bernard Berelson and Ronald Freedman, "A Study in Fertility Control," *Scientific American,* 210 (May 1964), 29-37 (in Taiwan).

Gunilla Bjeren, *Makelle (Ethiopia) Elementary School Drop-Out 1967,* Research Report No. 5, Scandinavian Institute of African Studies, Uppsala, Sweden, 1969.

Robert O. Blood, Reuben Hill, Andree Michel and Contantina Safilios-Rothschild, *Comparative Analysis of Family Power Structure: Problems of Measurement and Interpretation* (Paper at 9th International Seminar on Family Research, Tokyo, 1965) printed in *International Yearbook of Sociology.*

J. L. Boutillier and J. Causse, "Les budgets familiaux, mission socio-economique du fleuve Senegal," Dakar, 1958.

J. C. Caldwell, "Fertility Attitudes in Three Economically Contrasting Rural Regions of Ghana," *Economic Development and Cultural Change* 15 (Jan. 1967), 217-238.

Dominion of Canada, Royal Commission on Banking and Finance, *Consumer Survey* (Conducted by McDonald Research Limited in spring 1962 and published by them).

Dominion of Canada, Dominion Bureau of Statistics. *Farm Family Living Expenditure: 1958,* (Catalogue N 62-523 Occasional) Dominion Printer, Ottawa, Jan. 1966.

Dominion of Canada, Dominion Bureau of Statistics. *Urban Family Expenditure: 1959,* (Catalogue No. 62-521, Occasional) Dominion Printer, Ottawa, March, 1963.

Dominion of Canada, Dominion Bureau of Statistics, *Urban Family Food Expenditure, 1962* (Catalogue No. 62-524 Occasional) Dominion Printer, Ottawa, December, 1965.

Central Treaty Organization, *Symposium on Household Surveys,* Dacca, East Pakistan, 1966 (reports on surveys in Turkey, Pakistan, Iran).

Ceylon, Central Bank, *Survey of Ceylon's Consumer Finances, May, 1953,* The Central Bank, Colombo, Ceylon, 1954.

Michael Chaput and Ladislav Venys, *A Survey of Kenya Elite,* Occasional Papers No. 25, Program of East African Studies, Syracuse University, May 1967.

University of Chile, *Family Incomes and Expenditures in Greater Santiago-Experimental Survey,* Santiago, Institut de Econ. Econ Pub No. 85, 1966.

Paul Clerc, *Grands Ensembles. Banlieues Nouvelles, Enquête Démographique Et Psycho-Sologique,* Presses Universitaires De France, Paris, 1967.

George E. Cumper, "Expenditure Patterns, Kingston, Jamaica, 1954" in *Social and Economic Studies* 7 (June 1958) 166- (N = 1180, a later 1957-8 study appears only as a government document, N = 355).

Thomas Dow Jr., "Attitudes Toward Family Size and Family Planning in Nairobi" *Demography* 4 (1967) 780-797.

J. M. Due, "Post War Family Expenditure Studies in Western Europe," *Journal of Farm Econ.,* 38 (Aug. 1956), 846-856.

East African Statistics Department, *The Patterns of Income, Expenditure and Consumption of African Unskilled Laborers in Kampala, Sept. 1953,* 1954;

- - - - - - *The Patterns of Income, Expenditure, and Consumption of Africans in Nairobi 1957/58,* 1959;

- - - - - - *"Patterns of Income, Expenditure, and Consumption of African Unskilled Workers in Kampala, February, 1957,* 1957;

- - - - - - *The Patterns of Income, Expenditure, and Consumption of African Unskilled Workers in Mbale, Feb., 1958,* 1958;

- - - - - - *The Patterns of Income, Expenditure and Consumption of Agrian Unskilled Workers in Gulu, Feb. 1959,* 1959;

- - - - - - *The Patterns of Income, Expenditures and Consumption of African Unskilled Workers in Fort Portal, February, 1960,* 1960 (all Nairobi).

Europe, Office Statistique Des Communautés Européenes, *Budgets Familiaux,* 1963-64, No. 1, Luxembourg, No. 2. Belgique, No. 3 Nederland, No. 4, Italia, No. 5 Allemagne, No. 6 France, No. 7, Bruxelles, Belgique, 1966 or later.

European Coal and Steel Community, "Budgets familiaux des ouvriers de la C.E.C.A. 1956-7," *Informations Statistiques* Serie "Statistiques socials" No. 1, 1960. (See also *Informations Statistiques,* May-June 1959 and November, 1959 for results of a housing survey of 40,000 workers.)

Abdul Farouk, *Irrigation in a Monsoon Land,* University of Dacca, Bureau of Economic Research, Dacca, East Pakistan, 1958 (Economics of Farming in the Ganges-Kobadak).

Frederick C. Fliegel, Prodipto Roy, Lalit K. Sen, Joseph E. Kiflin, *Agricultural Innovations in Indian Villages,* National Institute of Community Development, Hyderabad, India, 1968.

Food and Agriculture Organization, *Review of Food Consumption Surveys,* FAO, Rome, 1958.

Phillips Foster and Larry Yost, "A Simulation Study of Population, Education, and Income Growth in Uganda," *American Journal of Agricultural Economics* 51 (Aug. 1969), 576-91.

Ronald Freedman, "Sample Surveys for Family Planning Research in Taiwan," *Public Opinion Quarterly* (Summer 1964), 373-382.

M. P. Gavanier, *Budgets Familiaux des Ouvriers de la Communaute Europeenne du Charbon et de L'Acier, 1956-7.* Luxembourg: C.E.C.A., December, 1959 (similar data for 6 countries, much attention to income in kind).

Ghana, Office of the Government Statistician, *Statistical and Economic Papers* (various surveys reported 1953-1960).

Great Britain, Ministry of Labour, *Family Expenditure Survey; Report for 1962,* Her Majesty's Stationery Office, London, 1962 (also reports for 1957-9, 1960-61, and individual years from 1963). See Ministry of Labour Gazette.

Greece, National Statistical Service, *Household Survey—Carried out in the Urban Areas of Greece, 1957-58,* Athens, 1961 (See also the NSS's *Monthly Statistical Bulletin,* IV (April 1959, 9-25 and July 1959, p. 9, 9-24. (Continuous surveys starting with 1958;9, 300 households, to be raised to 600).

Greece, National Statistical Service, *Preliminary Report on the 1963-64 Household Survey—In the Semi-Urban and Rural Areas of Greece,* Athens, 1965.

S. C. Gupta, *An Economic Survey of Shamaspur Village* (University of Delhi, Delhi School of Economics, Continuous Village Survey Series No. 2), Asia Publishing House, New York, 1959.

Peter C. W. Gutkind, *African Urban Family Life* (Publications of the Institute of Social Studies, Serios Minor Vol. III) International Institute for Social Studies, 's-Gravenhague. Mouton and Co, The Hague, 1963.

M. Habibullah, *Some Aspects of Productivity in the Jute Industry of Pakistan* Bureau of Economic Research, University of Dacca, Dacca, East Pakistan, 1968 (Interviews with workers and supervisors).

Donald F. Heisel, "Attitudes and Practice of Contraception in Kenya," *Demography* 5 (1968), 632-641.

Hungarian Central Statistical Office, *The Twenty-Four Hours of the Day* (Analysis of 12,000 time-budgets) English, summary, Budapest, 1965.

Gerald D. Hursh, Niels R. Roling, Graham B. Kerr, *Innovation in Eastern Nigeria, Success and Failure of Agricultural Programs in 71 Villages of Eastern Nigeria.* Diffusion of Innovations Research Report 8, Department of Communications, Michigan State University, East Lansing, Michigan, Sept. 1968.

Gerald D. Hursh, Allan Hershfield, Gramam B. Kerr, Niels G. Roling, *Communications in Eastern Nigeria: An Experiment in Introducing Change,* Diffusions of Innovations Research Report 14, Department of Communications Michigan State University, East Lansing, Michigan, July, 1968.

Alex Inkeles, "Making Men Modern," *American Journal of Sociology,* 75 (Sept. 1969) 208-225 (six countries).

International Labour Office, *Family Living Studies,* I.L.O., Rome, 1961 (reports in 14 surveys in 12 countries).

I.N.S.E.E. (French Statistical Office) "Un enquete sur les dépenses des menages des exploitants agricoles en 1952," *Bulletin mensuel de statistique,* Paris, Presses Universitaires de France) Nouvelle série, supplément July-Sept. 1954, pp. 45 ff.

Israel, Central Bureau of Statistics, *Family Expenditures Survey 1963-4,* Jerusalem 1966; see also *Statistical Bulletin of Israel:* English Summary, April-July 1958 for 1956-7 survey; and Bank of Israel, Savings Survey 1963-64, Jerusalem, 1967.

Israel, Central Bureau of Statistics and Bank of Israel, *Saving Survey 1963-4,* Jerusalem, 1967.

Ivory Coast, Service de la Statistique et de la méchanographie de la Cote d'Ivorie *Enquete nutrituion-niveau de vie, Subdivisionde Bongouanou,* Paris, 1958.

Italy, Institute Centrale di Statistica, *Primi Risultati Dell' Indagine Sui Bilanci Di Famiglia,* Anni 1963-4, Roma, Aprile, 1966.

Jamaica, Department of Statistics, *Household Expenditure Survey 1957-8,* Government Printer, Kingston, 1959.

Japan, Bureau of Statistics, Office of the Prime Minister, *Family Income and Expenditure Survey,* Tokyo, yearly.

Joseph A. Kahl, *The Measurement of Modernism: A Study of Values in Brazil and Mexico,* University of Texas, Austin, 1968.

Kenya, Republic Of, Ministry of Economic Planning and Development, Statistics Division, *Economic Survey of Central Province* 1963-4, Nairobi, 1968.

Kenya Government, Ministry of Finance and Economic Planning, *The Patterns of Income, Expenditure, and Consumption of African Middle Income Workers in Nairobi, July, 1963, 1964,* Nairobi.

Joseph E. Kivlin, *Correlates of Family Planning in Eight Indian Villages,* Research

Report 18, Project on the Diffusion of Innovations in Rural Societies, National Institute of Community Development, Hyderabad, India, May, 1968.

J. B. Knight, "Earnings, Employment, Education and Income Distribution in Uganda," *Bulletin of the Oxford University, Institute of Economics and Statistics* 30 (Aug. 1968) 267-297.

Korea, Ministry of Public Information, *Report of the First Nation-Wide Public Opinion Survey,* by Ministry of Cabinet Administration, December, 1960; *Report of the Seoul City Public Opinion Survey,* June 1961; *Final Report of the Second Nationwide Public Opinion Survey,* August, 1961.

Irving Kravis, "International Differences in the Distribution of Income," *Review of Economics and Statistics,* 42 (Nov. 1960), 408-416, extensive bibliography.

Simon Kuznets, "Quantitative Aspects of the Economic Growth of Nations: Parx VIII Distribution of Income by Size," *Economic Development and Cultural Change* 11 (Jan. 1963) 80 pp. (summarizes international data from 16 countries).

Nissan Liviatan, *Consumption Patterns in Israel,* Falk Project for Econ. Res. in Israel, Jerusalem, 1964.

Nigeria. *Urban Consumer Surveys of Nigeria,* Government Printer, Lagos, 1959, 1963.

Malawi, *Housing Income Survey for Major Urban Areas,* Government Printer, Zomba, 1967.

Benton F. Massell, "Consistent Estimation of Expenditure Elasticities from Cross-Section Data on Households Producing Partly for Subsistence," *Review of Economics and Statistics* 51 (May 1969), 136-142.

Benton F. Massell and Judith Heyer, "Household Expenditures in Nairobi: A Statistical Analysis of Consumer Behavior," *Economic Development and Cultural Change* 17 (January 1969), 212-233.

P. K. Mukherjee and S. C. Gupta, *A Pilot Survey of Fourteen Villages in U.P. and Punjab,* Asia Publishing House, New York, 1959.

National Council of Applied Economic Research, *All India Rural Household Survey,* Vol. I, Methodology, August, 1964; Vol. II, Saving, Income and Investment, July 1965; Vol. III, Basic Tables with Notes, January 1966; and *Urban Income and Saving,* New Delhi, 1962.

Netherlands, Central Bureau of Statistics, *Savings Survey of the Netherlands, 1960,* Part I, Methods and Definitions, and Part II Results and Specifications, Zeist, Amsterdam, 1963.

W. S. Mann and J. C. O. Nwanko, *Rural Food Consumption Surveys in Eastern Nigeria* (mimeo), Ministry of Agriculture, Enogu, Eastern Nigeria, 1963.

K. S. Palda, "A Comparison of Consumer Expenditures in Quebec and Ontario," *Canadian Journal of Economics and Political Science* 33 (February 1967), uses 1959 government budget survey data).

J. O. Retel, *Logement Et Vie Familiale* (2 Tomes) Centre D'Etudes Des Groupes Sociaux, Paris, 1965.

J. Reyer and L. Goreau, *Review of Food Consumption Surveys,* F.A.O., Rome, 1959 (45 post-war surveys).

H. Riedwyl and F. Thomet, "On the Determination of Saturation Levels" (Zem Problem der Sättingung), *Schweiz. Zeitschr. f. Wolkwirtschaft und Stat.* 102 (June, 1966), 157-178. (Cross section of Swiss households in 1963).

Everett Rogers, *Modernization Among Peasants,* Holt, Rinehart and Winston, New York, 1969 (Summarizes a variety of data, some previously unpublished).

Everett M. Rogers and Ralph E. Neill, *Achievement Motivation among Colombian Peasants,* (Diffusion of Innovations Research Report 5), Department of Communication, Michigan State University, East Lansing, Michigan, 1966.

J. Ross and S. Bang, "Predicting the Adoption of Family Planning," *Studies in Family Planning* 9 (January 1966), 8-12.

Prodipto Roy, Frederick B. Waisanen, and Everett M. Rogers, *The Impact of Communication on Rural Development,* U.N.E.S.C.O., Paris, 1969.

Harold T. Shapiro and Gerald E. Angevine, "Consumer Attitudes, Buying Intentions and Expenditures: An Analysis of the Canadian Data," *Canadian Journal of Economics* 2 (May 1969), 230-249.

James R. Sheffield, Ed., *Education, Employment and Rural Development* (Conference at Kericho, Kenya, Sept. 1966), East African Publishing House, Nairobi, Kenya, 1967 (especially chapters by H. E. Ijnen, Koff, Moris, Somerset).

Miyohei Shinohara, *Growth and Cycles in the Japanese Economy,* Kinokuniya Bookstore, Tokyo, 1962. (Includes some survey data not generally available in English).

Andrzej Sicinski, "Public Opinion Surveys in Poland," *International Social Science Journal* 15 (1963), 91-110 (Includes surveys of leisure and recreation, attitudes to work and private property.)

Stanislaw Skrzypek, "The Political, Cultural, and Social Views of Yugoslav Youth," *Public Opinion Quarterly* 29 (Spring, 1965), 87-106.

R. H. Stroup and R. G. Marcis, "Analysis of Income and Expenditure Patterns in Rural South Vietnam," *Western Economic Journal* 6 (December, 1967), 52-64. (1964 AID survey).

Burkhard Strumpel, "Preparedness for Change in a Peasant Society," *Economic Development and Cultural Change* 13 (January 1965), 203-216.

Thailand, *Household Expenditure Survey* (Done in 1962-3) Published, no date, in 1968 with English subtitles.

Suresh D. Tendulkar, "Econometric Study of Monthly Consumption Expenditures in Rural Uttar Pradesh," *American Journal of Agricultural Economics* 51 (February 1969), 119-137.

Sten Thore, *Household Saving and the Price Level,* National Institute of Economic Research (Konjunctur Institutet) Stockholm, 1961.

M. A. Tremblay, G. Fortin and M. LaPlante, *Les Comportements Economique de la Familie du Quebec.* Les Presses de L'Universite Laval. Quebec, Canada, 1964.

K. Tsujimura, "Family Budget Data and the Market Analysis," *Bulletin of the International Statistical Institute* 38 (1961), 215-242.

Uganda Government, *The Patterns of Income, Expenditure and Consumption of African Unskilled Workers in Kampala, February, 1964,* Statistical Branch, Ministry of Planning and Community Development, Entebbe, Uganda, 1966.

Uganda Government, *The Patterns of Income and Expenditure of Coffee Growers in Buganda, 1962/3,* Statistics Division, Ministry of Planning and Economic Development, Entebbe, Uganda, January, 1965.

M. Upton, "Socio-Economic Survey of Some Farm Families in Nigeria," *Bulletin Rural Econ. Sociol.* 2, 127-183.

F. B. Waisanen and Jerome T. Durlak, *A Survey of Attitudes Related to Costa Rican Population Dynamics,* Program Interamericano de Informacion Popular, American International Association for Economic and Social Development, San Jose, Costa Rica, 1966. (AID funded) (Has annotated bibliography of 62 similar items.)

U.S. Department of Commerce, Bureau of the Census, *The Soviet Statistical System: The Continuous Sample Budget Survey,* International Population Reports Series P-95, Washington, January, 1965.

Ursula Wallberg, *Hushållens Sparande år 1957,* Konjunkturinstitutet, Stockholm, 1963 and same in 1958, published in 1966, also a 1955 pilot study publ. in 1959.

Gordon C. Whiting, William A. Herzog, Gustavo M. Quesada, J. David Stanfield and Lytton Guimaraes, *Innovation in Brazil: Success and Failure of Agricultural Programs in 76 Minas Gerais Communities,* Diffusion of Innovations Research Report 7, Department of Communications, Michigan State University, East Lansing, Michigan, January, 1968.

Gordon C. Whiting and John A. Winterbon, *Methodological Background of the Phase 1, MSY-AID Brazil Diffusion Project,* Technical Report 6, Department of Communications, Michigan State University, East Lansing, Michigan, May, 1968.

Gordon H. Wilson, *An Evaluation of Three Years of Rural Development and Change at Samia-Kabondo-Bomet, Rural Development Survey* (prepared for Ministry of Cooperatives and Social Services Dept. of Community Development) Nairobi, 1968. (Changed interviewers and selection of final units led to biases).

F. C. Wright, *African Consumers in Nyasaland and Tanganyika,* H.M.S.O., London, 1955. (Inquiry carried out in 1952-3.)

Charles Y. Yang, "An International Comparison of Consumption Functions," *Review of Economics and Statistics* 46 (Aug. 1964), 279-286.

Footnotes to Chapter IV

1. See *Statistical Reporter,* July, 1959.

2. For some history, see Gertrude Bancroft, "Current Unemployment Estimates of the Census Bureau and some Alternatives," in *Measurement and Behavior of Unemployment,* Princeton University Press, Princeton, New Jersey, 1957.

   For a report on difficulties when a sample was changed, resulting not from sampling but from interviewer training and procedures, see Robert W. Burgess, "Report of Special Advisory Committee on Employment Statistics," *American Statistician* 8 (Dec. 1954), 4-6 and Stanley Lebergott, "Measuring Unemployment," *Review of Economics and Statistics* 36 (November, 1954), 390-400.

   For a report on the current definitions, see U.S. Congress, Joint Economic Committee, Subcommittee on Economic Statistics, *Unemployment: Terminology, Measurement, and Analysis,* U.S. G.P.O., Washington, D.C., 1961; and also U.S. Department of Labor and U.S. Department of Commerce (Bureau of Labor Statistics and Bureau of the Census), *Concepts and Methods Used in Manpower Statistics from the Current Population Survey,* B.L.S. Report No. 313, Current Population Series P-23, No. 22, U.S. G.P.O., Washington, D.C., June, 1967.

3. G. Allen Brunner and Stephen J. Carroll, Jr., "Weekday Evening Interviews of Employed Persons are Better," *Public Opinion Quarterly* 33 (Summer, 1969), 265-7.

4. One study of unwed mothers found more "public answers" in personal interviews, particularly from low-status respondents replying to middle-status interviewers: Dean D. Knudson, Hallowell Pope, and Donald P. Irish, "Response Differences to Questions on Sexual Standards: An Interview-Questionnaire Comparison," *Public Opinion Quarterly* 31 (Summer 1967), 290-297; see also Ralph H. Oakes, "Differences in Responsiveness in Telephone versus Personal Interviews," *Journal of Marketing* 19 (October 1954), 169 (more suggestions given in person than on phone).

5. Jay Schmiedeskamp, "Reinterviews by Telephone," *Journal of Marketing,* Vol. 26, No. 1, January 1962, pp. 28-34.

6. There is some evidence that preliminary phone calls improve response rates for mail surveys. See Neil M. Ford, "The Advance Letter in Mail Surveys," *Journal of Marketing Research,* Vol. IV, May 1966, pp. 202-204.

7. G. Allen Brunner and Stephen J. Carroll, Jr., "The Effect of Prior Telephone Appointments on Completion Rates and Response Content," *Public Opinion Quarterly* 31 (Winter 1967-68), 652-4.

8. Charles F. Cannell and Floyd J. Fowler, "Comparison of a Self-enumerative Procedure and a Personal Interview: A Validity Study," *Public Opinion Quarterly* 27 (Summer 1963), 250-264. See also Charles F. Cannell *Comparison of Hospitalization Reporting in Three Survey Procedures,* U.S. Dept. of Health, Education and Welfare, National Health Survey, P.H.S. Publ. No. 584-D8. Washington, D.C., 1963.

9. W. F. F. Kemsley, "Interviewer Variability in Expenditure Surveys," *J.R.S.S.,* Series A, Vol. 128, 1965, pp. 118-137. See also Life Magazine, *Life Study of Consumer Expenditure,* Time, Inc., New York, 1952.

10. Herbert N. Hyman, *Interviewing in Social Research,* University of Chicago Press, 1954, pp. 182-185.

11. See Hyman, *op. cit.,* for citations.

12. Leon Festinger, (cited by Hyman, pp. 182-185).

13. John B. Lansing, Gerald Ginsburg, and Kaisa Braaten, *An Investigation of Response Error,* Urbana, Bureau of Business and Economic Research, University of Illinois, 1961.

14. Christopher Scott, "Research on Mail Surveys," *Journal of the Royal Statistical Society,* Series A, Vol. 124 (1961), 143-195, The discussion on pp. 196-205 contains additional experience by other researchers who were the discussants.

15. See the discussion in Joseph Waksberg and Robert Pearl, "The Current Population Survey: A Case History in Panel Operations," *Proceedings, Social Statistics Section, American Statistical Association,* 1964, pp. 217-228.

16. *Ibid.* See also U.S. Bureau of Census *The Current Population Survey, A Report on Methodology,* Technical Paper No. 7, U.S.G.P.O., Washington, D.C., 1963.

17. Stephen B. Withey, *Consistency of Immediate and Delayed Report of Financial Data,* Ph.D. Thesis, University of Michigan, Ann Arbor, Michigan, 1952.

18. See John Neter and Joseph Waksberg, *Response Errors in Collection of Expenditure Data by Household Interviews: An Experimental Study,* U.S. Dept. of Commerce, Bureau of the Census, Technical Paper No. 11, U.S.G.P.O., Washington, D.C., 1965 (contains an extensive bibliography).

19. Lansing, Ginsburg, and Braaten, *op. cit.* See also Robert Ferber "Does A Panel Operation Increase the Reliability of Survey Data? The Case of

Consumer Savings," *Proceedings of the Social Statistics Section,* American Statistical Association, 1964, pp. 210-216; see also Robert Ferber, *Collecting Financial Data by Consumer Panel Techniques,* Univ. of Illinois, Bureau of Economic and Business Research, Urbana, Ill., 1964.

20. Waksberg and Pearl, *op. cit.*

21. Marion Sobol, "Panel Mortality and Panel Bias," *Journal of the American Statistical Association,* 54 (March, 1959), 52-68.

22. Cannell and Fowler, *P.O.Q.,* 1963.

23. P. W. Haberman and J. Elinson, "Family Income Reported in Surveys: Husbands Versus Wives," *Journal of Marketing Research* 4 (1967), 191-194.

24. E. Wohlgast, "Do Husbands or Wives Make the Purchasing Decisions?" *Journal of Marketing* (Oct. 1958), 151-8. See summary of this and others in Morgan, "Household Decision Making," in *Household Decision Making,* Nelson Foote, ed. New York University Press, 1961.

25. James N. Morgan, "Some Pilot Studies of Communication and Consensus in the Family," *Public Opinion Quarterly* 32 (Spring, 1968), 113-121; see also John A. Ballweg, "Husband-Wife Response Similarities on Evaluative and Non-Evaluative Survey Questions," *Public Opinion Quarterly* 33 (Summer 1969), 249-254; Robert Ferber, "On the Reliability of Responses Secured in Sample Surveys," *Journal of the American Statistical Association* 50 (1955), 788-810; John Neter and Joseph Waksberg "Effects of Interviewing Designated Respondents in a Household Survey of Home Owners Expenditures on Alterations and Repairs," *Applied Statistics* 12 (1963), 46-60; and Shirley A. Star, "Obtaining Household Opinions from a Single Respondent," *Public Opinion Quarterly* 17 (Fall 1953), 386-391.

26. Kenneth Arrow, *Social Choice and Individual Values,* John Wiley and Sons, New York, 1951.

27. George Levinger, personal communication.

28. C. S. Lewis, *The Screw-Tape Letters,* Macmillan, New York, 1944.

29. Monroe G. Sirken, E. Scott Maynes, John A. Frechtling, "The Survey of Consumer Finances and the Census Quality Check," in *Studies in Income and Wealth,* Vol. 23, *An Appraisal of the 1950 Census Income Data,* Princeton University Press, 1958, pp. 127-168.

30. Harry V. Kincaid and Margaret Bright, "Interviewing the Business Elite," *American Journal of Sociology* 63 (Nov. 1957), 304-311.

31. Robert B. Pearl, *Methodology of Consumer Expenditure Surveys,* Working Paper 27, Bureau of the Census. U.S. Department of Commerce, Washington, D.C., March, 1968.

32. Bernard Berelson and Ronald Freedman, "A Study in Fertility Control," *Scientific American* 210 (1964), 29-37.

33. Frederick G. Lasley, Elmer R. Kiehl and D. E. Brady, "Consumer Preference for Beef in Relation to Finish," *Research Bulletin* 580, Missouri Agricultural Experiment Station, University of Missouri, Columbia, Missouri, March 1955.

34. Donald J. Baker and Charles H. Berry, "The Price Elasticity of Demand for Fluid Skim Milk," *Journal of Farm Economics* 35 (February 1953), 124-129.

35. R. N. Morris and John Mogey, *The Sociology of Housing,* Routlege and Kegan Paul, London, 1965.

36. B. P. Emmett, "The Design of Investigations into the Effects of Radio and Television Programmes or Other Mass Communications," *Journal of the Royal Statistical Society* 129 (1966), 26-49, with discussion on pp. 50-60.

37. Philip Converse, "The Shifting Role of Class in Political Attitudes and Behavior," in *Readings in Social Psychology,* Eleanor Maccoby, Theodore Newcomb and Eugene Hartley, Eds., 3rd Edition, Henry Holt and Co., New York, 1958, pp. 388-399. See also Angus Campbell and Warren E. Miller, "The Motivational Basis of Straight and Split Ticket Voting," *American Political Science Review,* 51 (June, 1957) 293-312 (Effect of State Laws).

38. For the best statement yet, see Charles F. Cannell and Robert L. Kahn "Interviewing" in Gardner Lindzey and Elliot Aronson, eds., *Handbook of Social Psychology* Vol. II, Addison-Wesley, New York, 1968 (526-595) or the earlier more extensive books: Robert Kahn and Charles Cannell, *The Dynamics of Interviewing,* Wiley, New York, 1957; and Herbert H. Hyman and others *Interviewing in Social Research,* University of Chicago Press, Chicago, 1954.

39. B. M. Bass, "Authoritarianism or Acquiescence?" *Journal of Abnormal and Social Psychology* 51 (November 1955), 616-623.

Raymond A. Bauer and Stephen A. Greyser, *Advertising in America: The Consumer View,* Cambridge, Harvard University Press, 1968 (demonstrated by a number of conflicting statements, both agreed to).

I. A. Berg and G. M. Rapaport, "Response Bias in an Unstructured Questionnaire," *Journal of Psychology* 38 (Oct., 1954), 475-581.

Urie Bronfenbrenner, "Personality and Participation: The Case of the Vanishing Variables," *Journal of Social Issues* 16 (1960), 54-63.

Donald T. Campbell, Carole R. Siegman and Matilda B. Rees, "Direction-of-Wording Effects on the Relationships between Scales," *Psychological Review* 68 (November 1967), 293-303.

A. Couch and K. Keniston, "Yeasayers and Naysayers: Agreeing Response Set as a Personality Variable," *Journal of Abnormal and Social Psychology* 60 (1960) 151-174.

A. Paul Hare, "Interview Responses: Personality of Conformity?" *Public Opinion Quarterly* 24 (Winter, 1960), 679-685.

Harry A. Landsberger and Antonio Saavedra, "Response Set in Developing Countries," *Public Opinion Quarterly* 31 (Summer 1967), 214-229.

Gerhard Lenski and John Leggett, "Caste, Class and Deference in the Research Interview," *American Journal of Sociology* 65 (March 1960), 463-467.

Samuel Messick and Douglas N. Jackson, "Acquiescence and the Factorial Interpretation of the MMPI," *Psychological Bulletin* 58 (July 1961), 299-304.

David Horton Smith, "Correcting for Social Desirability Response Sets in Opinion-Attitude Survey Research," *Public Opinion Quarterly* 31 (Spring 1967), 95-102.

Hans J. Eysenck, "Response Set, Authoritarianism, and Personality Questionnaires," *British Journal of Social and Clinical Psychology* 1 (1962), 20-24.

J. B. Knowles, "Acquiescence Response Set and the Questionnaire Measurement of Personality," *British Journal of Social and Clinical Psychology* 2 (1963), 131-137 (argues against "balancing" questions).

John Martin, "Acquiescence—Measurement and Theory," *British Journal of Social and Clinical Psychology* 3 (1964), 216-225 (distinguishes between sets for acquiescence and social desirability).

40. James Morgan, Ismail Sirageldin and Nancy Baerwaldt, *Productive Americans,* Survey Research Center, University of Michigan, Ann Arbor, 1966; see also Alan C. Kerckhoff, "Nuclear and Extended Family Relationships: A Normative and Behavioral Analysis" in Ethel Shanas and Gordon Streif, eds., *Social Structure and the Family; Generational Relations,* Prentice-Hall, Englewood Cliffs, N.J., 1965, p. 112.

41. George Katona, *Mass Consumption Society,* McGraw Hill, New York, 1964.

42. Barbara B. Reagan, *Condensed v. Detailed Schedule for Collection of Family Expenditure Data,* U.S.D.A., Agricultural Research Service, Home Economics Research Branch, March 1954, Washington, D.C.

43. M. Brewster Smith, J. S. Bruner and R. W. White, *Opinions and Personality,* Wiley, New York, 1956, p. 286. (A study of ten men.)

44. Robert Eisner, Review of Robert A. Gordon and Lawrence R. Klein, ed., *Readings in Business Cycles,* Richard D. Irwin, Homewood, 1965, in *American Economic Review* 56 (Sept. 1966), p. 928.

45. See Kahn and Cannell, "Interviewing," in Gardner Lindzey and E. Aronson, *Handbook of Social Psychology,* Addison Wesley, New York, 1968, pp. 526-595; A. N. Oppenheim, *Questionnaire Design and Attitude Measurement,* H. Cineman, London, Herbert Hyman, and others, *Interviewing in Social Research,* University of Chicago Press, Chicago, 1954;

    Robert Kahn and Charles Cannell, *The Dynamics of Interviewing,* Wiley, New York, 1957.

46. Herbert H. Hyman, *op. cit.*

47. Cited by Hyman, p. 197. (See *International Journal of Opinion and Attitude Research,* IV, 1950, p. 391.)

48. See Hyman, *op. cit.,* p. 199.

49. Hyman, *op. cit.,* p. 218.

50. Morris Axelrod and Charles F. Cannell, "A Research Note on an Attempt to Predict Interviewer Effectiveness," *Public Opinion Quarterly,* Vol. 23, No. 4 (Winter 1959), pp. 571-575.

51. Seymour Sudman, "Quantifying Interviewer Quality," *Public Opinion Quarterly,* Vol. 30, Winter 1966, pp. 664-667.

52. Matthew Hauck and Stanley Steinkamp, *Survey Reliability and Interviewer Competence,* Bureau of Economic and Business Research, University of Illinois, Urbana, 1964. See also S. Steinkamp, "The Identification of Effective Interviewers," *Journal of the American Statistical Association* 59 (December, 1964), 1165-1174.

53. U.S. Department of Commerce, Bureau of the Census, Evaluation and Research Program of the U.S. Censuses of Population and Housing, 1960 Series ER 60 No. 7 *Effects of Interviewers and Crew Leaders,* Washington, D.C., 1968.

54. Ann Cartwright and Wyn Tucker, "An Attempt to Reduce the Number of Calls in an Interview Inquiry," *Public Opinion Quarterly* (Summer 1967), pp. 299-302.

55. Marjorie N. Donald, "Implications of Nonresponse for the Interpretation of Mail Questionnaire Data," *Public Opinion Quarterly,* Vol. 24 (Spring 1960), pp. 99-114.

56. See W. F. F. Kemsley, "Some Technical Aspects of a Postal Survey into Professional Earnings," *Applied Statistics* 11 (June 1962), 93-105; *Salaries and Selected Characteristics of U.S. Scientists* (preliminary report based on 1968

National Register of Scientific and Technical Personnel, U.S.G.P.O., Washington, D.C., Dec. 1968.

57. Walter E. Boek and James H. Lade, "A Test of the Usefulness of the Post-Card Technique in a Mail Questionnaire Study," *Public Opinion Quarterly,* Vol. 27 (Summer 1963), pp. 303-306.

58. Percy S. Gray and Elizabeth A. Parr, "The Length of Cigarette Stubs," *Applied Statistics* 8 (June 1959), 92-103.

59. Charles F. Cannell and Morris Axelrod, "The Respondent Reports on the Interview," *American Journal of Sociology,* Vol. 62 (September 1956), pp. 177-181.

60. Kenneth J. Gergen and Kurt W. Back, "Communication in the Interview and the Disengaged Respondent," *Public Opinion Quarterly,* Vol. 30 (Fall 1966), pp. 385-398.

61. Charles F. Cannell and Floyd J. Fowler, "Comparison of a Self-enumeration Procedure with a Personal Interview: A Validity Study," *Public Opinion Quarterly* 27 (Summer 1963), 250-264.

62. Herbert H. Hyman, *Interviewing in Social Research,* The University of Chicago Press, 1954. See page 155 ff.

63. But, Martin David found black respondents more likely to admit to white interviewers that they were on welfare, see Martin David "The Validity of Income Reported by Families Who Received Assistance During 1959," *Journal of the American Statistical Association* 57 (September 1962), 680-685.

64. Dan Katz, "Do Interviewers' Bias Poll Results?" *Public Opinion Quarterly* 6 (Summer 1942), 248-268.

65. James M. Hund, "Changing Role in the Interview Situation," *Public Opinion Quarterly,* Vol. 23, No. 2 (Summer 1959), pp. 236-246.

66. June Sacher Ehrlich and David Riesman, "Age and Authority in the Interview," *Public Opinion Quarterly,* Vol. 25 (Spring 1961), pp. 39-56.

67. Rainald K. Bauer and Frank Meissner, "Structure of Mail Questionnaires: Test of Alternatives," *Public Opinion Quarterly,* Vol. 27 (Summer 1967), pp. 307-311.

68. Paul W. Haberman and Jack Elinson, "Family Income Reported in Surveys: Husbands Versus Wives," *Journal of Marketing Research,* Vol. 14 (May 1967), pp. 191-194.

69. Barbara A. Powell, "Recent Research in Reinterview Procedures," *Proceedings, Social Statistics Section, American Statistical Association,* 1966, pp. 420-433.

70. Allen F. Jung, "Shopping Techniques for Collecting Price Data," *Public Opinion Quarterly* (Summer 1964), pp. 303-311.

71. Herbert H. Hyman, *Interviewing in Social Research,* The University of Chicago Press, 1954, pp. 228-242.

72. See U.S. Department of Agriculture, *Response Variation Encountered with Different Questionnaire Forms,* Marketing Research Report No. 163, U.S.D.A., Washington, D.C., 1957.

73. Kent Marquis, "Effects of Social Reinforcement on Health Reporting in the Household Interview," *Sociometry* 33 (June 1970) 203-215. For a development of theory toward this, see Kahn and Cannell, in Festinger and Katz, *Research Methods in the Behavioral Sciences,* Dryden, N.Y., 1953, then in *Dynamics of Interviewing,* Wiley, New York, 1957, and finally in their chapter in the *Handbook of Social Psychology,* Lindzey and Bronson, Ed., Addison Wesley, New York, 1968.

74. Joseph Waksberg and Robert B. Pearl, "The Current Population Survey: A Case History in Panel Operations," *Proceedings, Social Statistics Section, American Statistical Association,* 1964, pp. 217-228.

75. Lolagene Coombs and Ronald Freedman, "Use of Telephone Interviews in a Longitudinal Fertility Study," *Public Opinion Quarterly,* 28 (Spring 1964) 112-117. The women interviewed were recently married or had one, two, or four children.

76. Jeanne E. and John T. Gullahorn, "An Investigation of the Efforts of Three Factors on Response to Mail Questionnaires," *Public Opinion Quarterly,* 27, (Summer 1963), 294-296. But see Scott, op. cit. for a discouraging summary of varying methods of using mail.

77. Durbin and A. Stuart, "Differences in Response Rates of Experienced and Inexperienced Interviewers," *Journal of the Royal Statistical Society,* A114 (1951), 163-205; W. F. F. Kemsley, "Interviewer Variability a Budget Study," *Applied Statistics* 9 (June 1960), 122-128.

78. For other data on differences according to number of calls required, see Leslie Kish, *Survey Sampling,* Wiley, New York, 1965, pp. 532-547, and S. S. Zarkovich, *Quality of Statistical Data,* F.A.O., Rome, 1966, pp. 145-151, 167, and pp. 173-180.

79. Marion Gross Sobol, "Panel Mortality and Panel Bias," *Journal of the American Statistical Association* 54 (March 1959), pp. 52-68.

80. Philip E. Converse, "Discussion," part of a session on "Evaluation of Panel Operations," *Proceedings, Social Statistics Section,* A.S.A., 1964, pp. 229-231. For another report on panel losses, see R. Kosobud and J. Morgan, Eds., *Consumer Behavior of Individual Farmers over Two and Three Years,*

Institute for Social Research, University of Michigan, Ann Arbor, 1964, Appendix B by A. M. Marckwardt.

81. Lee N. Robins, "The Reluctant Respondent," *Public Opinion Quarterly* 27, (Summer 1963), 276-286.

82. Charles S. Mayer and Robert W. Pratt, Jr., "A Note on Nonresponse in a Mail Survey," *Public Opinion Quarterly* 30 (Winter 1966), 637-646.

83. See Hazel Gaudet and E. C. Wilson, "Who Escapes the Personal Investigators?" *Journal of Applied Psychology* 24 (1940), 773-777;

T. P. Hill, "A Pilot Survey of Incomes and Savings," *Bulletin of the Oxford University Institute of Statistics* 22 (May 1960), 131-142;

T. P. Hill, L. R. Klein and K. H. Straw, "The Savings Survey of 1953, Response Rates and Reliability of Data," *Bulletin of the Oxford University Institute of Statistics* 17 (Feb. 1955), 89-126;

Lee N. Robbins, "The Reluctant Respondent," *Public Opinion Quarterly* 27 (Summer 1963), 276-286;

H. Lawrence Ross, "The Inaccessible Respondent: A Note on Privacy in City and Country," *Public Opinion Quarterly* 27 (Summer 1963), 269-275;

Frederick J. Stephan and Philip J. McCarthy, *Sampling Opinions,* Wiley, New York, 1963, pp. 235-272;

Edward A. Suchman, "An Analysis of Bias in Survey Research," *Public Opinion Quarterly* (Spring 1962), 102-111.

84. Edward A. Suchman, *op. cit.*

85. Robert Ferber, "Item Nonresponse in a Consumer Survey," *Public Opinion Quarterly* 30 (Fall 1966), 399-415.

86. L. Kish and J. Lansing, "Response Errors in Estimating the Value of Homes," *Journal of the American Statistical Association* 49 (Sept. 1954), 520-538. For estimates of non-money incomes, see J. Morgan, M. David, W. Cohen and H. Brazer, *Income and Welfare in the U.S.,* McGraw-Hill, New York, 1962; and J. Morgan, I. Sirageldin, and N. Baerwaldt, *Productive Americans,* Survey Research Center, University of Michigan, Ann Arbor, 1966.

87. See Lee J. Cronback, *Essentials of Psychological Testing,* second edition, Harper and Bros., New York, 1960.

88. John A. Ballweg, "Husband-Wife Response Similarities on Evaluative and Non-Evaluative Survey Questions," *Public Opinion Quarterly* 33 (Summer 1969), 249-254.

P. W. Haberman and J. Elinson, "Family Income Reported in Surveys: Husbands Versus Wives," *Journal of Marketing Research* 4 (May, 1967), 191-194.

Robert Ferber, "On the Reliability of Responses Secured in Sample Surveys," *Journal of the American Statistical Association* 50 (Sept., 1955), 788-810.

James Morgan, "Some Pilot Studies of Communication and Consensus in the Family," *Public Opinion Quarterly* 32 (Spring 1968), 113-121.

John Neter and Joseph Waksberg, "Effects of Interviewing Designated Respondents in a Household Survey of Home Owners Expenditures on Alterations and Repairs," *Applied Statistics* 12 (March, 1963), 46-60.

Shirley A. Star, "Obtaining Household Opinions from a Single Respondent," *Public Opinion Quarterly* 17 (Fall 1953), 386-391.

Elizabeth H. Wolgast, "Do Husbands or Wives Make the Purchasing Decision?" *Journal of Marketing* (October 1958), 151-158.

89. Wolgast, *op. cit.*

90. John Neter and Joseph Waksberg, "A Study of Response Errors in Expenditure Data from Household Interviews," *Journal of the American Statistical Association* 59, 1964, pp. 18-55. J. Neter and J. Waksburg, *Response Errors in Collection of Expenditure Data by Household Interviews,* U.S. Bureau of the Census, Technical Paper No. 11, Washington, D.C., 1965.

91. Robin Barlow, J. Morgan and G. Wirick, "A Study of Validity in Reporting Medical Care in Michigan," *Proceedings of the Business and Economics Statistics Section,* American Statistical Association, Aug. 1960, pp. 54-65.

Nedra B. Belloc, "Validation of Morbidity Survey Data by Comparisons with Hospital Records," *Journal of the American Statistical Association,* 49 (December, 1954), 832-846.

Michael E. Borus, "Response Error in Survey Reports of Earnings Information," *Journal of the American Statistical Association,* 61 (Sept. 1966), 729-738.

Gerhard Brinkman, *Berufsausbildung und Arbietseinkommen,* Duncker und Humblot, Berlin, 1967 (grades in school).

Arthur L. Broida, "Consumer Surveys as a Source of Information for Social Accounting," in *The Flow-of-Funds Approach to Social Accounting,* (Studies in Income and Wealth, Vol. 26), Princeton University Press, Princeton, 1962, pp. 335-381.

Charles F. Cannell, Gordon Fisher, and Thomas Bakker, *Reporting of Hospitalization in the Health Interview Survey* (Health Statistics, Series D, No. 4), U.S. Public Health Service, Washington, D.C., May 1961.

Martin David, "The Validity of Income Reported by a Sample of Families Who Received Welfare Assistance During 1959," *Journal of the American Statistical Association,* 57 (Sept., 1962), 680-685.

Robert Ferber, "The Reliability of Consumer Surveys of Financial Holdings: Demand Deposits," *Journal of the American Statistical Association,* 61 (March, 1966), 91-103.

Robert Ferber, *The Reliability of Consumer Reports of Financial Assets and Debts,* University of Illinois, Bureau of Economic and Business Research, Urbana, June, 1966.

Gordon Fisher, "A Discriminant Analysis of Reporting Errors in Health Interviews," *Applied Statistics,* 11 (Nov. 1962), 148-163.

Percy G. Gray, "The Memory Factor in Social Surveys," *Journal of the American Statistical Association,* 50 (June, 1955), 344-363.

Harold M. Groves, "Empirical Studies in Income Tax Compliance," *National Tax Journal,* XI (December, 1958), 291-301 (Reverse purpose—to check official records accuracy).

Lawrence D. Haber, "Evaluating Response Error in the Reporting of the Income of the Aged: Benefit Income," *Proceedings of the Social Statistics Section,* American Statistical Association, 1966, 412-419.

Einar Hardin and Gerald L. Hershey, "Accuracy of Employee Reports on Changes in Pay," *Journal of Applied Psychology,* 44 (Aug., 1960), 269-275.

W. Horn, "The Milli-RPS," an Investigation into the Nature and the Behavior of RPS Savers," transl. from HETP.T.T. bedrift, Vol. VIII (Aug., 1957).

David L. Kaplan, Elizabeth Parkhurst, and Pascal K. Whelpton, "The Comparability of Reports on Occupation, from Vital Records and the 1950 Census," U.S. Dept. of Health, Education and Welfare, Public Health Service, Office of Vital Statistics, *Special Reports,* 52 (June, 1961).

E. Keating, D. G. Paterson and C. H. Stone, "Validity of Work Histories Obtained by Interview," *Journal of Applied Psychology,* 34 (Feb., 1950), 6-11.

Leslie Kish and John Lansing, "Response Errors in Estimating the Value of Homes," *Journal of the American Statistical Association,* 49 (Sept., 1954), 520-538.

John B. Lansing, Gerald Ginsburg, and Kaisa Bratten, *An Investigation of Response Error,* University of Illinois, Bureau of Economics and Business Research, Urbana, June, 1961.

E. Scott Maynes, "The Anatomy of Response Errors: Consumer Saving," *Journal of Marketing Research,* 2 (November, 1965), 378-387.

E. Scott Maynes, "Minimizing Response Errors in Financial Data," *Journal of the American Statistical Association,* 63 (March, 1968), 214-227.

Joseph F. Metz, Jr., *Accuracy of Response Obtained in a Milk Consumption Study,* Methods of Research in Marketing, Paper No. 5, Cornell University, Agricultural Experiment Station, Storrs, July, 1956.

Saad Nagi, "Congruency in Medical and Self-Assessments of Disability," *Industrial Medicine and Surgery,* 38 (March, 1969), 22-33.

Twila E. Neely, *A Study of Error in the Interview,* Ph.D. Thesis, Columbia University, New York, 1937 (Summary of older data).

Robert C. Nuckols, "The Validity and Comparability of Mail and Personal Interview Surveys," *Journal of Marketing Research,* 1 (February, 1964), 11-16, (life insurance).

Mistuo Ono, George F. Patterson, and Murray S. Weitzman, "The Quality of Reporting Social Security Numbers in Two Surveys," *Proceedings of the Social Statistics Section,* American Statistical Association, 1968, p. 197-205.

Fred Østergård, *De Aeldres Levelilkar, I, Indkomsterne,* Socialforskings-instituttets, Publikationer 17, København, 1965 (Danish National Institute for Social Research). (A check of incomes of aged against tax returns.)

Alfred Politz, *Description of Operational Design and Procedures,* Vol. 4, Life Study of Consumer Expenditures, 1958 (Recall of supermarket bill that evening).

Lee N. Robins, *Deviant Children Grow Up,* Williams and Wilkins, Baltimore 1966, Chapter 12, reports on past behavior).

Barkev S. Sanders, "How Good Are Hospital Data from a Household Survey?" Paper at Statistical Section, American Public Health Association, October, 1958. (See other publications of this author.)

M. G. Sirken, E. S. Maynes, and J. A. Frechtling, "The Survey of Consumer Finances and the Census Quality Check," in *An Appraisal of the 1950 Census Income Data* (Studies in Income and Wealth, Vol. 23) Princeton University Press, Princeton, 1958.

Kaare Svalastoga, "Interviewets gyldighedsproblem: En Prøve" *Sociologiske Meddeleser* 5 (1960) 64-67 (Danish) Income checked by records.

U.S. Bureau of the Census, Evaluation and Research Program of the U.S. Censuses of Population and Housing; *Record Check Studies of Population Coverage;* Series ER 60 N' 2, Washington, D.C., 1964.

- - - - - - *Accuracy of Data on Housing Characteristics,* Series ER60, No. 3, Washington, D.C., 1964.

- - - - - - *Accuracy of Data on Population Characteristics as Measured by CPS-Census Match,* Series ER 60, No. 5, Washington, D.C., 1965.

------ *The Employer Record Check,* Series ER 60, No. 6, Washington, D.C., 1965.

Carol Weiss, *Interviewing Low-Income Respondents,* Columbia University, Bureau of Applied Social Research, Oct. 1966 (A survey of the literature).

David J. Weiss, Rene V. Davis, George W. England and Lloyd H. Lofquist, *Validity of Work Histories Obtained by Interview,* (Minnesota Studies in Vocational Rehabilitation XII), University of Minnesota, Industrial Relations Center, Minneapolis, 1961.

92. John Neter, E. Scott Maynes, and R. Ramanathan, "The Effect of Mismatching on the Measurement of Response Errors," *Journal of the American Statistical Association* 60 (December, 1965), 1005-1027.

93. Grover Wirick, *op. cit.*

94. Morris H. Hansen, William N. Hurwitz, and Max A. Bershad, "Measurement Errors in Censuses and Surveys," *Bulletin of the International Statistical Institute,* Vol. 38, part 1, 1961, pp. 359-374.

95. Leslie Kish and John B. Lansing, "Response Error in Estimating the Value of Homes," *Journal of the American Statistical Association,* 49 (Sept. 1954), pp. 520-538.

96. Robert Ferber, "Reliability of Consumer Surveys of Demand Deposits," *Journal of the American Statistical Association,* 61 (March 1966), pp. 91-103.

97. Ronald Freedman, "Sample Surveys for Family Planning Research in Taiwan," *Public Opinion Quarterly,* 28 (Summer 1964), pp. 373-382.

98. Thomas Rhys Williams, "A Critique of the Assumptions of Survey Research," *Public Opinion Quarterly,* Vol. 23, Spring 1959, pp. 55-62. See also L. Rudolph and S. H. Rudolph, "Surveys in India: Field Experience in Madras State," *Public Opinion Quarterly,* 22, (Fall 1958), pp. 235-244. See also the above issue of *Public Opinion Quarterly,* Fall 1958 and *Journal of Social Issues,* 1959-63, especially E. C. Wilson, "Problems of Survey Research in Modernizing Areas," *Public Opinion Quarterly,* 22 (Fall 1958), pp. 230-234, and A. G. Jones, "The Survey Methods in Under-Developed Countries," *International Social Science Bulletin,* 5 (1953), pp. 530-531.

99. For a description of interviewing difficulties in a Pakistan industrial setting, see M. Habibullah, *Some Aspects of Productivity in the Jute Industry of Pakistan,* Bureau of Economic Research, University of Dacca, Dacca, East Pakistan, Sept. 1968, pp. 19-21.

100. Elmo C. Wilson, "Problems of Survey Research Modernizing Areas," *Public Opinion Quarterly,* Vol. 22, Fall 1958, pp. 230-234.

101. Frederick W. Frey, "Surveying Peasant Attitudes in Turkey," *Public Opinion Quarterly,* Vol. 27, Summer 1963, pp. 335-355.

102. Lloyd and Suzanne Rudolph, "Surveys in India: Field Experience in Madras State," *Public Opinion Quarterly,* 22, Fall 1958, pp. 235-244.

103. Roe Goodman, "Survey Sampling and Implementation for Development Programs," *Proceedings,* Social Statistics Section, American Statistical Association, 1960, pp. 2-4.

104. Robert O. Carlson, "To Talk with Kings," *Public Opinion Quarterly,* Vol. 22, (Fall 1958), pp. 224-229.

105. Ralph Lewis and Helen M. Crossley, "Opinion Surveying in Korea," *Public Opinion Quarterly,* 28 (Summer 1964), pp. 257-272.

106. William John Hanna and Judith Lynne Hanna, "The Problem of Ethnicity and Factionalism in African Survey Research," *Public Opinion Quarterly,* Vol. 30 (Spring 1966), pp. 290-294.

107. Henry A. Landsberger and Antonio Saavedra, "Response Set in Developing Countries," *Public Opinion Quarterly,* 31 (Summer 1967), pp. 214-229.

108. Raymond D. Gastil, "Middle Class Impediments to Iranian Moderization," *Public Opinion Quarterly,* Vol. 22 (Fall 1958), pp. 325-329.

109. Howard Stanton, Kurt W. Back, Eugene Litwak, "Role-Playing in Survey Research," *American Journal of Sociology,* Vol. 62, (Sept. 1956), pp. 172-176.

110. On this point, see Lloyd and Suzanne H. Rudolph, *op. cit.*

111. See Raymond Firth, *Elements of Social Organization,* Watts and Company, London, 1951.

Chapter V

GETTING DATA READY FOR ANALYSIS

Introduction: Strategy

The most neglected and often the most unscientific part of the whole survey process is the quantification of the information and its preparation for analysis. While many economic magnitudes are already quantified, others are not, and many of the explanatory variables introduce problems of quantification. As we see in Chapter VI, new computer methods of analysis reduce the need for making all the variables into numerical scales, but many problems still remain.

We have already suggested that since the time and cooperation of the respondents is the scarcest resource, it should be economized, by postponing to a later stage any work that can be postponed. It is also wise to limit the time, attention, and work of the interviewer in the same manner.

In fact, one can argue that as one progresses from respondent to the computer, each stage is more specialized but less expensive, so that the basic strategy should be that wherever a task is simple enough to move forward to a more specialized and cheaper operation (and resource-demand), it should be moved. Respondents vary but are in possession of the basic information. Interviewers have been trained to handle a wide variety of different problems intelligently, including motivating respondents to cooperate, knowing how much to probe, organizing travel, developing and using sampling materials, etc. Editors, coders, keypunchers, and computers, are each in succession less broad in their outlook and decision-making powers, but speedier and more efficient in doing simpler and simpler things.

Technical considerations urge us to push tasks closer and closer to the respondent where they can be handled more intelligently and with more discretion; but economic considerations urge us to push tasks closer and closer to the computer where they can be handled rapidly, systematically, and with minimum cost. The final decision depends also on the volume of work, the number of interviews, and whether there will be other studies that can use the same procedures, since heavy investment in developing more mechanical procedures must be amortized. Pushing a task to a later stage without adequate planning and development can lead to major breakdowns.

213

An additional strategic consideration has to do with the cost of errors. Since each step builds upon the work of the preceding steps, any errors not found until after later steps have been completed will require repeating all those steps. There is a great premium on knowing that each step is working properly before proceeding to the next. But since it would be time-consuming, hence expensive, to wait till one step is done before going on, one must engage in immediate and continuous checking of each step, often tailored to the parts of the task most likely to be error-prone, or most likely to cause later trouble if they are wrong.

So, we try for the advantages of division of labor and specialization, and at the same time by dividing up the tasks attempt to accomplish each by the most systematic and specialized resources consistent with intelligent and proper handling of the data. The larger the study and the more similar studies to come, the greater the payoff to specialization. A small, one-time study might well be better handled with the researcher himself doing a great deal of the editing and coding, and, as we shall see, even generating his analysis variables as he codes so that the data are immediately ready for analysis.

For example, if it were important to know how far each respondent lived from the center of the nearest Standard Metropolitan Statistical Area (city of 50,000 or more), it would be unwise to use interviewing time and respondent energy by asking it directly. The interviewer, with her less precious time before or after the interview, and her knowledge of maps and the area, could easily estimate it along with the other observational items she adds to the questionnaire. Indeed, since the interviews come in clusters, the same estimate will apply to several other respondents.

Another example is the adding of income components to get total income. One might ask the interviewer to add them and check the total with the respondent. But interviewers are often not good at addition, and do not like to interrupt the flow of the interview. And respondents often do not know what the total should be, and will agree that a total is right even when it was added incorrectly. The whole process was wasteful of scarce resources with little or no gain. Editors in the central office can do it more efficiently while they are estimating income taxes.

Strategy in data handling once the interviews arrive at the central office depends, of course, upon the kind of computer equipment that is available, and the kind of manpower available. If the computer facilities are primitive, and there is great need to get results in a hurry, then the editing and coding of data can be designed to prepare the data fully, so that they are ready for analysis as soon as they are machine-readable. Assuming the study is small, or competent editor-coders are available, it should be possible to keep almost up to date with the field work. If there is no need for weighting the data, or getting rid of all the bad codes or discrepancies, one could get tables only a few days after the last interview comes in.

On the other hand, if one wants to do a careful job of editing and cleaning data or generate complex variables, it may be best to postpone some tasks to the computer, saving the time and energy of editors and coders. Coding things the way one wants to use them often means complex codes which slow down the coders and multiply the coding errors. (We already pointed out that questionnaires which make the respondent or the interviewer do their own coding also slow them down and multiply their errors.)

In the historical development of computers, perversely enough, the more powerful computers that first started using tape input rather than cards, were much less flexible when it came to data manipulation, particularly generating new variables or correcting errors. It was fairly simple to sort out cards with errors and correct them, or to select subgroups of cards and gang-punch new codes for them. But for many years it was difficult to change tapes. It is still true that even the smallest change usually requires rewriting the whole set of data on a new tape reel. The situation is now changed in the newest computers with adequate software, so that a very large number of fairly complicated tasks can be postponed and done on the computer. The computer is excellent for simple tasks that have to be repeated over and over again, such as adding up components, computing ratios, or looking for inconsistencies. It is also good for tasks which are only relevant and required for small sub-parts of the sample, where it does not seem profitable to train a whole set of editors to watch for the few cases they may come across.

On the other hand, there are some things that must still be done by editors because they require judgment, or complex decisions, or using look-up-tables where interpolation or extrapolation may be necessary. For example, assigning values where information on minor components of a total are missing, or calculating income taxes, or using tables where the number of items to be looked up for one interview varies and must be kept open-ended, are still done more efficiently by human beings.

One recent development in computers means that postponing complex tasks to the computer may not create as much delay as one might think. Modern computers are card-programmed. Hence it is possible to take small batches of data through each of the steps as they come in, including cleaning and variable generation. Each step then gets improved, debugged, and ready to apply very rapidly and efficiently on the last few interviews when they come in. The major delay is the time it takes to look up cases and correct errors, and that goes rapidly with the few final cases. Hence, batch-processing of material as it comes in greatly reduces the delay in getting the data ready after the last interview is in, and allows more time in the field to get those last difficult interviews.

We turn now to a discussion of the steps that must take place once the interviews arrive in the central office. The steps are:

1. Field controls, check-in and initial quality-check
2. Editing and check editing
3. Coding and check coding
4. Cleaning of wild codes, inconsistencies, and extreme cases
5. Generating new variables
6. Response rate analysis and weighting

Field Controls

Any probability sample requires a check to make sure that the sample is properly accounted for. This requires a set of sample books with each sample address or designation as a separate item in the book with an identifying number. In the case of area probability samples these books are usually arranged alphabetically by county, or by region of the country and by county within it. The interviewer has a copy of her pages from the sample book. The sample book number can be so organized that one of its digits represents the region, another the city size, and another whether or not the particular location is within a standard metropolitan statistical area or not. As the questionnaires come into the office the sample book number is generally on the cover sheet attached to the questionnaire, but is transferred to the questionnaire before they are separated. The questionnaire is also given a serially-assigned interview number. This number is used for control purposes, checking, putting interviews in batches for coding and editing, and generally for identifying each interview from this step forward. One might think the sample book number could be used for these purposes, but it turns out to be very useful to have a sequence number also. At the same time, a certain amount of pre-editing is done. This needs to be kept right up-to-date: making sure that the questionnaire is properly filled out, that it does not have to be sent back to the field for more work, that it is indeed a response and not a non-response. This requires some strategy in deciding how much information has to be available in order for a questionnaire to be considered a response, rather than thrown out as a non-response.

At the same time, a certain amount of other sample information is transferred from the cover sheet or the sample book to the questionnaire form so that the cover sheet, which has identifying information, can be physically separated and locked up—preserving the confidentiality of the information.

Some cover sheets will come in for non-response, refusals, not part of the sample, and no one at home. The information about them has to be coded from the cover sheet for an analysis of the non-response, which we shall discuss later. A different set of serial numbers is usually assigned these non-response cases. If it does not upset the coding too much, it sometimes turns out to be simpler to code a single card for each of the valid interviews, containing the same kind of information that is available for the non-response, so that it is very easy to compare the response and the non-response on the variables that are available for both of them. In any case, as we shall see later, it is also necessary to be able to list the response and non-response cases in order by sample book number in order to check out the completion of the sample and make sure there are no addresses unaccounted for.

If a *limited* amount of information about the local area (county, census tract, school district) is to be used, it may pay to transfer it from sample books to questionnaires at this stage. It is essential to do it at this stage if the areas are too detailed to be identified by the sample book number alone.

Editing

In most complex interviews division of labor is still an important advantage. It pays to do an editing operation before one tries to code the questionnaires. This is particularly true of economic surveys where there may be components of the economic measures that are wanted scattered throughout the questionnaire. They need to be combined or added. The editors scan the interview again for problems and once more decide whether, even after the first screening, it is a non-response case rather than an interview. Where the wrong respondent is accepted, e.g. wife when the head is called for, the editor must decide whether to accept her answers to attitude questions or treat them as "not ascertained," and check that the work and income of "head" and of "wife" are properly recorded.

Where only certain items are missing, the editors assign them unless they are to be left as "not ascertained" in the coding.[1] Assignment is important where there are very few missing values for a particular variable and where the variable is a major explanatory variable often used on controls of stubs of tables. It is also important where many components are added together to make a total and any one of the components may be missing. One does not want to throw away the total simply because some minor component is not there. The best source of assignments is previous similar surveys, particularly if things are not changing very rapidly. Building assignment tables or estimates from the same survey tends to slow down processing. In the Surveys of Consumer Finances it has been customary to use a number of previous surveys, indeed, in a distributed-lag function created by averaging the most recent survey averages for assignment groups with the previous *assignment* values, which means that preceding surveys are each weighted half of the one that follows. Hence, half of the weight of assignments come from the previous year and a quarter from the year before that and an eighth from the year before that and so on. The strategy problem here is to develop assignment tables which are based on enough cases from previous surveys to be stable and not increase the sampling variance too much, but which are small enough groups to be reasonably precise in estimating what the number should be for the case in which it is missing, that is similar to the missing case.

A number of problems arise in assignments; for instance, if there is both a question of whether a man has a particular item at all and if so how much it is, it is usually necessary to make two separate assignments. If he does not answer either question, one goes first to a probability table and some random numbers to assign whether or not he has a car, for instance, and if the assignment is that he has a car, one goes to a second table to assign its value. The reason for this, of course, is that if one took only the average value of all people in a particular sub-group including the non-owners, it would be very difficult to know what to do in cases where you knew the man was an owner. If one assigned the average value including non-owners, yet in other cases where it was clear the man did not own, you assigned zero, the result would be a set of biased estimates.

Similarly, when an important concept like income is made up of a whole set of sub-components, strategy decisions are necessary as to whether to assign the total or to assign each component. If one assigns the total only, then in many cases known complements will add up to more than the assignment. If one then succumbs to the temptation to use the known total whenever it is larger than the assignment, but the assignment whenever it is smaller, again one ends up with biased estimates. Consequently, it is much better to have assignment procedures for each of the components so that one assigns whatever components are missing and then adds together all the given and assigned data to get the total. No matter how careful one is there is always a problem of whether to use certain side information that may be available. Sometimes it is quite obvious from other information in the interview that the man could not possibly own a car. The thing to keep in mind in any such use of outside information is to reduce the possibility that it will produce bias, e.g., by only allowing corrections in one direction.

Sometimes it makes sense to assign only a class interval value for a variable, so that the bracket code can be used in tables without having a "not ascertained" group, while the missing information is not used when the variable is used as a dependent or independent variable in an analysis (where the assignments would spuriously increase the correlation with the variables used in the assignment process, but not with other variables). Sometimes it makes sense to do the reverse: assign the detailed amount, so that optimal estimates of means and aggregates can be made, but keep the "not ascertained" code in the class interval code as a record of how many assignments were required, as a method of eliminating them from any analysis, and because some statistical procedures allow them to be treated as a separate group.

In general, whenever complex information must be added or assembled from various parts of the questionnaire, it is useful for editors to use a worksheet designed so that the numbers entered on it can be keypunched directly rather than going through a separate coding operation. We have provided here one example of a fairly complicated four-page worksheet which puts together components, sub-totals, and totals of work hours, income, food consumption, calculation of food-need standards, and certain other items about housing and the journey to work.

These worksheets illustrate some decisions about the kinds of things that are properly done at the editing stage. In particular where there are components, many of which are zero for substantial parts of the population and where only the total is relevant, it is often useful to add them together and code only the total. The food-need standard is another kind of situation where one must enter a complex table based on age and sex for each individual in the family, but where the number of people in the family may vary from one to thirteen or more. It would be very cumbersome and expensive to do this by machine because one would have to have coded in the main file the ages and sexes of whatever maximum number of people one would expect, and then would have to engage in a machine table-look-up operation. On the other hand, after once estimating the total unadjusted food needs for the family, the computer was used in this case very effectively to make adjustments for family size (economies of scale) and for farm-nonfarm differences. Note that no missing data are allowed—assignments are made wherever necessary—but each variable has next to it a separate indicator of its accuracy, including whether it was assigned.

Another example on these same worksheets is the estimation of income taxes for the family—a very complex procedure that has so far proved intractable to economical machine programming, (particularly since tax rules change every few years). In other economic surveys expenditure on durables, total debt, and total debt payments have been added by the editors. They are thus not only able to make sure the numbers look reasonable and to avoid double counting, but can add up a variable number of items without leaving space in the computer tape record for an unlimited number of separate items, many of which would be a zero.

Another example, of course is entering the values of people's cars. Not only does one usually want the value of all cars owned by the family but sometimes having a simple set of tables available requires one to interpolate or extrapolate to estimate the value of cars that are quite rare or do not fit the usual categories. In general, it is useful to use a worksheet where some of the components of a total are useful and are to be analyzed, and the total is useful and needs to be analyzed, but some of the minor components are not. In this case one can make the important components and total machine-readable from the worksheet but does not have to use up space, time, and energy with all the minor components.

The editors have a major advantage in that they have looked through the whole questionnaire, have assembled the information, and made sure that it was

SURVEY RESEARCH CENTER   1968 SURVEY OF FAMILY ECONOMICS   WORKSHEET 1.

| 7 | 6 | 8 | | 0 | 1 | | | | |
| 1 | 2 | 3 | | 4 | 5 | | 6 | 7 | 8 | 9 | 10 |

SAMPLE BOOK #   EDITOR   CHK. EDITOR

HOUSING

OWNERS   Property taxes

1. HOUSE VALUE   (A6)   A. ☐☐☐☐☐   X ———————— = B. ☐☐☐☐☐ ☐
                              11 12 13 14 15   (rate, table A)   16 17 18 19   20

2. - MORTGAGE   (A9)   ☐☐☐☐☐   Imputed rent   ☐
                                                                        21

3. = NET EQUITY   ☐☐☐☐☐   X 0.06 = C. ☐☐☐☐☐ ☐
                                                    22 23 24 25   26

4. MORTGAGE PAYMENTS   (A8)   _____ X 12 = D. ☐☐☐☐☐ ☐
                                                    27 28 29 30   31

RENTERS

5. RENT   (A 11)   _____ X 12 = E. ☐☐☐☐☐ ☐
                                                    32 33 34 35   36

OTHERS

6. RENT VALUE IF RENTED   (A 16) _____ X 12 = F. ☐☐☐☐☐ ☐
                                                      37 38 39 40   41

7. WORK IN RETURN FOR HOUSING?   /YES/   /NO/   IF YES, F ÷ 2 =   Hrs

ALL

8. APPROXIMATE UTILITIES   (A5/ A13 / A18)   G. ☐☐☐☐ ☐
                                                  42 43 44   45

9. VALUE OF A & R DONE SELF (A23, 24)   H. ☐☐☐☐☐ ☐ Hrs
                                              46 47 48 49   50

10. A & R PAYMENTS (A 27)   _____ X 12 = I. ☐☐☐☐☐ ☐
                                                      51 52 53 54   55

ALL CARS

11. CAR INSURANCE   (C12 or C16) _____ X _____ = J. ☐☐☐☐ ☐
                                                          56 57 58 59   60

12. CAR DEBT PAYMENTS   (C 13)   _____ X _____ = K. ☐☐☐☐ ☐
                                                          61 62 63 64   65

13. SAVED ON CAR REPAIRS   (C 21, 22)   L. ☐☐☐ ☐
                                              66 67 68   69

14. HOW MUCH TIME DID THAT TAKE?   (C 23)   M. ☐☐☐ ☐ Hrs
                                                  70 71 72   73

OTHER DEBT

15. MONTHLY PAYMENTS ON OTHER THINGS   (D 1, 2) _____ X 12 = N. ☐☐☐☐ ☐
                                                                    74 75 76 77   78

SURVEY RESEARCH CENTER   1968 SURVEY OF FAMILY ECONOMICS   WORKSHEET 2.

| 7 | 6 | 8 | | 0 | 2 | | | | | | |
1   2   3   4   5   6   7   8   9   10

INDIVIDUAL FOOD COSTS:
USE LISTING BOX AND TABLE B

TABLE B. INDIVIDUAL FOOD STANDARD (LOW COST)

AGE	MALE	FEMALE
Under 3	3.90	3.90
4 - 6	4.60	4.60
7 - 9	5.50	5.50
10 - 12	6.40	6.30
13 - 15	7.40	6.90
16 - 20	8.70	7.20
21 - 35	7.50	6.50
35 - 55	6.90	6.30
55 +	6.30	5.40

1. _____
2. _____   SAMPLE BOOK #
3. _____
4. _____   EDITOR
5. _____
6. _____   CHK. EDITOR
7. _____
8. _____
9. _____
10. _____
11. _____
12. _____
13. _____

FAMILY SIZE   A. [ ]
                  11

TOTAL UNADJUSTED _____

SEE TABLE FOR FOOD AND NEED STANDARDS FOR THE ABOVE FAMILY SIZE AND UNADJUSTED FOOD TOTAL

ANNUAL FOOD STANDARD   B. [| | |]   ANNUAL NEED STANDARD   C. [| | | |]
                          12 13 14 15   16 17 18 19 20
                                                                          ANNUAL AMOUNT
FOOD EXPENDITURE

1. SPENT EATING OUT (E 2)   _____ X _____ = _____

2. COST OF MILK (E 4)   _____ X _____ = _____

3. OTHER FOOD   (E 5)   _____ X _____ = _____

4. FOOD BILL SUBTOTAL (1 + 2 + 3)   _____

5. ALCOHOL (E6) _____ X _____ = D. [| |] IF INCLUDED(E7)   _____ [ ]
                                         21 22 23   ENTER AT RIGHT   24

6. CIGARETTES (E9) _____ X _____ = E. [| |] IF INCLUDED (E10) _____ [ ]
                                          25 26 27   ENTER AT RIGHT   28
CORRECTED FOOD BILL

7.   SUBTRACT 5, 6, FROM FOOD BILL IF INCLUDED   F [| | |] [ ]
                                                              29 30 31 32   33
NON MONEY FOOD

8. HOME GROWN FOOD (E12) SEE SUPERVISOR   G [| |] [ ]   Hrs 4
                                                34 35 36 37

9. CLOTHES MADE AND MENDED (E17, 18)   H [| |] [ ]   Hrs 5
                                                38 39 40 41

10. FOOD RECEIVED ON THE JOB (J30, page 24) I [| |] [ ]
                                                 42 43 44 45

11. SAVED ON FOOD STAMPS (J32, page 24)   J [| |] [ ]
                                                 46 47 48 49

SURVEY RESEARCH CENTER   1968 SURVEY OF FAMILY ECONOMICS   WORKSHEET 3.

7	6	8		0	3					
1	2	3	4	5		6	7	8	9	10

SAMPLE BOOK #   EDITOR   CHK. EDITOR

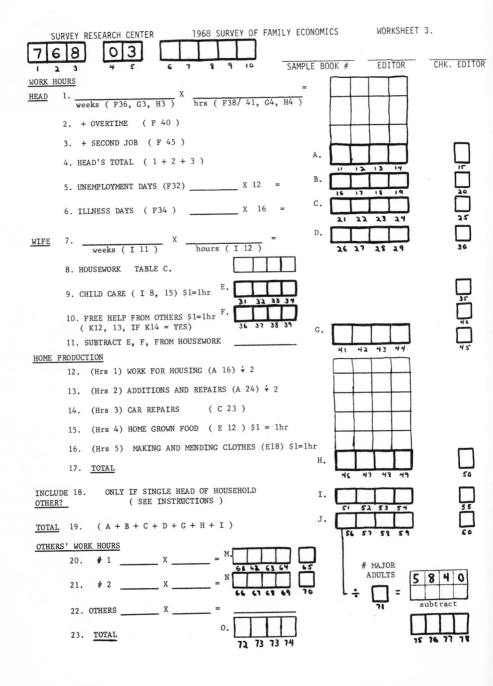

WORK HOURS

HEAD   1. _____ X _____ =
           weeks (F36, G3, H3)   hrs (F38/ 41, G4, H4)

       2. + OVERTIME   (F 40)

       3. + SECOND JOB (F 45)

       4. HEAD'S TOTAL (1 + 2 + 3)

       5. UNEMPLOYMENT DAYS (F32) _____ X 12 =

       6. ILLNESS DAYS (F34) _____ X 16 =

WIFE   7. _____ X _____ =
           weeks (I 11)   hours (I 12)

       8. HOUSEWORK   TABLE C.

       9. CHILD CARE (I 8, 15) $1=1hr

       10. FREE HELP FROM OTHERS $1=1hr
           (K12, 13, IF K14 = YES)

       11. SUBTRACT E, F, FROM HOUSEWORK _____

HOME PRODUCTION

       12. (Hrs 1) WORK FOR HOUSING (A 16) ÷ 2

       13. (Hrs 2) ADDITIONS AND REPAIRS (A 24) ÷ 2

       14. (Hrs 3) CAR REPAIRS   (C 23)

       15. (Hrs 4) HOME GROWN FOOD (E 12) $1 = 1hr

       16. (Hrs 5) MAKING AND MENDING CLOTHES (E18) $1=1hr

       17. TOTAL

INCLUDE 18.   ONLY IF SINGLE HEAD OF HOUSEHOLD
OTHER?   (SEE INSTRUCTIONS)

TOTAL   19.   (A + B + C + D + G + H + I)

OTHERS' WORK HOURS

       20. # 1 _____ X _____ =

       21. # 2 _____ X _____ =

       22. OTHERS _____ X _____ =

       23. TOTAL

MAJOR ADULTS

| 5 | 8 | 4 | 0 |
subtract

SURVEY RESEARCH CENTER   1968 SURVEY OF FAMILY ECONOMICS   WORKSHEET 4.

7	6	8		0	4						
1	2	3		4	5		6	7	8	9	10

HEAD'S LABOR INCOME

1. LABOR PART OF FARM INC. (J4*)
2. LABOR PART OF BUS. INC. (J7*)
3. WAGES   (J 8)
4. BONUS, OVERTIME, COMM. (J10)
5. PROF., PRACTICE, TRADE (J11a)
6. LABOR PART OF ROOMERS ETC. (J11b*)

7. TOTAL (SUM OF 1 to 6)   A

                     11 12 13 14 15

WIFE'S LABOR INCOME

8. WIFE'S INCOME FROM WORK (J15*)   B

                     16 17 18 19 20

CAPITAL INCOME, HEAD AND WIFE

9. ASSET PART OF FARM INC. (J4*)
10. ASSET PART OF BUS. INC. (J7*)
11. ASSET PART OF ROOMERS ETC.(J11b*)
12. RENT, INT., DIV., ETC. (J11c)
13. WIFE'S INCOME FROM ASSETS (J15*)

TAXABLE INCOME OF HEAD AND WIFE
14. (A + B + CAPITAL INC.)   C

                     21 22 23 24 25

TAXABLE INCOME OF OTHERS (J19 + J22)
15. OTHER WITH HIGHEST INCOME   D

                     26 27 28 29 30

16. NEXT HIGHEST INCOME   E

                     31 32 33 34 35

17. STILL OTHERS WITH INC. ?

OTHERS' TOTAL INCOME
18. (15 + 16 + 17)   F

                     36 37 38 39 40

TRANSFERS (TOTAL FAMILY)
19. A.D.C. A.D.C.U. (J11d)   G

                     41 42 43 44 45

20. OTHER WELFARE (J11e)
21. SOCIAL SECURITY (J11f)
22. OTHER RETIREMENT (J11g)
23. UNEMP., WORKMENS' COMP. (J11h)
24. ALIMONY (J11i)
25. HELP FROM RELATIVES (J11j)
26. ANYTHING ELSE? (J11k*)
27. WIFE'S TRANSFER INCOME (J15*)
28. OTHERS' TRANSFER INCOME(J19,22*)

TOTAL FAMILY MONEY INCOME
29. (C + F + G + OTHER TRANSFERS)   H

                     46 47 48 49 50

TAX EXEMPTIONS   SAMPLE BOOK #
OF HEAD AND WIFE

☐ ADULTS   EDITOR

+ ☐ CHILDREN   CHK. EDITOR

+ ☐ BLIND,
    65 & OVER

+ ☐ OUTSIDE FU ____ ENTER DOLLAR
    (J45)   AMOUNT (J46)

ENTER TOTAL
EXEMPTIONS

                     51 52 53 54

HEAD & WIFE

   OTHERS
             CIRCLE
             TABLE USED

                      TAX FROM TABLE

☐   M S HH J

☐   M S HH K

☐   M S HH L

TOTAL FAMILY TAX   M
(J + K + L)

                     55 56 57 58 59

CHILD CARE (I8,15)   N
(SEE BOX E, SHEET 3)

UNION DUES (K18)   O

COST OF INCOME   P
(M + N + O)

                     60 61 62 63 64

ASSIGNMENTS

0 none / 1 minor / 2 major

A ☐   B ☐   C ☐   D ☐
  65   66   67   68

E ☐   G ☐   I ☐
  69   70   71

consistent and meaningful. Generally, the first thing the editors do is to read a little description—called a "thumbnail sketch"—in the back of the interview which describes the situation and anything about it the interviewer thought would be useful in interpreting what went on.

A final thing that editors may be called upon to do occurs when the analysis is not all to be done with the same unit of analysis. Sometimes one interviews spending units but wants to do some analysis on a family basis. In this case it may be important to combine the information from more than one questionnaire into family totals. Some of this can be done by machine, but in some cases—particularly for consistency and to avoid double counting—it is useful to have a family editing operation. The definition of family head and coding his age, is an example. Problems arise, of course, where one spending unit within a family was a non-response. This can become a very difficult matter to handle.

A more usual problem, however, has to do with subunits where one may want to do some analysis that treats each individual in the family, or each nuclear family in a larger family, as a separate unit. Indeed, the unit may not be a person but a transaction or an event or an object owned. Analysis has been done, for instance, of all the disabled individuals in a sample, or of all the purchases of durables (where one may want a price distribution of individual durables run against the income of the family that bought the durable), or all the cars owned in a family, or all the hospitalization experiences, or all the auto accidents. Indeed, wherever there is a problem of a varying number of items per interview, it may be useful to consider whether some analysis should not be done with each of these items as the unit of analysis. One may want to ask people about airplane trips, but some people would have one trip, and some two, and some ten. It would be very cumbersome to leave space on each record in a computer tape for an indefinite number of trips, particularly if one wanted to analyze the characteristics of trips by the people who took them and separately to analyze people according to how many trips they took. If there is to be a separate analysis by a different unit, then the editors may have to have worksheets—one for each of these units—where the material is entered to facilitate or bypass the coding operation. We will come back to this when we discuss coding.

At the end of editing there will be a complete questionnaire with assignments made of missing information, with some worksheets filled out, and with a general agreement that these are acceptable questionnaires. There is then usually a check-editing procedure which starts with very thorough check-editing at the beginning of the editing period. As the evidence that things are under control increases, check-editing is gradually reduced to the point where it is done only on a sample of the interviews, or only on some troublesome items. Check-editing needs to start early in order to correct procedures and reduce future errors. It needs to continue in order to detect diverging procedures or other, rarer, errors.

Much more complex editing may be in order in the case of reinterviews or panels, where one not only wants to analyze changes in many things, but may want a prior look at their reasonableness. Some combining of information from the two questionnaires may reveal discrepancies which one does not want to leave in the data, or even cases where the wrong person was obviously interviewed the second time.

When three or more interviews have been taken with the same family, the need for some flexible look at how the information fits together is obvious. If an income is reported for a secondary earner in some years and not others, but no mention is made of any change in his status, one is tempted to assume that there has been response error, rather than change in income.

What one never does in any editing operation, however, is to impose the editor's judgement to change answers, unless there is persuasive evidence not only that there was an error, but also what a better answer would be. One of the experiences with reinterviews has been that first-year answers which seemed odd, turned out, upon assembling the additional information, to be not only correct but meaningful—once one understood the situation.

If one should not change answers much, why edit? For one thing, errors in interpreting data can be avoided. In addition, it is possible to add some new variables representing the editor's judgement as to the quality of the data as was done on the worksheets reprinted here. Then analysis can be run excluding cases judged to be dubious, whenever the precision of the data is important, that is, when one is estimating amounts or the shapes of relationships, rather than looking for patterns.

There is very little printed material about the editing of survey data. There is one article by Walter Stewart on the experience with Bureau of Labor Statistics.[2] The Census Bureau uses a complex machine called FOSDIC in editing the Current Population Surveys. The machine reads microfilms of pre-coded questionnaires. The microfilms are done at several locations in the field to avoid bottlenecks. FOSDIC not only converts them to machine-readable form but edits the material and assigns missing information at the same time. This seems to work very well with the Standard Current Population Survey. It sometimes breaks down seriously when used on new and more complex questionnaires. Experience in the Survey Research Center has been a gradual movement from hand editing to computer work as the computer seems to be able to handle it, but a great deal is still done by editors because the sample sizes are small enough to make this feasible and the material is complex enough to make it essential. It may even pay to postpone to the computer editing operations that only need be done on a very small fraction of the cases, to reduce the number of different things editors must keep in mind.

Coding

The coders have now had their work very much simplified, both by the worksheets (with which they do not have to do anything at all) and by the editor's careful work on the questionnaire and assigning of missing information. The process of developing codes is a complex one which should be done in advance on the basis of the pretest questionnaires, even though some changes and additions may have to be made along the way.

Some specialization may be useful even within the coding operation. The classic example is "occupation" which is so complex that it is often coded for all the questionnaires by a single person who has memorized the Census Standard Occupation Code.

For purposes of easing the coder's job it is very important to have conventions and standards which are uniform, not only within a survey but from one study to the next. For instance, it is very useful to use the code "0" uniformly when the particular item is inappropriate or inapplicable for that person and to use "9" for N.A. (not ascertained) or missing information. This not only simplifies the coder's job but it makes possible computer software which automatically takes account of these two kinds of situations. In the case of yes/no questions it is useful to choose some uniform convention such as "1" for yes and "5" for no, so that the coders gradually memorize many of the simpler codes. Similarly with attitude or reasons codes, it is often useful to use a standard five-point Likert scale:

"1" is unqualifiedly favorable or positive,
"2" is positive with qualifications,
"3" is a pro-con (on the one hand, on the other hand, kind of answer),
"4" is a negative or a con answer with qualifications,
"5" is an unqualified negative,
"9" is uncodable answer or answer in the wrong frame of reference,
"0" means the question was inapplicable to this particular person.

Once again, the general principle of postponing work to the point where it can be done at least expense applies in coding where one might be tempted to combine the answers to two questions, "Do you have one?" and "How much is it worth?" in a single code, because that is what is needed in the analysis. But it is much easier and faster for coders to code an answer for each question: "yes" or "no" to the first question and an amount for the second. Later the computer can combine this in the form it is to be used in the tables. There is not much on coding in the published literature. Perhaps the best treatment is that by Cartwright in the Festinger-Katz Book.[3] We do not need to pay too much attention here to the problems of quantifying the answers to relatively unstructured questions. But even in economic surveys there are going to be questions about reasons or attitudes or expectations about the future which raise coding problems. Cartwright gives two general characteristics that any code has to satisfy. First, the categories need to be exhaustive; and secondly, they need to be mutually exclusive. Many people set up categories that do not meet these criteria. Cartwright gives an example where people were asked where they were solicited to buy war bonds. The categories include: work, home, store, bank, and post office. If a man works in a bank, what does he do? Or, if he were solicited on the way to work what does he do? A more recent example is a mailed questionnaire where people were asked about breakdowns of their washing machines. They were asked to indicate why the washing machine broke down by checking categories like: it made a noise, fan belt broke, it did not pump out the water, man replaced the motor. Some of these are symptoms and some are diagnoses, some are repairs and, of course, sometimes two or more of them apply.

In the case of "reasons" codes, there are two kinds of problems. First, how many categories should be used; and second, how many different reasons should be coded for each person? In categorizing anything, one can try to impose structure by categorizing reasons into "reasons for" and "reasons against" or into economic and non-economic reasons. Of course, it is a mistake to code so much detail that there are codes into which almost no one falls. It is very useful to be able to specify in advance the combinations of reasons the analysis will use and group them together. Any reduction of the total number of categories, of course, involves imposing some structure and, if the structure has too many dimensions, trouble ensues. For instance, if one wanted to categorize reasons into economic and non-economic reasons, then one would have to leave a third category for reasons that are not clearly economic or non-economic. And if one wants to code reasons for and reasons against, it is necessary to leave another category for cases where it is not clear whether they are for or against, and the combination of these two triplets already requires nine categories into which reasons fit. One way to deal with this, of course, is to leave one place in the record for each of these nine categories and then code components within each one. The difficulty, of course, is that the same answer or something that seems like the same answer may appear in any one of the nine places.

Sometimes it is possible to use a code with no particular structure to it and only a few categories by simply putting the stereotyped answers into the main groups in which they fall. With some questions where people seem to give *only* stereotyped answers this may be the best thing to do. In the early days when we asked people how they felt about installment credit there were many who said, "It is the only way to buy things," others, "It is the way to establish your credit," and others gave more moralistic answers, "It is bad because you tend to spend too much." Nobody gave moralistic answers in favor of it, and very few gave institutional answers against it; so there would be no point allowing all the combinations. Sometimes after a code is put into use a large number of cases are in the category labelled "other"—it does not fit anywhere else. When this happens, it may be necessary to go back and reread these answers to see whether there is some important new category that should be established.

Whenever one wants to allow more than nine different kinds of reasons, there is a strategic question whether to use a two-digit reasons code, which often causes trouble in the computer, or whether to try to break the reasons up into two categories, code them separately, and then combine them later. The latter is usually better.

A second problem, of course, is how many different reasons to allow any one person to give. Allowing for many reasons per case greatly increases the amount of space that is taken up and it is particularly annoying if only a few people give more than one or two reasons. The result is a lot of 0's, just to get a few non-0's cases handled.

One way to avoid the need to code all reasons given is to put them in some kind of priority order. In a study of the affluent a major question was whether or not the individual used tax considerations as a reason for any one of a number of things he did. A priority rule was used. If taxes were mentioned as a reason they were always coded first. If they were not mentioned, then a number of other things were eligible to be mentioned. In this way, even if a man gave four reasons and we left room for only one or two or three, we still did not lose the fact that he mentioned taxes.

Another example of a priority code was a situation where respondents were asked what kind of things they did when they repaired their own car. The study was concerned with the level of difficulty of the things they did, not with categorizing specifically what part of the car was repaired or what was done. Consequently, a priority code was used. If a man did something very difficult or complicated he was coded "1," if he did something somewhat complicated requiring a certain amount of skill, he was coded number "2," and so on down to the code at the very bottom which was very simple things like washing and waxing. (See Appendix A to this chapter.)

Sometimes people are tempted to code combinations of things—a kind of a geometric code—where if there are three things that can be mentioned, whether they are reasons or things owned, the "1" code is for a, "2" code for b, "3" code for c, "4" code for a *and* b, "5" code for b *and* c, "6" code for a *and* c, and a "7" code for a *and* b *and* c. So:

1. a only	5. b and c
2. b only	6. a and c
3. c only	7. a, b, and c.
4. a and b	

These codes often turn out to be cumbersome and difficult to handle. Ordinarily one wants to know how many of the three things were true, or whether any one of them was true, rather than all the combinations. This is a case of saving space on the record in a way that may make things more complicated instead of easier.

It is often tempting to try to build other kinds of pattern codes out of several variables. This turns out to be dangerous if it gets very complicated or has too many dimensions, and it is prone to coding error. We know it is prone to error because if we code the components too, and then by computer find out how many people have each of the combinations, the results do not agree very well with the "pattern coding" that was done. On the other hand, there are some simple examples where it is fairly easy. One can combine sex of head and marital status because there are only three categories—married couples, single females, and single males. This is a mutually exclusive code that exhausts the population.

When analyzing data, of course, one wants codes where there are a reasonable number of cases in each category. Sometimes it may be useful to allow somewhat more categories than necessary and then collapse the code by computer, combining adjoining items that have very few cases. With quantitative material such as income or values of assets, one can wait until after he has seen the data before generating brackets (class intervals) that spread the sample fairly evenly. On the other hand it is often very useful to have codes at either end of the scale which distinguish a fairly *small* part of the population—say five or ten percent—since they may turn out to be quite different from the rest of the population in other ways. One thing that should be avoided if possible is coding dichotomies when one can code three, four, or five groups, since it is a known statistical fact that you can maximize the chance of showing a significant effect of a particular variable if you compare the one-third of the group at one end with the one-third at the other end and leave out the middle. The middle may contain a lot of people for whom the question is meaningless anyway.

There is a great temptation to code everything the first time through just in case anybody wants it. In the case of economic surveys this often leads to the absurd situation of coding five- and six-digit dollar fields for things which are zero for ninety-five or ninety-eight percent of the population. Such a variable cannot be used as a dependent variable and probably not even as an explanatory variable since it is badly skewed and dominated by a few cases. One is far better off in situations like this with an interval code that distinguishes zero, small amounts, and large amounts. When anyone wants to look at the large amounts, he can look them up individually and write case studies on them. Even where five to twenty percent are non-zero it may be more sensible simply to code a crude bracket code, rather than try to preserve all the detail. Or one may decide to code one card only for some subgroup who were asked certain questions. A special smaller sample analysis can be done with them after transferring to that card some of the other information.

Another general strategy problem is whether to code several things which must be internally consistent, rather than build one of them out of the others. For instance, in the case of dollar fields and brackets one could code both the dollar field and the bracket code and then check by machine to make sure they agree. This may reveal some errors. In practice it turns out that for the most part the errors are errors in the coding of the bracket code, so that the gain was negligible, hence we have generally given up this practice. Similarly, when one has income taxes, total income, and income after taxes, one could code all three. It then becomes necessary to check to make sure that income after taxes plus taxes is equal to income before taxes. Unless there is some particular reason to believe that this will help uncover errors, it makes more sense to code only two of the components and get the third one by computer later on. On the other hand, where a very large number of components are to be added up later, it may pay to have the editors add that sum and code it as a single sum to check the accuracy of coding of all the components, particularly where each of the components is assigned where necessary so that the addition always holds.

Another temptation is to code the answers to questions which were not asked. It is difficult to interpret volunteered information since it is only volunteered by some people and one really does not know about the others. For instance, one might ask a question, "How many hours during a week day do you spend watching television?" Some people will reply, "I do not have a television." Now this *implies* that they do not watch it, but it also gives an additional piece of information—that they do not have one. The problem is that we did not ask the other people whether they had a television set or not, and we cannot really infer it from whether or not they watch television. Someone else who said he watched several hours a night may not own a television; he may watch it in the bar. Another man may simply say he does not watch television even though he owns one. Consequently, in general it does not pay to code information for which there is not an explicit question.

An allied problem is the temptation to write in the Interviewers' Instructions requests for information that is not included in the questions the interviewers are to ask. This puts the interviewer in an intolerable situation since she is asked to find out whether the man owns a television set, for instance, and there is no question in the questionnaire. She must either guess, invent a question, or not provide the information.

In general, the code should reflect the purposes of the study just as the questions should, and a question should not be asked if it is not necessary. Therefore, there should not be any uncertainty about whether to code the answers. There are, however, some exceptions where a question is simply asked to introduce a subject. In practice, however, such questions are often coded just in case someone may want the information, or simply to make the coder's life simpler because he has a general rule of coding one answer to every question.

The actual process of coding usually begins with a discussion of one or two examples of the completed questionnaires and codes. Then there is a process of check-coding, again done very heavily at first and less heavily later on, as the consensus develops about how to handle things and that things are under control. But at least some partial check-coding is continued right through the whole process. Sometimes problems arise later on or arise in fairly rare cases but need to be communicated to the other coders.

One advantage of both check-editing and check-coding is that records can be kept of the percent disagreement, even if one does not want to worry about who is right. There are, of course, problems as to the meaning of the number of such disagreements, because the more categories a code has, the more possibility there is for disagreement; and, of course, some disagreements have to do with whether the answer should be coded "not ascertained" or "don't know" or whether it actually is a codable reason. In general, a question with a high percent of disagreement is a troublesome question. It is either a bad question, a question that is answered in several frames of reference, or a question the interviewer is not handling properly.

On the other hand, one may keep a question year after year that has problems in coding, because it fits some theoretical objectives and for at least a substantial part of the population is bringing meaningful responses. Perhaps the classic example is one of the questions used by George Katona to assess the state of consumer confidence. It reads,

> Now about the big things people buy for their homes—such as furniture, house furnishings, refrigerator, stove, television, and things like that. *Generally speaking,* do you think now is a good or bad time for people to buy major household items?

This question attempts to tap the state of people's feelings and, although it is flabbergasting to some people and some give funny kinds of answers, there is clearly something being asked that is important. A question which seemed to be clearer or easier to code might fail to get what one was after in this kind of situation.

We have pointed out that sometimes when there are variable numbers of things to be reported one may want to do a separate analysis with each of them as a separate unit: each person, each child, each appliance, each hospitalization, etc. On the other hand, even in this case, one may want some kind of summary codes to describe the whole family situation. Take the composition of the family, for instance. One may not want to code the age, sex, relation to head, etc. of each member of the family where this number may vary from one to fifteen but may want to economize by coding some summaries such as the total number of people in the family, the number of children eighteen or under, the age of the youngest child, the age of the oldest child, the number of children in school, whether any of the children are *not* the natural children of the head and wife, etc. The age of the youngest child is of particular relevance in economic surveys because it indicates whether someone needs to be home during the day to take care of children, or whether they are all in school, or whether they are all old enough to take care of themselves. And if the youngest is 12 or older, the family is unlikely to have any more children in the future. Similarly, one may ask someone to list the organizations he belongs to and what kind they are but may be content to code the total number of organizations and/or the total number of organizations that are other than sheer amusement organizations. Sometimes when people come up with this problem it results from the fact that they have failed to cut out of a questionnaire things they really do not need. If it is only necessary to know *how many* different organizations the man belongs to, it wastes his time to ask him to list them all and describe what they do.

Numerical fields require decisions about the treatment of missing information (if not assigned) and about cases which exceed the field width. The indication of missing information depends on the computer software available. It is often a series of nines, but that is dangerous if someone innocently ignores the code and the missing cases are treated as the largest possible value. Cases that exceed the field raise more substantive issues, that is whether they should not be truncated to a number within the field anyway, given their rarity in a sample, and the damage they would do to any least-squares statistical analysis. We suggest that one should not attempt to use the detail on extreme amounts, and should truncate them, even at the expense of some distortion of means and aggregates, in most analytic surveys.

There is also a question whether to code "don't know" separately from "didn't answer." Separation certainly seems called for with attitudes and expectations.

In summary then, the basic strategy in coding is to code things that are relevant to the analysis of the study and to keep the level of accuracy up. If errors are made, they may never be found unless they are caught either in check-coding or in later inconsistency checking. Consequently, all the expensive field work can be lost if poor work is done in quantifying the answers. It helps to standardize codes; it helps to keep them as simple as possible; and, as we will see below, it also helps to check up later on things that obviously are inconsistent. It is probably best to do a good deal of recoding and variable generation in the computer and keep the coders work as simple and straightforward as possible in order to reduce errors and increase speed. This depends very much on the computer facilities available and how complex the material is.

There have been various attempts to make the initial questionnaire easier to code, or suitable to be sent directly to keypunchers, or even machine readable (by putting black marks in boxes). We have argued that this puts a burden on interviewers and even on respondents, for a relatively small gain later, except where a relatively simple set of answers, mostly quantitative, is asked repeatedly of rather large samples (as with the Current Population Survey). The formats of such questionnaires almost always are more difficult to read and follow, and errors are likely to creep in. Faced with the problem of holding down the costs of a labor-intensive operation, the survey director will be under increased pressure to bypass the coding and/or keypunching operation; but he may merely find himself spending more on the costly labor involved in correcting errors, or the costs of lower response rates. Worksheets are another matter. They can be designed to be easy for editors and still suitable for direct keypunching. When machines allow keypunchers to write directly on tape, records of unlimited length, this will be a major improvement, obviating the need for match-merging decks of cards.

Treatment of Non-Response

We have already seen that the editors can assign missing items of information, and have pointed out the strategy problem: whether one uses a large group on which to base the assignment, making it somewhat less precise in terms of the individual being assigned, but more stable in terms of sampling variability. Sometimes assignments are made by actually copying a number from another interview with a similar "matched" family. This, of course, makes the assignment very explicit and appropriate for the individual, but subject to amplified sampling variance.

There are also situations where the whole interview is missing. In the flow chart presented here notice that information on the non-response is coded, keypunched, and verified, not only to check out the sample books but also so that one can compare distributions fo the response and the non-response on whatever kinds of information are available for both, to see whether the non-response are systematically different from the response cases. If they are, it may be necessary to weight the data, weighting up subgroups of the population that are more underrepresented than others in the sample. Whether such weighting for differential non-response is needed depends on the purpose of the survey. If the purpose is to make estimates of amounts or distributions or proportions, then weighting is necessary if the non-response are different from the response on the items which are to be estimated. On the other hand, if the purpose of the survey is analytical, estimating relationships between variables, then one needs to worry about non-response bias only if the non-response are systematically different in terms of these relationships, in other words, if there are things associated with non-response which interact with the explanatory variables of the study, altering their effect on the dependent variables. For instance, if the non-response is biased

Processing Flow—From Receipt of Questionnaires to Data Ready for Analysis

Decision whether to accept,
reject, or return to field
↓

Sample information onto non-response forms	Sample book entry as response ↗	Sample information onto questionnaires
Assign serial numbers ←— or non-resp.		↓ Assign serial numbers

↔ Editing of subunit information

Coding Check-coding	Editing Check-editing	Check-editing
	↓ Coding	↓ Coding
	↓ Check-coding	↓ Check-coding
↓ Keypunching Verifying	↓ Keypunching Verifying	↓ Keypunching Verifying

List in order by sample book number	List in order by sample book number	Merge card files onto tape	Merge card files onto tape
	Compare listings with sample books Every address accounted for?	↓ Wild code check	↓ Wild code check
		↓ Corrections Rerun check	↓ Corrections Rerun check
	↓ Corrections	↓ Consistency check	↓ Consistency check
Distribution of non-response by all available variables	Distribution of of response by all information available also for non-response	↓ Corrections Rerun check	↓ Corrections Rerun check
		↓ Extreme case check Corrections	Extreme case check Corrections
	Non-response analysis. Computation of weights if necessary	↓ Add dictionary	↓ Add dictionary
		↓ Generate new variables (brackets, deciles, combinations, county data, indexes)	↓ Generate new variables
		↓ Transfer in weights	↓ Transfer in weights and variables from larger unit
		↓ Main file ready	↓ Subunit file ready
		↓ Analysis	↓ Analysis

in terms of income, but one is using income to predict or explain some expenditure, then the mere fact that there are too few people in some income groups should not bias that relationship. On the other hand, if the response underrepresents the single people or the old people and they have different income elasticities, then some weighting for differential non-response may reduce the bias of these estimated relationships.

The same kind of strategy problem involved in assigning individual items of missing information arises in assigning weights for non-response. If one uses very small groups, then the people whose weights are increased to take account of the non-response are more like the non-response because they are more carefully specified, *but,* if one gets widely varying weights this way, one may increase the sampling variance and trade a small reduction in bias for a large increase in sampling variance. This may not be wise. The extreme procedure again is to find *one* other family matched as much as possible to the one who is missing and simply duplicate his record. If this person turns out to be a millionaire or is unusual in some other way, of course, one can see what potentially disastrous results might occur. On the other hand, if one is very concerned with preserving not only unbiased estimates of means and proportions but unbiased estimates of the variances, one may want to make individual assignments with the greater variance. Taking a whole group and weighting them up may tend to reduce the variance of the sample in the same way that using an average of some other group to assign missing information may reduce that variance. The general experience has been that unless response rates vary quite widely and systematically, weights often make very little difference and are probably not worth the trouble. They create problems not only in simple analysis but also in complex analysis where one may want to apply significance tests, because the sum of the weights is different from the number of degrees of freedom. But an analysis of response rates is called for in any case. An example is given in Appendix B to this chapter.

The only analysis of response rates that can be done is for characteristics that can be measured for both the response and the non-response. This usually means locational items (city size), type of dwelling, and things the interviewer can guess: race, house value, or rent level. On the other hand, given good national data in several dimensions on the numbers of families, it might be possible with national samples, to estimate response rates without any direct information about the individual addresses where no interview was taken, and to produce weights on that basis.

There is a final kind of missing information which occurs when the sample does not cover the population properly. One may miss whole dwellings in a sample of dwelling units, either because of new construction or because of hidden dwellings in basements or above garages or without an outside door. A solution to this problem, which largely affects estimates of aggregates but may also affect other things, is to use outside data to estimate the total number of households for expanding from survey averages to estimates of aggregates. There may be situations where it is useful to develop the weighting procedures from outside estimates of the population distribution where one is particularly concerned about potential biases from missing whole dwellings plus potential biases from non-response.

Where different sampling fractions were used, or where one develops some data on a larger unit than that sampled (where the probability of selection varies with the number of elements combined) then weights are essential, of course.

Cleaning the Data

We have already discussed several processes intended to maintain the accuracy of the data: check-editing, check-coding. With each succeeding step of the process additional checks should be built in to maintain this quality. Here again, of course, there is a strategy problem and a problem in resource allocation. It may or may not be wise to invest very large amounts of money getting rid of a few small random errors. Sometimes it seems as though we pay attention to them out of all proportion to their real importance simply because they are so annoying or, in the final report, so embarrassing. On the other hand, there are a number of instances where people have gotten half way through the analysis stage and decided they had to go back, throw out all they had done, clean out the data first, and start over again.

Once the coding is done the data go to the keypunching operation, and the keypunching is verified by redoing it on a similar machine. Keypunching is a very straight-forward, rapid, and reasonably error-free procedure, but the verifying reduces the errors still more. Then in a major study where quality is important there follows a series of procedures for cleaning the data. Under present technology this is often done after the data are merged and put on tape. In a major study there may be anywhere from two to ten or fifteen computer cards full of material for each interview and the computer technology still requires putting the material on cards first. These decks then have to be put in order by some serial (interview) number, merged, and written on tape before one can use the data easily. It pays to do this before the cleaning process starts, if it is easy to make tape corrections.

The first step is usually to get rid of "wild codes," codes that are not in the original list of codes and thereby unacceptable. Sometimes, of course, codes have been added or altered during the coding process and one has to be careful to allow them. The process of finding wild codes is quite easy with a computer, but the process of looking up all the cases, deciding what the code should be and ordering the corrections is time consuming. In recent years the procedure has been to take the first few hundred interviews, do the wild code check and make corrections, and then continue to do wild code checks in batches as the data come in, rather than wait until the very end and have all the work piled up. This also leads to improvements in the coding process, since wild codes sometimes arise because the coders are doing something wrong. It is worth rerunning the wild code check after the corrections have been made. Sometimes the corrections are not made properly. Sometimes new errors are created in the process of making corrections. And once the program is ready to go, it is very simple and fast to rerun it.

The next step is "consistency checking" where one makes sure that if a man has a mortgage he has a house on which to have a mortgage, for example. One of the problems in writing requests for consistency checks is that some consistencies are one-way and some are two-way. Sometimes B is true *if and only if* A is true; sometimes B has to be true if A is true, but the reverse need not hold. This means that writing computer language for making such consistency checks is quite complicated, and only a fairly sophisticated set of computer software allows it to be done with ease. The problem arises, of course, even if the consistency checking is being done on a sorter; one has to remember to specify in advance exactly what the consistency is. In many cases, things that are thought to be inconsistent when writing the specifications turn out to be perfectly legitimate. On the other hand, sometimes things show up which are inconsistent because there are some real problems with the conceptual definitions or with the editing procedures. This often leads to real improvements in the data. Again, once the corrections are made, it pays to rerun the check to make sure they have been done right. When possible, it pays to do consistency checking in batches because it is a time-consuming process because sometimes improvements can be made in the interviewing, editing, or coding process on the basis of information secured during the early batches of consistency checking.

It also pays to look up the extreme cases to see whether there is something wrong with them. This used to be done as part of the regular consistency checking, but it is often better to hold it as a separate operation, because only a small fraction of the selected cases need correcting, but the listings need to be preserved. Any case that is extremely large or extremely small or unusual in the sense that it is possible but very unlikely is looked up to see whether there is something wrong.

One kind of check that has not traditionally been done but theoretically could be, particularly as computers get more powerful, is to run a multivariate analysis on each of the major dependent variables and sort out the cases that deviate substantially from what might be expected on the basis of three or four explanatory variables. One would then look them up to see if there was something wrong with them—either absolute errors or conceptual problems. Since in a later multivariate analysis the extreme cases might either have to be eliminated, or handled specially, this may save some later problems. It may also uncover some real errors. There is the theoretical difficulty that it might introduce certain biases by eliminating some kinds of errors and not others, and it would certainly spuirously increase a correlation if the errors were actually distributed up and down the range but the only ones that were discovered were the ones that reduced the correlation with certain explanatory variables.

At about this stage in the processing it may be useful to add a dictionary at the head of the set of data, naming the variables, specifying their tape locations, and perhaps specifying certain "inapplicable" or "missing data" codes for the convenience of the computer. Computer programs now exist which will actually pick up twenty-four letters of alphabetical description of each variable and print it along with the machine output in analysis runs. Also the dictionary allows a very easy way of designating variables by number in ordering a computer run without having to specify their dictionary titles every time. It also keeps the names of variables consistent.

Another decision that has to be made all the way through the processing stages is how many safety precautions to take in terms of back-up tapes or extra decks of computer cards. Since every time corrections are made to a tape, a whole new tape is written, the back-up tape then gets out of date and it would have to be rewritten too. Clearly, there must be some compromise between continually writing two tapes, and letting the back-up tape get so out-of-date that if anything happens to the main tape it would be very costly to redo it. Even the sheer record-keeping gets difficult, since any minor change in a tape requires writing a new tape, so that the identifying number of the tape reel changes many times.

Where the number of variables and required consistencies are small, it may pay to check for wild codes, inconsistencies, and extreme cases all in one operation. In general, however, trying to do too many things at once leads to trouble, even though sequences of steps seem cumbersome.

Variable Generation or Creation

Once the originally coded data have been cleaned up and are on a computer tape, it is generally necessary to create some new variables and add them to the tape. First there are variables containing information not collected in the interview or inserted by the interviewer, but having to do with the area in which the respondent lives (assuming they were not put on the questionnaire when checking it into the sample books). These tend mostly to be data about the country or the state or the region usually taken from the United States Census Bureau or other government agencies. Knowing which county each respondent lives in, one can add information about the employment level, median level of education, etc., in his county.

A second kind of added variable consists of class interval or bracket codes or deciles on quantitative information. It is generally useful to have the family income in dollars, but for many purposes when one wants to use income as the stub of a table or even in multivariate analysis, one may want eight or ten income brackets, or ten deciles (breaking up the population into ten equal groups arranged in order according to the size of their income). Deciles are difficult and complex to build because the data must be sorted in order by size of the variable to be "deciled." It requires a separate sorting for each variable. Even on a modern computer sorting several thousand cases on a five-digit variable is not a simple matter. Then one must allocate cases tied at the boundaries to one subclass or the next, in an unbiased way.

A third kind of variable to be generated consists of combinations of other variables. The classic example, of course, is stage in the family life cycle which combines information about age of the head, marital status, presence of children, age of the youngest child, and sometimes, whether the head is still in the labor force. With modern computer programs that look for interactions, it is somewhat less necessary than it once was to build variables containing interaction possibilities in them, but they are still very useful where there is a good theoretical base for them.

A fourth kind of variable that is often generated is what might be called an "aggregated variable," such as the mean of some characteristic for a whole subgroup of the population (or sample) to which the respondent belongs. These can be created right out of the sample. Or one might generate a residual from this mean indicating by how much the individual was above or below the rest of some group. The group might be expected to be a reference group for him. There are difficulties, of course, in the interpretation of such variables. Take the classic case in economics where one may want to separate a man's income into three components. One might first introduce a variable which is the mean income of people in the same education, race, and sex group as the respondent, a kind of proxy for a permanent lifetime income. One might add a second variable representing the deviation of the mean income of people in his age, education, race, and sex group from the first variable, representing the extra earnings or lower earnings that might be expected because he is in a particular age group too. And then one could add a third variable, the deviation of the individual's own income from the composite of the first two. The difficulty with assuming that these three represent expected lifetime earnings, extra expected current earnings of his reference group, and his own deviations from the sum of these two, is that they are basically representations of race, age, education, and sex. Several other interpretations can be given to them. And it can be argued that one should introduce all these variables into an analysis directly, find out which combinations matter in explaining the behavior to be studied, and then try to interpret whether the permanent income notion makes more sense than several other alternative explanations of what education and age and race mean. Furthermore, the individual deviations from expected income may represent *not* "transitory income" but permanent differences based on differential skill or motivation. There are many other possibilities of introducing as variables either the group average of some characteristic or the individual's deviation from that average. There are still difficult computer problems in creating such variables and adding them to each individual record, however.

Finally, and perhaps the most troublesome of all, one may want to generate various *indexes* combining a set of attitudinal questions or several different evidences of a particular behavior pattern. (See Chapter IV.) The literature in psychology is full of very complex procedures for getting a reduced set of variables out of several hundred, based largely on their intercorrelations. Factor analysis is perhaps the most commonly known of these but there are others of more modern variety such as "Least space analysis." All of them involve a great deal of computer work. All of them are based almost entirely on the intercorrelations among the items. None of them pay any explicit attention to the effects of these components on some variable that one is trying to explain. At the other extreme from this inductive approach are indexes built up with a great deal of theoretical structure giving a man points for various things and adding them up or perhaps putting on even more complicated weighting schemes.

One should view the problem differently depending on whether one is combining various bits of information to generate a *dependent* variable or an *explanatory* variable. In the case of a dependent variable it may be quite essential to do some thorough investigation before combining variables. There may even be some justification for a factor analysis, generating some weights to be applied to build a new dependent variable for analysis. In the case of explanatory variables, however, there are differences. For one thing, one may not want to be combining two or three things because they are correlated, if they have effects on the dependent variable in opposite directions from one another. Secondly, one certainly does not want to combine things that are negatively correlated with one another. But that does not mean that it is necessary to go through an elaborate procedure of weighting according to the size of correlation.

A strong case can be made for building fairly simple additive indexes to be used as explanatory variables. Once such a simple additive index is built out of components that are not negatively correlated (so that they will not offset one another) one can then use the bracket levels of this index as a set of dummy variables in an explanatory analysis, and look to see whether the effect is linear or not. If the effect is linear, then the assumption of additivity is maintained. If the effect is curved and concave from above so that nothing happens to the dependent variable until the index is very high, the assumption is justified that the components to the index are complementary because it takes many of them before anything happens, that is, they reinforce one another. If, on the other hand, the effect is curvilinear and convex from above, the implication is that the components are substitutes for one another. Any one or two of them will have as much effect as all of them together. In any case, there is great scanning efficiency in building such an index because if it has no effect at all and the components are all zero or mildly positively intercorrelated, one can be reasonably sure that none of the components have any effect either. If it has a strong effect, one can first check to see whether the components are additive, complementary, or substitutes, and one can also go back and search the detail to see which of the components is really having most of the effect.

There are great efficiencies in generating variables all in one batch on the computer with some preplanning rather than doing them as one goes along. Every time one generates a variable in a computer it is necessary to rewrite the whole tape. This means that the operation is rather expensive. It costs little or nothing more to generate a whole set of variables.

When new variables are generated, they are likely to be at least as important as the ones originally coded, and should be subjected to many of the same checks. Extreme cases should be looked up, and the distribution examined. This is doubly important if some variables are generated, from which still others will be created. It may be useful to get a distribution or average of each new variable, tabulated against one or more explanatory variables to see whether the results look reasonable.

How does one keep track of all these variables, so that it is easy to find where they are (on which tapes), or even against what other variables they have been run? Extremely elaborate and costly indexing systems could be devised, but they are quite likely to break down. Some try for an alphabetic card-file of variables by name, on which is entered all the data tapes where that variable exists, and even all the computer runs (by number) in which it was used. A sequential file of tabulation requests, with attached lists of the variables involved has proven the most useful way of keeping track at least during the main processing. Sometimes the tabulation requests are given different sequences of numbers depending on their purpose, i.e. whether file building, or which type of dependent variable.

In panel studies the process of variable generation is a great deal more complicated, because one generates a set of variables for each year, but when the next wave comes along a very large number of possibilities open up for generating variables which reflect changes from one year to the next, either absolute difference or percentage changes. If one wants to analyze changes, the change is always correlated positively with the second year's value and negatively with the first year's value. So, it may seem important to generate the average of the two years as a second independent variable (uncorrelated with the first) so that one can find out whether it is the over-all level, or the change, in this particular variable that is doing the work. For numerical variables these change variables and average level variables are not too difficult except for the amount of space they take but, if one wants to generate measures of changes in categorical variables, the problems are much more complicated. How does one develop a new variable reflecting change in occupation for instance?

Finally, a mechanical problem results from the fact that most computer software has been developed to handle records of a length up to a thousand variables. Any one survey may have several hundred variables. A panel study may easily reach the thousand limit with the first reinterview when the "change variables" are added. After that one has the same problem that existed with IBM cards i.e., the necessity for generating a *lot* of work tapes once one runs over the limit for a single file. This requires a good deal of planning, and some restriction on the total number of variables one wants to carry, from the sheer mechanics of staying within the restraints of the machinery.

The same process of consistency checking, corrections, and generating new variables may take place on the other files if they are separate files of subunit information. It is also possible to transfer information from one file to another, e.g. put family income on the record for each individual in that family.

At this point we are still not ready to analyze the data. There may be weights necessary to allow for variations in either sampling rates or response rates or both. As one can see from the flow diagram, a whole side process has been going on during the consistency check operations, checking the variations in response rates to see whether weights are necessary to allow for variations in response rates. If there were variations in the sample rates, weights would be necessary in any case. A simple way to put the weights on is to put them onto the unit that was sampled, namely a household or a family, and then transfer them into the subunit files from there. This has a certain efficiency because at the same time one can transfer *information* about the larger unit into each of the subunit records as well. For instance, if one has a record for each individual in the sample, one will want to have available alongside each individual's record, his family income and perhaps other information about the family. This information, together with the proper weights, can be transferred in at the same time. It should be fairly clear to those who understand sampling that whatever weight is appropriate for a family is appropriate for each of its members because it was the family that was sampled, not the individual members.

We now have one or more files of data ready for analysis, perhaps with a dictionary at the beginning, certainly with the data all cleaned up, and probably with a set of additional variables, brackets, indexes, etc., added at the end to make the analysis easier. We turn in the next chapter to the description of some of the problems of analysis and interpretation of the survey data.

A final note of warning: The importance of meticulous care and proper record keeping through the data cleaning and variable generation process cannot be exaggerated. One result of the process should be a code for each of the variables, including the newly generated ones, with notes on conceptual problems or extreme cases discovered in the cleaning process, and ideally with distributions of the categorical variables and means and variances of the numerical ones. At this stage, one or more back-up tapes should be written, hopefully with some mechanism to prohibit anyone from writing on them by accident. Any errors in the weights or in the generated variables will affect all the subsequent analysis, and if discovered later may require redoing a great deal of work.

Particularly since the data may well be used by other people, the codes and attached documentation should be sufficient to guard against most errors. Most surveys of any size are the joint work of a number of people, so procedures that assure that each of them knows what the other has done are important. A single master code is probably better, for this reason, than separate copies for each researcher, at least until the data are ready for analysis.

Records of the Process

Part of the documentation of any study should be a summary of the experience in editing, coding, and cleaning. A list of the codes for which the percent disagreement in check-coding was the highest is useful. Some account of the distribution among interviews of the number of uncodable answers per interview also helps, as well as some notion how many cases had to be assigned—unless a special code was added indicating assignments. Sometimes a bracket code is used with a category for missing information, even though the amount field contains assignments for those cases. Where no assignments are made, there is usually a code for missing information and a distribution of each code tells the reader how much of a problem there was with missing data.

Similarly, there should be a report from the editors on the areas of greatest difficulty in check-editing, and the kinds of problem cases or conceptual difficulties that were encountered.

If the checks for wild codes, inconsistencies, and extreme cases, were done by computer, there should at least be information on the number of corrections required, and perhaps a discussion of the kinds of codes which seemed to lead to trouble.

Under the pressure of work, it is often difficult to insure that proper notes are made of problems, hence it is even more important that the account be written as soon as possible after the end of the process. Presentation of such material in survey reports should not only improve the understanding of each report, but provide the base on which to improve the processing of future surveys.

Even narrative accounts of problems may be worth preserving. A brief list of some irritating and vexing problems we have faced may be useful here:

Corrections that were not properly made, or that introduced further inconsistencies or errors.

Difficulties and delays because of coding errors in interview numbers, scrambling data from two different interviews.

Discovery of errors after variables had been used to create other variables, or had been transferred to other decks or tapes, requiring multiple corrections, and redoing of later steps.

Picturesque variable names that misled or confused, like "remaining installment debt" for the total amount left to pay, including service charges, or "debt payments" including only installment debt payments to institutions.

Work decks or tapes not adequately documented, but not destroyed either.

Creation of a sequence of data tapes, each altering the tape location and variable number of each variable, but without creating a new code for each or maintaining in the variable name a reference to its original code location, so that locating the code detail requires translating through several transformation lists—those lists not with the codes but buried in piles of machine output.

Retention of the same variable name after the variable has been altered, truncated, corrected, etc., but with the old variable still on other tapes or cards.

Failure to date the completion of each step, so that one cannot tell whether an analysis run was done before or after certain corrections or changes in variables.

Regressions or other least squares analyses run with variables containing extreme cases, because the distribution had not been examined in advance.

Failure to save the computer instruction cards, so that one cannot tell which subgroup was selected (by filters, or sorting) for the analysis.

A decision to postpone one operation from editing to the computer was forgotten, and only noticed when some tables were run, partly because the master code did not contain a note, or a label for the variable indicating that it had not had one final adjustment made to it.

Footnotes to Chapter V

1. John Lansing and Thomas Eapen, "Dealing with Missing Information in Surveys," *Journal of Marketing,* 24 (Oct. 1959), pp. 21-27.

2. Walter J. Stewart, "Computer Editing of Survey Data—Five Years of Experience in BLS Manpower Surveys," *Journal of the American Statistical Association* Line 61 (June 1966), pp. 375-383.

   See also: Kenneth Janda, *Data Processing* (Applications to Political Research), Northwestern University Press, Evanston, Illinois, (second edition) 1969.

3. Dorwin Cartwright, "Analysis of Qualitative Material," in Leon Festinger and Daniel Katz, *Research Methods in the Behavioral Sciences,* Holt, Rinehart, and Winston, New York, 1953.

   See also A. N. Oppenheim, *Questionnaire Design and Attitude Measurement,* Basic Books, New York, 1966.

APPENDIX A

SOME EXAMPLES OF HOW RESPONSES FROM THE
COMPLETED INTERVIEWS ARE PROCESSED

Specifically, we shall follow the step-by-step processing of a series
of question on car repairs and food expenditures.

Car Repairs

The first section to be discussed is that on car repairs. The first
question in this series (C19), "Do you (or your family) do any of your own
repair work on your car(s)?" is merely a screening question separating those
who do repair work on their cars from those who do not.

The code for this question is also shown on the next page. Code categories "1" and "5" are, through convention at the Survey Research Center, used
for "Yes" and "No" replies respectively. The "9" category is traditionally used
for the "not ascertained" category. Usually, for a question so simple as this
one is, the "not ascertained" category is used when the question is inadvertently
not asked when it should have been asked. The "0" category is used for those
cases where the family does not own a car, and hence not asked whether or not
they made repairs to their car.

The replies to the second question about car repairs, "What kinds of
things have you done on your car(s) in the last year?" are classified into
categories fitting the conceptual scheme of the study. Note that for this code
(next page) Col. 35 the phrase "PRIORITY CODE," appears. This means - in the
given example - that if a respondent gives a reply that fits into both categories
1 and 2, that we would code it into the 2 category, indicating that he had done
some work on his car requiring some skill and ignoring the fact that he may have
done some work requiring little or no skill.

A response we received such as "I owned different cars, and so did lots--
1st one overhauled engine 4 times--always grease car; tune it up;" would be coded
in "5" category on the grounds that the fact the respondent overhauled the engine
4 times takes priority over the fact that he also greased and tuned up the car,
since overhauling the engine takes more skill than greasing the car or tuning it
up. Another response such as "minor motor tuneup" would be coded 3.

The next 3 questions in this sequence (Qs. C21, C22, and C23) are
handled in the editing stage. The amount of money saved is considered one
of the nonmoney components of income.

Once the data from each of these interviews has gone through the editing
and coding stages, key punched onto IBM cards and put onto tape, it can be
utilized for analyses.

One of the most common ways of presenting the data we collect is in table
form. Still using the information on car repairs, the table on the following
page shows the difficulty of car repairs by family income. You will note that
the categories indicating the degree of complexity come from the code.

C19. Do you (or your family) do any of your own repair work on your car(s)?

☐ YES   ☐ NO (GO TO D1)

(IF YES)

C20. What kinds of things have you done on your car(s) in the last year?

_____

_____

C21. In the last year do you think you saved more than $50 that way?

☐ YES   ☐ NO (GO TO D1)

C22. (IF YES) About how much do you think you saved? $_____

C23. About how much time did that take you altogether? _____

(HOURS)

34

<u>C19 Do you (or your family) do any of your own repair work on your car(s)?</u>

1. Yes

Code 0
in Cols. ——5. No, or none in the last year
35-39

9. N.A.

0. Inap., family does not have car (Coded 0 in Col. 16)

35

C20 (If yes) What kinds of things have you done on your car(s) in
the last year?

PRIORITY CODE - highest number

5. Yes, complex repairs that usually take a skilled mechanic
(rebuilt engine or transmission)

4. Yes, extensive repairs, taking much skill (rings, valves, bearings,
install factory rebuilt engine, king pins, ball joints, transmission
work, motor work, or "I do anything that needs doing"

3. Yes, some skill required, (brakes, wheel bearings, exhaust system,
starter)

2. Yes, some skill (tune-up, points, plugs, adjust carburetor, fuel pump)

1. Yes, little or no skill, mostly maintenance (oil change, greasing,
tire switching) (touch-up painting)

9. N.A. whether or kind of repairs

0. Inap., family does not have car, does no repair work

7. Yes, but not in the last year.

Dollars saved put on worksheet 1, and become part of non-money income.

Hours spent go on worksheet 3, and become part of total work hours, and reduce
estimated leisure time.

DIFFICULTY AND COMPLEXITY OF CAR REPAIRS BY TOTAL FAMILY MONEY INCOME

Difficulty and Complexity of Car Repairs	Total Family Money Income								
	Less than $1000	$1000 -1999	$2000 -2999	$3000 -3999	$4000 -4999	$5000 -7499	$7500 -9999	$10,000 -14,999	$15,000 or more
Complex repairs requiring a skilled mechanic	1%	1%	1%	2%	1%	2%	2%	3%	2%
Extensive repairs taking much skill	1	3	4	5	7	6	9	7	4
Repairs requiring some skill	3	2	2	3	6	8	12	10	5
Repairs requiring some skill of a lesser amount	1	2	3	5	6	11	17	15	13
Repairs requiring little or no skill	0	1	1	1	2	4	5	4	4
Not ascertained	1	1	1	1	1	2	1	1	1
No repair work	93	90	88	82	76	66	53	58	69
Made repairs but not last year	0	0	0	1	1	1	1	2	2
Total	100%	100%	100%	100%	100%	100%	100%	100%	100%
Percent who own no car	78	67	57	45	36	22	10	5	4
Percent of those with a car who repaired it	27	27	26	27	34	40	50	41	29

Expenditures on food

The calculation of expenditures on food involved an editing stage, which we will illustrate in the next few pages.

From the listing box of the interview we determine the weekly food requirement for each individual in the FU according to his age and sex. We then total this for all individuals in the FU and convert this total to an Annual Food Standard which also makes allowances for economics in feeding large families. Assuming that a family spends 1/3 of its total income on food, we then multiply the Annual Food Standard by 3 to get the annual income need standard which we label the "Annual Need Standard." Thus, we have arrived at our standards.

Having arrived at our standards, we can now see how our FU compares with our standards. To do this we need the FU's total food consumption. Total food consumption consists of the total Food Expenditure plus the total Non-Money Food consumed. Under Food Expenditure we have:

1. (Amount) Spent Eating Out taken from Question E2 of last year's questionnaire

2. Cost of Milk from E3

and 3. (Cost of) Other Food from E5.

The total of these three expenditures gives us the Food Bill Subtotal.

To obtain the total food expenditure labeled the "Corrected Food Bill" we must subtract any alcohol or cigarette expenditures which may have been included in the Food Bill. We now have the total Food Expenditure and must add to this the Nonmoney Food consumed to obtain total food consumption.

Nonmoney Food consists of:

1. Home Grown Food taken from E12 of last year's questionnaire

2. Food Received on the Job from J30

and 3. (Amount) Saved on Food Stamps from J32.

Adding the total of these three items to Food Expenditure, we finally arrive at total consumption figure which is in dollars. All of this information is edited on Worksheet 2, except the total Food Consumption, which is assembled in the computer.

We can now compare our FU's actual total Food Consumption with its Annual Food Need Standard. We do this in ratio form by placing Food Consumption over Food Need Standard. If this ratio is less than one, then this implies that the FU's Food Consumption in below the Standard. If the ratio equals one, then the Standard is just met. If the ratio is greater than one, then it means that the FU's Food Consumption is above the Standard.

However, this ratio is used for more than just comparisons. This ratio as well as other items (measures) are conveniently used in tables as summary statements of our data. These tables are very important in the analysis of our data and are used to make crucial policy decisions by policy makers. We have two such tables using this food consumption data for you to scan today. The table summarized the relationship between Family Size and Ratio of Food Consumption to Food Standard. We see that smaller families spend more on food, especially one person families - probably single men. The chart also indicates that larger families economize more; but we find that these larger families have a higher percentage of those who consume less food than the standard.

4

SECTION B

B1. How many people live here altogether? _Four (4)_____

(LIST ALL PERSONS, INCLUDING CHILDREN, LIVING IN THE DU, BY THEIR RELATION TO HEAD)			(ASK B3 FOR THOSE AGED 5-25 (EXCEPT HEAD AND WIFE)	(ASK B4 IF ANSWER TO B3 IS "NO")
B2. How old are they and how are they related to you?	Age	Sex	B3. Is (he/she) in school?	B4. How many years of school did (he/she) finish?
1. HEAD OF DWELLING UNIT	26	M	▨▨▨▨▨	▨▨▨▨▨
2. Wife	25	F	☐ YES ☒ NO ⟶	12
3. Son	5	M	☐ YES ☒ NO ⟶	00
4. Daughter	3	F	☐ YES ☒ NO ⟶	00
5.			☐ YES ☐ NO ⟶	
6.			☐ YES ☐ NO ⟶	
7.			☐ YES ☐ NO ⟶	
8.			☐ YES ☐ NO ⟶	
9.			☐ YES ☐ NO ⟶	
10.			☐ YES ☐ NO ⟶	

B5. Anyone else? (LIST ABOVE)

_____

8

E2. About how much do you (FAMILY) spend in a week eating out, including lunches at work (or at school)?

$ _CO_____

E3. Do you have any of your milk delivered to the door?

☒ YES   ☐ NO - (GO TO E5)

E4. About how much do you (FAMILY) spend on that milk in a week or month?

$ _5_____ per _month___

E5. About how much do you spend a week on all the (other) food you use at home?

$ _20_____

E6. How about alcoholic beverages -- how much do you (FAMILY) spend on that in an average week?

$_____   ☒ NONE - (TURN TO E8)

E7. Is that included in the food bill?

☐ YES   ☐ NO

E8.   Do any of you smoke?

   ☒ YES   □ NO (GO TO E11)

> E9.   (IF YES)   About how many cigarettes do you (FAMILY) smoke in a day or week?
>
> _____4 Packs_____ per _____Week_____
>   (CIGARETTES, PACKS, OR CARTONS)   (DAY, WEEK)
>
> E10.   Is that included in the food bill?   ☒ YES   □ NO

E11.   Are there any special ways that you try to keep the food bill down?

   ☒ YES   □ NO (GO TO E14)

E12.   (IF YES)   What special ways do you have for keeping the food bill down?

We try to catch sales. We clip Coupons
from the paper.

E13.   Anything else? _No_____

E14.   (ASK IF 2 OR MORE PEOPLE IN FAMILY)   How much of the time does the family sit
down and eat the main meal of the day together? _Once every day_

J30.   Did anyone here get more than $50 worth of food or clothing
as a part of their pay?   _$5 per week (food)_

   ☒ YES   □ NO (GO TO J32)

J31.   (IF YES)   About how much would that be worth? $ _250_

J32.   Did you (FAMILY) get any free food, clothing, or food stamps
worth $50 or more in 1967?

   □ YES   ☒ NO (GO TO J34)

J33.   (IF YES)   About how much did that save you last year? $_____

SURVEY RESEARCH CENTER   1968 SURVEY OF FAMILY ECONOMICS   WORKSHEET 2.

7	6	8		0	2		$\mathcal{O}$	$\mathcal{O}$	$\mathcal{O}$	$\mathcal{O}$	$\mathcal{O}$
1	2	3		4	5		6	7	8	9	10

INDIVIDUAL FOOD COSTS:
USE LISTING BOX AND TABLE B

TABLE B. INDIVIDUAL FOOD STANDARD (LOW COST)

AGE	MALE	FEMALE
Under 3	3.90	(3.90)
4 - 6	(4.60)	4.60
7 - 9	5.50	5.50
10 - 12	6.40	6.30
13 - 15	7.40	6.90
16 - 20	8.70	7.20
21 - 35	(7.50)	(6.50)
35 - 55	6.90	6.30
55 +	6.30	5.40

1. _3.90_
2. _4.60_
3. _7.50_
4. _6.50_
5. _____
6. _____
7. _____
8. _____
9. _____
10. _____
11. _____
12. _____
13. _____

SAMPLE BOOK #

EDITOR

CHK. EDITOR

A. | 4 |
FAMILY SIZE   TOTAL UNADJUSTED _22.50_

SEE TABLE FOR FOOD AND NEED STANDARDS FOR THE ABOVE FAMILY SIZE AND UNADJUSTED FOOD TOTAL

ANNUAL FOOD STANDARD   B. | 1 | 1 | 9 | 6 | ANNUAL NEED STANDARD   C. | 0 | 3 | 5 | 8 | 8 |
                          | 12 | 13 | 14 | 15 | | 16 | 17 | 18 | 19 | 20 |

ANNUAL AMOUNT

FOOD EXPENDITURE
1. SPENT EATING OUT (E 2)   ___ X ___ = ___
2. COST OF MILK (E 4)   _5_ X _12_ = _60_
3. OTHER FOOD   (E 5)   _20_ X _52_ = _1040_
4. FOOD BILL SUBTOTAL (1 + 2 + 3)   _1100_

5. ALCOHOL (E6) _____ X _____ = D. | 0 | 0 | 0 | IF INCLUDED(E7)   ___ | 0 |
                                       | 21 | 22 | 23 | ENTER AT RIGHT | 24 |

6. CIGARETTES (E9) _____ X _____ = E. | 0 | 8 | 3 | IF INCLUDED (E10) _83_ | 1 |
                                          | 25 | 26 | 27 | ENTER AT RIGHT | 28 |

CORRECTED FOOD BILL
7.   SUBTRACT 5, 6, FROM FOOD BILL IF INCLUDED   F. | 1 | 0 | 1 | 7 | | 0 |
                                                            | 29 | 30 | 31 | 32 | | 33 |

NON MONEY FOOD
8. HOME GROWN FOOD (E12) SEE SUPERVISOR   G. | 0 | 0 | 0 | | 0 | Hrs 4
                                                | 34 | 35 | 36 | | 37 |

9. CLOTHES MADE AND MENDED (E17, 18)   H. | 0 | 0 | 0 | | 0 | Hrs 5
                                                | 38 | 39 | 40 | | 41 |

10. FOOD RECEIVED ON THE JOB (J30, page 24) I. | 2 | 5 | 0 | | 0 |
                                                 | 42 | 43 | 44 | | 45 |

11. SAVED ON FOOD STAMPS (J32, page 24)   J. | 0 | 0 | 0 | | 0 |
                                                | 46 | 47 | 48 | | 49 |

Table I

RATIO OF FOOD CONSUMPTION TO FOOD STANDARD
BY NUMBER OF PEOPLE IN FAMILY

Ratio of Food Consumption to Food Need Standard	Number of people in family								
	1	2	3	4	5	6	7	8	9 or more
Less than .75	6%	3%	5%	6%	6%	8%	18%	25%	41%
.75 - 1.24	21	20	31	33	39	46	45	57	42
1.25 - 1.74	25	27	33	36	33	32	30	19	14
1.75 - 2.24	19	25	18	17	15	10	6	4	3
2.25 - 3.74	22	21	12	8	6	4	1	0	0
3.75 - 6.24	6	4	1	0	0	0	0	0	0
6.25 - 9.74	1	0	0	0	0	0	0	0	0
9.75 - 14.24	0	0	0	0	0	0	0	0	0
14.25 or more	0	0	0	0	0	0	0	0	0
Total	100%	100%	100%	100%	100%	100%	100%	100%	100%
Number of Cases	791	1103	731	671	565	348	224	153	211

ECONOMIC SURVEY METHODS

RATIO OF FOOD CONSUMPTION TO FOOD NEEDS STANDARD BY TOTAL FAMILY MONEY INCOME

Ratio of Food Consumption to Food Needs Standard	Total Family Money Income								
	Less than $1000	$1000 -1999	$2000 -2999	$3000 -3999	$4000 -4999	$5000 -7499	$7500 -9999	$10,000 -14,999	$15,000 or more
Less than .75	21%	18%	13%	10%	12%	6%	3%	1%	0%
.75 - 1.24	42	38	37	42	36	35	27	18	9
1.25 - 1.74	24	23	27	30	28	31	33	33	24
1.75 - 2.24	7	13	12	11	13	16	22	25	25
2.25 - 3.74	6	7	10	6	8	10	13	21	34
3.75 - 6.24	0	1	1	1	3	2	2	2	7
6.25 - 9.74	0	0	0	0	0	0	0	0	1
Total	100%	100%	100%	100%	100%	100%	100%	100%	100%
Number of Cases	154	496	510	507	419	998	649	707	344

APPENDIX B

AN EXAMPLE OF A RESPONSE RATE ANALYSIS

Survey Research Center   1967 Survey of Consumer Finances
Economic Behavior Program   Project 763
                                                October 1967

THE RESPONSE RATE OF THE 1967 SURVEY OF CONSUMER FINANCES[1]

by Alice Pruss and John Sonquist

This memorandum reports the analysis of the response rate statistics

for the 1967 Survey of Consumer Finances (first Debt Panel wave). The prelim-

inary response rate was revised and made higher by the NAH replacement proce-

dure described in P. 763 memo of September 6, 1967, "Response Rate Revisions,

1967 SCF." Selected tables were rerun with the revised data.[2]

---

[1]This memo supersedes the September, 1967 memo with this same title.

[2]There were 91 households of P. 753 (1966 Survey of Consumer Finances)
where no member of the dwelling unit was contacted at any time during the interviewing period or some member of the dwelling unit was contacted, but the
financially responsible member of the family unit was not contacted and no
interview was obtained. These households were visited as part of the P. 763
sample; 45 interviews were obtained. There were 46 non-interviews, some of
which were refusals, no one at home, non-sample and non-eligible respondents.
The 46 non-interviews should never have been included in the non-interviews
for P. 763. Their non-interview number was obtained from Sampling and they
were removed from Deck 99.
     Replacement of 45 non-interviews of P. 763 by the 45 interviews obtained
was as follows: P. 763 non-interviews where no one was at home were listed
in order of PSU (P. 763, MTR 106). The PSUs where the 45 interviews were
taken were obtained from Sampling. One-to-one replacement was attempted;
that is, a NAH non-interview in a particular PSU was replaced by an interview
in that PSU. The random half indicator (circled line) was chosen to be identical for both. If there was no way of replacing a non-interview in a PSU by
an interview in the same PSU preserving the random half indicator, then one
from a nearby PSU in the same region was substituted. Similar regions were
substituted if the same region could not be used. About half of the 45 substitutions involved judgements. (See P. 763, MTR 107 for an 80 x 80 listing
of non-interviews removed from Deck 99.)
     In conclusion, all 91 of the P. 753 NAH's are accounted for by removing
Deck 99 cards. The overall revised response rate is accurate. However,
response rate by belt (P. 763, MTR 106) or other variables may be of
questionable accuracy due to the "fudging" necessary to replace the non-
interviews.

Computation: NER's (7000 series, non-eligible respondents) were considered like non-sample (9000 series) for both response rates and subtracted
from all addresses to give interviews and non-interviews. The computations
are as follows:

	Preliminary	Revised[3]
Addresses	5234	5163
Secondaries	56	56
Addresses & Secondaries	5310	5219
Non-sample (9000 series)	710	703
NER (7000 series)	667	659
Actual interviews	3165	3165
Non-interviews (8000 series)[4]	768	692
To compute response rate:	5310-710-667 = 3933	5219-703-659 = 3857
	$1 - \dfrac{768}{3933} = 80.5\%$	$1 - \dfrac{692}{3857} = 82.1\%$

The preliminary response rate of 80.5% and the revised rate of 82.1%
for the 1967 Survey of Consumer Finances represent a slight, but continued
decline over the past few years. As in past years the rates tend to be lowest in the big city metropolitan areas. However, the response rate differen-
tials do not appear to require assigning weights to compensate for the slight
under-representation of big-city respondents. Table 1 shows the preliminary
response rates by PSU. The following PSU's had rates less than 60%:

            San Francisco and Oakland Cities
            St. Louis City
            Washington City

In addition, the following PSU's had response rates between 60% and 70%:

---

[3]Takes account of replacement NAH's, Respondents Absent.

[4]All respondents that refused to give information for the listing box
on the face sheet were coded as refusals (8000 series) regardless of whether
they occurred on circled line numbers or not. Hence, there may have been a
few FU's with the head aged 60 or over in the "circled" half of the sample
who were classified as sample refusals rather than as NER's.

Chicago City North
Chicago City South
Cleveland City
New York suburbs in New York State
Jersey City and Newark, New Jersey

Philadelphia City
Baltimore suburbs
Harris, Texas

Santa Clara, California

Mercer, New Jersey
Worcester, Massachusetts
Onondaga, New York

Table 2 indicates that the preliminary response rate varied by region, ranging

from 76.1% in the Northeast to 83.1% in the South. The North Central, South,

and West regions were almost identical. The Northeast was slightly lower.

Revisions to Table 2 increased the response rate in the South and North Central

regions by about 2% as compared to about a 1% increase in the West and North-

east. Variations were somewhat greater when tabulated by size of place

(Tables 3 and 4). As in previous years, the highest response rates occurred

in rural areas. The next highest rates occurred in urban places ranging from

2500 to 50,000 in population. The lowest response rates occurred in the

central cities of the twelve largest SMSA's. These areas had a preliminary

rate of only 70.2%, and a revised rate of 72.7%. Revision increased the rates

in the central cities more than it did in other areas. The other large cities,

of population 50,000 and over exclusive of the twelve largest SMSA's had pre-

liminary response rates of 74.8% and revised response rates of 77.1%. The

urban-rural differential in response rates is reflected when the statistic is

tabulated by Belt Code. The suburban areas of the 12 largest SMSA's can be

seen to be lower in response rate than the suburban areas of other SMSA's.

The relevant preliminary statistics are 78.5% and 85.1%, respectively; the

revised rates are 79.0% and 86.5%. The central cities of the twelve largest

SMSA's, as indicated before, had a preliminary rate of only 70.2%, compared

with 73.8% for the central cities of other SMSA's. The revised rates are
72.7% and 76.3% respectively. Distance from the center of a central city is
another variable used to explain the response rate for addresses which are in
SMSA PSU's but not inside the central city. The lowest response rates tend
to be within eight miles of the center of the central city. Higher response
rates are found between eight and 15 miles, and then the response rate drops
off again between 15 and 25 miles from the center of the central city. Revision increased the rate fairly equally throughout. Differential preliminary
response rates by household composition existed, but are difficult to interpret.
When divided in this fashion, rates range from 82% to 100%; however, almost all
of the non-interview situations occurred in households in which it was not
possible to ascertain the household composition. Therefore, it is not clear
whether these households have the same composition as others for which interviews were obtained.

When broken down by interviewers' estimates of the family income, the
preliminary response rates range from 80.1% to 93.2%, the revised rates range
from 81.5% to 93.7%. Those having an estimated income of $10,000 or over
have the highest response rate. This might be expected in view of the distribution of interviews over urban-rural areas. A large fraction of the refusals
occurred in households in which the interviewer was not able to obtain enough
information about the family to make an estimate of their income. There was
no significant variation in response rate by race. Revision increased the
rate the most for Negros. The preliminary rate is 84.3%, the revised rate
is 86.5%.

Though there is slight variation in response rates by age, the preliminary ranging from 81.3% to 88.0% and the revised rate ranging from 81.9% to
89.1%, there is not enough to warrant compensation by weighting. The response

rate of young people under 25 increased from a preliminary rate of 87.5% to a
revised rate of 89.1%. When preliminary response rates are computed for
households living in various types of structures, considerably more variation
is apparent. Less than 70% of the families living in apartment houses of four
or more stories and containing five or more units were interviewed successfully.
On the other hand, 88% of those living in two family houses with two units
side by side were interviewed. The response rate problems clearly occur in
multiple-family dwellings (see Table 5).

The preliminary response rate by number of calls was tabulated. The
probability of obtaining an interview drops off very rapidly after the fourth
call. The number of calls made by interviewers was tabulated according to
the belt code location of the household. Getting the response rate in the
central cities of the twelve largest SMSA's up, even to the point where it is,
requires an extremely large number of calls. Of the interviews obtained in
these areas, some 43% were obtained after making four or more calls.

Types of non-sample addresses were also tabulated. There are no significant differences from data obtained in the previous year's Survey. About
80% of the non-sample addresses turned out to be unoccupied dwelling units.
Another seven or eight percent of the non-sample address classifications
resulted from dwellings which were either non-habitable, destroyed, or damaged,
or a trailer moved. There was a slight decline in the proportion of addresses
not occupied because of new construction. In 1966 this was 5.6% of the non-
sample addresses; in 1967 it was only 3.9% (preliminary rates). Changes in
the amount of new construction resulting from increased mortgage interest
rates during the past year do not appear to have affected sample characteristics noticeably.

The non-interviews were tabulated according to the reason for disposition of the schedule as a non-interview (Table 6). From 1964 to 1967, the

percentage of refusals has increased from 11.5% in 1964 to 12.6% in 1967.

In 1967, 2.7% of the non-interviews resulted from no one being at home during the entire study period. The percentage was 2.8% in 1964. In 1965 and 1966, the proportion dropped to about 2%. In 1966, 1.3% of the non-interviews occurred because the interviewers could not contact any of the financially responsible adults in the family. This proportion increased to 2.0% in 1967. There are no significant differences in reasons for non-response between the two years.

Taken together, these data appear to indicate that though we continue to have some troubles with our response rates in the central cities of the large SMSA's, these do not yet appear to be sufficiently bad as to warrant compensatory weighting.

Table 1

RESPONSE RATE BY PSU

Preliminary

P S U	All addresses N	Ints. + Non-Ints. N	Interviews N	Response Rate (1) %	Response Rate (2) %
Los Angeles City	81	60	49	60.5	81.7
Los Angeles Suburbs	123	99	86	69.9	86.9
San Francisco and Oakland Cities	36	23	13	36.1	56.5
San Francisco Suburbs	50	42	34	68.0	81.0
Chicago City, North	85	66	41	48.2	62.1
Chicago Suburbs	93	69	56	60.2	81.2
Chicago City, South	42	30	19	45.2	63.3
Cleveland City	32	25	16	50.0	64.0
Cleveland Suburbs	30	26	20	66.7	76.9
Detroit City	55	41	32	58.2	78.0
Detroit Suburbs	68	59	49	72.0	83.1
St. Louis City	19	15	8	42.1	53.3
St. Louis Suburbs	36	27	21	58.3	77.8
New York City, Bronx, Queens, Brooklyn, Manhattan	221	174	131	59.3	75.3
New York Richmond	6	4	4	66.7	100.0
New York Suburbs (in New York State)	79	66	46	58.2	69.7
Jersey City & Newark, N.J.	15	13	8	53.3	61.5
New York Suburbs (in N.J.)	107	89	65	60.7	73.0
Boston City	22	14	12	54.5	85.7
Boston Suburbs	66	51	41	62.1	80.4
Philadelphia City	71	51	32	45.1	62.7
Philadelphia Suburbs	53	41	32	60.4	78.0
Pittsburgh City	17	14	10	58.8	71.4
Pittsburgh Suburbs	48	37	27	56.3	73.0
Baltimore City	30	20	17	56.7	85.0
Baltimore Suburbs	36	29	20	55.6	69.0
Washington City	27	25	11	40.7	44.0
Washington Suburbs	33	31	27	81.8	87.1

Table 1 - continued

P S U	All addresses N	Ints. + Non-Ints. N	Inter- views N	Response Rate (1) %	Response Rate (2) %
Harris, Texas	83	72	44	53.0	61.1
Atlanta, Georgia	66	51	39	59.1	76.5
Jefferson, Kentucky	41	34	25	61.0	73.5
Dade, Florida	51	37	33	64.7	89.2
Tulsa, Oklahoma	49	41	30	61.2	73.2
Richmond, Virginia	59	48	41	69.5	85.4
Pulaski, Arkansas	56	43	30	53.6	70.0
Taylor, Texas	53	36	31	58.5	86.1
Montgomery, Alabama	50	39	31	62.0	79.5
Richland, South Carolina	48	37	33	68.8	89.2
Orange, Florida	48	38	28	58.3	73.7
Fayette, Kentucky	52	42	36	69.2	85.7
Sarasota, Florida	112	61	56	50.0	91.8
Pitt, North Carolina	55	46	45	81.8	97.8
Pulaski, Virginia	47	36	33	70.2	91.7
Mississippi, Arkansas	46	35	31	67.4	88.6
Erath, Texas	91	50	45	49.5	90.0
Clark, Arkansas	66	47	46	69.7	97.9
East Carroll, Louisiana	52	32	26	50.0	81.3
Rankin, Mississippi	50	36	30	60.0	83.3
Muhlenberg, Kentucky	86	56	52	60.5	92.9
Hickman, Tennessee	64	39	36	56.3	92.3
Watauga, North Carolina	55	36	34	61.8	94.4
Currituck, North Carolina	83	55	48	57.8	87.3
Franklin, Nebraska	58	37	31	53.4	83.8
Stoddard, Missouri	58	39	32	55.2	82.1
Crawford, Iowa	73	51	44	60.3	86.3
Marshall, Indiana	74	53	40	54.1	75.5
St. Joseph, Michigan	52	44	42	80.8	95.5
Adair, Missouri	62	50	45	72.6	90.0
Logan, Illinois	41	26	21	51.2	80.8
Knox, Ohio	75	54	47	62.7	87.0
Hancock, Ohio	62	45	36	58.1	80.0
Sheboygan, Wisconsin	57	35	32	56.1	91.4

Table 1 - continued

P S U	All addresses	Ints. + Non-Ints.	Interviews	Response Rate (1)	Response Rate (2)
	N	N	N	%	%
Minnehaha, South Dakota	46	26	23	50.0	88.5
Butler, Ohio	44	35	30	68.2	85.7
Black Hawk, Iowa	57	51	45	78.9	88.2
Genessee, Michigan	56	46	39	69.6	84.8
Toledo, Ohio	55	41	33	60.0	80.5
Marion, Indiana	54	43	36	66.7	83.7
Hennepin, Minnesota	86	74	58	67.4	78.4
Montgomery, Ohio	77	66	48	62.3	72.7
San Diego, California	31	23	20	64.5	86.9
San Bernadino, California	30	20	19	63.3	95.0
King, Washington	44	36	28	63.6	77.8
Salt Lake, Utah	66	50	44	66.7	88.0
Maricopa, Arizona	54	40	33	61.1	82.5
Santa Clara, California	33	28	19	57.6	67.9
Lane, Oregon	63	54	44	69.8	81.5
Whatcom, Washington	64	44	38	59.4	86.4
Tulare, California	58	39	30	51.7	76.9
Logan, Colorado	50	31	29	58.0	93.5
Plumas, California	108	57	45	41.7	78.9
Susquehanna, Pennsylvania	53	30	27	50.9	90.0
York, Maine	98	53	49	50.0	92.5
Ulster, New York	49	34	28	57.1	82.3
Lycoming, Pennsylvania	65	44	37	56.9	84.1
New London, Connecticut	39	29	25	64.1	86.2
Luzerne, Pennsylvania	61	42	35	57.4	83.3
Mercer, New Jersey	44	42	29	65.9	69.0
Fairfield, Connecticut	44	34	26	59.1	76.5
Worcester, Massachusetts	59	43	29	49.1	67.4
Onondaga, New York	66	56	39	59.1	69.6
TOTAL	5310	3933	3165	59.6	80.5

NOTE: Response Rate (1) = Interviews divided by all addresses (if secondary FU in DU, address counted twice, etc.).

Response Rate (2) = Interviews divided by (Interviews + Non-Interviews), NER's are treated as non-sample (9000 interview series).

P. 763: MTR 4 and F. O. Memo.

Table 2

RESPONSE RATE BY REGION

(percentage distribution of family units)

Preliminary and Revised

| Region | Interviews + Non-Interviews | | Interviews | Response Rate (2) | |
	Preliminary	Revised[a]		Preliminary	Revised[a]
	N	N	N	%	%
Northeast	961	945	731	76.1	77.3
North Central	1174	1149	944	80.4	82.1
South	1152	1125	958	83.1	85.1
West	646	638	532	82.3	83.4
TOTAL	3933	3857	3165	80.5	82.1

NOTE: Response Rate (2) = Interviews divided by (Interviews + Non-Interviews).

[a]See P. 763, MTR 107.

P. 763: MTR 18

Table 3

RESPONSE RATE BY SIZE OF PLACE

(percentage distribution of family units)

Preliminary and Revised

Size of Place (1960 Census Classification)	Interviews + Non-Interviews			Interviews		Response Rate		
	1966 N	Revised[a] 1967 N	Prelim. 1967 N	1966 N	1967 N	1966 %	Revised[a] 1967 %	Prelim. 1967 %
Central Cities of 12 largest SMSA's	442	557	577	324	405	73.3	72.7	70.2
Cities 50,000 & over (except central cities of 12 largest SMSA's)	654	863	889	500	665	76.5	77.1	74.8
Urban Places 10,000 - 49,999	474	665	672	409	550	86.3	82.7	81.8
Urban Places 2500 - 9999; urbanized areas not included above	569	818	827	488	688	85.8	84.1	83.2
Rural, in an SMSA PSU	175	183	187	147	160	84.0	87.4	85.6
Rural, not in an SMSA PSU	612	771	781	551	697	90.0	90.4	89.2
TOTAL	2926	3857	3933	2419	3165	82.7	82.1	80.5

NOTE: Response Rate = Interviews divided by (Interviews + Non-Interviews)

[a] See P. 763: MTR 107.

P. 763: MTR 18

Table 4

RESPONSE RATE BY BELT CODE

(percentage distribution of family units)

Revised

Belt Code (1960 Census Classifications)	Interviews + Non-Interviews		Interviews		Response Rate[a]	
	1966 N	1967 N	1966 N	1967 N	1966 %	1967 %
12 largest SMSA's						
Central Cities	442	557	324	405	73.3	72.7
Suburban Areas	448	604	371	477	82.8	79.0
Other SMSA's						
Central Cities	521	689	401	526	77.0	76.3
Suburban Areas	436	621	355	537	81.4	86.5
Other Areas						
Adjacent Areas	499	671	447	580	89.6	86.4
Outlying Areas	580	715	521	640	89.8	89.5
TOTAL	2926	3857	2419	3165	82.7	82.1

NOTE: Response Rate = Interviews divided by (Interviews + Non-Interviews).

P. 763: MTR 106.

Table 5

RESPONSE RATE BY TYPE OF STRUCTURE

(percentage distribution of family units)

Preliminary

Type of Structure	Interviews + Non-Interviews		Interviews		Response Rate[a]	
	1966	1967	1966	1967	1966	1967
	N	N	N	N	%	%
Detached single family house	2014	2711	1705	2245	84.7	82.8
2-family house, 2 units side by side	132	150	113	132	85.6	88.0
2-family house, 2 units one above the other	113	227	94	171	83.2	75.3
Detached 3-4 family house	95	116	75	84	78.9	72.4
Row house	106	147	75	114	70.7	77.5
Apartment house (5 or more units, 3 stories or less)	173	245	137	172	79.2	70.2
Apartment house (5 or more units, 4 stories or more)	127	149	87	102	68.5	68.5
Apartment in a partly commercial structure	48	66	40	50	83.3	75.7
Trailer	83	80	75	65	90.4	81.3
Other	25	42	18	30	72.0	71.4
Not Ascertained	-	-	-	-	*	*
TOTAL	2926	3933	2419	3165	82.7	80.5

[a]Response Rate = Interviews divided by (Interviews + Non-Interviews).

*All Not Ascertained cases were assigned.

P. 763: MTR 18, 18a step 1.

Table 6

REASONS FOR DISPOSITION AS NON-INTERVIEW

(percentage distribution of interviews and non-interviews)

	1967[a] N	1967[a] %	1966 N	1966 %	1965 N	1965 %	1964 N	1964 %
Refusal[b]	495	12.6	350	12.0	187	11.6	213	11.5
No one at home	107	2.7	58	2.0	30	1.9	52	2.8
Respondent absent	80	2.0	39	1.3	17	1.1	21	1.1
Other	86	2.2	60	2.0	24	1.5	30	1.6
Total non-interviews	768	19.5	507	17.3	258	16.1	316	17.0
Total all interviews and non-interviews	3933	100.0	2926	100.0	1607	100.0	1856	100.0

[a]Figures for 1967 are preliminary.

[b]Includes partial refusal i.e. respondent answered some interview questions, but not enough to be considered by the analysis staff as an interview.

P. 763: MTR 18.

Chapter VI

ANALYSIS

It is appropriate at the start of the analysis of survey data to refer back to the objectives of the project. As set forth in Chapter I, there are four general categories of purposes for a project: prediction, explanation, evaluation, and description. A particular investigation will include some combination of these four types, and analysis plans should be developed with that in mind. It is also useful to be as clear as possible about any potential social usefulness of the findings, whether they are expected to be relevant to the management of the economy as a whole, to some broad social problem, or to some specific policy.

The discussion which follows is divided into three parts. The first concerns the construction of variables and the second, the estimation of statistical relationships within analytical models. The third section considers the organizational aspects of analysis and the practical problems of manipulating survey data.

It is not possible nor would it be useful to present here a complete discussion of the topics mentioned. Much important material is covered in textbooks on statistics or elsewhere in the literature. We will indicate what topics are of particular importance for the analysis of economic surveys and why. For a systematic and detailed coverage of most of the topics the reader will be referred to the appropriate specialized literature. An attempt will be made to refer both to introductory and advanced discussions of each topic to allow for differences in readers' backgrounds and interests.

Construction of Variables

Theoretical Variables and Measured Variables: The analyst confronted with the data obtained from a sample survey has at his disposal a set of measurements on a certain number of variables, operationally defined. He knows, in principle at least, the precise methods which were used to obtain those measurements. If the project was well designed and well executed, he knows what was done by the people who drew the sample, took the interviews, and coded the answers.

The analyst also has in mind a theory, a set of theoretical concepts and propositions concerning the relationships among those concepts. The theory

269

may be more or less completely worked out. It may be exclusively economic theory, or it may include elements from psychological or sociological theory. Even in descriptive studies, there will be some consideration given to conceptualization, to organizing the data in ways which have potential theoretical meaning.

It is important to recognize that there will always be a gap between the measured variables and any theoretical variable. The two are never identical.[1] The analyst, however, should seek to reduce the gap to a minimum. He should try to arrange the data at his disposal so that the measured variables are close approximations to theoretical variables.

The importance of these considerations has been brought home to economists by the discussion of "permanent income," "temporary income," and "measured income."[2] It has been argued that the theoretically relevant variable, "permanent income," is poorly approximated by "measured income." It has also been argued that close attention should be paid to what is sometimes called "non-income income." That is, one should consider the total flow of resources which become available to a household including such items as goods and services provided by employers, gifts, and capital gains, as well as those flows more commonly counted as income. A single theoretical variable may well be constructed from answers to several questions. A clear distinction should be drawn between a "variable" in the sense of answers to a question and a "variable" in the sense of the closest operational approximation to a theoretical variable. For example, answers to many questions may be combined to produce estimates of a single variable, income. The answers may simply be added together, as one adds income from interest to income from wages. But simple addition by no means exhausts the logical possibilities of combination. Whether or not a receipt is counted as income, for example, may be decided on the basis of a question about its origin.

The same kinds of consideration apply to consumption, to saving, to net worth, and so forth, as well as to income. In each case it will be appropriate to consider carefully the exact nature of the theoretically relevant construct and to raise the question of how the measured variable may be brought as close as possible to the theoretical variable.[3]

These considerations also apply to non-economic variables. For example, stage in the family life cycle is a single variable from a sociological point of view. The variable represents the stages through which individuals pass, defined in terms of the formation, changing composition, and dissolution of nuclear families. The stages may be defined in more or less detail according to the purpose: for example, one may or may not wish to distinguish families with a single child from those with two or more children. But it will remain true that families are being placed on a continuum which originated in sociological theory.

Psychological theory also provides examples. The sense of personal effectiveness is a psychological construct developed from the theory of ego-strength. Several questions or items may be used to develop an operational variable intended to measure personal effectiveness. That variable will be more satisfactory the stronger the evidence that it does in fact measure to a close approximation the theoretical construct. Yet, philosophically, a gap will always remain: the measurements are not the constructs which they represent.

They may even represent more than one thing. Take "ability to pay," and "need for housing," for instance. The more people there are in a family the more housing they need, but the less income per capita they have for any given family income. We might build an "ability-to-pay" variable by dividing family income by the number of people in the family. And we might use the number of people in the family as another variable indicating the need for housing. The only trouble is that these two variables are highly negatively correlated with one another since one of them is in the denominator of the other. Family size represents two conflicting forces.

Another example is the attempt to decompose the income into expected average lifetime income, expected current income deviation from the lifetime average, and transitory deviations from the sum of the other two. We can obtain such a measure by developing estimates of lifetime incomes for people according to education, race, sex, and then we can develop expected income for a group of this *age* by using education, sex, and race *and age*. Then we can get a measure of the deviation of actual income from that estimate which we could then call transitory income. The difficulty is that each of these concepts has used other variables which have effects of their own. It may be misleading to label these variables: "Permanent income," "permanent short-run income," and "transitory income." If a man is making $1000 more than his group, perhaps he is the kind of person who makes that much *more* all the time. Hence there may be more variation from year to year in terms of general lifetime changes in income than there are in the so-called transitory effect.

The problem of measurement and variable generation is different for dependent variables and for explanatory variables. It is absolutely essential that the dependent variable be well-measured, well-distributed, and have enough variance so that it can be explained, and relate to some theoretical construct with minimal error. With the possible exception of canonical correlation with dummy variables, it is not possible to scale the dependent variable in the process of the statistical analysis, as it is with the explanatory variables. Hence, much of what we say in the next pages about scaling applies largely to dependent variables. And since in economic surveys, the dependent variables are often numerical magnitudes which require no scaling, the whole issue is less important than in the other behavioral sciences. There are, however, economic behaviors which one may want to study and which would require the generation of variables: e.g., interest in early retirement, receptivity to change, or leadership in acquiring new products.

Level of Measurement: The discussions of cardinal versus ordinal utility have familiarized economists with one of the basic distinctions in the theory of measurement, the distinction between an *ordinal* scale, in which rank orders are known, and an *interval* scale, in which the distances between positions on the scale are also known. There are additional levels of measurement, however, which it is useful to distinguish.[4]

The simplest type of measurement consists in the construction of *nominal* scales, that is, the mapping of objects into categories. What is required is the ability to distinguish between objects which belong to a certain category and those which do not. Some variables of interest in economic surveys are such simple dichotomies. For example, an individual may be classified as a Negro or not a Negro. Many classifications, such as occupation, region of the country, or marital status, have neither order nor quantitative measure.

Between nominal scales and fully ordered ordinal scales Coombs introduces a category of partially ordered scales. In such a scale the members of one class *may* bear some relationship to the members of another class. One position may be "more than" or "greater than" another position. A complete ordering, however, is not possible. This situation may arise when there are two or more fully ordered scales which underlie the scale under consideration, but there is no exact set of equivalences between the underlying scales. Coombs' example is a scale of socio-economic status based on measures of income and education. If A has both more income and more education than B, his status is higher; if he has less of both, his status is lower; but if he has, say, more income but less education, his relative status is not clear. Only a system of equivalence between education and income will produce an answer to the question.

It is possible, of course, to introduce an arbitrary system of equivalences. One might say that one year of education is equivalent to $2000 in income. The resulting ordinal scale, however, would contain a corresponding arbitrary element.

There is a strong tendency for analysts to make such assumptions. Manipulation of the data is greatly facilitated if it is in the form of ordinal scales, or, better, interval scales. It may be possible to find some theoretical or empirical basis for the methods used to specify equivalences.

The risks involved, however, may be serious. It is very easy to become accustomed to the use of imperfect scales and to forget their weaknesses. Consider, for example, level of education. The number of years of formal education which a person has received is a variable which is not only an *interval* scale but, in Coombs' terminology, a *ratio* scale, since it has a meaningful zero point. Suppose it is desired to analyze the effect of education on income and to examine whether income has the same effect on the income of Negroes as of whites. There might be interest in whether Negroes earn lower incomes than whites of the same level of education as a result of discrimination in the job market. One might, therefore, propose to look at the relation between education and income for each racial group separately, and compare the results.

The proposed analysis, however, rests on the assumption that years of education are equivalent. The underlying social reality, unfortunately, does not support the assumption. The data actually represent two scales, one of which refers to years of formal education in one set of schools, and the second, to years of formal education in a second set of schools. What the analyst has at his disposal is two scales, a quantity scale and a quality scale. He must face the problem of equivalence between them.

If he does not do so he will then discover that Negroes earn less than whites of the "same" education. He may infer discrimination in the job market. If he does, he may be wrong. The market might be valuing people's services impartially when the quality as well as quantity of education is taken into account. Or, of course, lower incomes of Negroes than whites with the same number of years of education may be partly the result of job discrimination and partly of educational quality.

This line of reasoning may be applied more generally. School systems are not identical in different regions of the country, in different states, or even in different parts of the same city. They certainly differ over time: there are considerable differences between the instruction represented by a high school diploma in 1928 and 1968. Also, colleges and universities vary in quality. Closely considered, number of years of formal education is not a ratio scale, an interval scale, or even an ordinal scale: it is a partially ordered scale.

The same general considerations apply to other measurements familiar to economists. The entire discipline of accounting represents essentially a set of rules and procedures for reducing widely different situations to sets of numbers in the form of ratio scales.

One of the important implications of the existence of variables with different levels of measurement is that the statistical methods appropriate for analysis depend upon the level of measurement. We shall not attempt a detailed discussion of this subject here. In general, however, such techniques as rank-order correlation methods have been developed for use with ordinal scales.[5] Multiple regression was originally restricted to variables measured as interval or ratio scales, but has been extended even to nominal scales for the explanatory variables through the use of sets of dichotomous or "dummy" variables. Measurement theory also has implications for the development of practical techniques of measurement and the construction of variables.

Dummy Variables: Dichotomous or "dummy" variables have come into wide use in survey analysis in working with predictors (explanatory variables) which are not interval scales or which have a non-linear relation to the dependent variable. Specifically, dummy variables are frequently used as predictors in regression analysis. Analogous techniques also exist for the treatment of dependent variables. One of the basic attractions of the method of dummy variables is that the level of measurement required is only that represented by a nominal scale. That is, what is required is that "likes" be grouped together. The method is flexible enough so that the "likes" may be defined on two (or more) dimensions. For example, the individuals to be placed in one category might be college graduates who live in the Northeast.

It should be recognized that even these minimal conditions are not always easily met. For example, there is some question, as suggested earlier, as to the appropriateness of grouping together graduates of all colleges. A man who spent three years at a first rate institution but did not graduate may be better educated than one who spent four years at a marginal institution and did graduate. In practice one cannot expect to be perfectly successful in grouping "likes" into one category and "unlikes" into another, and the results must be interpreted accordingly.

When a dummy variable is used to represent a simple dichotomy, the procedure is simply to define a variable which takes the value 1 for all individuals falling into the category, and 0 for all others. For example, the variable might be sex, with all females assigned a score of 1, and all males, 0.

The method has been extended to classifications in which there are three or more categories. The usual procedure then is to define a *set* of dummy variables, the number of variables being one less than the number of categories. The reason for this is the k-1 dichotomies contain all the information. If the individual is known to be, or not be, in each of three regions, we know whether he is in the fourth. A fourth dummy variable would be identical to a linear function of the other three, so the four would give a determinant =0 in the denominator in solving the normal equations of regression. Like any case of perfect correlation among predictors, the system is insoluble. Consider, for example, a system of classification into four regions and the values which would be taken by each of the three dummy variables needed to represent the regions each individual:

Dummy Variables

Region	X_1	X_2	X_3
Northeast	1	0	0
Northcentral	0	1	0
South	0	0	1
West	0	0	0

When these three dummy variables are introduced as predictors in a regression, a regression coefficient for each will emerge from the calculations. These coefficients will measure for any individual the effect on the score on the dependent variable of being in a category *rather than the omitted category.* For example, the coefficient for X_1 would measure the effect of living in the Northeast *rather than the West.* For the West, of course, the coefficient is zero. The predicted scores for individuals in the West, however, will be included in the constant term. If a different region had been omitted the calculations would have yielded different regression coefficients and a different constant term, but the predicted score for any individual would have been identical. A simple linear transformation can be used to create *four* adjusted coefficients so that the weighted sum of the *four* coefficients (one for each region) is =0. Four such coefficients are easier to interpret than three where the fourth is constrained to zero. (See below) Thus, this procedure in effect makes it possible to introduce into a regression a system of classification without requiring a level of measurement even as high as a partially ordered scale.

The dummy variable technique also may be used in working with variables which are measured as interval or ratio scales to allow for curvilinearity in the relationship. In effect, the dummy variable can approximate a curvilinear relationship by a step function. If there is reason to believe that the true relationship actually is a step function, so much the better. For example, the exact age of an individual may be known, and it may be desired to include age as a predictor, say, of income. Age is a variable measured at a high level—age in years forms a ratio scale. But there is every reason to believe that the effect of age on income is not a straight line—people's incomes rise after they leave school but decline after retirement. Age in years can be divided into a set of dummy variables and treated exactly as in the above example for region. The regression coefficients will then be free to reflect the curvilinearity in the relationship. For a more comprehensive discussion of the technique, see the writings of Daniel B. Suits and Arthur Goldberger.[6]

The success of this device has reduced the interest of economists in scaling, a subject to which a great deal of attention has been given by psychologists. It is less important to achieve a higher level of measurement if one has available techniques which give reasonably good results with a lower level of measurement. The problem of dimensionality, however, to which reference has been made above, arises at any level of measurement. And, in addition, there is a gain in information and, hence, in predictive power when it is possible to place individuals on a finely graduated scale. For example, there is an advantage in knowing the income of a family to the dollar compared to knowing only in which of five classes their income falls. The importance of this advantage will depend upon the shape of the relation of income to the particular dependent variable under consideration. Compare expenditures on goods A, B, and C in the graph on the following page.

For analysis of A, the exact income would be useful. For analysis of B, at low levels no detail is needed but at high levels of income detail is essential.

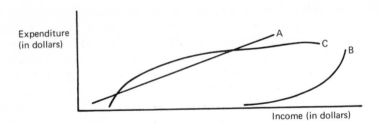

C, there is no need of detail at high levels of income. For other predictors presumably similar considerations apply. Consider the effect of substituting on the graph, "psychological attribute" for income. The vertical axis may be left "expenditure in dollars" or, more generally, may measure any type of economic behavior. It might read, "probability of buying a new car in a given period." Without knowledge of the nature of the relationships under study it is not possible to say how fine a system of classification is needed for a problem. However, the extent to which one loses precision by categorizing a numerical variable into a set of classifications is usually exaggerated. If, for instance, a predictor has a linear relationship with some dependent variable, accounting for some M percent of its variance, then dummy variables representing as few as five subclasses of the explanatory variable will account for ninety-five percent of that potential M percent, and ten subclasses will account for ninety-nine percent of the total possible.[7] And if in fact the relationship is not linear, a set of dummy variables may easily account for *more* of the total variance than a linear regression using the full numerical detail.

An additional advantage of dummy variables is that they allow flexible handling of missing information. A separate dummy variable accounts for the "not ascertained" cases of each classification or interval code. This saves all the other information available about these cases, and even indicates whether there is something peculiar about those who did not answer a particular question.

Note that the use of dummy variables as discussed above is as *predictors*. Economists are likely to use psychological or sociological variables as predictors. When the dependent variable is a dummy variable, other problems arise. Yet it *is* possible to have sets of dummy variables on both sides of an equation, as we see below when discussing canonical correlation.

Cumulative Dummy Variables: Where the classes represent an ordered scale, then it is possible to define a set of dummy variables representing "this level or less."[8] For instance, with education one could define the following variables:

Variable	Value = 1 if:	Years
X1	Less than 5 years of education	(0-4)
X2	Less than 9 years of education	(0-4 + 5-8)
X3	Less than 12 years of education	(0-4 + 5-8 + 9-11)
X4	Less than 16 years of education	(0-4 + 5-8 + 9-11 + 12-15)
X5	Not college graduate	(16 or more, no degree, or less)
X6	No advanced degree	(College graduate or less)
X7	Advanced degree or less	Everyone

Anyone coded 1 for variable X7 would also be coded 1 for variables X1 through X6, i.e. the variables form a Guttman scale.

Algebraically the results can be translated back into the other kind of dummy variables where each one represents a mutually exclusive group (level of education), though the intercorrelations among the dummy variables are higher and positive, where with the exclusive dummies they are smaller and negative.

One might think that the differences between the incremental dummies would be better indicators of the marginal effects of moving to the next step, but in fact they would seem to mask the true marginal effect. Suppose, for instance that the true effects of each level of education were as given in the first column of the table below. If the population were evenly spread, twenty percent in each group, then the cumulative coefficients would be as given in the second column, and the differences would understate the true payoff to additional education:

Educational Achievement	Income Coefficient (adjusted by regression)	Income Coefficient (for that level or less)	Income Coefficient (for that level or more)
0-6 grades	$ 2,000	$2,000	$ 6,000
7-11 grades	4,000	3,000	7,000
High school (12)	6,000	4,000	8,000
Some college	8,000	5,000	9,000
College degree	10,000	6,000	10,000

The "cumulative" coefficients are not themselves marginal payoffs to more education, nor are their first differences.

If the cumulation were defined the other way, so much education or *more*, the marginal payoffs would still be underestimated, except under the argument that the advantage of each level should include the option value of allowing further education. That is, finishing the first level has a value which includes the value of going on times the probability of doing so. It is not a convincing argument.

Hence, even though the regression coefficients and the calculated standard errors are a mathematical translation of those with the usual dummy variables, the data are in less usable form. Indeed, one might easily decide that the differences were not significant, as Rogers' dissertation seemed to do.

We return to a more detailed consideration of dummy (dichotomous) variables in regression later in this chapter.

Introduction of Measures of Price: A technique of special interest to economists is the introduction of data about prices with the purposes of converting variables which are measures of quantity into new variables which are measures of value. The survey may be used to provide the measures of quantity while other sources may provide the measures of price. For example, Houthakker and Haldi used published price data on cars to develop measures of households' inventories and investments.[9] The same technique has been used for years in the Surveys of Consumer Finances. Its usefulness arises from the added information gained. For example, one knows more about a family's situation if he knows that its stock of cars is worth $100 than if he knows only that it posseses one car.

The procedure requires a known set of prices which can be mapped into the data about quantities. The goods in question may have values which vary depending on their characteristics, e.g. the make, year, model, body style, and equipment of a car. The survey must contain information about the commodity which corresponds at least approximately to the data required to enter the price list. Inaccuracies in the price information, of course, will be reflected in the newly calculated variables and reduce correlations. Systematic variations in prices not taken into account can introduce systematic error in these variables. One must also be clear that it is market price he wants, not use value.

The possibilities of this type of procedure are best, therefore, when complete information about prices is published and the published prices are the actual prices. Also, the simpler the price structure, the easier the estimation. Price data for airline tickets, for example, meet the criteria of publication and close agreement between published and actual prices. To estimate the cost of particular trips, however, would present problems arising from the need to distinguish among classes of service and various types of special fares as they may apply to particular origins and destinations. In some situations one might ask about expenditures, and use price information to estimate quantities.

For goods and services subject to wide variations in price from customer to customer, from time to time, from place to place, and the like, an investigator may prefer to obtain his price data by developing questions to obtain it directly from the respondent. Alternatively, he may proceed by obtaining information about prices both from the interview and from outside sources.

Variables Representing an Individual's Subgroup: Another kind of variable often generated after the data are assembled, represents the mean of some characteristic measured over some subgroup to which the individual belongs. The rent level of his area, if there are large enough sample clusters to allow its estimation, is an example, or one might want to know the average value of cars owned by people in a person's age, education, income, and city size group, and each individual's deviation from that group average. Sometimes outside data about the subgroup may be available, e.g. median income in the county.

Panel Variables Representing Change versus Level: With reinterviews, possibilities open for generating variables representing change, absolute or relative, in some measure, such as the family income. Since the initial state (in the case of debt, or assets) is important as well as the change, problems arise because of the negative correlation between the two. As we have suggested, one solution is to generate two orthogonal (uncorrelated) variables: the average level (sum of the two measures) and the change (difference).

Scaling

When we have a number of measures each of which may be an imperfect measure of some theoretical construct, we may prefer to combine them rather than rely on any one. And if a set of measures are thought in various combinations to measure several theoretical constructs, we may seek some optimal way of developing several combinations, each uncorrelated with the others. The first problem is generally called scaling, and the second, factor analysis.

Scaling has a long history in psychology and sociology. It will be possible to include here only the bare elements of the subject.[10] The more complex procedures have in common the use of a battery of questions or scale items. There are problems, then, of constructing the individual items, and of selecting the best possible items from those that may be suggested for inclusion in the final scale. There are also problems of how best to combine the information from the items into a single scale.

The earliest of the basic approaches was developed by L. L. Thurstone. The first step in this procedure is to collect a large number of statements about a given subject. Each judge then independently sorts the statements into eleven piles. The piles are to be equal distance apart and to range from most favorable to least favorable. Since there are many judges, it is possible to compute for each item a median rank, and a measure of the dispersion of the assigned rankings, such as the interquartile range. The smaller the dispersion, the better the item. The final scale, then, can be constructed from the twenty or so best items. Respondents then express agreement or disagreement with each item. They should agree only with those in a limited range. The score on the scale for any respondent is the average of the scale values with which he agrees.

This procedure is open to objections. It rests upon the doubtful ability of the judges to perceive equal distance between items. It also rests upon the assumption that respondents and judges have the same frame of reference. Empirically it has been shown that some respondents when given Thurstone scales agree with statements that have widely different scale values. In such situations the meaning of average scores is doubtful.[11]

A second basic type of scaling procedure was originally developed by Likert and is now widely used. People are asked to respond to each item, not simply by agreeing or disagreeing, but by indicating the degree of agreement or disagreement. Typically, five steps are given between extreme agreement and extreme disagreement. No judges are used. In the development of a scale, people similar to the eventual respondents are the subjects.

The method of combining items is to add the scores for the items without regard to whether one item may appear to be different from another. A score of +1 may be assigned to extreme agreement, and +5 to extreme disagreement, on any item. Such scores are summed to give a total score for the test. The procedure is fast and simple.

The items used in the test may be selected from all items suggested for inclusion on the basis of correlation analysis. The criterion may be selection to yield high intercorrelation among the items. Alternatively, items with low intercorrelation with each other but high correlation with an outside criterion may be selected.[12]

These procedures remove some of the disadvantages of Thurstone scales, but also are by no means ideal. There is an arbitrary element in the system of weighting. The criterion of a high degree of agreement among items is imperfect in view of the possibility that the items may differ in their position on some underlying continuum. Again, the items may indeed be correlated, but this correlation is not in itself enough to establish that they belong on the same underlying continuum.

A third type of scale has been developed by Guttman. Guttman's scalogram analysis was developed to deal especially with the problem of unidimensionality.[13] He seeks to use the data obtained from a group of respondents to solve the two problems of ordering the items and ordering the respondents. The test of unidimensionality is whether the answers given by respondents do in fact order themselves systematically. Ideally, when the work is complete, respondents at a given scale position will give favorable replies to all statements up to that position and unfavorable replies to all statements farther along the continuum than their position. In preparing a test, items are selected which tend to fit into such a pattern. Stress is laid on achieving a high "coefficient of reproducibility." This coefficient is the proportion of responses to items which can be predicted correctly knowing the scale position of the respondents. The difficulty with this coefficient is that it tends to look too good—it can seldom fall below .80 and is affected by extreme marginals or large numbers of items.

In the development of a Guttman scale the procedure is to prepare a matrix with a column for each item and a row for each respondent. The entry in each cell may be a + or - sign, depending on whether that individual responded positively to that item. The analyst then rearranges the rows in optimal order, and also the columns in optimal order, optimal order being defined as that which yields the highest coefficient of reproducibility. It is possible, of course, that there is no arrangement which will produce a higher coefficient than should be attributed to chance. One would expect that result either if the items do not belong on a single continuum or if the respondents have no attitude on the topic.

There has been a considerable amount of attention to the question of circumstances in which a high coefficient of reproducibility might be achieved but the procedure might still be unsatisfactory, and Guttman has suggested taking into account additional considerations as well as the value of the coefficient. It is particularly desirable that some items which divide the population about evenly should be included instead of just items which almost everyone accepts or rejects. Also, the *pattern* of errors should be random and not systematic.

Guttman further proposes that intensity of feeling should be asked for each item. He suggests that a natural zero point on the scale may appear where intensity of feeling is low. The scale itself is an ordinal scale.

This procedure also has limitations. It may prove difficult to construct items which will "scale" satisfactorily unless the items are very similar. One approaches a procedure which may not be so very different from the Likert-type technique of asking people to place themselves in one of five categories from "agree strongly" to "disagree strongly" with a single statement.

It is by no means certain that people will feel strongly about something only if they hold an extreme position. A person might believe passionately that a middle position was correct. In such a situation no zero point could be discovered by Guttman's procedures.

The procedures reduce but do not eliminate the subjective judgment of the investigator. The rearrangement of rows and columns and the choice of items for elimination in the preparation of the test might be done differently by different researchers. It is possible that a scale will be satisfactory for one type of respondent but unsatisfactory for other respondents at another time or place or from a different socio-economic category.

An example of a Guttman scale comes from replies to a question we ask about whether it is all right for someone "like yourself" to borrow money for each of several purposes: eighty percent thought it was all right to borrow to cover illness expenses, seventy-seven percent to finance educational expenses, sixty-five percent to finance purchase of a car, fifty-two percent to finance the purchase of furniture, forty-three percent to pay piled up bills, forty percent to cover living expenses when income is cut, nine percent to cover vacation expenses, and four percent to finance purchases of a fur coat or jewelry.

When such a wide differentiation appears, the problem is, is there anyone who would approve of credit for jewelry but not for illness? There are very few. The coefficient of reproducibility indicates essentially how many people violate the proper ordering of a scale like this. But one must remember that this coefficient can get fairly high, when there is still a fairly bad scaling.

Scaling techniques are universally based on the interrelations among the components or potential components, usually with the imposition of assumptions of additivity and linearity. This is acceptable when the new variable is to be used as description (a measure of intelligence) or as the dependent variable in analysis. But where the new variable is to be used as an explanatory variable, there are problems:

1. The components may not operate additively, but in some more complex fashion.
2. Regardless how they are correlated with one another, the components may have opposite effects on the dependent variable. Combining two factors positively correlated with one another, but with opposite effects on the dependent variable, will produce a scale or index which will have no effect at all.

Of course, combining two factors negatively correlated with one another but both with positive effects on a dependent variable, will also produce an index with no apparent effect on the dependent variable.

A simple test should be considered prior to any elaborate scaling operations of an explanatory variable: First examine the gross relationship of each element with the dependent variable to be sure its effect is in the expected direction. Then build a simple additive scale by adding one to a sum for each component element that is positive. This produces an index ranging from zero for those who give positive responses to none of the items to a number equal to the number of items.

If one then looks at the *shape* of the relationship of this new index or scale with the dependent variable, one can tell whether the additivity assumption is valid.

1. If the relationship is linear, then the components are probably additive. Whether they occur in an ordered sequence can only be tested by some Guttman-like procedure, but may not be crucial anyway.
2. If the relationship is convex from above, then the components are probably substitutes for one another, any two or three of them

produce the effect. In this case it makes sense to ask whether it is the same two or three—which is not the same as asking whether a Guttman scale exists, for effects only of a subset could exist without any ordering of the items.

3. If the relationship is concave from above, then the components are complementary—it takes all or nearly all of them before any effect appears.

A final consideration is that, provided one combines items which are not negatively correlated with one another, and seem to have effects on the dependent variable in the same direction, the weighting of the components will make very little real difference. If any of them have an effect, the weighted sum will have an effect. One might do better to think of indexes or scales as rapid ways of testing whether *any* of a set of items have any impact, returning to the details only if there is some indication that it will be useful.

On the other hand, if the problem is to develop a *dependent* variable to be explained, then a great deal more attention may have to be paid to its proper scaling.

The possible procedures in developing scales are by no means limited to those discussed above. An example of a sophisticated approach to the subject is Coombs' Unfolding Technique.[14] This method, unlike Guttman's scalogram, is designed to produce information about the *distance* between scale positions as well as an ordering of the positions. It is included here for its intrinsic interest although it has been rarely if ever used by economists. The method will be described in two stages: data collection and analysis.

The underlying hypothesis, in simple uses of the approach, is that there is a single underlying continuum and that there are, say, five stimuli ranged along it, probably at unequal distances from one another. We may think of people as each having a unique preferred position on this continuum, which probably will not exactly coincide with that represented by any stimulus. Still, each person will feel that the stimuli differ in how closely they are to his true feelings. The problem is to find how the five are arranged on the *true* scale.

There are different tasks which we can ask people to perform for us. We might ask, simply, that each person tell us the statement closest to his own position. We might ask for the two closest statements, or the three closest. The unfolding technique requires that we ask him both to select and to rank them according to how close they are to his position. If there were five items, in effect we have asked the respondent to omit two and order the others. Coombs calls this method "Order 3." (We might have asked the respondent to "Order 4," but here we restrict attention to the simpler task.)

The crucial point about this method is that the information thus collected includes information about metric relations—about distances on the underlying continuum—as well as about rank order. We may observe, for example, that some people pick position BCA but nobody picks BCD.

The implication is that the distance between A and the region in which B is first choice and C is second choice is less than the distance between D and the region in which B is first choice and C is second choice. On the above scale B is first choice anywhere between 1 and 2. B is first *and* C is second only for a person located between 2 and a point half-way between A and C, indicated by ac. People who pick B and C will always select A rather than D as third choice only if A is closer than D to the BC range.

The rank order of the stimuli to a respondent will depend on the distance they would be from his position if the scale were folded at his exact location. Hence, the name of the procedure, the "unfolding technique."

The important notion is that there is one true but unknown linear ordering of the stimuli. If all individuals accept that ranking, their ranking of the items shows where they are on the scale, but more important, analysis of many individual rankings will reveal what the basic ordering is, and even some of the metric.

The analysis consists, first, in the arrangement of the data in rows and columns as in the Guttman method, except that numbers, 1, 2, or 3, or a blank, appear in the cells for the items rather than + or -. Also as in the Guttman technique, the rows and columns are permuted until a matrix with desirable properties is achieved. These properties Coombs specifies as follows.[15]

1. The entries in the rows (i.e. for each individual) and in each column (i.e. for each stimulus), must be adjacent with no blanks.
2. The entries in the first row and first column must monotonically increase from left to right and top to bottom, respectively.
3. The entries in the last row and last column must monotonically decrease from left to right and from top to bottom, respectively.
4. The entries in all other columns must monotonically decrease and then increase from top to bottom.

The method provides the necessary information for a much more detailed ordering of individuals than is possible if all that is known is their first choices. For example, it distinguishes, among those for whom B is first choice, those who prefer A to C from those who prefer C to A. Thus, the group with B as first choice can be divided. Similar divisions are possible among those who select C or D as first choice. It is unlikely that actual data will satisfy these stringent requirements exactly, and there will be problems of how much deviation from the correct pattern to tolerate. The method calls attention to the individuals with patterns of response which do not fit the general pattern for the group as a whole. The question can be examined whether such individuals are very frequent in some subgroups of the population. One might conclude, for example, that a scale was satisfactory for people with high education but not for people of low education. This conclusion could not be drawn from responses to a simple Likert scale since the data do not contain enough information.

Coombs also suggests an ingenious way of checking whether there is indeed a single underlying continuum on which people find themselves. The trick is to ask people to name the choice the *farthest* from their position. That choice should be at *one end or the other* of the true scale, depending on the individual's position, hence there should be only two choices, representing the two ends, which get all the votes as least preferred. If the choices scatter all over, there is presumably no underlying continuum and one need not bother with unfolding, or scaling.

In building any kind of index, arbitrary or not, there is a question whether to rely on attitude questions or on reported behavior. When people were asked about their attitudes toward new products, and their self perception of whether they use them or not, their answers did not correlate very well with how many of ten specific new products they actually used. In another study nine normative items about task sharing in the family did not correlate well with an index based on actual task sharing. The author concluded that there is considerable deviation between normative definitions and actual behavior of the family studied.[16]

Finally, another way to build a scale is to order how *salient* a particular response is by designing a series of questions which lead into the subject gradually. The individual is then scored on how far one must push him before he responds. One might ask a sequence of questions about whether it was a good idea to have bought bonds in World War II and then mention the fact that price levels have gone up and say, "How about that?" and finally say, "How about common stock?" Then one can use, as an index of awareness of inflation and of the need for hedging against it, the stage in this process where a man says that buying something whose value would go up with the price level (like common stock) would have been a better idea. This gives some notion of how *salient* the notion of hedging against inflation is to the individual and may be a good predictor of whether he is likely to buy stock. However, an old finding in nutritional studies is that if you ask people what is needed for good nutrition they often fail to mention milk first because it is so obvious. So this technique of salience may be misleading in some cases. Another method is to ask for reasons and then say, "Well, which of these is the most important?" In a very large number of cases, it was the second or third reason given that turned out to be the most important by the man's own statement, not the first one.

This introduction to the subject of scaling is far from complete. No attempt has been made to cover all techniques in common use. Such topics as Lazarsfeld's latent structure analysis and the semantic differential have been omitted entirely. The reader is referred to the references cited above.

A brief word may be added in conclusion concerning basic methods of assessing scales. It is common to assess the reliability of a scale by the "split-half" technique. The procedure is to divide the items into two groups, compute scores for each half, and estimate the correlation coefficient. It is especially adapted to scales based on substantial numbers of items which are combined by simple addition of scores. The objection is sometimes made that a low correlation between halves may indicate either unreliability of the test or lack of unidimensionality.

Reliability may also be assessed by repetition. The assumption must be made that the observed changes over time measure the unreliability of the instrument rather than actual changes in the true position of the individuals on the scale. This assumption can best be defended when there is theoretical reason to expect stability and when the time interval is short. For example, psychologists would not expect intelligence to change over short periods.

Validity is sometimes checked against behavior. The behavior may be in the future, so that a measure of attitudes at one date is used to predict subsequent behavior. This type of check is especially relevant when the principal purpose of the attitude measurement is prediction. There is a sense, however, in which it begs the question of the relation of attitudes to behavior. To examine that question, strictly speaking the validation of the measurement of the attitudes should be made independently of the behavior. Otherwise one assumes that the attitude cannot exist unless it predicts behavior.

Factor Analysis: Extensive use has been made in psychology of principal components analysis or factor analysis. There has been some interest in the application of the procedures to problems of interest to economists, but little work actually has been done. The subject will be treated here only briefly.

The method was developed by Hotelling.[17] A systematic discussion of the theory may be found in Anderson, and for an application of the method to an economic problem see Stone.[18]

The purpose of principal components analysis is the compression of information. For example, a psychologist might have information on the replies to a large number of test items by a sample of individuals. He might seek to characterize those persons in terms of a limited number of attributes or factors.

The method begins with the covariance matrix measuring the relationship between each item and every other item. Mathematically, the principal components are the characteristic vectors of the covariance matrix.

The usefulness of statistical procedures for developing principal components is likely to be greatest at an early stage in the development of a field when there is little available theory. When the theory is better developed, an investigator is likely to be able to specify in advance the variables he wishes to measure rather than to discover them as a result of principal components analysis. His problem, then, becomes one of measurement, and he will devote his energies to the construction of variables which he has reason to believe are relevant to his analysis. He will not invent a large number of items more or less at random and later seek to sort them out.

There may be areas of inquiry at an early stage of development, however, with a plethora of measurements believed to be of independent variables. For example, one might have data on accident rates for each of fifty states, and measures of, say sixty characteristics of the states believed to be possible causes of accidents. Principal components analysis might then be considered as one way of compressing the sixty characteristics into a manageable number of variables. There is one difficulty with the technique which may be mentioned. The results will depend on the units in which the initial measurements are expressed. It is possible to make an arbitrary decision to divide each measurement by its own standard deviation and work with data thus standardized. A corresponding arbitrary element will enter the results.

Factor analysis was originally designed not just to economize on variables but to find out whether a large set of items could be broken down into a smaller set of components that had some meaning. For instance, the items in an intelligence test could be analyzed and they might fit into clusters which could then be considered components of intelligence: things like verbal facility, abstract reasoning, mathematical abilities, etc.

What factor analysis really does is to *assume* linear additive combinations. Start with the simple matrix of correlations among a whole set of items. There is no dependent variable and nothing is said about the relations of any of them to a dependent variable. There is then a statistical method by which clusters are identified and a set of weights determined so that a weighted sum of the items in any one cluster, forms a new variable or factor. These weights are called factor loadings. The factors can be derived so that they are uncorrelated with one another. This means that one can regard factor analysis as a method of taking fifty attitudinal items and converting them into three or four new variables that are nicely uncorrelated with one another and easy to put into an analysis to explain something.

There are the same two major difficulties. One is the assumption of additivity in the components of these factors, and the other is that in building them, no attention is paid to the relationships they have with the dependent variable. It is quite possible to have two items which are highly correlated with one another, and end up with large positive weights on one of these factors, but they have opposite effects on the dependent variable. In this case, this factor would have no correlation with the dependent variable since it is made up of two things which have opposite effects, and information is thrown away.

There has been very little use of factor analysis in economic surveys because by the time one collects the basic economic information (which is easy to combine by adding) there is not enough interviewing time left to ask fifty attitudinal questions. Consequently we are more likely to rely on five or ten.

Arbitrary Indexes of Attitudes or Behavior: In many economic studies the legitimate components of some index are relatively obvious and the number of candidates so small, that it is doubtful that elaborate and time-consuming methods of scale construction are justified. In a study of deliberation in purchase decisions, Mueller made use of several indexes created by giving the respondent a point for each of a list of activities, and then created a summary index as the sum of the component indexes.[19]

In a study of a number of aspects of economically adaptive or progressive behaviors, a number of indexes of attitudes or behavior were created, again as arbitrary sums of points given for various forms of behavior or of attitudinal (or self-assessing) responses.[20]

The logical basis of this procedure is partly theoretical and partly empirical. The theoretical basis is an argument, more or less carefully worked out, that the specific items in question are similar, or form a coherent typology or syndrome. There is an assumption that the set of behaviors can be used to predict other things, or can as a set be efficiently predicted, or both.

The empirical basis is that each of the components is related in the same direction to the other variables to which the index is to be related, whether explanatory or dependent, *and* that the components are not negatively correlated with one another. If either of these were in fact violated, the index would not work, that is it would not be easy to explain as a result of other variables, or be useful as a variable in predicting another variable.

It is not, however, necessary that an index combine things which are *strongly* positively correlated with one another. Indeed, if the components are *very* strongly positively correlated, one might use fewer of them, whereas one might very well want to combine into one index a number of statistically unrelated but theoretically similar things. Hence all that is required is that components not be negatively correlated, so that they will not cancel one another out, and that they have effects in the same direction.

A common reason for combining several items is that each one may be relevant, and revealing, for some part of the population, but provide no information for others. Indeed some of the components may actually be *alternatives* where it would be difficult to do both. For instance the husband might get a second job *or* let the wife go to work in the evening while he watched the children. The index, hopefully, contains at least some items relevant to each member of the population. It is a problem, however, to deal with the respondents for whom an item is inappropriate. Ideally, one should assign them the mean value for the rest of the sample. For instance, if a risk avoidance index gave a point for fastening seat belts, what about people with no car, not asked the question? If fifty percent of the car owners fastened their seat belts, the non-owners could be neutralized by giving them half a point. Or one could use even digits by giving two points to those who fastened belts, one point to those with no car, and no points to those with cars who did not fasten their seat belts. (This is the same as giving 0 to the non-owners, and -1 and +1 to the owners who did not or did fasten.) In practice, with digits added for indexes, it is tempting to use the 0, 1, 2 sequence even though 1 is not really the average of the other two groups. In this case the neutralization is not quite precise.

A second problem arises when some components are felt to be more important than others. Here again, it is possible to assign them larger weights in an index, remembering that the weighting of any index has relatively little effect.

Such indexes are, of course, arbitrary, and no better than the judgment that went into their composition. And it is difficult to describe them briefly without seeming to imply a great deal more theory than one wants.

An important justification for such arbitrary indexes, however, is their economy and efficiency. If the components are not negatively correlated with one another, and have effects on the dependent variable in the same direction, then either the index helps predict the dependent variable or it does not. If it does not, we can be reasonably sure that *none* of its components would have much predictive value separately. If it does have some effect, then we can pursue it further as we suggested earlier:

Treat the index as a set of dummy variables, and see whether its effect is linear or not. If it is linear, then presumably the components are operating additively, and one may only want to look at them separately, to sort out which ones are most useful. One might then, for instance, put each component into a regression as a separate dummy variable.

But if the effect is non-linear, it may mean that the components operate either as substitutes or in complementary fashion accentuating one another. If the relationship is concave from the top, the index having little effect until it reaches substantial values, then the implication is that it takes all the components or a large set of them, to have any effect, that is that they operate multiplicatively. If it is convex from the top, the implication is that any one or two of the items are enough to produce an effect, the others adding little, i.e. that the components are substitutes for one another. In any case, further decomposition of the index would then seem worth while, but in the non-linear case, only with techniques which allow for interaction effects now known to exist.

Frequently however, indexes made up either of attitudes, or of self-reports, or of supposedly revealing behavior, do not predict the dependent variable at all, and the rapid creation and use of a relatively arbitrary index serves to eliminate a whole set of hypotheses quickly and efficiently.

There is, of course, a problem if one wants to assess the relative importance of a number of indexes and other explanatory variables by looking at their contribution to reduction in the unexplained variance of some dependent variable. Some variables may be measured better than others. One might think, for instance, that if he had used factor analysis or some other technique to build an index, it might have explained more of the variance. This problem exists even in comparing simple variables for their relative power, of course. And again it is possible to exaggerate its importance. A variable or an index that is really important in explaining behavior, will show through some relatively bad measurement errors.

Estimation of Relationships

Given a set of measured variables, loosely connected with some theoretical constructs, how do we proceed with the analysis?

The process is really a search for structure of relations among the measured variables, and an interpretation in terms of the theoretical constructs that they represent. There may be situations where one should follow the conventional wisdom: embody the explanatory hypotheses in a model and test it, but we submit that this is rare. There are usually a substantial number of competing hypotheses, even at the theoretical construct level, and when we move to the measured variables, adding uncertainty about what represents what, the credibility of any one *a priori* model is rather low, and the need for showing that it is more credible than a number of competing alternatives is high.

We say this in the face of a burgeoning literature in both econometrics and in sociology that works out elaborate procedures for measuring relations or testing hypotheses, both because of the relatively primitive state of our knowledge and theory about human behavior, and because of the demands that the assumptions of these methods put on the data and the theory. They nearly all require at least some of the following assumptions:

> Sampling and measurement errors reasonably small, uncorrelated, normally distributed, and without too heterogeneous variances
>
> Measurability of variables (no scaling problems)
>
> Linearity of effects
>
> Additivity of effects (or very simple easily represented cross-product effects)
>
> Ability to specify causal directions
>
> A recursive system

All the relevant variables are included
The system is just identified.

Of course the last two compete with one another, and one is tempted to leave out variables or invent some in order to make the system tractable. Recently some have suggested checking for inconsistency of the separate estimates in an over-identified system as an indication of distortions caused by different and imperfect proxies for the real variables. (See Costner, Note 73.) It is doubtful that survey data have the characteristics, particularly the precision, to hold up the elaborate structures of many of these procedures.

Indeed, it is not obvious that the least-squares criterion on which *all* the statistical procedures are based, is appropriate. Are errors important in proportion to their square? Errors in survey data are often not so much normally distributed as rectangular—a large error being about as likely as a small one, say from misplacing a decimal. And the larger the discrepancy, the more likely that there is some conceptual difficulty or misunderstanding, such as mixing up a man's business affairs with his household accounts.

All this is not to say that one is not to use whatever theory he can, and whatever reasonable assumptions will make things easier. Whenever there are clear one-way causal directions or intermediate stages in the causal process, a basic structural model must take account of them. But within those broad bounds, we are really searching for better evidence about the structure of relationships, and about which variables really account for the variation in others. And beyond that we are attempting to interpret this structure and these relationships in terms of relationships among the theoretical constructs for which the measured variables serve as proxies.

Analysis of One Dependent Variable with One Level of Explanatory Variables

A great deal of analysis can be systematically organized and done in terms of what it is that is being described, explained, evaluated, or potentially predicted. Conversely, it is not usually efficient to organize research or analysis around an *explanatory* variable. Anything that is learned about one explanatory variable must be learned separately for each dependent variable, and in a multivariate context if we are to be sure it is not spurious.

The first step, often overlooked in the analyst's haste to get this multivariate analysis done, is to examine the distribution of the dependent variable. Two-way tables against the more important explanatory variables will reveal whether there are problems. The two main problems are kurtosis and heterogeneous variance. Skewness is less of a problem, and if it appears can usually be handled by some transformation, or even ignored. But extreme cases (leptokursis) play havoc with any least squares analysis.

Extreme cases should be examined in detail. They may be errors, for the distribution of errors made in processing data is not a normal distribution—very large errors are as likely as small ones. Extreme values may represent conceptual or measurement difficulties which would justify their elimination from the sample, or truncation to some large but not extremely large value. Or, one may take the square root or the log of the dependent variable, if there are no zeros or negative numbers.

Even a reasonably well-distributed dependent variable might have widely different variances in different parts of the population. In practice this has not turned out to be much of a problem, and in any case it affects significance tests most, parameter estimates somewhat, and analysis of variance (which explanatory variables account for the most variance) least of all. G.E.P. Box uses the term "robustness" for a procedure which is not badly affected by departures from its assumptions. He refers to tests for homogeneity of variance as rather like putting to sea in a rowboat to see whether it is safe for an ocean liner to set sail.[21]

Most distributional problems with the dependent variable can be located by inspection of tables. This does mean that even if the variable is numerical, a categorical (bracket) code should be created in order to investigate its distribution, overall, and in tables against the main explanatory factors.

The layout and labeling of tables is a matter of importance if readers are to see the results easily and clearly. Any table is a distribution of some kind of *unit* (families) according to some *dependent variable* (food expenditures per person) within subgroups classified by some *explanatory characteristic* (family size, income etc.), for the whole *sample* or some subpopulation thereof. Perhaps the best procedure, since the unit and often the subpopulation remain constant over many tables, is to put the variable of interest, and the classifying variable in the title, and the unit and subpopulation in the subtitle: Food Expenditures Per Person by Family Size (For Urban Families).

Such a convention, combined with consistency in the words used to label each variable, will be a great help to everyone concerned. It is also useful to have tables right-side-up on the page, not turned sideways, so that the percentages add to 100 percent at the bottom, and the number of cases is always easily found below the row of 100 percent's. The stability of a percentage depends on the number of cases on which it is based, so those numbers should be easily available. Sometimes where the same classifying variables are used many times and for the same sample, the frequencies can be relegated to an appendix.

A final convention, irritating to purists but nonetheless necessary, is to "fudge" the figures so that the percentages in each column add to 100 percent or 100.0 percent. (It is doubtful that in most surveys, carrying data beyond the nearest percentage is justified except where there is a large inappropriate group and someone may want to repercentagize the table omitting them.) The general rule is to force up, or down as necessary, the percentage closest to xx.50, but

where several are very close, one may prefer to shift the larger of the two percentages so that the *relative* error is kept small.

The purposes of examining a table are to observe the shape of the distribution of the dependent variable, and whether that shape persists in subgroups, and
second to see whether there is an association between the classifying variable
(family size) and the dependent variable (food expenditure per person). If the
dependent variable is reasonably well distributed, then one can move to using its
average, or "whether the respondent is in a selected set of subclasses" as a variable, vastly simplifying the subsequent analysis. It is much easier to present a
table of *average* food expenditure per person for families classified jointly by
both income and family size, than to present the full distribution.

But there may also be substantive interest in the degree of association in
the cross-classifications. It should be possible to state in a single sentence what a
table shows, and sometimes to state in a second sentence something which indicates the magnitude of the relationship. First, the table is scanned to find the division of just two classes of the explanatory characteristic for which the differences in the dependent variable are the greatest, then again to find the level of
the dependent variable at which the proportions differ the most. For instance,
one might find that the greatest difference in food expenditure per person was
between single person families (who eat out a lot) and all other families:

Weekly Expenditure Per Person by Family Size
(For All Families)

Food Expenditure Per Person Per Week	Actual		Cumulative		
	Single Persons	Families of Two or More	Single Persons	Families of Two or More	Difference
Under $2.00	5	10	5	10	5
$2.00-3.99	5	15	10	25	15
$4.00-5.99	5	25	15	50	35
$6.00-7.99	10	15	25	65	40
$8.00-9.99	10	10	35	75	40
$10.00-11.99	15	10	50	85	35
$12.00-13.99	25	5	75	90	15
$14.00-15.99	15	5	90	95	5
$16.00 and over	10	5	100	100	0
	100	100			
Number of cases	200	1800			

The difference can then be stated simply as follows: Three-fourths of the single people spend eight dollars a week or more on food, but only a little more than a third of the families of two or more spend that much.

Since a search took place for the largest difference in such a pair of percentages, one cannot simply apply a significance test to the difference between two percentages. And since in practice one first selects the two subclasses with the maximum difference in cumulative percentages, even the Kolmogorov-Smirnov test is not quite appropriate, though it is better.[22]

Actually it is not significance that matters, but importance (how much does it matter?), and the investigator's problem is really which classifying variable produces the greatest differences in the dependent variable. For this purpose, a comparison of the differences in cumulative percentages is a fast approximation.

There is a great deal of discussion in the literature about more sophisticated measures of association for cross-classifications. Where the two "variables" or characteristics have natural ordering, and one expects a monotonic relationship, then various kinds of rank correlation coefficients are appropriate, the best probably being Kendall's Tau beta.[23]

Kruskal's Gamma, and Kendall's three Tau measures of rank correlation are all based on a kind of trick: one considers *all possible pairs,* and asks which of them are concordant with the notion of a positive association, which discordant, and which are tied on X or Y or both. A simple diagram will show how these are computed:

The small letters represent proportion of the table total in that cell:

	X_1	X_2	X_3
Y_1	a	b	c
Y_2	d	e	f

Proportion concordant: $a(e + f) + b(f) = P$ $\quad\begin{cases} \text{i.e., number of pairs where if second is} \\ \text{higher X class, then also higher Y class.} \end{cases}$

Proportion discordant: $c(d + e) + b(d) = Q$

Proportion tied on X: $ad + be + cf = Xo$ $\quad$ Pairs where X is same.

Proportion tied on Y: $a(b + c) + bc + d(e + f) + ef = Yo$

Proportion tied on both $1/2 [a(a - 1) + b(b - 1) + c(c - 1) + d(d - 1) + e(e - 1) + f(f - 1)]$

$$\text{Gamma} = \frac{P - Q}{P + Q} \qquad \text{Tau}_\alpha = \frac{P - Q}{n\frac{(n - 1)}{2}} \qquad \text{Tau}_\beta = \frac{P - Q}{\sqrt{(P + Q + Xo)\,(P - Q + Yo)}}$$

$$\text{Tau}_y = P - Q\,\frac{2n}{n^2\,(m - 1)} \qquad \begin{cases} \text{where } m = \text{number of rows or columns,} \\ \text{whichever is smaller} \end{cases}$$

It is clear that Tau gamma is intended to deal with cases where one or the other characteristic has very few classes, that Tau alpha is to deal with very small samples, and that Tau beta, which is intended to deal with tied rankings, is probably the most appropriate to use with survey data. It is probably better than

Gamma since there can be vast differences in the number of ties in different cross-classifications.

Where one does not want to assume order and a monotonic relationship, the problem becomes more complicated, and the best judgment is that the method of choice depends on what you want to do.[24]

The most commonly used measure in the past has been chi-square, the sum of squared deviations of actual from expected frequencies divided by the sum of expected frequencies, but it has a number of disabilities, including instability when frequencies get small. Cramer proposed a measure "V" which adjusts for this: $V = X^2/N$ divided by R-1 or C-1 whichever is smaller.[24]

As another example of difficulty, there is Kruskal's Lambda, which is based on the relative reduction in the probability of predicting wrong a single case selected at random. If one knows only the overall distribution, one has to predict the modal value, which may contain m% of the cases, and has a probability of being wrong of (100-m)/100. If one knows which subgroup on some explanatory characteristic the individual is in, then one uses the modal value of the dependent characteristic for that subgroup. The sum of the fractions of the total sample in those modal subgroups, $\Sigma m_i n_i$ may be greater than m (it can never be smaller), and the gain is measured by $\Sigma m_i n_i - m/100 - m$, the increase in the probability of a correct guess, as a fraction of the original probability of a wrong guess. But sometimes even when there is a clear association the modal group is the same for each classifying group. For instance, the modal hourly earning rate is the same for whites and blacks in the United States, yet the distributions are skewed in opposite directions. Lambda would be zero, when there is clearly an association because the focus on predicting a single case is not proper. We want to know the error in predicting a random sample of cases. The stochastic element must be preserved. In fact, for most purposes where it is the predictive *power* that is wanted, the ideal measure would seem to be the size of a canonical correlation coefficient, treating the subclasses of the two classifications as a set of dichotomous (dummy) variables on both sides of an equation. (Canonical correlation estimates the coefficients of the variables on both sides such as to maximize the correlation between the two weighted indexes. It is not the coefficients that matter, but the ability to predict one distribution [set of coefficients] from the other distribution [set of coefficients].) One article has actually presented such a set of canonical correlation coefficients among the pairs of the explanatory characteristics used in its analysis as a guide for the readers as to the extent to which the explanatory power of one might be imbedded in another, but more recently, it turns out that Cramers V is identical in the limit (for large samples) with the mean square of all the canonical correlations.[25]

This means that the computational problems are simpler, since Cramer's V is based on a chi-square computation, whereas the calculation of a whole series of canonical correlations (each orthogonal to the rest) is quite a task. (Canonical correlations are computed sequentially so long as one more orthogonal set of co-efficients adds anything, much the way factor analysis proceeds to weaker and weaker factors.)

Limited Dependent Variables: Any truly multivariate analysis must necessarily compress the dependent variable to a number, though it may take only the values 1 and 0. For example, a household owns its home, or it does not. It may be a qualitative variable which can assume one of only three or more values. For example, workers in a certain area may be able to make the journey to work by car, bus, or train, but no other method of transportation may be possible. It may be a variable which has the value 0 for a large segment of the population, but may take any of a wide range of values for the remainder. For example, value of owned homes is 0 for non-owners but for owners may take any of a large number of values. It is, indeed, about as common to work with such dependent variables in survey analysis as with variables which are normally distributed, or nearly so. The classical normal linear regression model, however, assumes that the distribution of the error term is homoscedastic. This assumption is clearly violated when y can no longer take on any value. Questions arise as to what are the most appropriate statistical procedures in such circumstances.[26]

The most widely used method with a dichotomous dependent variable is to proceed as in an ordinary regression analysis. The calculated value of y is treated as a conditional probability, and the regression equation is referred to as a linear probability function. Thus, the predicted score on the dependent variable, for individuals with a particular set of scores on the independent variables, might be, say, .75. The interpretation would be that 75 out of 100 such individuals would be expected to have a score of 1 on the dependent variable, and the remaining 25, a score of 0. It is safest if the proportions for most subgroups are between .20 and .80 where departures from normality of subgroup proportions are least.

This procedure is also open to the objection that some of the predicted scores, hopefully only a few, may fall outside the range from 0 to 1. Probabilities of less than 0 or more than 1 are embarrassing. To see how this situation can arise, consider the following diagram, which is a graph of a possible sample of actual observations with the straight line of best fit. (We assume that the independent variable is continuous. It might be income.)

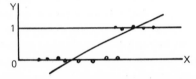

All the observed points necessarily fall on either the horizontal axis or the line parallel to it corresponding to y = 1. The regression line is very likely to intersect both of the "railroad tracks." Hence, there will be values of X for which the predicted value of y is negative or larger than 1.

One method of dealing with this difficulty has been proposed by Orcutt. He develops a transformation from expected values to probability estimates. The method is designed essentially to plot the average expected proportion who have a characteristic against the average observed proportion. The results may appear somewhat as follows:

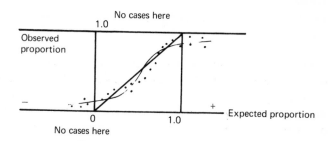

We would expect the straight line of best fit to be a ray from the origin with a slope of forty-five degrees. The observed proportions, however, may differ systematically from the expected proportions, since the latter can be less than 0 or greater than 1.0. These discrepancies can be computed by grouping the sample observations according to the expected proportion, computed from the regression equation (or related technique), and calculating the observed proportion for each group these formed. (Alternatively, if the residuals are computed for each sample observation, the sum of the residuals can be computed for each of the groups.) If the departure from linearity is systematic, as in the above graph, an appropriate S-shaped curve can be fitted.[27] Predictions, then, can be made on the basis of the expected proportion as adjusted. Note that this method will not lead to any adjustment in the regression coefficients, which also retain their usual interpretation. Even when there is no intention to adjust the predicted values, the procedure may be enlightening as to the quality of the fit of the linear equation.

There are other approaches to the problem which introduce the transformations earlier in the calculations and lead to different equations to estimate the relationship. Two such methods are the use of probits and logits.

The probit method has a long history in biological research. It has been discussed in detail by D. J. Finney.[28] It has been used in studies of the effects of insecticides, where it is known that a sufficiently large dose of poison will kill all of a batch of insects and it is desired to estimate the percentage kill for different doses. Interest attaches both to the *median* effective dose, that is, the dose that will kill half the insects, and to the *variance* of the resistance to the poison. The method involves the transformation of percentages into probits, which are based

on the standard normal cumulative distribution. Instead of a linear relation between the concentration of the poison and the percentage kill, the transformation leads to a linear relation between the concentration of the poison and the
probit, which in effect is equivalent to fitting a S-shaped curve to the raw data
rather than a straight line. The probit of a proportion, P, is defined as the
abscissa which corresponds to the probability, P, in a cumulative normal distribution with mean 5 and variance 1. It is y where:

$$P = \frac{1}{\sqrt{2\pi}} \int_{-\infty}^{y-5} e^{-1/2\mu^2 d\mu}$$

The logic of the method may be sketched by outlining the graphic procedure described by Finney. The first step is to assemble the basic data, which
include the percentage kill for each dose. The percentages are then converted to
probits, using tables which have been calculated and published for the convenience of those using the method. The probits are plotted against the dose. (Actually, the log of the dose is ordinarily used.) A straight line then may be drawn to
fit the points as plotted. It is possible to estimate graphically the slope of the
line and other measures as desired, such as the dosage at which y = 5, corresponding to a fifty percent kill. It should be mentioned that the procedures for calculation require iterative methods of estimating the probits corresponding to each
dose. For a more complete account including the statistical theory which under-
lies the method and computational procedures to obtain more exact results the
reader is referred to Finney.

The statistical theory underlying probit analysis is based on maximum likelihood. Berkson has advocated the use of the logistic function rather than the in-
tegral of the normal curve, and the least squares criterion rather than maximum
likelihood.[29] The logistic curve will also produce an S-shaped relation between
the dose and the mortality rate. Berkson proposes that for each dose the logit
should be evaluated, i.e. the natural logarithm of the percentage kill. He then fits
a straight line by least squares to estimate the relation between the dose and the
logit of the mortality. Each observation is weighted in the calculation by a factor
$W_i = N_i P_i Q_i$, where N_i is the number of insects in batch i, P_i is the proportion
killed, and $Q_i = 1 - P_i$. The result is a close approximation to a least squares solution of the logistic function, $Q = \frac{1}{1 + e^{a-bx}}$, where Q is the estimated mortality,
and a-bx is the equation of the line of relationship. A closer approximation can
be obtained by successive approximations. Berkson compares results from fitting
probits and the logistic curve for several studies, and shows that the findings are
similar.

Warner has compared results from calculations using several different methods applied to the problem of choice of mode for the journey to work, and Theil

has proposed and illustrated the use of logit specifications with an information-theory interpretation.

Theil has pointed out the nice transformation provided by the natural log of the odds (that is, of p/1-p). It approaches minus infinity as p approaches 0, and it approaches positive infinity as p approaches 1. (One must be dealing with proportions or probabilities, of course.)

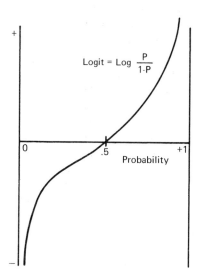

Theil then suggests that the measure of explanatory power be the "average conditional entropy," a concept from information theory, defined as minus the log of the probability, weighted by the probability of being in that row or column, summed over the marginal distribution of probabilities.

Warner recommends the use of the function:

$$Pn(X) = E^{L(X,N)}/(1+e^{L(X,N)})$$

Where Pn (X)   is the probability that an observation at X from a sample of size N is from population 1, X being an explanatory row vector;

and   L (X,N)   is a function which may be estimated with a limited amount of computation, given the results of the usual calculation of a linear probability function.

This approach is much easier from a computational point of view than the use of logits or probits since the solution is reached without procedures requiring iteration. The estimated probability approaches zero as $e^{L(X,N)}$ becomes small, and approaches one as that expression becomes large.

Work has been done by Tobin on the problem of how to handle in one calculation the analysis of mixed dependent variables of the class represented by the value of owned homes. He proposes a combination of probit analysis and multiple regression analysis.[31] Most analysts have approached this problem by splitting it into two separate problems, and analyzing, first, the factors which determine whether a unit does or does not own its home (or whatever the dichotomy may be), and second, the factors which determine for owners the value of the home. More widespread use of Tobin's approach may follow the increasing availability of high speed computers with large capacities and the development of appropriate software. But the choice also depends on which is the appropriate model—are the factors leading to home ownership different from those which determine house value for owners?

Discriminant Analysis: To this point in the discussion we have emphasized the approach to limited dependent variables through regression analysis. An alternative approach to the problem is through discriminant analysis. The logic of discriminant analysis is quite different but the calculations are the same. The starting point is the problem of assigning individuals to categories on the basis of their characteristics. In regression analysis the independent variables are regarded as fixed, while the dependent variable is regarded as fixed in discriminant analysis.

The procedures in discriminant analysis are developed on the basis of standards of good classification. The statistician seeks to make as few errors as possible. He may take into account the cost of different errors, as well as the number of errors, and seek to minimize the cost of misclassification.[32] Anderson's example of a discriminant problem is the selection of students for a college with a limited number of openings. There may be a battery of tests administered to each prospective student. The problem is to sort the prospects into two groups, those who will complete college training successfully and those who will not. We may note that the two possible errors of misclassification need not be evaluated as equally costly. That is, the college administration might not be concerned about rejecting applicants who should have been admitted, arguing that they could go elsewhere, but it might wish to be quite sure to accept only applicants who would succeed.

It is a noteworthy result that the linear discriminant function which minimizes the errors of classification is proportional to the function which is the result of application of the method of least squares, that is the statistical results are the same as regression with a 1-0 dependent variable.[33]

Discriminant analysis has been extended to cover the situation in which there are more than two possible values of the dependent variable. Regression analysis is not able to handle this situation except when the dependent variable is an interval scale. The problem of classifying individuals into one of three or more groups has been discussed in detail by Rao, who includes examples drawn from biometrics.[34] The procedures have been little used in economics, but would seem to be of potential value for survey data when the dependent variable is essentially a system of classification, a nominal scale.

Since the method is not in general use the logic of the procedures for the three category problem will be described briefly. (For a complete discussion, see Rao or Anderson.) The method requires calculation of the discriminant functions for any two pairs of categories. If the categories are A, B, and C, the function might be calculated for A vs. B, and for A vs. C. An indefinite number of separate measurements of characteristics for each individual may be available for use in these equations. Let X and Y, respectively, be the discriminant scores obtained from these equations.

Using these X and Y scores it is possible to define three regions whose boundaries are defined in terms of values of X and Y, as in the sketch below.

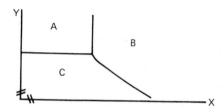

The boundary between A and B is based on scores on X; the boundary between A and C, on scores on Y; between B and C, on scores on X plus Y. Specifically, the average of the mean score on X for groups A and B is the boundary between A and B, and similarly for the other boundaries. It is also of interest to plot on the diagram the point representing the mean X and mean Y for members of category A, and similarly for the other categories.

This approach has been extended to allow for calculation of the boundaries of doubtful regions. The procedures just sketched make it possible to allocate any individual about whom the necessary measures are available to one of the three regions. It is also possible to define three regions specifying three constraints which limit the proportion of the population classified in each region in error. Thus, within region A, there will be a region A' in which the constraint is satisfied. There will also be a doubtful region, A'', containing that part of region A not included in A'. This method of analysis has not been applied to economic surveys, but it might well prove enlightening to know the equations which specify the boundaries of regions such as A and A'.

It may be useful to create categories A, B, and C out of the extreme ends and the middle of a measured dependent variable. The analysis of A vs. B and B vs. C may then reveal an assymetry of the causal force.[35]

Sometimes the dependent variable is unevenly distributed because it really represents the result of a set of decisions which need to be analyzed separately. We return to this problem near the end of this chapter.

Selection of Explanatory Variables: The analysis of survey data involves both the selection of explanatory variables to consider and the specification of the relationships among these variables. The two processes are interrelated, but may be separated for discussion.

The selection of variables is in large part a problem of survey design. Yet, even the analyst who is confronted with an existing body of data and has a restricted set of variables from which to choose may be able to create from the mass of data at his disposal a wide variety of analytical variables. The range of choice confronting him is still broad. The same general considerations apply as at the design stage.

The criteria for selection of variables must be based upon the objectives of the project. Four considerations may be relevant.[36]

(1) *Accuracy of measurement.* Between two variables of equal merit from other points of view, the variable which is measured more accurately is preferred. There may be some variables which are measured with so little accuracy that they must be discarded for that reason alone. When errors of measurement do occur in a variable, it will be particularly important to ask whether there are errors of measurement in other variables to be included in the analysis and whether the errors of measurement in these variables are correlated. In forming sets of variables for inclusion in a relationship, that set is to be preferred for which there is least correlation among errors of measurement. (The subject of errors in variables is further considered below.)

(2) *Availability for prediction.* Between two variables of equal merit from other points of view, the variable which is more likely to be available for prediction is to be preferred. In work whose principal purpose is prediction, this consideration may be of overriding importance. It is not of much practical help in such a situation to know that one could predict accurately if one knew something which one does not know. For making predictions which are conditional upon other basic predictions, it will be necessary to select variables which can be fitted into the framework of the basic prediction. For example, if a forecast is to be contingent upon a basic forecast of the level of income, the variable should be consistent with those used in that basic forecast. Of course the explanatory variable must also be expected to change over time, so some change can be predicted.

(3) *Theoretical appropriateness.* Between two variables of equal merit from other points of view, the variable which has the greater theoretical relevance is to be preferred. Theoretical relevance may be defined as appropriateness in terms of the best available theory concerning the causal processes which produce the phenomena under consideration. The subject of causal sequences will be further

considered below. An example of a situation in which one variable would be preferable to another is one in which the theory indicates that variable X causes Y and Z. In that situation in order to explain Y, the analysis should include X in preference to Z.

(4) *Parsimony.* The simplest possible explanation of a phenomenon using the least number of variables is to be preferred. The inclusion of large numbers of measured variables without close consideration of the theoretical meaning of the variables and of the logical interrelationships among them may produce results which defy comprehension and are equally useless for prediction. In an investigation in which the purpose is explanation, it may be argued that completeness is a virtue, in the sense that attention should be paid to the complete set of known interrelationships among the variables related to the phenomenon under consideration. Once the theory and the measurements are developed to the point where the underlying causal mechanisms are understood, however, it may be possible to simplify the model. For example, in the simple model above, it would be possible to eliminate Z from consideration and consider only the effect of X on Y.

Data Analysis: Having selected a set of explanatory variables, and assuming that they are all at the same causal level so that we can think of a single-level multivariate analysis, there is the problem of discovering just which variables, in what pattern, explain (and hence presumably predict) best. While the problem is often stated initially as though all the variables were cardinal scales (numbers), it is really more common to think of all the explanatory factors as sets of subclasses, ordinal scales.

Once there is a single valued dependent variable without some of the problems just discussed, analysis can most simply be thought of as reducing the unexplained variance, or the summed squared errors in predicting the dependent variable for each of a sample of cases. One can argue that it is the absolute errors that matter, not their squares, that an error of 100 is not 10,000 times as bad as an error of 1, but squaring produces nice statistical properties. If one tried to outwit the usual statistical procedures by using the square root of the dependent variable, one minimizes the absolute errors, but at the expense of fitting parabolic functions to it:

$$\sqrt{Y} = a + bX$$
$$\text{implies: } Y = a^2 + 2abX + b^2X^2$$

Any text in statistics can give the justifications for mean square error analysis.

It is instructive to avoid skipping to numerical fitting of functional forms and calculating of regressions, since that already imposes assumptions which may not be appropraite. Let us start more simply:

If we knew only the average of the dependent variable we should predict average for everyone and our errors in predicting the individuals in our sample would be:

$$\sum_{1}^{N} (Y - \overline{Y})^2 \equiv \Sigma Y^2 - 2\overline{Y}\Sigma Y + NY^2 \equiv \Sigma Y^2 - 2\overline{Y} \left(\frac{\Sigma Y}{n}\right) N - N\overline{Y}^2$$

$$\equiv \Sigma Y^2 - 2\overline{Y}^2 N + N\overline{Y}^2 \equiv \Sigma Y^2 - N\overline{Y}^2 \qquad \text{(a)}$$

For large samples this is also an estimate of the error variance in predicting the population not just the sample, for small samples one multiplies it by $N/(N-1)$.

The simplest application of information to reduce predictive error is to know which of two subclasses each individual is in. In this case, there are predictive errors around the *two* group means which are used for prediction:

$$\Sigma Y_1^2 - N_1\overline{Y}_1^2 + \Sigma Y_2^2 - N_2\overline{Y}_2^2 = \Sigma Y^2 - N_1\overline{Y}_1^2 - N_2\overline{Y}_2^2 \qquad \text{(b)}$$

and the gain over using one overall mean is:

$$N_1\overline{Y}_1^2 + N_2\overline{Y}_2^2 - N\overline{Y}^2 \qquad \text{(a)-(b)}$$

This is known as the "between sum of squares," and the first term above, (a), as the "total sum of squares," the phrase "around the mean" being understood. And (b) is the "within group sum of squares." The ratio of the additional explanation (a-b) to the original unexplained variance (a), is the square of the correlation ratio, eta, or the proportion of the variance (in the sample) explained by knowing which of two groups the individual is in. This is easily expanded to k groups and put in a form known as analysis of variance, and of variance components.

The total sum of squares (around the mean) is the same, and the gain or "explained sum of squares," or "between group sum of squares" for k subgroup means is:

$$\sum_{1}^{K} N_2 Y_1^2 - N\overline{Y}^2,$$

the weighted sum of squares of the subgroup means minus the standard correction factor. The simple one-way analysis of variance with k subclasses is given in Figure G-1. The divisor $\overline{n}$ is an adjustment for unequal group sizes, an approximation provided by Ganguli, which *is* the group size if they are all equal but progressively smaller if they are unequal:

$$\overline{n} = \frac{1}{K-1} \left[N - \frac{1}{N} \Sigma n_i^2\right]$$

so
$$\sigma_B^2 = \frac{\dfrac{B}{K-1} - \sigma_\mathcal{E}^2}{\bar{n}}$$

What this means is that the proportion of the population variance accounted for by groups, $\sigma_B^2/(\sigma_B^2 + \sigma_\mathcal{E}^2)$, can be estimated from the sample as:

$$\frac{\left[\dfrac{B}{K-1}\right] - \left[\dfrac{W}{N-K}\right]}{\left[\dfrac{B}{K-1}\right] - \left[\dfrac{W}{N-K}\right] + \bar{n}\left[\dfrac{W}{N-K}\right]}$$

which is different from the proportion of the *sample* variance explained. It is lower, the larger the error variance, and lower, the more varied the subgroup sizes. The explained sum of squares in a sample, in other words, is biased upward by containing an error component itself, and upward by unequal subgroup sizes.[37] Figure G-1 summarizes all this.

We have focused on components of variance, estimates of which are relatively robust under departures from normality and homogeneity of variances. Tests of significance consist of treating the mean squares as estimates of the variance, equal if the groups were all the same, and computing the F-ratio $B/(K-1)$ divided by $W/(N-K)$, which is not only more sensitive to the basic assumptions, but also assumes simple random sampling which is rare in surveys.

At this level, the investigator's interest is often not so much in significance, or in predicting back to the population, as in comparing the explanatory power of the K subgroups of one classification with the L subgroups of some other classification, representing a different explanation. For this purpose, the total sum of squares remaining the same, all that need be compared is the "between group" sum of squares, or the mean square, adjusted for the number of subgroups. If one has a reasonably equal number of subgroups, it is only the size of $\sum\limits_{1}^{L} n_i \bar{Y}_i^2$ that matters, which requires knowing only the subgroup means and the number of cases in each.

Where the dependent variable is a dichotomous variable taking only the values 1 and 0, the same relations hold, although some of the formulas simplify and look strange:

$$\text{Total} = NP(1 - P)$$

$$\text{Between groups: } \sum\limits_{1}^{k} n_i P_i (1 - P_i)$$

But a computer program designed to handle a numerical dependent variable can take one with values 1 and 0, without altering the terminology.

FIGURE G-1

ONE WAY ANALYSIS OF VARIANCE AND COMPONENTS OF VARIANCE

	Sum of Squares	Degrees of Freedom	Mean Square (Estimate of Variance)	Mean Square is an Estimate of the Population Value of:
TOTAL (Around the Mean)	$\sum_1^N Y^2 - \dfrac{(\Sigma Y)^2}{n} = T$	$N - 1$	$\dfrac{T}{N-1}$	$\sigma^2 Y$
BETWEEN GROUPS (Accounted for by Group Means)	$\sum_1^K N_i Y_i^2 - \dfrac{(\Sigma Y)^2}{n} = B$	$K - 1$	$\dfrac{B}{K-1}$	If No Effect: $\sigma^2 Y$ Otherwise: $\sigma_{\mathcal{E}}^2 + \bar{n}\sigma^2 B$
WITHIN GROUPS ("Error") or "Unexplained"	$T - B$	$N - K$	$\dfrac{T-B}{N-K}$	If No Effect: $\sigma^2 Y$ Otherwise: $\sigma_{\mathcal{E}}^2$

No-Effect Hypothesis $\dfrac{B}{K-1} = \sigma^2 Y = \dfrac{T-D}{N-K}$: F-Ratio $= \dfrac{\dfrac{B}{K-1}}{\dfrac{T-B}{N-K}}$

Components of Variance: $\sigma_{Total}^2 = \sigma_{Between\ groups}^2 + \sigma_{Error}^2$
—in population

Sample Estimates: $\sigma_{\mathcal{E}}^2 = \dfrac{T-B}{N-K}$

$$\sigma_B = \dfrac{\dfrac{B}{K-1} - \sigma_{\mathcal{E}}^2}{\bar{n}} \quad \text{where } \bar{n} = \dfrac{1}{K-1}\left[N - \dfrac{1}{N}\Sigma N_i^2\right]$$

$$= \dfrac{\dfrac{\Sigma N_i \bar{Y}_i^2 - \dfrac{(\Sigma Y)^2}{N}}{K-1} - \dfrac{\Sigma Y_2 - \dfrac{(\Sigma Y)^2}{N} - \left[\Sigma N_i \bar{Y}_i - \dfrac{(\Sigma Y)^2}{N}\right]}{N-K}}{\dfrac{1}{K-1}\left[N - \dfrac{1}{N}\Sigma N_i^2\right]}$$

NOTE: $\bar{n} = N/K$ if groups are all the same size, $< N/K$ if not. So between groups sum of squares exaggerates the explained variance by $\sigma_{\mathcal{E}}/\bar{n}$, and exaggerates it by $\dfrac{n}{\bar{n}} = \dfrac{\text{Actual}}{\text{Estimate}}$.

The analysis of subgroup means need not take only means classified according to a single explanatory variable at a time. If one were analyzing food expenditure, per family not per capita, then the explanatory power of income groups, or family size groups, or even the sum of the two would be considerably lower than that of the KxL groups classifying people *both* by income and family size. Indeed, comparison of the explained variance using the KxL subcells with that explained by the K plus that by the L subgroups provides a rough indication of the extent of interaction effects, although the former can be smaller than the latter sum if the two characteristics are highly correlated, their explanatory power overlapping.

We have departed from the usual approach of using numerical explanatory variables and then discussing possible problems, on the grounds that with surveys it makes more sense to treat all the variables, or nearly all, as sets of discrete classes rather than continuous numbers. Most of the statistical literature, however, is written as though all the variables were numerical, and some of our discussion of problems will have to be in these terms, even though the regression coefficient for a numerical variable may in practice be the shape of a set of dummy variable coefficients.

We turn now to a series of problems in multivariate analysis, and various ways of dealing with them.

Non-linear Relations: Non-linear relationships present no problem with dummy variables, as we shall see below. With numerical variables there are, broadly speaking, two statistical approaches to the problem of detecting non-linearities. The first strategy is to go ahead and fit a linear relationship, and then check to see whether the straight line fits the data. The second strategy is to proceed as if the relationship were non-linear and check to see whether evidence of the non-linearity does appear. The choice between the two approaches usually depends on what the investigator knows about the matter before he starts his analysis, and on the importance of departures from linearity for the problem at hand. He may believe that, while there no doubt is some departure from linearity, a linear relationship is a good approximation.

The basic procedure, if the first strategy is followed, is to analyze the residuals. That is, one fits the relationship, calculates for each individual in the sample the predicted score and the actual score on the dependent variable, and subtracts. Predicted scores, of course, may be estimated using multiple regression or any other procedure which yields an estimated relationship. If a linear relation has been erroneously assumed, there will be a systematic relationship between the independent variable and these residuals. The situation might be as sketched below:

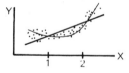

In this situation the average of the residuals below X = 1 will be positive, from X = 1 to X = 2 negative, and above X = 2, again positive. The analyst could detect this situation by dividing the data into groups according to the value of X and computing the mean residual for each group of observations. Or he could simply plot the residuals, or a sample of them, as in the sketch.

It may be possible to come to a conclusion on the question of linearity without using a formal statistical test. Such tests are available, however: Prais and Houthakker propose use of a statistic more familiar in time series analysis, the Durbin-Watson d. This statistic will provide a test of the degree of serial correlation between residuals when the residuals are arranged according to the magnitude of the determining variable, rather than by data as in time-series analysis where it originated.[38]

If an analyst follows the second strategy, proceeding as if the relationship were known to be non-linear, he has several options. He can transform one or more of the variables, using, for example, the log of income instead of income, he can fit a polynomial using, say, the square and the cube of the independent variable, he can introduce dummy variables, or he can break up the data, sorting on the independent variable, and fitting his entire equation separately for different ranges of values of the independent variable. He may also use a combination of these approaches.

The most common transformation of a variable is the use of its log. The log of a variable like income is particularly convenient because the original variable is highly skewed. The use of a complete multiplicative model, in which all variables are converted to log form is not necessary to cure non-linearity in a single variable. Another transformation which is sometimes used is to divide the individuals in the sample into groups of equal size and assign a score to each individual according to the tenth or decile of which he is a member, or even according to the mean of the dependent variable for that subgroup. Ratios are also commonly used, for example, the ratio of assets to income.[39]

In principle, any power of an independent variable can be introduced into a regression. It is unusual, however, to use higher powers than the square and the cube. Guthrie has provided an example of several methods to deal with non-linearity in the relation of liquid assets to income. The basic facts are that liquid assets are high in relation to income at low income levels and also at high levels but not at intermediate levels. Guthrie used as dependent variable the liquid asset-income ratio. As independent variables he used the income decile score of each unit and the square of that score.[40]

The use of dummy variables has been discussed earlier and will be treated fully later. Essentially, they permit the approximation of any curve by a step function. The number of dummy variables which can be used is limited only by considerations of the statistical reliability of the estimates. If a close fit is required, it may be possible to improve on the step function by fitting a continuous curve once the general shape of the relationship is known from the calculations using the dummy variables. How much improvement is possible could be estimated by the use of residuals in the manner outlined above for checking for departures from linearity.

To fit the entire relationship—the complete regression equation—for each of several ranges of the values of an independent variable will reveal non-linearity in the relationship between that variable and the dependent variable. The dummy variable technique, however, is more economical if non-linearity is the only problem. The complete re-fit is needed only when there are interactions in the data, as will be discussed below.

Much of the historic treatment of non-linearity was with time series data where there were very few degrees of freedom, and it was necessary to impose restrictive assumptions on the data. With survey data, there are enough cases so that even for numerical variables the most appropriate method in most cases is to convert each predictor into a set of dummy variables and let the output of a multiple regression indicate whether the effect is linear or not. There may be exceptions to this when some strong theoretical reasoning specifies the shape of some relationship, or when measurement of an elasticity is sought, but in general it would appear unwise to assume linearity or any other functional form when it is so easy to let the regression analysis decide the issue. The non-linearities in survey data are frequently bothersome: (a) discrete jumps, where completion of some type of schooling is more important than the number of years completed, (b) extreme effects of the extremes, where residence does not matter, except for the genuinely rural areas, and the very centers of the largest cities, or (c) non-monotonic effects, where the middle-aged earn more than the young *or* the old.

Errors in Variables and Their Effects on Relationship: The evidence is clear that there are substantial errors of measurement of some of the variables in survey estimates. Therefore, it is necessary to consider what effect these errors may have on the estimation of relationships. Fortunately, the relevant econometric theory has been worked out reasonably well. The theory, however, is rarely taken into account in the literature reporting the results of sample surveys. This compartmentalization of knowledge has produced a situation in which users of survey results are left uninformed as to whether reported regression coefficients (or related statistics) are biased as a result of errors in measurement of the independent variables. The simplest statement found in many statistics books, is that errors in the dependent variable can reduce the correlation but do not cause bias in the estimate of the relationship. But errors in an explanatory variable produce a downward bias in the regression coefficient (slope of the regression line). Actually, the problem is more complicated than that.

The reader is referred for a more complete treatment to J. Johnston's *Econometric Methods* or to Kendall and Stuart.[41] Johnston calls attention to a parallel between the theory of errors in variables and Friedman's analysis of the consumption function, a comparison which may assist economists to an understanding of the subject.

Consider a situation in which there are two variables, each of which is observed with error. If x and y are the true variables, the observed variables, X and Y, are equal to the true variables plus errors:

(1) $X = x + u$

(2) $Y = y + v$

The true variables are assumed to be related to each other in a simple linear relationship:

(3) $Y = \alpha + \beta X$

We may then find the relation between the observed variables by substitution:

$$Y - v = y$$

$$X - u = x$$

(4) $Y - v = \alpha + \beta (X - u)$
       $Y = \alpha + \beta x - \beta u + v$

Hence,   (5) $Y = \alpha + \beta x + w$, where $w = v - \beta u$

But w is not independent of X. It includes the term, $-\beta u$, and u is a component of the observed value, x. Thus, ordinary least squares procedures will yield biased estimates of α and β even if the sample is infinite and even if the mean values of the error terms are zero.

More generally:

(6) $\varepsilon\{w[X - E(X)]\} = \varepsilon(uv) - \beta u^2$

Thus, the covariance of X and w depends upon—(1) the covariance of the errors of observation, and (2) a factor which is the product of the true regression coefficient and the variance of the errors of observation for X. It is not surprising that the covariance of the errors of observation enters the expression. Any systematic relationship between the errors might well distort the estimate of the true regression coefficient.

It is instructive to consider the effects of the errors on the estimator of β from a sample of size n. The estimate of β would be as follows:

$$(7) \quad \beta_n = \frac{\sum_{i=1}^{n} (X_i-\bar{X})(Y_i-\bar{Y})}{\sum_{i=1}^{n} (X_i-\bar{X})^2}$$

If we introduce the error terms, the expression becomes:

$$(8) \quad \beta_n = \frac{\Sigma(x-\bar{x})(y-\bar{y}) + \Sigma(x-\bar{x})(v-\bar{v}) + \Sigma(y-\bar{y})(u-\bar{u}) + \Sigma(u-\bar{u})(v-\bar{v})}{\Sigma(x-\bar{x})^2 + 2\Sigma(x-\bar{x})(u-\bar{u}) + \Sigma(u-\bar{u})^2}$$

The estimate of β_n, therefore, will depend upon the following:

(a)   Whether u and v are independent of one another. (See the last term in the numerator.)

(b)   Whether each of the true variables is independent of the error in the other variable. (See the second and third terms in the numerator.)

(c)   Whether x is independent of the error in x. (See middle term in the denominator.)

(d)   The magnitude of the variance of the errors of observation of x. (See the last term in the denominator.)

It is, therefore, not possible to say in general whether β will be biased upward or downward. One must know the sign and the magnitude of each of the five terms in (8) which involve u or v or both.

We can, however, consider what is known about errors in sample surveys and its probable implications for these terms.

(a)   In sample surveys there is reason to expect u and v not to be independent. The same individual is reporting under identical circumstances. We would expect him to report both x and y accurately, or to report neither accurately. If u and v are *positively* correlated, the effect will be to *increase* β_n. This situation is likely to be a common one: for example, both income and savings may be understated. If, however, u and v are *negatively* correlated, the effect will be to reduce β_n. For example, income might be understated and charitable contributions overstated.

(b)   In sample surveys there may well be association between the true value of one variable and the error in the other. There is reason to believe, for example, that high income people report savings accounts more completely than low income people. If there is a *positive* correlation between a true variable and the error in the other variable, the effect will be to increase β_n. If the correlation is *negative,* the effect will be to *reduce* β_n.

(c) In sample surveys there may well be association between the true value of an independent variable and whether that variable is reported accurately. For example, in the measurement of total income, high income people tend to have income from property, which is typically underreported, while low income people have only income from wages, which is reported correctly. If there is a *positive* correlation between the true value of x and its error of measurements, β_n will be *reduced;* if there is a *negative* correlation, β_n will be *increased.*

(d) In sample surveys the error of measurement in the independent variable may be substantial. The *larger* the squared error of measurement of x, the *smaller* the estimate of β_n. This may well be the most important problem.

As the preceding comments suggest, it may be possible to obtain estimates of the terms of equation (8) by conducting validity studies.

Johnston proposes three general approaches to the problem of how to conduct statistical analysis of data subject to errors of measurement. The first, or "classical," approach, involves stringent assumptions about the error terms. The specific procedure depends upon what is known about the errors. It will be discussed briefly below. The second approach involves grouping the data, plus making less stringent assumptions about the error terms. We admit to some uncertainty as to whether this method is as effective as it appears, and will simply refer the interested reader to Johnston and the references there cited. The third approach, the method of instrumental variables, will be discussed below.

The first approach is developed more fully by Kendall and Stuart, who discuss four cases which differ according to what is known or can be ascertained about the errors. The "classic solution" requires knowledge of the ratio of the variance of the errors. Given this information, and zero covariance terms, the problem becomes manageable. Instead of the ratio of the variance, the available information may be the actual variance of one or the other of the error terms, or, it may be that the variances of both error terms are known. We emphasize that it is generally impossible to know the covariance terms of equation (8) above, or even the distributions of the errors of each variable considered separately.

The method of instrumental variables may prove to be of practical value for some problems of survey work, and we shall discuss here the nature of the requirements it places on the process of data collection. Consider again the situation in which the following expressions apply:

(9) $Y = \alpha + \beta X + w$

   $w = v - \beta u$

We introduce a variable Z, which is independent of both errors, u and v. We use as an estimator:

(10) $\quad \hat{\beta} = \dfrac{\sum\limits_{i=1}^{n} Y_i Z_i}{\sum\limits_{i=1}^{n} X_i Z_i}$

Note that:

(11) $\quad \hat{\beta} = \dfrac{\beta \Sigma Y_i Z_i + \Sigma Z_i (w_i - \overline{w})}{\Sigma X_i Z_i}$

The second term in the numerator will tend to zero as n becomes large because Z is not correlated with the errors u and v. Note that Z must have a fairly high correlation with x. If it does not, the denominator in (10) will be near zero, and the estimate of β will be near infinity.

The logic of the method requires that we estimate the relation between y and x by taking the ratio of the relation between y and z to that between x and z. There may be other independent variables at work, which influence the relationship, but in principle we can take them into account in a multivariate calculation.

Johnston noted three major problems with the method of instrumental variables. First, the choice of instrumental variables is arbitrary, and there is a possibility of variations in the resultant estimates as a consequence. It would be desirable to try two or more instrumental variables and compare the results to check this possibility. Second, there is the difficulty of checking that the instrumental variables actually are independent of the errors of observation, and that they are exogenous, not dependent on X or Y. We may note that in survey work some variables are measured a great deal more accurately than others. It is also possible, on occasion, to introduce into an analysis variables which are measured outside the survey. Third, Johnston notes that the approach places great stress on the importance of consistency of the estimate. This stress may prove warranted in surveys—one needs more information to be sure.

Another interpretation, suggested by Theil, focuses on the problem of shocks affecting both X and Y and producing an extraneous relationship rather than an over-determined system.[42] He proposed removing the error or random element from X by regressing it on some exogenous variable Z and treating the residuals from that regression as the random shock elements. In fact this amounts to using the predicted value of X from that regression, instead of the actual X, in finding its relation to Y, and is algebraically equivalent to the method of instrumental variables.

$$\hat{X} = a + bz$$

$$Y = c + dx$$

Again there is the problem of finding something which affects X but is not affected by either X or Y, and a question whether different Z choices would produce different estimates. The method is called "two-stage least squares" but
should be carefully distinguished from analysis of residuals, and from step-wise
least squares procedures.

These two solutions, instrumental variables, and two-stage-least-squares,
assume that the focus is on the best estimate of *the* relationship between two
variables, though others may be in the model additively. If there are interaction
effects then there is no single relationship anyway. And if we are assessing the
relative power of a number of explanatory variables, extending the methods is
cumbersome.

The remaining problems in the one-level analysis of a dependent variable
have to do with the multivariate nature of the problem—the fact that one is attempting to sort out the effects of a number of variables simultaneously, not
just get the best unbiased estimate of the effects of one of them. These problems
can be categorized into three main parts, intercorrelations among the predictors,
interaction effects, and the "one dominant variable" problem.

Intercorrelations among the Predictors: If the predictor variables are completely uncorrelated with one another, then their simple correlations and regression coefficients are all that is needed. If any one predictor, at the other extreme
is perfectly correlated with one of the others, or any linear combination of the
others, then clearly there is no way at all to separate their influences, or attribute the explained variance to one or the other of them. (In solving the normal
equations of multiple regression, a determinant in the denominator of one expression becomes zero, and the computer stops.) In between, the usual procedure for sorting out separate effects is that of multiple regression. Although
the usual computing procedure for estimating multiple regression coefficients is
by solving a set of so-called normal equations, it is easier to see what is really involved by describing an algebraically equivalent process in which they are estimated in a series of iterations. This process is itself most easily described when
the explanatory variables are categorical—sets of dummy variables.

Suppose one had a dependent variable, income, and two explanatory
characteristics: age and education. One could estimate a relationship between
age and income (mean income for each age group) and one between education
and income (mean income for each education group). These means are expressed
as deviations from the overall mean. The coefficient (deviation) for the young,
say, is adjusted for the fact that a smaller proportion of young than old are uneducated. This is done by multiplying the proportion of young uneducated by

the income deviation for uneducated and the proportion of young educated by the income deviation for educated, dividing by the sum of the proportions, and subtracting the result from coefficient for young (that much being accounted for by the fact that a larger proportion of the young are educated and get paid more for that reason). Similar adjustments for the old would be smaller and in the other direction since more of them are uneducated. One then goes to the coefficients for educated and for uneducated, adjusting them for the disproportionate age compositions. The result is four new coefficients, adjusted once for intercorrelations among the predictors (the fact that a subclass of one is not distributed across the other in the same way as the whole population). The process can then be repeated, until the marginal adjustments are so small as to be negligible, and the resulting coefficients are now an additive set which will predict income with minimum error variance.

Note that we actually started with a set of subgroup means and adjusted them for possible distortion by the effects of disproportionality on other factors. If two predictors (subclasses) are identical (two subclasses one from each of two predictors) then the process does not converge, but goes into a set of oscillating, reversing corrections, the analogue of the zero denominator in the determinant solution of the normal equations.

With numerical predictors, one can think of plotting the scatter diagram, fitting a simple regression line, taking the residuals case by case and plotting (or running) them against the second predictor, taking those residuals in turn and running them against the first predictor again, and so forth until there is no relation left. This can be done graphically with small data sets, to get the feel for what happens.[43]

The price one pays for the powerful simultaneous determination of the effects of many variables in multiple regression is the required assumption of additivity and universality. That is, any variable which affects the dependent variables does so with the same impact in all subparts of the population, so that its effect can be added, across the whole population, to the effect of each of the other variables. But if this assumption is met, or can be approximated by judicious redefinition of variables, and if the intercorrelations among the predictors are not so high as to lead to unstable estimates of the regression coefficients, then multiple regression is a powerful tool indeed.

Furthermore, as we have said, it is not necessary to assume linearity of the effects of each predictor in order to use regression, provided one has enough cases to allow the use of dummy variables.[44]

If the direct algebraic solution to the normal equations of regression is to be used, one must either constrain the coefficients of each set of dummy variables so that their weighted sum is zero, or constrain one of them to zero. The latter is easier with computer programs already written. One merely omits one of each set. The result is that remaining coefficients are all in terms of differences from the excluded group, and the effects of being in the excluded groups are pooled into the constant term.

In the simple example with two predictors, of two classes each, Age (young and old) and Education (Uneducated or Educated), and a dependent variable, Income, the computer regression then becomes:

$$\text{Income} = \text{Constant} + A \text{ (if young)} + B \text{ (if uneducated)}$$

The only information an additive regression model needs is the simple variances and covariances (correlations) among all the variables including the dependent one. Where the explanatory variables take only the values 1 and 0, however, their covariances with the dependent variable are simple functions of the mean of the dependent variable for the subgroup that is non-zero on that dummy variable. And the covariances among the predictors when they only take values 1 and 0 are the two-way frequency tables of the pairs of explanatory characteristics. The data needed for the example are:

	Mean Incomes			Frequencies	
By Age		**By Education**		Uneducated	Educated
Young $6200		Uneducated $4600	Young	10	40
Old $5800		Educated $7400	Old	40	10
		All: $6000			

Variances: Of dummies, NPQ where P is proportion non-zero; Q = (1-P)

Of income, calculated from data. For our example we assume there is no "error" variance, that is, that the basic data are as follows:

Mean Incomes

	Uneducated	Educated	
Young	$3000	$7000	(No variance within groups)
Old	5000	9000	

But the regression model does not use this information, being content with the one-dimensional subgroup means and the overall variance of the dependent variable.

If one actually calculates a regression using the subgroup means and the two-way frequency table, it will come out:

Income = $9000 - $2000 if young - $4000 if uneducated; R = 1.00

This is the form in which dummy-variable regression is usually presented; unfortunately so, since it is most misleading. The coefficients are in terms of differences from the excluded group, not from some known and stable base. If the excluded group is small, say the non-ascertained cases, all the other coefficients can have a very large, and somewhat erratic shift when the excluded group has a widely deviant mean. And the constant term can also be erratic. It is a bit like standing a triangle on its end.

A much better form, mathematically identical is:

$$\text{Income} = \text{Average income} \quad \begin{array}{ll} + a1 \text{ if Young} & + b1 \text{ if Uneducated} \\ \\ + a2 \text{ if Old} & + b2 \text{ if Educated} \end{array}$$

The transformation for each set of dummies is by simply adding a constant (C or K) to each coefficient (including the zero one) so that their weighted sum will equal zero, subtracting the same constant from the constant term:

Age	Education
50 (-2000 + C) + 50 (0 + C) = 0	50 (-4000 + K) + 50 (0 + K) = 0
100C = 100,000	100K = 200,000
C = 1,000	K = 2,000

	- 1000 if Young	- 2000 if Uneducated
so: Income = 9000 - 1000 - 2000		
	+1000 if Old	+2000 if Educated

Another advantage of this form appears when one wishes to compare similar regressions computed for another sample or a different time or place. One can observe changes in the mean, and then check to what extent they can be attributed to:

(a) Changes in the proportions in each subgroup with no change in the *effects* of subgroup belonging (the coefficients).

One multiplies the original a and b coefficients by the new population proportions in those groups to see how far the result departs from zero. Perhaps
changing incomes simply result from more college graduates and more older people, with the payoffs to education and experience remaining unchanged.

(b) Changes in the structural relations, which may be behavioral responses,
or effects of background conditions.

One multiplies the original population proportions times a new set of a and
b coefficients, again to see how far the sum departs from zero.

These two experiments can be done separately for each explanatory characteristic (set of dummy variables) since the model assumes independent additive
effects.

When the number of predictors, and the number of subclasses of each, becomes large, presentation of the results becomes a problem. In order to see the
effects of adjustments for intercorrelations among the predictors carried out by
the regression analysis, the following form is useful:

INCOME

Predictors	Unadjusted		Adjusted (by regression)		Number of Cases
	Means	Deviations	Deviations	Means	
Young	$6200	+200	- 1000	5000	50
Old	5800	- 200	+1000	7000	50
Uneducated	4600	- 1400	- 2000	4000	50
Educated	7400	+1400	+2000	8000	50

What has happened is that the negative correlation between education and
age (experience) has led to spurious reductions in the apparent effects of each,
which the regression then eliminated. We made this an extreme case, where the
apparent effect of age was actually reversed. The young seemed to be making
more, but it was only because they were so much better educated. Taking account of education, they made less. In terms of simple correlations we have:

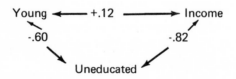

The small positive correlation is a classic example of spurious correlation result-ing from the positive product of two high negative correlations with lack of edu-cation. (If we had defined a dummy variable "educated," rather than "unedu-cated," we should then have talked about two high positive correlations with being young and with high income.)

By adding the mean to the adjusted deviations we can say what the mean income of that group would have been if it were like the whole sample on all the other dimensions.

It is also important to present the column of frequencies, since the sampling variances of the means and deviations, unadjusted or adjusted, are mostly affected by the varying sizes of the subgroups on which they are based. If the predictors are perfectly uncorrelated, each subclass of each predictor being distributed like the population across the classes of every other predictor, then the simple regres-sions, or the subgroup means in the case of categorical variables, are unbiased estimates of the effects, and multiple regression is unnecessary. In the iterative process, not even the first iteration would make any adjustments. If the young were exactly half uneducated and half educated, the weighted product of their deviations by education subclass would be zero. In fact, however, they are mostly educated, so the weighted sum is a substantial positive number which is then subtracted from the estimated deviation for "young," since it is attributable to education, not youth. The same adjustments are made for each subclass of each predictor, producing a set of first-adjusted deviations. The process is then re-peated using these deviations to calculate new adjustments, and second-adjusted deviations. The process is continued until no adjustments show more than some very small amount (absolutely not relative to the size of the coefficient itself since some adjusted deviations will be close to zero). The resulting final-adjusted deviations are, as we have said, algebraically identical with the results of the dummy variable regression calculations, except that they are already in the more meaningful form, with no subclasses omitted. Each adjusted deviation is a de-parture from the overall mean attributable to membership in that subclass, and not to the fact that the subclass differs on some of the other characteristics.

Usually the adjusted coefficients are smaller than the unadjusted ones, be-cause the variables are usually positively correlated with one another, and with the dependent variable. But if two explanatory variables positively correlated with each other have opposite effects on the dependent variable, then simple re-lations understate both effects and multiple regression should produce more striking regression coefficients. Similarly if two variables each positively affect-ing the dependent variable are negatively correlated with one another (age and education on earnings), then again each effect would be underestimated by the simple unadjusted subgroup means or simple regressions.

If the regression must be run on a standard program, forcing one of each set of dummy variables to have a coefficient of zero, the chances are also that the program will *not* give the mean of the dependent variable for each subgroup (not = 0 on that dummy variable). Yet an interpretation of the regression is improved if one sees just what the adjustment for intercorrelation among the predictors did. Hence, having gotten the regression coefficients expressed as subgroup deviations from the grand mean (adjusted by regression), one would like to compare them with the deviations of the unadjusted subgroup mean from the grand mean. Most regression programs do not provide this information, but they do provide data from which it is derivable, namely the simple correlations among all the variables, the means of all the variables, and the number of cases.

What we want is the mean of Y for the group where $x_i = 0$, which is: $\dfrac{\Sigma X_i Y}{\Sigma X_i}$

since X_i is = 1 for cases in the subgroup, otherwise = 0. What we have is:

$$r^2 = \frac{\text{cov } X_i Y}{(\text{var } X_i)\,(\text{var } Y)}$$

where

$$\text{cov } X_i Y = \Sigma X_i Y - \frac{\Sigma X_i\, \Sigma Y}{N}$$

$$\text{var } X_i = \sigma^2_{X_i}$$

$$\text{var } Y = \sigma^2_{Y}$$

So

$$\frac{\Sigma X_i Y}{\Sigma X_i} = \frac{\left(\Sigma X_i Y - \dfrac{\Sigma X_i\, \Sigma Y}{N} + \dfrac{\Sigma X_i\, \Sigma Y}{N}\right)}{\Sigma X_i} = \frac{\text{cov } X_i Y + \dfrac{\Sigma X_i\, \Sigma Y}{N}}{\Sigma X_i} = \frac{\text{cov } X_i Y}{N\overline{X}} - \overline{Y}$$

$$= \frac{\dfrac{\text{cov } X_i Y}{\sigma^2_{X_i} \sigma^2_{Y}} \cdot\; \sigma^2_{X_i}\, \sigma^2_{Y}}{N\overline{X}} - \overline{Y}$$

$$= \frac{r^2_{X_i Y} \cdot \sigma^2_{X_i}\, \sigma^2_{Y}}{N\overline{X}} - \overline{Y} \;=\; \text{mean of Y for } X_i \neq 0.$$

If the covariances are available, the next to last term provides the mean of the dependent variable for the subgroup not = 0 on x_i, but if only the correlations are available, the last term provides it.

This mean can be compared with the "adjusted mean," or one can subtract the grand mean from it and compare it with the "adjusted deviation," the multiple regression coefficient for x_i when they have been adjusted so that the weighted sum of each set of coefficients is equal to zero.

The use of standard regression packages with dummy variables entails a considerable amount of hand work for the results to be ready for easy interpretation by the reader. He needs the effects of each dummy variable (membership in some subgroup in the population) expressed as deviations from the grand mean (not from other subgroup arbitrarily selected to have its coefficient zero). And he needs to compare this with the subgroup's deviation from average, unadjusted by any consideration of its disproportionate membership in other subgroups. Or he may want both numbers expressed as averages, not deviations, i.e. with the grand mean added to both of them.

Let us take a somewhat more complex example, with less symmetry and with three subclasses, so that one uses two dummy variables, for each of two predicting characteristics. Again, all the regression uses is the one-dimensional subgroup means, and the two-way frequency distributions of the predictors, are the overall variance.

Means			Frequencies			
	Income			Uned	H.S.	College
Young	$ 8,000		Young	5	10	15	30
Middle-aged	10,571		Mid.	10	15	10	35
Uneducated	4,200		Old	20	15	5	40
High School	6,750						
				35	40	30	105

(We have made the data realistic, if rounded, and with additive effects.)

If one uses a regular regression program, again one must eliminate one subgroup of each classification (since it is totally predictable from knowing whether each individual is in either of the other two subgroups). Suppose we eliminate the middle groups, and use four dummy variables, called Young, Old, Uneducated, and College. From the subgroup means one can calculate the simple correlations of each predictor with income:

$$r$$

Correlation of income with "Young"	=	.1456
"Old"	=	- .7000
"Uneducated"	=	- .6513
"College"	=	.7282

And from the two-way frequency tables, one can calculate the simple correlations among the pairs of predictors:

	Old	Not		Uneducated	Not		College	Not
Young	0	30		5	25		15	15
Not	40	35		30	45		15	60
	r = -.4961			r = -.2236			r = +.3000	

	Old	Not			College	Not
Uneducated	20	15		Uneducated	0	35
Not	20	50		Not	30	40
	r = +.2774				r = -.4472	

	College	Not
Old	5	35
Not	25	40
	r = -.2791	

Using only this information, and assuming additivity, the regression analysis might produce the following:

$$\text{Income} = 10,000 \quad \begin{matrix} -4,000 \text{ if Young} & -3,000 \text{ if Uneducated} \\ -6,000 \text{ if Old} & +5,000 \text{ if College} \end{matrix}$$

These coefficients represent deviations from the excluded groups (middle aged, or high school graduates) not from the mean, and the constant term is not the mean, but the mean plus the effects of the two excluded groups. Again a linear transformation, to make the weighted sum of the three coefficients equal to zero for each of the two explanatory characteristics gives a better equation.

If C is an adjustment added to each of the three age coefficients to make them have a weighted sum of 0, we have:

$$\begin{matrix} \text{Young} & \text{Old} & \text{Middle Aged} \end{matrix}$$

$$0 = \frac{(C - 4000)\ 30\ +\ (C - 6000)\ 40\ +\ (C + 0)\ 35}{105}$$

(See Frequency Table for Weights)

    C = 3429

So we have - 571 if young
          +3429 if middle aged
          -2571 if old

    A similar process for education gives a constant of -429, and we have the "adjusted deviations" in column 3 of the table below. Note that if the two adjustments are also made to the constant term, it becomes the overall mean: 10,000 - 3429 + 429 = 7,000, and we have the more meaningful predicting equation:

$$\text{Income} = 7000 \quad \begin{array}{l} - 571 \text{ if Young} \\ +3429 \text{ if Middle Aged} \\ - 2571 \text{ if Old} \end{array} \quad \begin{array}{l} -3429 \text{ if Uneducated} \\ - 429 \text{ if High School} \\ +4571 \text{ if College} \end{array}$$

And for each group, using the next-to-last column of the table, we can say what their average income would be if they were "average" on the other characteristic.

	Unadjusted		Adjusted		
	Means	Deviations	Deviations	Means	Number of Cases
Young	$ 8000	$+1000	$- 571	$ 6429	30
Middle Aged	10571	+3571	+3429	10429	35
Old	3125	- 3875	- 2571	4429	40
Uneducated	4200	- 2800	- 3429	3571	35
High School	6750	- 250	- 429	6571	40
College	12000	+5000	+4571	11571	30

    The regression coefficients came out as they did because we built the model into the data without any interaction effects (non-additivities) as in the data table below. We also allowed no (error) variance within any of the nine groups, so the multiple correlation coefficient came out 1.00.

MEAN INCOMES AND FREQUENCIES

	Uneducated	High School	College	All Educations
Young	$3,000	$ 6,000	$11,000	$ 8,000
	5	10	15	30
Middle Aged	7,000	10,000	15,000	10,571
	10	15	10	35
Old	1,000	4,000	9,000	3,125
	20	15	5	40
All Ages	4,200	6,750	12,000	7,000
	35	40	30	105

The differences between the unadjusted and the adjusted deviations in the prior table are of course the adjustments for intercorrelation among the predictors (unequal frequency distributions). Notice that three of them are smaller in absolute amount, indicating the elimination of some spurious correlation, while two are larger, indicating the elimination of some spurious lack of correlation, and one even changes direction! Take the sign reversal for illustration, and use correlation diagrams:

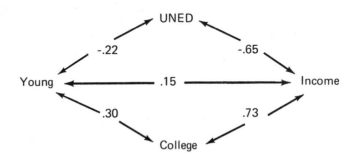

The simple small positive correlation between being young and having a high income is the spurious result of high positive products of correlations of the two through the two education variables. Young people have higher incomes because they are less likely to be uneducated (they avoid that negative effect), and more likely to have a college degree (they get that positive effect) but if they were only average on education, their incomes would be lower than average. The unadjusted effect of being young is distorted up by their high education (multiply the education deviations by the proportions of young in each educational class).

The question often arises whether one does not lose information by converting a numerical predictor into a set of subclasses which are assigned dummy variables. Actually the flexibility (non-linearity) allowed is achieved with very little loss in precision. As few as eight subclasses will explain almost all the variance the full detail will explain, and even more if there is non-linearity. Indeed, with most survey data, errors of measurement are sufficiently large so that some of the "lost precision" is spurious, and the extreme cases which tend to dominate the results of numerical least-squares estimates, are particularly likely to contain either conceptual or measurement errors. For example, using a single dummy variable for everyone whose house is worth more than $30,000 may keep some one person coded as having a house worth $500,000 (perhaps erroneously) from dominating the estimates.

In interpreting the results of dummy variable regression, one is usually interested in the relative *importance* of the various predictors, thought of as characteristics like age, education, and the like, and not interested in the importance of each subgroup by itself. The same is true with questions of statistical *significance,* though we argue that with substantial samples (1,000 or more) of the size to allow dummy variable regression, anything worth looking at (in terms of importance) will be significant anyway, and the crucial issue is the explanatory *power* of the predictors.

How then can we assess the explanatory *power* of a whole set of dummy variables associated with one characteristic, like education? There is a relatively simple answer by analogy with the partial beta coefficient of numerical regression, often used as an approximate indicator of the relative power of the predictors. The ideal indicator of course is the partial correlation coefficient, or the increase in the multiple correlation (squared) achieved by adding the predictor in question (the *set* of dummy variables) after all the others are already in. The true partial correlation coefficient can best be thought of as the simple correlation between two sets of residuals, residuals of the dependent variable after removing the effects of all the other explanatory variables except X1, and residuals of X1 after removing the effects from it of all the other explanatory variables. There is a great deal of confusion generated by the terminology and by the fact that the simple *regression* coefficient using these two sets of residuals is mathematically identical with the "partial beta coefficient" of a single multiple regression. However, the simple *correlation* coefficient between the two sets of residuals, which is equal to the partial *correlation* coefficient, cannot be derived from a single multiple regression analysis, unless the analysis also estimates the standard errors of the regression coefficient (b's) in which case:

$$r_{12.345}^2 = \frac{(b_{12.345})^2}{(b_{12.345})^2 + (\sigma_{b12.345})^2 (D/f)}$$

$$= \frac{t^2}{t^2 + D/f}$$

where D/f = N - K - 1 with N cases and K predictors.

The regression coefficients of a numerical multiple regression become "partial beta coefficients" when multiplied by the standard deviation of the explanatory variable in question and divided by the standard deviation of the dependent variable:

$$\beta = \frac{b_i \, \sigma_{X_i}}{\sigma_Y}$$

They are a kind of "standardized" regression coefficient, in standard deviation units, i.e. How many standard deviations ones the dependent variable move when the explanatory variable changes by one standard deviation?

The analogue to the partial beta coefficient in the case of dummy variables is simple and obvious. The dummy variables can be thought of as a new scale, new sets of numbers. If each individual were assigned the coefficients instead of the 1-0 dummy variables, and a regression computed with the same dependent variable, the regression coefficients would be 1.00 for each of these new "variables." The partial beta coefficients are then simply 1.00 times the standard deviation of the new "variable" (square root of the weighted sum of squares of the dummy variable coefficients in the set) divided by the standard deviation of the dependent variable which is known. Therefore the "partial beta coefficient" for a set of coefficients, Ai is:

$$\beta_A = \frac{1.00 \sqrt{\frac{\Sigma \, n_i A_i^2}{\Sigma \, ni}}}{\sigma_Y}$$

The main difference is that the signs of the A's have already taken account of direction of effects so this analogue beta is always positive.

It is useful in presenting the results of a regression using sets of dummy variables, to first list the predicting characteristics, in order of their "partial beta coefficients," then to present the tables of unadjusted means and deviations and adjusted deviations and means, for the more important predictors.

Readers are often interested not only in the power of each set of dummy variable in the multivariate context, but also its power if used alone. Again it is possible to use a standard statistic, Eta, the correlation ratio, which is directly comparable with the partial beta, except that it is calculated using the unadjusted deviations rather than the adjusted ones.

$$\text{ETA} = \eta = \sqrt{\dfrac{\dfrac{1}{n}\sum_{i=1}^{K} N_i\,(\overline{Y}_i - \overline{Y})^2}{\dfrac{1}{n}\sum_{i=1}^{N} (Y_i - \overline{Y})^2}} = \dfrac{\sqrt{\dfrac{\sum_{i=1}^{K} N_i\,(\overline{Y}_i - \overline{Y})^2}{\Sigma N_i}}}{\sigma_Y}$$

Indeed, eta is really the result of a one-way analysis of variance, using subgroup means, and relating the "explained sum of squares" explained by those means to the total variance (total sum of squares around the mean). Using the example on pp. 4-6, we can calculate η and β for "age" as follows: (remember we allowed no variance within the subgroups)

$$\eta = \sqrt{\dfrac{\dfrac{(200)^2\cdot 50 + (-200)^2\cdot 50}{100}}{\dfrac{(-3000)^2\cdot 10 + (1000)^2\cdot 40 + (-1000)^2\cdot 40 + (3000)^2\cdot 10}{100}}} = \sqrt{\dfrac{40,000}{2,600,000}} = \sqrt{.0154} = .124$$

$$\beta = \sqrt{\dfrac{\dfrac{(-1000)^2\cdot 50 + (1000)^2\cdot 50}{100}}{\dfrac{(-3000)^2\cdot 10 + (1000)^2\cdot 40 + (1000)^2\cdot 40 + (3000)^2\cdot 10}{100}}} = \sqrt{\dfrac{1,000,000}{2,600,000}} = \sqrt{.3846} = .620$$

It is unusual to have β larger than η, because spurious correlation is more common than spurious lack of it.

Ideally, then one would present the etas and "partial betas" indicating the explanatory power of each predictor (set of subclasses) separately and in a multivariate analysis.

Purists from the regression school may ask what about the assumptions of normally distributed explanatory variables. How can something which takes only the values 0 and 1 be normally distributed? Actually regression, particularly if interpreted in terms of power in reducing unexplained variance, not as a set of significance tests, is relatively robust under departures from this normality assumption. Trouble arises when for some subclass almost everyone is either 0 (no cases, so high sampling variability) or 1 (no variance so no explanatory power), but these problems become obvious if the tables give the number of cases.

Regression can also be used where the dependent variable is a dichotomy, such as whether or not the person owns a home. Again the depatures from normality are most serious when the average proportion is close to zero or to one hundred percent. Otherwise, the analysis can proceed, and the calculations are the same as though one were conducting a discriminant analysis, though the assumptions about errors are different. It is best to think of the final equation as predicting a probability, rather than classifying a whole group "Yes" or "No" as discriminant analysis does.

Indeed, it is often useful to create dichotomous dependent variables, even when there is a well distributed dependent variable. For instance, one might want to check whether the things that make a man more likely to be at one end of the distribution (on the dependent variable) are different from those that put him at the other end.[45]

Where dichotomous dependent variable possibilities do not seem appropriate, but the dependent variable is still not normally distributed, then as discussed earlier various solutions have been proposed:

> Transformations, such as logs or square roots, to reduce skewness, or allow elasticity interpretations of coefficients, or reduce the impact of extreme cases.
>
> Probit analysis, where one posits a normally distributed resistance to the explanatory forces, and wants to estimate both the mean and the variance of that distribution.

Actually one of the main problems with a dichotomous dependent variable is that it is often based on a single bit of information (answer to one question) and has relatively little real variance, and substantial error variance (reporting errors, etc.). In many cases, it pays to get some additional dimensions with other questions, build an index combining the answers to several questions (however arbitrary the index), so as to have some additional variance to explain and also to average out some of the error variance. When this was done with early retirement, adding three other indicators, and giving an extra point for planning to retire *very* early, the correlation with expected cash retirement income quadrupled (from $r^2 = .04$ to .15) and the relationship become much more nearly linear.[46]

One difficulty with the additivity assumption of regression appears at this stage, because the predicted value of some of these subgroups may be impossible, less than zero, or in the case of dichotomous dependent variables treated as probabilities, an expected probability greater than one.

Of course, such impossible cases appear even more easily if one uses the multiple regression coefficients to predict individual cases. It is easy to make such predictions if the output is in the form suggested: One starts with the grand mean and for each predictor adds or subtracts an amount depending on which subclass of that predictor the individual is in. An individual who is in the group on each predictor with the largest negative coefficient, may well end up with a predicted value less than zero for some quantity which cannot be negative.

The sampling errors of dummy variable regression coefficients have some special properties which make it somewhat easier to approximate them. Suppose we consider them as subgroup means, to which some adjustments for intercorrelations have been made. Then their stability certainly depends directly on the square root of the number of cases in the subgroup that was not zero on the dummy variable, i.e. the group that provided the mean. When sampling errors were calculated for dummy variable regression coefficients by the method of balanced repeated replication discussed in the previous chapter on sampling, they did fit $\sigma\sqrt{N}$ rather well. In other words, differences in variance among subgroups were much less important than differences in their sizes. Hence, it is very important that one present the subgroups sizes as well as the unadjusted and adjusted coefficients, enabling the reader to discard the non-significant ones. Indeed, one could, in a well-designed survey, assume some design effect, perhaps 1.05 to be conservative, and then use the following approximations:

Sample error of unadjusted deviations $\doteq \dfrac{(1.05)\,(\sigma_Y)}{\sqrt{N_i}}$
(subgroups means)

Sampling error of adjusted deviations $\doteq \dfrac{1.05\,\sigma_Y\sqrt{(1 - R^2)}}{\sqrt{N_i}}$
(dummy variable coefficients)

When there is no previous work on the design effects of the sample being used for the dependent variable in question, then a number of sampling errors can be calculated using balanced repeated replication, in order to establish an approximate design effect, to replace the 1.05 above.

So multiple regression with dichotomous variables handles the problems of intercorrelations among predictors (if they are not too high) and non-linearities in their effects. It does *not* handle non-additivities. If the effect of one explanatory factor depends on the level of another, we are unlikely to find it by regression. If we wanted to check for a limited number of such effects, we could build them in, but the total possibilities are astronomical, particularly if one allows for higher-order interactions. The figure on the next page shows a dramatically different "effect" of income on home ownership depending on age and family size among the young, or living in central cities (with apartments but few private homes) among the old. There was also so much stepwise non-linearity, that the particular groups account for most of the potential variance. Separate dummies for each of the ten groups would work out well, if one knew in advance to define them that way.

In other words, multiple regression is not really multivariate analysis. It throws away the rich matrix of information, keeping only the simple correlations among pairs of variables. The assumption of additivity is very powerful statistically in reducing complexity, but it is commonly violated in the real world. Running separate regressions on subgroups of the sample is a cumbersome way to look for these non-additivities, but is a useful first step. Prior analysis with more flexible data searching programs may be more efficient.

Figure 1

Percentage Who Own Their Own Home, by Income Decile, for Four Subgroups

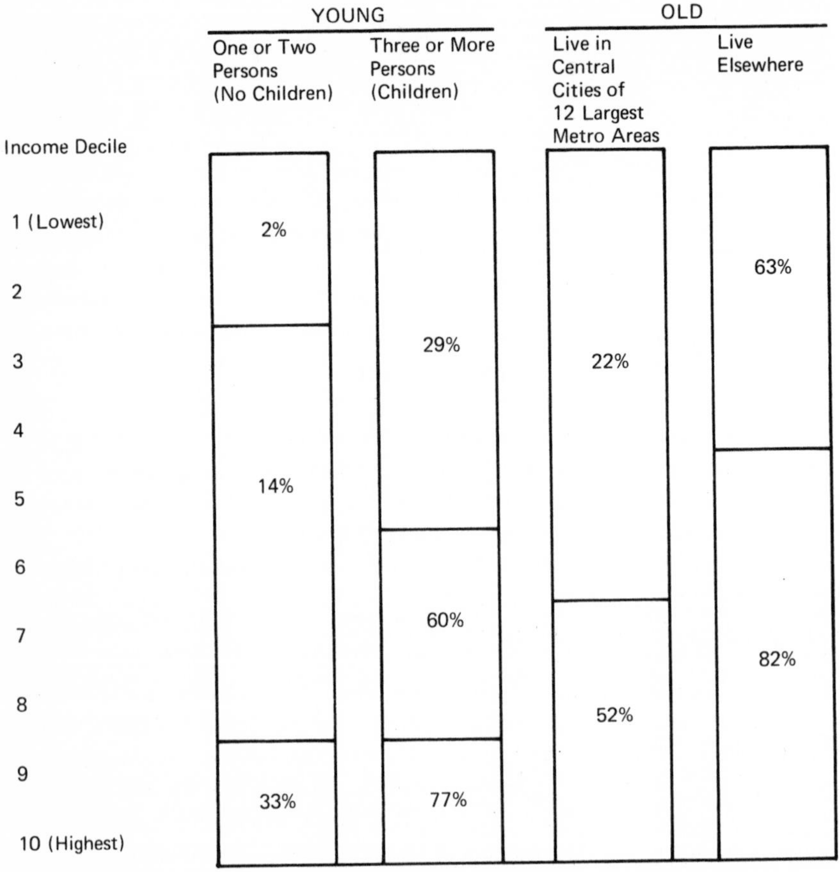

Income Decile	YOUNG		OLD	
	One or Two Persons (No Children)	Three or More Persons (Children)	Live in Central Cities of 12 Largest Metro Areas	Live Elsewhere
1 (Lowest)	2%			
2				63%
3		29%	22%	
4				
5	14%			
6				
7		60%		
8				82%
9			52%	
10 (Highest)	33%	77%		

Source: George Katona et al 1967 Survey of Consumer Finances, Survey Research Center, The University of Michigan, Ann Arbor, Michigan, 1968.

As we shall see, these searching strategies deal with intercorrelation in a different way: sequentially. What influence is left to other predictors after one actually removes some of the effects of one predictor (by dividing the sample, and hence implicitly only looking at deviations from the means of groups defined according to that predictor)? Where prediction is more important than untangling the causal structure, such a sequential approach may make sense even for the intercorrelation problem. One may want to know the cheapest (in terms of variables) way to predict (optimal disaggregation), and if one variable incorporates the influence of another, the second can be omitted.

Stepwise Procedures: There are many ready-made multiple regression programs which have "stepwise" procedures, for adding variables according to some strategy. This does not make much sense with dummy variables, or even with numerical variables. If one merely wants to know how much each variable would add to the total explanation, if it were added after the others were already in, then one needs only the partial correlation coefficients, and these are easily derivable from the multiple regression coefficients and their standard errors.

It would seem preferable to eliminate variables on the basis of this statistic rather than on some earlier determination. Certainly one should not eliminate variables on the basis of their simple correlations with the dependent variable. There is always the possibility of spurious lack of correlation. Suppose for instance that both A and B really have effects on Y, but in opposite directions, and are highly positively correlated with each other. Then the simple correlations might be:

$$r_{AB} = +.70$$

$$r_{YA} = .00$$

$$r_{YB} = .00$$

Both variables would be eliminated by a researcher focusing on reducing the number of explanatory variables. It might have been better to combine A and B somehow, if it were really essential to cut the number of variables. With samples of 1000 or more, the whole need for restricting explanatory variables is considerably reduced anyway.

The same logic that led to the proposed "partial beta coefficient" measure of the power of a whole set of dummy variables reflecting a single characteristic, might be thought to lead to a method for measuring this marginal contribution more directly. Suppose one treated the coefficients of the subclasses as a new variable, assigning to each individual a value for that variable equal to the coefficient for the subgroup to which he belongs. One could then recalculate the regression using not r sets of characteristics with k_i subclasses each, but with r new "variables." The regression coefficients must all come out to be 1.000, but the standard errors provide a measure of the partial correlations using the following relationship:

$$R^2yx.wz = \frac{(b_{yx.wz}/\sigma_{b_{yx.wz}})^2}{(b_{yx.wz}/\sigma_{b_{yx.wz}})^2 + N - K - k}$$

With:
N = cases
K - predictors
So:
N - K - 1 = Degrees of Freedom

With simple numerical multiple regression, this formula provides a way of getting the partial correlations without actually recalculating the regression K times, each time leaving out one of the predictors. But with dummy variables, repeating the regression with the new scales, the formula exaggerates the marginal contribution of each, because it is equivalent to rerunning the regression leaving out one set of dummies, but *not allowing the coefficients for the others to change within the sets.* (The new regressions would only allow a uniform shift up or down in a whole set.)* In practice, however, these partial correlations using the new scales turn out to provide a closer approximation to the true partial correlations than the betas.

When we have actually rerun the regressions leaving out each set of dichotomes separately, the reductions in the multiple correlation which are the true measure of the partial correlations, turn out to be closely approximated by the set of estimates from a single recomputation using the new scales, and fairly well approximated by the partial beta coefficient described earlier.

Interaction Effects: It is important to be clear about the difference between interaction effects on the one hand, and intercorrelation among the predictors on the other. We simplify the discussion by making one of the two

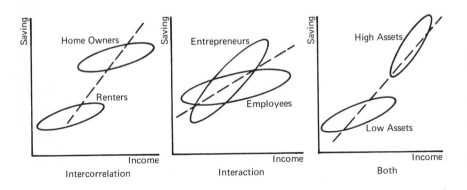

explanatory variables a dichotomy. Where the two groups on that dichotomy have different levels but the same slope (intercorrelation only), the simple saving-income regression would be spuriously high, but a multiple regression would introduce a shift-variable for home-ownership and give the proper income effect.

Where the two groups do not differ on income, but do have different income elasticities of saving (interaction effect) the simple saving-income regression is a compromise and adding a "entrepreneur or not" variable to make a

*We are indebted to W. H. Locke Anderson and Daniel Suits for this warning.

multiple regression would have no effect, self-employment appearing to have no influence. Only a covariance search, or a search for groups with different means (using income groups) would uncover the truth.

Where we have both intercorrelation and interaction effects, multiple correlation will measure neither of them properly. Only the more flexible search procedures will find the two effects, unless of course one suspects them and builds a linear model that incorporates them. But the number of possible interaction effects is almost unlimited and they are often higher order—for instance the people who do the most home-production (do-it-yourself work) are those who are home-owners *and* well educated *and* live in the country *and* have children *and* do not have any babies in diapers.[47]

With cardinal variables, interaction means that the relation between X1 and Y is different for different values of X2 (in which case the relation between X2 and Y will differ for different values of X1). Hence describing interaction effects is difficult since they can be stated either way, and it is impossible to know in most cases which way the causal influence goes (or whether it goes both ways).

In numerical regression, a common practice when interaction is suspected is to put in cross-product terms such as X1X2. This is a very restricted expression which may not fit the particular interaction that exists. It has the statistical disadvantage that it is highly correlated with both X1 and X2, and the substantive disadvantage that if there really is an interaction effect, then the meaning of the coefficients of X1 and of X2 is unclear, if not misleading. The interested reader would do well to read the literature on design of experiments and the testing for interaction effects in factorial designs.

The meaning of interaction effects is easier to see with categorical predictors, and a simple test for their presence easier to understand. Take a simple case without any interaction effects:

		X1		
		0	1	
X2	0	$1	$3	$2
	1	$3	$5	$4
		$2	$4	$3

Assume equal numbers exist in each of the four possible combinations, (no intercorrelation among the predictors), so that the overall average, and the X1 and X2 averages are simple to relate to the subcell averages. The test for interaction is whether one can predict the interior of the distribution from the marginals. For instance the $X1 = 0$, $X2 = 0$ combination is predicted by noting that for X1 the 0's are $1 below average, and for X2 the 0's are $1 below the average of $3, so $3 minus 1 minus 1 is $1. This is the technique for estimating data from missing cells in factorial designs in experimental work often called the "Yates missing plot technique."

Now suppose, in fact, that in addition to the separate effects of X1 and X2 there is an extra twelve dollars resulting from having both positive, then the inside of the table is not derivable from the marginals:

X1

		0	1	
	0	1	3	2
X2				
	1	3	17	10
		2	10	6

Using the marginals to make an additive prediction of the interior of the table would have the following expected values:

	0	1
0	-2	7 ·
1	7	14

and the following residuals from expected (additive) values:

	0	1
0	+3	-3
1	-3	+3

which are systematic and large, revealing that there is an interaction effect.

Now a dummy variable regression using X1 and X2 would still leave a substantial unexplained variance of 36, from the last figure. Suppose we had put in a cross-product term X1X2 which had the value 1 when X1 and X2 were both 1? We could not also put in X1 and X2, since either one along with X1X2 would determine the other (perfect intercorrelation among the predictors). If we put in one of the main effects, say X1, and the corner term, we still do not uncover the original model. Indeed, there are three chances out of four of getting the wrong corner. Now one might say, why not put in dummy variables for three of the four subcells, that would reproduce all the information exactly, and one could tell everything? This is true, but in the real analysis of survey data, where we have many predictor classifications and many subclasses of each, to put in a dummy variable for each subcell (except one) of each K_1 by K_2 table for each pair of predictors, rapidly exhausts even the capacity of present day computers, to say nothing of the patience of the person examining the output. If one thinks of attempting to select a few cross-product terms, then the probability of getting the right one is clearly one in four for two dichotomies, and one in nine for two trichotomies, one in twenty-seven for three trichotomies, and one in a hundred for two decile codes!

Furthermore, we have been talking only about first-order interaction effects. There is no reason why the effect of X1 should not depend on the joint distribution of X1 and X3.

In other words, the initial specification of each interaction as a separate variable so that one can stick to a linear model and use regression, is extremely difficult because there are so many possible kinds of interactions. The cross product of two numerical variables assumes that a particular form of synergism occurs, but it is equally possible to have the reverse, that is, a very low value of Y only when both X1 and X2 are small, and this would require a different specification of the interaction variables.

Systematic Search for Interactions: In practice, careful investigators searching a body of data for interactions have traditionally done so by sequential steps, separating the sample according to some important main effect variable, and seeing whether the two parts responded differently to some third variable. This procedure has been formalized in a computer program, with the advantage that the search analysis, usually thought of as idiosyncratic and artistic, can be specified as a strategy and replicated on the same or a different set of data.[48]

A brief description of the computer program's algorithm may be useful: There is a dependent variable and a set of explanatory predictors (each a set of categories or subclassifications). For each explanatory classification, the computer examines the explanatory power achievable by using it to divide the data into two subgroups. Power means reduction in unexplained variance, indicated by the "between sum of squares" of a simple analysis of variance with one degree of freedom (the weighted sum of squares of the subgroup means minus the usual correction factor, $N(\bar{X}^2)$. For a predictor with K classes, maintained in some logical or optimal order, there are k-1 possible ways to use it to dichotomize the sample, and the one with the greatest explanatory power is retained, while the computer goes on to repeat the process with each of the other predictors. The best overall division is then the best of the best (best split on the best predictor). That split is actually carried out, and the process repeated separately on each of the two subgroups thus formed.

Whether a predictor is maintained in its original order, or reordered optimally depends on whether it has a natural order. If not, then the optimal ordering is one according to the mean of the dependent variable for that subgroup. Of course this vastly increases the possibilities for idiosyncratic splits and is generally to be avoided.

Hence at each stage, the group with the largest remaining internal sum of squares is examined and if possible, divided again. The sample is divided by sequential branching into a series of mutually exclusive subgroups like the roots of a tree, with no assumption of symmetry (universality of effect) nor of equal effects (interaction effects absent). The process can be stopped when there are a stated number of final groups, or when no group contains more than some small percentage of the original total sum of squares, or, best, when no further split could reduce the unexplained variance by as much as some small fraction of the original sum of squares, say .005.

Even if predictors are maintained in order, there are $\sum_{i=1}^{n} (K_i - 1)$ possible divisions at each split, with n predictors of k subclasses each, so that it is useless to talk about tests of significance. If a predictor is reordered, there are of course, k! possible orders, times k-1 ways of splitting into a dichotomy after the reordering. So the computer is selecting a branching diagram in many cases among as many as a trillion possibilities. What can one say about the stability properties of such results—the possibilities of getting a similar result from a different sample?

The best way to look at this question is to note that the selection of a particular split competes with splits on each of the other variables, and clearly the closer the nearest competitors in terms of their explanatory power, the more likely that in another sample one of the others would win out. So it is a matter of the difference between variances (or sums of squares) relative to the standard error of that difference. (There are also competitive splits on the same predictor using different groups on each side, but such differences are minor and unimportant compared with using an entirely different predictor.) The probability of getting a different split is then the sum of the probabilities of getting each of the various alternative splits. In practice most of the competitors are not within twenty percent of the same sum of squares, but a sum of small probabilities can still be important. And the probability of getting the same branching diagram is the *product* of the probabilities of getting the same split at each stage:

(1 - probabilities of getting a competitor at first split)
(1 - probabilities of getting a different split at second stage)
(1 - probabilities of getting a different split at third stage) etc.

Clearly this can be very small for a complex branching using many predictors, if there are many close competitors.

In a sense the greatest power of the program is its ability to eliminate a variable as not important. If the variable has no effect on the whole sample, nor on any of the various subgroups generated because they differ on the dependent variable, then it can be said with some confidence that that variable does not matter. Actually the output produces the means of the dependent variable for each subclass of each predictor, for each subgroup which it generates, so one can see how the apparent effect of a variable is altered, accentuated, or attenuated, as other variables are taken into account by dividing the sample by them.

It might seem inefficient to "take account" of a variable by making a single dichotomous split on it, but the process can easily proceed to make several splits in a row on the same predictor, and as we have seen, a relatively few divisions on a variable will have nearly as much variance-reducing power as its full detail.

Experience has shown that many interesting variables do not affect the whole population, but only some susceptible (or unconstrained) part of it. A measure of achievement motivation, for instance, proved to be powerfully related to hourly earnings of the individual, but only for middle aged college graduates, presumably the group most able to alter its own earnings.[49] Again, the utilization of medical and hospital services proved to be related to insurance coverage, but only for middle-aged women, the others presumably having less discretion (particularly the children).[50] Perhaps the most startling example of non-additivity is one where the forces keeping people from engaging in home production appeared to be substitutes for one another, only those for whom everything was favorable engaging extensively in the activity.[51] Another analysis revealed that the effect of family size on food expenditures was different in rural and urban areas.[52]

There are certain balanced offsetting interaction effects which this search program could still miss, as when young women and old men go to the hospital more often:

Percent Who Go to the Hospital

	Men	Women	Both Sexes
Young	2%	4%	3%
Old	4%	2%	3%
All ages	3%	3%	3%

Having no incentive to split the sample on either age or sex, the program would have no way to discover this interaction. A new option is being developed which looks ahead a step or two and would find such things. It actually makes the best split on each predictor, however useless it looks, and then makes one or two more splits, looking for the largest explained sum of squares for the two-split or three-split sequence.

One might also prefer a symmetric branching diagram, unless the loss in explanatory power was severe (defined as an option) since it is so much easier to discuss and understand things which affect more than one subgroup. Again an option is being developed which, if one of a pair of groups has been split on a certain predictor using certain categories, will split the other group the same way (down to the subclasses on each side) so long as the symmetry does not explain less of the variance by as much as X percent.

A Simple Test for Non-Additivity: There are an extremely large number of possible interaction effects, even with relatively few predictors. With modern computers it is also easy to determine not only the shapes of the main additive effects of many predictors, but the proportion of the variance such an additive "multivariate" analysis explains. What is being omitted are the details of the interior of the tables, since multiple regression uses only the marginals, and the interrelationships among the predictors, throwing away all information except that imbedded in the table of all possible simple correlations. Consider a case with three predictors, with four, five, and eight subclasses respectively. Regression will provide estimates for the seventeen coefficients (provided each set is constrained to a weighted mean of zero rather than making one of each set zero). But we actually have information on 4 x 5 x 8 or 160 subcells in a three-dimensional table. We can consider the 160 subgroups in a one-way analysis of variance, and ask how much of the variance we could explain if we used those 160 subcell means to predict. The answer is simple, the explained variance is

$\sum_{i=1}^{160} N_i \overline{Y}_i$ around zero, or in more usual form $\sum_{i=1}^{160} N_i \overline{Y}_i^2 - N\overline{Y}^2$ around the grand mean.

Or as a proportion of the variance around the mean, the 160 groups account for:

$$\frac{\sum N_i \overline{Y}_i^2 - N\overline{Y}^2}{\sum \overline{Y}^2 - N\overline{Y}^2} = \eta^2$$

This can be compared directly with the R^2 from the additive multiple regression to see whether the 160 subcells do better than the seventeen coefficients. If they do considerably better, then clearly the additivity assumptions are incorrect. One must be careful, however, to take account of the degrees of freedom used. F-ratios are more appropriate. After all, with sufficient subclassification one might end up with only one case per subcell, and could then predict the sample perfectly.

The F-ratio is the ratio of two variance estimates, one based on grouping by predictors, one on the variance within groups. For computational simplicity the following is most useful:

Multiple regression:

$$F = \frac{\dfrac{R^2}{K - 1}}{\dfrac{(1 - R^2)}{N - K}} = \frac{R^2}{1 - R^2} \cdot \frac{N - K}{K - 1}$$

where there are N cases and k predictors (including those constrained to zero)

A set of subcell means:

$$F = \frac{\dfrac{\Sigma N_i \overline{Y}_i^2 - N\overline{Y}^2}{K - 1}}{\dfrac{(\Sigma Y_i^2 - N\overline{Y}^2) - (\Sigma N_i \overline{Y}_i^2 - N\overline{Y}^2)}{N - K}}$$

where there are N cases and k subcell means

each with K-1 and N-K degrees of freedom. The F-test here is not considered a significance test, to be compared with a null hypothesis, but a measure of importance or power of an analysis corrected for degrees of freedom used.

With a modern computer it should be very simple to impose a multiple sort and generate the weighted sum of squares of the subgroup means (or the equivalent $\dfrac{(\Sigma Y_i)^2}{n_i}$). All that is needed in addition is the total sum of squares, which is available from any of the additive regressions that may have been computed.

One Dominant Variable: A common problem arises when there is one variable which is of overwhelming importance, either because of its power, or because it is of substantive importance. In economic studies, it is usually income or education which fits this description, particularly income because the economic analyst or policymaker is primarily interested in the effects of income (or income elasticities). In studies of change, growth, or development, the initial state may be such a variable. The problem then is whether the relationship with this dominant variable is the same for all subgroups in the sample.

The traditional procedure in such a case is the analysis of covariance. Simply put, the analsyis of covariance fits a simple regression of the dependent variable against the dominant or control variable, separately for each of a set of subgroups of the sample, and partitions the variance into that accounted for by differences in the levels of the regression lines (subgroup means), that accounted for by differences in their slopes, and the remaining unexplained deviations from the regression lines. But in practice, one may want to *search* for which subgroups would be most useful in having the largest differences in regression slopes, for instance, which subgroups had the greatest differences in income elasticities of expenditure on cars.

For any single group, we have a total sum of squares which represents errors of prediction if one knows nothing. If one knows the grand mean, and predicts that for each case, the errors squared are then what is usually called the variance, or sum of squares around the mean:

Total sum of squares $\qquad\qquad\qquad \Sigma Y^2$

Sum of squares around the mean $\qquad \Sigma(Y - \overline{Y})^2 = \Sigma Y_i^2 - N\overline{Y}^2$

Reduction in error sum of squares
from knowing the mean: $\qquad\qquad N\overline{Y}^2 \equiv \dfrac{(\Sigma Y)^2}{N}$

If one adds information about the value of X for each case, and about the regression of Y on X, the error is reduced by a *fraction of the total sum of squares around the mean* equal to r^2. In more convenient computational form, the remaining error sum of squares knowing the regression x is:

$$[1 - r^2]\,[\Sigma Y_i^2 - N\overline{Y}^2] = \left[1 - \frac{\left(\Sigma XY - \dfrac{\Sigma X\,\Sigma Y}{N}\right)^2}{(\Sigma X^2 - N\overline{X}^2)\,(\Sigma Y^2 - N\overline{Y}^2)}\right][\Sigma Y^2 - N\overline{Y}^2]$$

and the gain, or explained sum of squares from knowing the regression, is:

$$r^2(\Sigma Y_i^2 - N\overline{Y}^2) = \frac{\left(\Sigma XY - \dfrac{\Sigma X\,\Sigma Y}{N}\right)^2}{(\Sigma X^2 - N\overline{X}^2)\,(\Sigma Y^2 - N\overline{Y}^2)} \cdot (\Sigma Y^2 - N\overline{Y}^2) = \frac{\left(\Sigma XY - \dfrac{\Sigma X\,\Sigma Y}{N}\right)^2}{\Sigma X^2 - N\overline{X}^2}$$

As a next step, having explained what we can knowing the mean of Y, its relationship with X, and the values of X, we break the sample into two groups, with different means, and different regressions on X. The gain in explanatory power (reduction in unexplained sum of squares) is in two parts: a gain from using two subcell means instead of one grand mean, and the gain from using two different regression *slopes* on X instead of one.

The error variance using two means instead of one is:

$$\Sigma Y_1^2 - N_1\overline{Y}_1^2 + \Sigma Y_2^2 - N_2 Y_2^2 \text{ but } \Sigma Y_1^2 - \Sigma Y_1^2 - \Sigma Y_2^2 = \Sigma Y^2$$

so the error is less than with one overall mean by:

(a) $\quad N_1\overline{Y}_1^2 \quad + \quad N_2\overline{Y}_2^2 \quad - \quad N\overline{Y}^2$

Expl. by	Expl. by	Expl. by
Mean of	Mean of	Grand
Group 1	Group 2	Mean

The error variance using two subgroup regressions instead of one overall regression is: $[1 - r_1^2][\Sigma Y_1^2 - N_1\overline{Y}^2] + [1 - r_2^2][\Sigma Y_2^2 - N_2\overline{Y}_2^2]$

which is a gain of:

(b)
$$\frac{\left[\Sigma X_1 Y_1 - \dfrac{\Sigma X_1 \, \Sigma Y_1}{N_1}\right]^2}{\Sigma X_1^2 - N_1\overline{X}_1^2} + \frac{\left[\Sigma X_2 Y_2 - \dfrac{\Sigma X_2 \, \Sigma Y_2}{N_2}\right]^2}{\Sigma X_2^2 - N_2\overline{X}_2^2} - \frac{\left[\Sigma XY - \dfrac{\Sigma X \, \Sigma Y}{N}\right]^2}{\Sigma X_2 - N\overline{X}^2}$$

Explained by	Explained by	Explained by
Regression of	Regression	Overall Regression
Group 1	of Group 2	Before Splitting
		Into Two Groups

The thing to keep in mind is that in discussions of explanation by regression, it is the sum of squares *around the mean* that is being decomposed into an explained and unexplained part indicated by r^2 and $1\text{-}r^2$. Hence the gain in going from one group to two is easily decomposible into a gain from using two means instead of one, and a gain from running regressions of two different slopes through those two different means, on the other. In comparing various pairs as candidates for splitting a sample, the third terms in expression (a) and (b) are constant over all possible splits and can be ignored. One seeks only for the division which makes the first two terms as large as possible.

The original computer search program maximized (a) at each split. It is easily possible to maximize (b) instead, or to maximize (a) plus (b).

If X is income, and Y is some expenditure (in logs if one likes to talk of elasticities), then splitting the sample to maximize (b) is a search for groups with the greatest differences in their responses to income, perhaps to find the optimal disaggregation. In that case one would argue that differences in level (means) between subgroups do not matter, only differences in their responsiveness to income.

On the other hand, there may be situations where one wants to locate groups which differ, whether by level (of Y) or slope (relationship to X), and that is also possible.

This modern variant of the analysis of covariance is much more flexible and makes use of the computer's capacity to carry out a programmed routine of investigative strategy tirelessly, and in a way which can be repeated on different data, or on the same data to check for errors or instabilities. Science seems likely to be best served by analysis strategies which are reproducible, just as is the rest of the research design.

The use of covariance analysis in the case of income elasticities is one approach to a problem which economists have struggled with for some time. Its most dramatic expression arose when it became obvious that income elasticities of total consumption expenditures calculated from cross-section data were substantially lower than those estimated from time series data, and always underestimated the growth of consumption over time as income increased. As we shall see below, one popular explanation advanced by Friedman, the "permanent income" hypothesis, essentially argued that there were errors in the measurement of income, the explanatory variable, which would have led to a downward bias in the regression slope. Permanent income, free from those short-run errors, would provide a better estimate of the true income elasticity of consumption. We shall return to this but it may be worth noting here that if the purpose is to predict the expenditure responses to changes in income, then a search for subgroups with differential responses does double duty—it allows one to find different responses according to conditions which may be token differences in permanent income, but it also allows one to find real differences in people's propensity to spend, for people in different situations. Prediction would then be improved by optimal disaggregation, asking to whom the income increases were going where it mattered.

In deciding on the best division of a sample or subsample, using differences in slopes only, a new problem arises, however. If the means of X and/or Y differ, and one is combining some of the k subclasses on a predictor into one group and the rest into another, it is possible for uniform slopes of several subgroups to be hidden by differences in their means. In the figures below, in both cases group B should certainly be isolated from the other two, yet the *pooled* slope through the clusters of A and C combined would not differ much from the slope for B alone, and the pooled slope criterion might easily segregate either A or C from the other two groups. Hence the computer program now being developed and

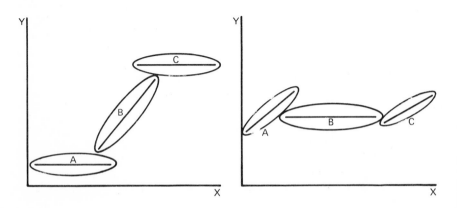

tested uses *weighted average* slopes as a criterion if one wants to focus on slopes, not full regressions.

The use of weighted average slopes for combinations of subgroups increases the possibility of idiosyncratic findings, however, since small subgroups can have their regression slopes dominated by a few cases. Hence we are finding that the search for different slopes must usually maintain the order of the subclasses of the predictors (allowing only the k-1 possible divisions along that ordering), and should also insist on a rather large minimum group size.

Special Problems in Estimating Income Elasticities: There has been more interest among economists in using sample surveys to estimate the effect of income on consumer behavior than the effect of any other independent variable. As a result of the close attention paid to income elasticities and related measures, the difficulties in estimating the theoretically relevant measures from survey data have been thoroughly discussed in the literature.

We may consider first the simple situation in which only two variables are involved, income and a measure of expenditures. From a theoretical point of view the simplest formulation is one in which both variables are in logarithmic form. The regression coefficient for income is then itself the income elasticity. This formulation assumes constant elasticity over the full range of income. It is doubtful whether this assumption can be defended in general—there are both theoretical and empirical objections—but it may be appropriate for some categories of expenditure.[53] Prais and Houthakker, after careful consideration, prefer a semi-log formulation for foodstuffs. It is also common to use income without a log transformation but to allow for curvilinearity in one of the manners discussed above.

When elasticity is permitted to vary, it is sometimes estimated at the mean, as a method of compressing the relationship of income to the dependent variable in a single statistic. There are theoretically any number of curves with the same slope at the mean, however, and it can be argued that the best procedure is simply to estimate and present the equation for the entire curve. It is also possible, of course, to calculate the elasticity at several points, depending on what one needs to know for the problem at hand. When the effect of the income is approximated by a step function, the calculation of point elasticity obviously requires curve fitting as an intermediate step.

The more fundamental problems in estimating income effects, however, concern the isolation of the effect of income from the effect of other variables. In the first place, the measurement of the effect of income on consumption requires the measurement of the effects of household size on consumption. This problem was carefully considered by Prais and Houthakker in the early 1950's by which time there was already a literature on the subject, and they were led to the development of unit-consumer scales. The objective was to adjust for the effect of household composition so that income effects could be isolated.[54]

An alternative to the use of equivalent adult scales is the separate analysis of families with different composition. For example, one might have a separate equation for married couples with one child, and estimate the effect of income on the consumption of some commodity for that segment of the population only.[55]

More recently attention has been drawn to the problems of isolating the effect of income from that of variables other than household composition. In particular, it is difficult to determine how to treat variables which may be correlated with "permanent" income. The problems are posed by the contention of Friedman that measured income is not a satisfactory approximation of the theoretically relevant income, nor, for that matter, is measured consumption satisfactory. The relevant income variable, he urges, is "permanent" income. Permanent income, empirically, is correlated with such variables as age and education. The analyst, therefore, is in an awkward position. If he chooses to think of age and education as essentially measures of tastes, or measures of factors which cause difference in tastes, then he should try to hold them constant since he would like to examine the effect of income for constant tastes. But if he thinks of such variables as related to permanent income he should not hold them constant. He must permit permanent income to vary if he wishes to measure its effect on consumption. If he thinks of these variables partly in the one way and partly in the other, he is faced with the problem of how to partial out their effects.[56]

One approach to the problem would seem to be to estimate permanent income directly. If income considerations other than those relating to current assets and current income influence how that income is allocated by consumers, logically these considerations must be in the nature of expectations. We may proceed by measuring these expectations and introducing them explicitly into the analysis. Then we may assert that any effect of, say, education, remaining after income expectations have been taken into account can be interpreted as the effect of education on tastes. This assertion, of course, is defensible in proportion to our ability to measure both education and the relevant expectations correctly. As an empirical fact, however, people's notions about their own future incomes are quite vague, and questions dealing with it elicit a large proportion of "don't know" answers. At any rate, if we are trying to measure a man's long-run economic status, expectations about future family obligations may be both more real and more powerful differentiators than differential income expectations.

Another possible strategy is to avoid asking questions about expectations and seek instead to approximate "permanent" income by using average measured income for several years. We may also prefer such an average measure for the entirely different reason that we hope the errors in our estimates of income will cancel out in the averaging process. This dual interpretation suggests again the close parallel between Friedman's analysis and the errors-in-variables problem discussed above.

In the same year that Friedman published *A Theory of the Consumption Function,* 1957, an article by Kuh and Meyer also analyzed the use of income coefficients from cross-section studies.[57] They were concerned in part with the types of consideration mentioned above, such as the problem of choice of functional form for the estimating equations. They also considered systematically the problems which arise in one important use of income coefficient from surveys, their inclusion in composite equations which combine cross-section with aggregate data.

The reasons for the development of this type of combined equation may be simply stated. In the analysis of consumer expenditure time series, estimates of price elasticity have been reasonably successful. Prices do vary over time; some prices vary considerably. It is more difficult, however, to estimate income coefficients from time series. Aggregate income changes slowly, and in a manner which may be hard to isolate from the effects of trends in other variables, such as trends in tastes, and is itself affected by changes in consumption. Income varies widely among families at a given point in time, however; while prices at any one time are likely to be the same for people at all incomes. Investigators have sought to use that variation to estimate income coefficients. Kuh and Meyer note, however, that the cross-section estimates of income elasticities of saving, usually have been lower than those obtained from time series. (This observation, of course, parallels Friedman's about the consumption function.)

Kuh and Meyer raise the question of whether people have adjusted their expenditure behavior to their income. There may be rigidities in spending behavior which lead to lags in adjustment, so that the relation between income and consumption may be a short run one for aggregate data but a long run for cross-section data.

We must conclude that satisfactory measurement of income elasticities from cross-section data requires more than simple bivariate calculations relating annual income and annual expenditures. We must also expect that similar close attention to other variables may reveal similar complications. It is quite possible that the imaginative application of the covariance search process described above particularly if used with panel data on changes in income and on spending will at least indicate where the differences are, from which a more realistic theory can be developed.

Analysis of Repeated Surveys: As the period for which sample surveys are available lengthens, there is increasing interest in the potentialities of analysing data from repeated surveys. For simple descriptive statistics it is possible to prepare measures of trend. One may examine, for example, the trend in the percentage of the population with income over a fixed level. Such comparisons require strict comparability of the survey procedures over time. Subtle differences in the questions asked, the method of sample, interviewer training, and the like, may influence the trends especially over periods of many years. It is also necessary to take into account changes in price levels. A twenty-year trend in median income, for example, obviously must take into account changing prices. And over long periods there are also changes in the demographic composition of households, including the average number of people per unit—such as the secular decline in the proportion of families containing two or more spending units. Careful comparisons must take these shifts into account.

One might think that the best way would be to measure all the variables in relation to the average levels that current year, but even aside from problems of calculating deciles of categorical items, this procedure would wipe out both changes in prices and changes in real incomes and expenditures. On the other hand, adjustments for price alone must face the fact that our ability to measure prices and price changes, particularly for components of expenditure, is not very good. The notion of calculating each year a measure of "real expenditure on cars" is likely to remain just an idea.

Repeated surveys allow somewhat better interpretation of age-related differences in behavior. If younger people in one survey are more receptive to the use of credit, is this because they are younger, or because they represent a new generation with new ideas which they will still hold when they are older; or do they represent a period of history in which they grew up so that their generation may be unique?

We can, with repeated surveys, sort out some of this, but not all. Suppose, for instance, that ten years later, the forty-five year olds, who were thirty-five ten years ago and favorable to installment credit, are now opposed to it. And suppose that the new group of thirty-five year olds are favorable to the use of credit. Then one might decide that it was age that made the difference. The age group, or generation, or cohort to use the demographer's word, did not have a stable attitude toward credit.

One should not count too much on the analysis of cohorts or generations in repeated surveys, because there are *three* hypotheses not two, and the three variables they imply are tightly interrelated: Is it the man's actual chronological age, his generation (when he was born), or the particular year of history that explains his attitude or behavior? One cannot sort out the relative influence of these three even with multiple regression, because any one of them is a strict linear function of the other two:

$$\text{Age} = \text{Present year of history} - \text{Year born}.$$

Only if one can assume that one of the three does not matter, is it possible using repeated survey data to separate the influences of the other two.

There has also been increasing interest in the comparison of relationship estimated at different dates. Miner has compared regression equations on consumer debt computed from repeated surveys.[58] Miner notes that there are three possible types of change in such an analysis: changes in the constant term in the regression equation, changes in the regression coefficients, and changes in the means of the predictors.

Changes in the *coefficients* reflect basic changes in behavior patterns. Multiplied times the original mean values of the explanatory variables, they provide an estimate of the aggregate or mean change that would have taken place if nothing but behavior patterns had changed.

Changes in the *means* of the predictors reflect changes in the situations people face, and multiplied by the original behavioral coefficients, provide an estimate of the overall change that would have taken place had nothing changed but the conditions people faced.

Residual changes in the grand mean, that is change in the mean minus the two estimates of changes accounted for by changes in behavior relations or in the situations measured, reflect changes unaccounted for in the analysis, often casually called "changes in taste." They are very difficult to interpret whether between years or between countries or between subgroups analyzed this way, because there are many hypotheses and only one degree of freedom.

Where dummy variables are used, the same analysis is possible, except that it is the proportions in subclasses which change rather than means of predictive variables, i.e., one deals with changing proportions in each income class rather than change in mean income. It is important, however, to have the data in the form suggested earlier, with coefficients for each subclass of each predictor, their weighted mean being zero, and the constant term being the overall mean. Otherwise the constant term has little meaning, being a composite of the means of the groups whose coefficients were forced to zero plus the grand mean; and changes in the other coefficients might well reflect not changes in behavior of that group, but in the behavior of the omitted group.

Such multivariate analysis of what accounts for overall differences in some dependent variable can be done not only with surveys at different points in time, but also with surveys in different countries, asking whether overall differences can be accounted for by differences in, say income or education levels, or differences in the effect of income or education on behavior, or are left to some other more global explanation (or to unmeasured variables). Similarly, one can analyze subgroups from a single survey in the same manner.

With expenditure analysis, one might want to regard the unexplained changes in the overall average as reflecting changes in the supply side of the market, including changes in price. But such changes might well affect different groups differently, so the problem would seem to require a more complete model.[59]

There is, of course, always the problem whether all the variables have been measured in the same way in successive surveys, and whether shifts in the other details of procedure have not introduced spurious changes. Strict probability sampling fully carried out is clearly essential. One study went back to the same geographic grids but allowed the interviewers to select every other dwelling "at random." The interviewers on the second wave were college students, and they interviewed younger, better educated people with larger farms, introducing all sorts of spurious change.

Where the repeated surveys use the same basic sample down to the rather small areas, added precision is provided for estimates of change even without re-interviews, because the correlation between first interview and second in demographic characteristics, etc. is higher than chance, and the negative covariance term in the formula for sampling error of the difference between two means (or two percentages) is larger, and so the sampling error is smaller than with two completely different random samples.

It is also possible to develop some semi-aggregated time series from a series of repeated surveys. One defines subgroups on characteristics that do not change much, and treats the mean income, saving, etc. of these subgroups as trends over time for the whole subgroups represented. The data are then subjected to econometric analysis like any set of time series. (Zellner forthcoming)

In a more general sense, analysis is possible on a within-year, between-year basis, where each variable is expressed as deviation of its actual value from its mean for all families that year, plus the overall deviation of the average that year for all families, from the average over all. By thus removing shifts attributable to the year, and to the individual family, what is left is presumably the revelation of short-run dynamic influences.[60]

Analysis of Reinterviews and Panels: There has been increasing recognition that reinterviews have important advantages for the analyst. The uses of reinterviews are diverse, and we shall keep clearly in mind that reinterviews may be undertaken for quite different purposes, and that it may be necessary to make a choice as to how a particular set of reinterview data is to be interpreted. If reinterviews are used primarily as a means of data collection, as in the work of Neter and Waksberg, the first interview may be used for purposes of "bounding" time intervals. Data from that first interview concerning the variable for which bounding is necessary cannot be used in analysis. Data from that interview on other variables, of course, may be used. It will be recalled that reinterviews may also be undertaken for purposes of sampling, such as reducing the sampling error of estimates of changes from repeated surveys. (The sampling error of a mean difference is about forty percent smaller than the sampling error of the difference between two means, though the gain over the surveys using the same sample structure is not that large.) Any gains in analytic potential which may result will be essentially by-products.

Reinterviews also may be undertaken primarily for the purpose of increasing analytic potential. The potential gains are of two basic types. First, the use of reinterviews makes it possible to focus attention on changes over time, and thereby to abstract from the stable characteristics of a unit. The resulting simplification may be advantageous. For example, Houthakker and Haldi were interested in the investment of families in automobiles. They set up an equation in which gross investment in a year is a function of income, initial stock, family characteristics, and an error term:

$$G_j = a + b Y_j + c S_j + d F_j + W_j$$

Where G_j = gross investment (for the j-th family)

Y_j = income

S_j = stock of cars (valued in dollars)

F_j = characteristics of the family

W_j = error.

They proceeded by setting up two such equations, one for each of the years under consideration, and subtracting the two. The F_j terms drop out.[61]

This method depends upon the assumption that the effects of the F_j terms, i.e., the family characteristics, are additive. If in fact there are interactions between these terms and the effects of income or stocks, the model is inappropriate. Whether there are such interactions is a question which must be considered for each model separately. But it seems unlikely that there will be important interactions. In principle one could include in such a model any such interactions, and any remaining stable characteristics of the family would still drop out.

It is possible that there may be *changes* over time even in the F_j, which will have additive effects. If such changes do occur, they will be reflected in changes in the constant term. The factors which drop out might be related to the location of the place of residence of a family for example. Over a period of two or three years, it seems reasonable to suppose that the characteristics of a location will not change. People who live in Manhattan will continue to be less likely to own cars than those who live in Connecticut. It is also quite reasonable that some people will continue to have a weakness for cars and allocate their income accordingly, while others are comparatively uninterested. Whether the income elasticity of the demand for cars is the same for these two groups seems more open to question.

The second basic way in which reinterviews may increase analytic potential is by their contribution to the problem of sorting out the sequence of causation. Several possible patterns may be used in analysis. In one pattern, conditions as measured in interview (1) are viewed as causes of one or more events in period (A) which is the period between interview (1) and interview (2). Interview (2) is needed only to measure the dependent variable. It may be brief. For example, in a study of the geographic mobility of labor, a major dependent variable was a measure of migration between an initial personal interview and a reinterview about a year later by telephone. The second interview was devoted essentially to ascertaining one fact, whether or not the family had migrated. Note that the analysis is based on two assumptions: (1) that the important causes of migration can be measured in advance, on the average, six months in advance. Causes that may operate close to the date of the move are ignored; (2) that the important causes can be measured at a single date. This type of analysis can be used either when the dependent variable is a discrete event, like moving to a new home, or a series of events, like saving money. Finally, note that any variable measured at interview (1) meets one logical requirement needed to qualify as a cause of events in period (A), the requirement of priority in time.

In the second two time periods are considered, (A) and (B). Events in (A) are measured in interview (1); events in (B), in interview (2). For example, Houthakker and Haldi examined the effect of income in (A) on investment in cars in (A), and the effect of income in (B) on the purchase of cars in (B). They found it useful, as noted above, to subtract the two equations to form a single equation involving the difference in value of the variables. The analysis relates changes in the variables.

This type of analysis assumes that the causes and effects are contemporaneous—e.g. income in a period influences outlay in that period. It is also possible to introduce stocks at the beginning of the period, relying on memory data. A variant on the scheme would measure the stocks in a preliminary interview at the start of the period (A). Then initial conditions plus contemporaneous events determine the dependent variable.

Wherever *change* in initial conditions (including attitudes and expectations), is supposed to cause *change* in subsequent behavior (a flow) then a third pattern involving three interviews is essential; (1) and (2) measuring initial conditions, and (2) and (3) measuring behavior (e.g., expenditures). It may be that the model believed to be relevant is one in which: (1) the crucial predictor or predictors are believed to operate with lags; and (2) the change in the value of the predictor is believed crucial. For example, a family which has experienced a decline in income may make a delayed adjustment. Then income may be measured for periods (A) and (B), and consumption for (B) and (C). The change in income from (A) to (B) may predict a change in consumption between (B) and (C). Then initial conditions plus events in the preceding period determine the dependent variable. This type of analysis obviously will be more or less revealing depending on the correctness of the assumptions as to what are the appropriate lengths of time periods and what are the appropriate lags. Periods often used are six months or a year, but either shorter or longer periods deserve consideration.

These three patterns, of course, by no means exhaust the possibilities. More complex schemes can be developed. This discussion is also incomplete in that it stresses only initial causes. An additional field for analysis is the causes of continuation of behavior, once initiated. It is widely believed that there are "ratchets" in consumer behavior—certain patterns of behavior, once established, tend to persist. (Compare, for example, the data on the effect of an initial experience on the propensity to travel by air.) We may expect increasing elaboration of analysis based on reinterviews.

Cagan has approached these problems in a different manner, relying on data from a single survey only.[62] His method is to use measures of wealth at time of the interview to estimate the average savings-income ratio in the past. The method requires an estimate of the relevant length of period, an estimate of the current value of net worth and an estimate of variations over time in the major independent variables, notably, in income. It also requires some method of dealing with changes in the price level and the associated capital gains (or losses). The method will tend to average out the effects of variables which fluctuate in the short run. Other factors which operate through their effect on the relevant lengths of period can also be omitted from explicit consideration. For example, some factors may operate through their influences on the data at which the family becomes the owner of its home. The essential idea implicit in the method is that careful consideration of the position of a family at a given point in time should be revealing as to the behavior of the family up to that date. In principle such information is available both to analyze the past and to predict the future. Hence, we may consider this method as a possible elaboration of the first pattern above.

In general before going to the vast expense and difficulty of reinterviews and panels, one should ask whether more extensive questioning in a single survey about events in the past would not produce as good a set of dated data for dynamic analysis. Substantial possibilities would seem to exist in studying the dynamics of changes in people's residences, and perhaps their cars, relying on their memories of past events.

It is quite possible for patterns of association found in static cross-sections to be the reverse of dynamic relations. For instance, various forms of economizing behavior are associated with lower than average incomes, presumably because people feel forced to adopt them. But over time, it may well be that those who do economize end up with increased incomes, a positive relation between an initial activity and the change. Or those who economize more than others in similar circumstances may end up with bigger income increases.

All this serves to dramatize another aspect of panels: some of the data are situations at time of interview: attitudes, rates of flow, but others are cumulative flows measured over a past period, such as last year's income and expenditure on durable goods. If one then has a hypothesis that changes in initial attitudes lead to changes in subsequent expenditures, we have already noted that it takes three interviews with the same people to provide the data to test this. The first two waves provide the initial stock and attitude data at the beginning of two years, and the second and third wave provide the after-the-period reports on actual behavior during the two years. A further difficulty with pursuing such dynamic analysis is the periodicity and lumpiness of many consumer decisions by which a powerful negative autocorrelation may be piled on top of a spurious positive cross-section correlation (through association of all variables with stage of the family life cycle), both of which make it difficult to find the dynamic correlation one seeks to measure.

When the data are for two different points in time for the same individuals, it is possible to convert an equation explaining the rate of change in some variable X_1 as a function of X_1 and X_2 to one which regresses its value at the second point in time on its value at the first point, and the value of other explanatory variables at that time. And the coefficients of such an equation can be related to the relationship between the dependent variable and the other explanatory variable in a static cross-section, if one is willing to assume that all the causal processes have resulted in an equilibrium state.[63]

Furthermore, given the regression of a dependent variable at the second time point on its value and the value of other variables at an earlier time point, if one takes a third wave of interviews, and uses only the third and first time points, then the mathematical model posits a difference between these coefficients and those using the time interval half as long. If there is nothing but measurement error, however, then the coefficients will be identical for the two time periods. In other words, one can estimate how much of the previously estimated dynamic relationship was pure measurement error and how much was a genuine dynamic relationship. Of course one must assume the basic relations have not changed, but at a minimum, this mathematical model suggests the importance of a third measurement on the same people in any study of change.

One way to deal with autocorrelation in panel studies is to use covariance analysis, treating the initial state or previous year's flow as the X variable, and searching for differences among subgroups in the regression slopes (rates of change). If, instead, one uses the change directly as a dependent variable, there will be a spurious negative correlation with the initial state if it is used as one of the explanatory variables:

$$(Y1 - Yo) = a + bYo + \ldots$$

or
$$Y1/Yo = a + bYo + \ldots$$

A similar problem arises with explanatory variables where one may want both the level and the rate of change in, say, income. The easiest way here is to generate two orthogonal (uncorrelated) variables (X1 + X2) and (X1 - X2) the first representing the level and the second the change. The same method can be used with two such highly correlated variables as the age of the head and wife. The mean and the difference make two better variables than the head's age and the difference, since the latter two are correlated.

The first step in looking at panel data would seem to be to generate as many first differences as possible, and find how they are related to one another. But ultimately some theoretical model is needed, such as the following, from a study of the dynamics of income change:

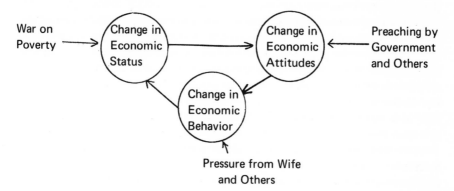

Such a working model allows flexibility and experimentation in the measurement of the major variables, and even if one can never really prove which way the causation runs, enough focus is put on how to look at the data, so that the model is helpful.

"Experiments" Natural and Real: The possibilities of experimenting with human populations are limited. Yet events occur spontaneously, and it may be possible for an investigator to obtain useful information from them as if he had instigated them. There are two types of events which have been studied, those that affect an entire population, and those that affect a part only of it. Study of the former requires measurement of the situation before and after the event, the investigator seeking to isolate the impact of the event from the consequences of any other forces which may have been operating. When the event affects only part of the population, there is the additional possibility of using the remainder as a control group.

There are three difficulties associated with the use of "natural experiments": (1) The "event" itself may not be equivalent to an experimental manipulation of the variables of theoretical interest. (2) Other forces may be operating whose consequences may be difficult to separate from those of the "event." (3) When the "event" affects only part of the population those affected may differ systematically in some important respect from those who are not affected. It may then be difficult or impossible to distinguish between the consequences of the event and the consequences of the factors which select those who experience it.

An example of an event which affected an entire population was the break in prices in the commodity markets which took place in the first week of February 1948. This event took place about the middle of the interviewing period on the 1948 Survey of Consumer Finances. The study had not been planned to include two halves which were random cross-sections, but an additional three hundred interviews, taken on short notice after the price break, were so distributed that the two halves were roughly comparable. It was possible, therefore, to compare the attitudes and expectations of consumers before and after the event. As would be expected, price expectations did shift. The percentage expecting prices to rise fell from fifty percent to fifteen percent. It turned out that the same proportions as before expected their own income to rise and expected good times to prevail.[64]

An example of an event which had a selective impact was the windfall of a refund or dividend on National Life Insurance policies of veterans. (This windfall resulted from unexpectedly low mortality experience.) The event was analyzed by Ronald Bodkin using data from the 1950 Consumer Expenditure Survey of the Bureau of Labor Statistics.[65] Bodkin was able to use data from this survey on income, expenditure, and saving to estimate the marginal propensity to consume out of the windfall. His conclusion was that this marginal propensity was about the same as that for all income—contrary to what might have been expected on the basis of Friedman's theories of consumer behavior.

Friedman took two of the logically possible positions to refute the conclusion. He argued that a hidden factor was at work in selecting those who received the windfall. Specifically, he argued that only those who kept up their policy after World War II received the dividend and whether the policy were kept up might well vary systematically depending on the economic position of the veteran—specifically, on his permanent income. Second, he argued that the dollar amount of the dividend as measured was not a satisfactory measure of the windfall since in later years annual dividends continued (even though these later dividends were not accumulative as was the first large payment). We are not here concerned with the force of these arguments; we note only that they are typical of the objections likely to be made to "natural experiments"—i.e. that they are "confounded."

The issue is not whether the groups exposed and not exposed to something differ as to their composition, age, etc., but whether they differ systematically according to the variable to be explained, and for some extraneous reason. For instance, two studies of the impact of private pensions (added to Social Security) on saving, were able to show an effect (the reverse of the economist's hypothesis) by arguing that individuals had no choice about whether they were included in such a plan, and had not had time to move to a job which suited their personal preferences about retirement provisions—the plans mostly being put in over a short period unilaterally or by union negotiations.[66] Differences in the earnings levels, ages, etc. of individuals could be taken care of by multiple regression or other multivariate analysis, leaving the effects of residual differences in saving associated with having or not having a private pension plan to be interpreted as the effects of plan or no plan.

As we indicated earlier in the chapter on design, there have been very few purposeful experiments designed to determine the effects of changes in explanatory variables. It is difficult to change things, and there are always other things not subject to control, so the result is not a controlled experiment but a semi-controlled one. Whether the statistical analysis can remove the effects of variations in the uncontrolled factors in order to see clearly the effects of those being manipulated, is always in doubt. But the analysis problem is clear. One has a whole set of explanatory variables, some with more than natural variation because of sampling to achieve that, or because of actual manipulation of the environment, and one desires to estimate the effects of these variables more precisely than in a representative sample in its natural situation, where the variables of concern may not vary much, or may vary too systematically with other things.

What must always be kept in mind in ranking the importance of different explanatory variables, is that variables which dominate the explanation of cross-section differences in behavior, may cancel out in the aggregates, or not move over time at all, and contribute very little to economic analysis which is essentially dynamic.[67]

Grouping as a Method of Dealing with Badly Distributed Dependent Variables: Particularly with expenditure data, we frequently have a large number of zeros, people who spent nothing during the period. This is true even for periods as long as a year, with durable goods. One way to average over a longer period of time, is to average over a group of people, on the argument that a random group of a particular type of family will contain those who just bought before the period started, those who bought during the period, etc., and that the proportion who bought measured the probability appropriate to the group, and the mean expenditure for all, the expected value. Indeed, with dichotomous dependent variables, only grouping converts to a proportion which can have a reasonable distribution for analysis.

The difficulty, of course, is that no matter how the groups are created, they average out certain variability which may be desired left in. If one averaged out much of the variability in family size, or age, or some other explanatory variable, then one reduces the possibility of finding the true effect of that variable, and increases the likelihood of erroneously concluding that it is not as important as some other variables.

Ideally one would want to group according to every explanatory variable jointly so that all their variance would be preserved. Of course one should not group by the dependent variable; this reduces the variation between groups of other unknown variables and raises the correlation and the regression slopes deceptively. Grouping on the explanatory variables can also reduce errors of measurement in them, and hence increase the regression coefficients.[68]

Since it is usually impossible to group on all the variables, one must at least be aware of the fact that those not used in the grouping will have much of their variance and explanatory power removed. If one groups by income, and regresses expenditure on income and family size, the latter will seem unimportant because the *average* family size in each income group varies little and effects of varying family size within the income groups have been averaged out and hidden. One must also keep in mind that any grouping hides some of the variation of the dependent variable and produces deceptive correlation coefficients. One can explain most of the variance of a set of *means* without explaining much of the basic variance of the variable.

Sometimes grouped data are used on the grounds that many of the explanatory variables actually operate on whole groups. For instance, one may study a number of villages, and be concerned with reasons why one village seemed to respond so much faster than another. Actually, it is often a mistake to use a larger unit of analysis on such grounds. One can always put into an analysis of family units, variables which are constant for the whole village. The only precaution, if one is using numerical variables measuring things affecting whole groups, is not to have them so detailed that knowing one specifies a sub-unit, and hence the value of all the other subunit information—this would mean perfect correlation among some predictors. But with some overlap to avoid this, it is possible to analyze data using variables at different levels of aggregation as explanatory variables. It is not necessary as studies of acceptance of innovation have sometimes done, to do one analysis at the village level, and another at the individual level that ignores the village variables.

Markov Processes: Whenever it is possible to assume some stability in survey-estimated relations between initial condition and subsequent change, the findings can be extrapolated over a number of periods into the future. One fascinating characteristic of the limits of such Markov processes is that they depend on the transition probabilities but not at all upon the initial states.[69]

For instance, if the probability of going from not owing a car to owning one is P, and the probability of a car owner becoming a non-owner is D, then whatever the initial proportion of car owners, the final proportion will be:

$$\frac{P}{P + D} \quad \text{owners}$$

because D% of the owners will drop out, replaced by P% of the non-owners:

$$D\left(\frac{P}{P + D}\right) = \frac{PD}{P + D} \text{ , and}$$

$$P\left(1 - \frac{P}{P + D}\right) = P\left(\frac{P + D - P}{P + D}\right) = \frac{P \cdot D}{P + D}$$

so the system is stable.

As an example, one can take a sample of adults, and relate their fathers' education to their own, and use this two-way table as an estimate of the matrix of transition probabilities.[70] Essentially one takes the marginal distribution of adults as a new set of fathers, estimates the distribution of their children's education, adds these distributions to get a new overall distribution of education for that generation, and so on. It is crucial to use adults and their fathers, not their children, to get the basic transition data since an adult has only one father, but a father can have several children. However, one might also want to improve the analysis by using different transition probabilities for families of different sizes.

If the transition probabilities vary for different but separate parts of the population, one can estimate the limit proportions separately and add. If the transition probabilities vary depending on other circumstances, then one has to move to a simulation model. Another example is suggested by Maisel in an analysis of the housing market.[71]

Maisel worked with data from the "1-in-1000" sample from the 1960 Population and Housing Census. The units are households. Each household faces a decision to move or not to move. If it moves it faces a decision to purchase or not to purchase. Estimates of choices made can be presented in the form of a probability tree. Trees can be estimated for the whole population, in Maisel's study the whole population of western Standard Metropolitan Statistical Areas over 1,000,000 in population. Estimates can also be made for those who at the start were owners, renters or new households. Maisel further breaks down the data by age, and also experiments with breakdown of the sample by income and by size of family (1 person, over 1 person). He reports the use of a form of matrix to project the state of households in Los Angeles at the next Census. He also notes that a satisfactory projection must include, in addition to a matrix which specifies choices by size of family, age, income, and tenure, a matrix which specifies demographic and income movements. The same type of analysis may be useful for other economic problems.

Actual simulation of livestock herds, or whole economies, can be done this way, with basic behavioral relations, and initial states, estimated from survey data (the former using reinterviews or memory to relate initial state to subsequent change or action). By then changing some of the relationships, such as a birth or death rate, one can quantify the effect of that change on the whole aggregate dynamics, such as the growth rate in Gross National Product.

The Problem of Aggregation: Many of the questions in economics have to do with the relation between two aggregates, such as disposable personal income and total consumption expenditures. The problem of how to go from micro-data about individual households to such aggregate data has been extensively discussed in the literature. Even where the individual micro-data are properly dynamic, there are problems, because a ten percent increase in income does not mean that each family's income increases ten percent. Even if it did, unless the income-expenditure relations are all linear, aggregate relations bear no simple relation to micro-relationships. Suppose, for instance, that whenever a family could count on $4,000 a year retirement income at age sixty-two, they would plan to retire early—a relationship which seems to appear in studies of people's retirement plans and behavior. Then increases in pension plan reserves, even if universally and equally distributed, would not relate to the amount of early retirement. One would have to know how many people's pension rights (combined with their Social Security) were passing the $4,000 per year threshhold.

The same problems exist, in spite of the elaborate algebra often presented, with attempts to use Engel curves from cross-section data to extrapolate and predict consumption patterns as national income rises. Changing income distribution (unequal distribution of income increases) or any non-linearities in the income-spending relations, will cause trouble. In addition, of course, there are the usual feed-back problems which have driven economics into structural equation models, so that going from micro-relations to aggregate dynamic systems requires complex simulation of the whole system.

Multi-Level Analysis of One Dependent Variable: All the preceding discussion operated on the assumption that the explanatory variables were at the same level of the causal process, that there were no one-way causal relations among them. If, however, one has two predictors one of which can affect the other but not vice-versa, there are difficulties with treating them at the same level in a multi-variate analysis. For example, one analyst used high school grades and whether the students said they planned to go to college to predict college attendance. In a multiple regression, the plans explained everything and it looked as though high school grades had nothing to do with going to college. Clearly the causal model was

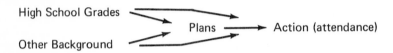

Only a true partial correlation, removing the effects of grades and parental background from both plans and acts and correlating the residuals would tell whether "plans" added anything not already in the other variables. This is difficult with classificatory variables. Correlating actual plans with residual actions not explained by grades and background, has a downward bias proportional to the correlation between plans and the background variables, but may sometimes be done for speed and economy.[72]

A similar problem of the explanatory structure arises when some of the explanatory characteristics are constraints or outside pressures, and others are motives or incentives.

In either case, one may want to engage in a two-stage analysis, first removing the effects of the causally prior variables, or the constraints, then entering into each individual's record the difference between his actual and expected value of the dependent variable, and then analyzing those residuals against another more immediate set of variables. Indeed, it is sometimes useful to make a third step, using the residuals from the residuals, and analyzing them against a new set of variables, held till this stage, because it is not even clear whether they affect the dependent variable or are affected by it. For those variables, one is still interested in their relationship, but does not want to let them dominate the explanation of the dependent variable.

The basic problem is not solved by such techniques as path analysis, which merely calculates a set of coefficients on the *assumption* of some particular pattern of causal forces, but does not really allow one to select among alternative models, except possibly by some "reasonableness of the coefficients" criterion. And things get much worse if we measure the theoretical variables only poorly or indirectly, particularly those at the middle or intermediate stages of causal paths.[73]

The structural models of econometrics should theoretically apply, but success in finding reasonable *and* identified models has been limited. One problem is too many explanatory variables. Another is the limited dynamism of the data.

Causal Sequences: The central problem in the analysis of survey data is how best to detect and exhibit complex causal patterns. As an introduction to the discussion of this problem, consider the possible patterns of relationship among three variables. There are five possible basic patterns, not counting the possibility that two, or all three, of the variables are unrelated. We also abstract from the problem of determining which variable fits at which point in each pattern. The five are as follows (arrows designate causation, not correlation):

(1)   *Spurious correlation.*

In this pattern B is a cause of A and also a cause of Y. A and Y will be correlated if considered as a pair. If the analyst has no knowledge of the part played by

B in the pattern, he may mistakenly conclude that there is a causal link between A and Y. There is always some danger that a new variable not heretofore considered will be found to be in the position of B in this sequence. It is also possible for a *real* effect of A only to be wiped out by a relation through B in the opposite direction!

(2)   *Causal sequence.*

$$A \longrightarrow B \longrightarrow Y$$

In this pattern A causes B, and B in turn causes Y. There is no effect of A on Y *except* through B. Note, however, that in this situation A does operate as a cause of Y. Analysts sometimes make the mistake of coming to the conclusion that A has nothing to do with Y—that is, they confuse this pattern with pattern (1) above. This confusion is easy because in both cases when B is taken into account statistically there is no remaining association between A and Y.[74]

(3)   *Compound causal sequence.*

$$A \longrightarrow B \longrightarrow Y$$

In this pattern A is a cause of B which is in turn a cause of Y, just as in pattern (2), but in addition A has a direct effect on Y. For example, education has an effect on income and income has an effect on the consumption of a certain commodity; in addition, education may form a taste for the commodity and influence its consumption directly. We may note that, in principle, it is possible that B influences A as well as A influencing B.

(4)   *Separate causation.*

It is possible for A and B both to influence Y. The simplest case is the one in which A and B are entirely independent of one another. It is this pattern which is the easiest for the analyst to discover.

(5)   *Interaction*

The relation of A to Y depends upon the value of B. This pattern is not easy to show with arrows. The pattern may be more easily illustrated by a graph showing one possible type of dependence:

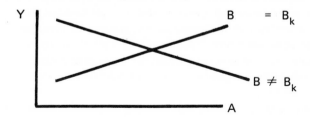

The slope of the line relating A to Y in this example is positive if $B = B_k$, but negative, otherwise. A great deal of elaborate discussion about causal paths starts out by assuming additivity (the absence of interaction effects), yet there is reason to believe that such interactions are quite important. And if both they and some one-way relations among the predictors exist, it often appears nearly impossible to tell from the data which causal model is appropriate.

The problem of the analyst is to discover *which* of these basic causal patterns is the appropriate one for his data. He is quite likely to have to concern himself with more than three variables, of course, but, as we see, he may have difficulties with only three. There are two basic strategies: he may rely on theory for guidance, or he may seek to learn from his data which causal pattern is the right one. It is possible to try both strategies, of course. The approach via theory emphasizes the attempt to construct a model which is consistent with what is already known to be true or believed to be true about the relationships under scrutiny. The approach via the data may involve an attempt to use the data to specify a more complete causal model or it may involve a special examination of timing. The specification of timing is extremely important for many problems, and we shall consider it first.

The central idea is the simple proposition that A cannot be a cause of B if B preceded A in time. There is a difficulty with this facile assumption in the case of dynamic (change) data. If in fact Y depends on the rate of change in X, then as X moves up and down in sinusoidal fashion, Y will always change direction *first* responding to the rate of change in X. This is a common problem with economic time series, but could occur in survey data too. In any case analysts turn their attention to the empirical question of which variables come first. For some, the answer is obvious. For example, the chronological age of an individual must be the result of the date of his birth and cannot be a consequence of anything that happened later. Events can influence whether he survives or not, but not his age.

For some variables it is possible to reconstruct timing on the basis of the data gathered in the interview. Special questions can be asked about the dates at which events take place. For example, we know that in a certain family the wife is working, and the family owns two cars. We set up the hypothesis that the second car was purchased *because* the wife needed it to get to work. We ask about timing, and are informed that the family has had two cars for five years, but the wife only started work last month. The hypothesis is greatly weakened. It is still barely conceivable that the wife bought the car in the expectation of going to work and has been on the verge of going to work for five years—but the suggestion strains our credulity.

There is always the possibility that the time of an event as reported in an interview is not precise. We may not be willing to accept the reported time as accurate enough to help us determine the causal pattern in which we are interested. It may then be necessary to establish time sequences through the use of reinterviews.

We return to the alternative use of data to help establish causation: the specification of a more complete causal model. A basic possibility is the addition of steps in the proposed causal sequence. The process by which, say, B causes Y, may be examined in detail. More detailed knowledge of the process will strengthen the interpretation that the causation is as hypothesized. It will reduce the possibility that the relationship may be found to be spurious.

The introduction of additional steps may be accomplished by adding psychological variables to the model. We may have an initial model in which the types of variables are as follows:

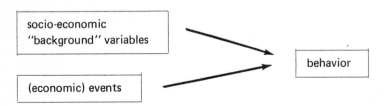

The more complete model may be as follows:

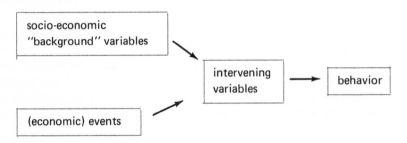

For example, the behavior may be the purchase of airline tickets by a family. The relevant background variables may be the demographic composition of the family. The "event" may be an increase in family income. We may observe repeatedly in successive surveys the relation between income change and purchases of tickets. It turns out that this relation is not constant—it shifts over time. We find that people's attitudes toward air travel can be measured. They are found to be shifting systematically as people shift from "non-fliers" to "fliers," that is, from the category of those who never have taken an air trip, to those who have done so. People who are "fliers" have a higher propensity to fly again. Knowledge of this shift helps us to understand the shift in the relation between income (and probably also, price) and the behavior.

Remember that we are still dealing with a situation where there is a single dependent variable to be explained, and the problem is that the explanatory variables are not all at the same stage in the causal process. The critical revelation of difficulty is that there are some pairs of predictors where one could be a cause of the other, but the reverse is not true. It is not simple intercorrelation that causes difficulty, but the one-way nature of the relationship.

In most survey work, for instance, there are some clearly exogenous variables whose relationship to one another cause no problems, but whose relationships to a second set can only be causal, not resultant: Year born, race, where grew up, can each affect a man's education, but cannot be changed by his education. His education in turn can affect his occupation, but a later occupation seldom changes the amount of formal education a person gets. How then can we take account of all this in accounting for a man's current wage rate?

One simple solution is to eliminate the variables except the most immediate proximate causes, and argue that the past is incorporated into occupation. But it is usually the case that we also believe that education, race, and age have direct effects on current earnings as well as the indirect effects through occupation. If that were all, one could do a stepwise analysis, first removing the effects of age, race, and where grew up, then relating the residuals to education, and relating the residuals from that analysis to occupation. But if the effect of occupation depends also on age, such a stepwise analysis which assumes additivity, at least between steps, is inappropriate. (Non-additivity at each stage can easily be handled by some variant of the sequential search strategy.)

And of course, one must believe the model. The use of residuals from one analysis in a second analysis, where the model is *not* sequential, produces a downward bias in the second-stage estimates, proportional to the degree of correlation between step one variables and the step two variables.[75] But one can still do a stepwise analysis where some causal directions are clear, putting in at later stages variables like age which may interact with later stage variables in their effects on the dependent variable.

The question becomes, how one selects the first stage variables, are they prior in time, clearly exogenous (not in turn affected by the dependent variable) unlike some of the other predictors, or what? Our preference is to eliminate at a first stage those clearly prior in time.

There are also constraints or overwhelming pressures, which one may want to consider eliminating before examining the effects of the more motivational (economic or psychological) variables. For instance, a man may be disabled, or a woman unable to work because she has small children and no husband. In these cases, an alternative procedure is to eliminate such cases from the sample for further analysis, since these constraints may affect not only the individual's earnings, but his capacity to have his earnings affected by any of the other variables.

Indeed, a common problem in survey research is that hypotheses about behavior really apply to those who are free to make choices, whereas a substantial part of the population may not be free. In that case, any real effect for the first group may be diminished by combining them with the constrained group.

It would be nice to recommend a simple recursive system, in place of stepwise analysis of a dependent variable, with the predicted values of each stage used in place of actual values, to predict a different dependent variable at the next stage. But this is not easy when many of the variables are categorical, and does not always seem to be a realistic model of the real world. We are left with the possibility of several stage residual analysis.

Complex Dependent Variables, or Joint Decisions: We pointed out earlier that sometimes when a dependent variable seems badly distributed, such as an expenditure when many people spend nothing, it can be decomposed into two parts, each with a more tractable distribution: whether the individual spent anything, and for those who did, the amount of the expenditure. The two alternatives, elaborate statistical procedures to deal with limited dependent variables, or grouping subsets of individuals to average over time by averaging over people, both have their drawbacks. From a purely statistical point of view, the probability of two things happening, such as a man buying a car, and buying it on credit, can be expressed as the product of two probabilities, without loss of information:

$$P(ab) = P(a|b) \cdot Pb = P(b|a)Pa$$

In a true joint decision, of course, one cannot say which decision came first, they may really have been made jointly. For instance, having once decided to buy a car, a man has to decide whether to buy a new one or a used one, and whether to pay cash or use credit, but the two decisions are not independent, since the greater price of a new car may make it more imperative to use credit. In practice, however, we can either analyze the new-used decision, and then analyze the cash-credit decision with the new-used decision as one of the explanatory variables, or we can reverse it and analyze the cash-credit decision regardless of new-used, and then analyze the decision whether to buy new or used, with the credit decision as part of the explanation.

These are examples of recursive systems, of course, applied to dichotomous dependent variables. In fact there are many consumer behavior areas where whole sets of decisions are involved, and a variety of analytical models can be applied. Let us take the car purchase decision and show some alternative models:

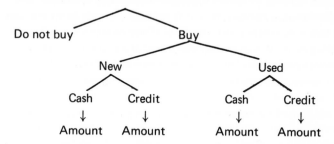

Here we analyze first the decision to buy, then the new-used decision for the buyers, then the cash-credit choice (for buyers) separately for new-used, or with new-used as one explanatory variable (preferably in a non-additive model). Finally we analyze the amount, either separately for the four groups, or with the new-used, and cash-credit decisions as part of the explanation (again preferably in an analysis which does not assume additivity).

But one could equally well have varied the order of the three decisions of buyers' new-used, cash-credit, and amount spent.

Indeed, one could produce a totally sequential line of decisions:

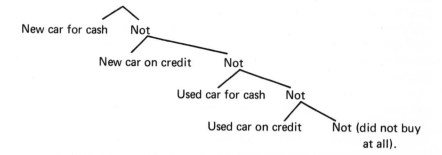

It can be shown that from the point of view of prediction, it does not make much difference which way one decomposes joint probabilities. But the interpretation of the behavior patterns is different, and one certainly would like a pattern of analysis which made intuitive sense. In the analysis of determinants of family income, we built up components starting with the head's hourly earnings, his work hours, moving to the wife's work, and then to other sources of income, and ending with an analysis of who moved in with relatives, or provided housing for relatives.[76]

Canonical Correlation: A totally different approach is possible if one is willing to impose several more assumptions: If one has a set of dependent variables, and a set of independent variables, one can ask what linear function of the first set and what linear function of the second set could be developed so that the correlation between the two functions would be a maximum. This is technically known as canonical correlation: It assumes that it is an appropriate model of the real world to create a weighted sum of the dependent variables with fixed weights, and to relate this to a weighted sum of the explanatory variables.

There has been some limited use of canonical correlations in the analysis of economic surveys and there may be further applications of the methods in the future.[77]

The purpose of canonical correlation is to exhibit the correlations between two sets of variates. It is useful to think of the analyst as starting with a single set of variates and the covariance matrix which shows the relationships between all possible pairs of these variates. He then partitions the list of variates into two parts, one of which he may wish to consider as a group of dependent variables, and the other, as independent variables. The statistical procedure is designed to reveal linear additive combinations of each of the two sets of variates. The desired linear combination of the dependent variates is that linear additive combination which can best be predicted; the desired linear additive combination of the independent variates is that combination which is the best predictor.

It is also possible to go on to find other pairs of linear combinations uncorrelated with the first pair which exhibit any further relationships which may exist between the two sets of variates. This extension of the calculations, however, has not yet been found useful in survey work. We may note, however, that there may be little to choose empirically between the first pair of combinations and the second or later pairs. Caution would suggest the extension of the calculations to check on this possibility. It is preferable to establish rather than to assume that little can be added to the initial results by the added calculations.

The development of canonical correlation, like the development of factor analysis, is due to Hotelling. A brief comparison of the techniques may be helpful. For both, the basic raw material is the covariance matrix. For both, the purpose is to "boil down" the data, to identify a limited number of factors which can account for what is observed. Both are most likely to be useful in fields of inquiry where the theory is poorly developed. Later on, presumably one knows what the basic variables are, and can develop measures of them.

There is, however, a basic difference between the two procedures. The criterion in canonical correlation is essentially a correlation coefficient. The magnitude of a correlation coefficient is not affected by the units of measurement employed. Factor analysis is so affected. In a canonical correlation, just as in any regression problem, it is possible to multiply any variate by an arbitrary constant without changing the final results of the analysis. In factor analysis the results would be changed by such a procedure.

Canonical correlation with dummy variables might be used in any problem in which the dependent variable is a nominal scale. In effect, the canonical correlation provides a method for scaling the dependent variable. This approach has been used in a problem in which the dependent variable was type of housing preferred, and respondents could select one of several possibilities.[78] Predictors included income and stage in the family life cycle.

An example of a problem to which the method might be applied is the prediction of interviewer performance. There are a number of possible measures of performance, as discussed in Chapter III, including completion rate, measures of response error, and reports from respondents about their reactions to the interview. There are also a variety of possible measures of interviewer characteristics, including performance on psychological tests, years of experience, age, sex, education, and so forth. Both sets could be handled in one canonical correlation.

Another example of a problem is the assessment of consumers' characteristics. A set of measures of behavior might be explained by a set of measures of psychological characteristics, with a view to developing a typology of consumers. In this problem, as in others mentioned, the statistical procedure becomes a method of developing scales. Thus, it is an alternative in some circumstances to the use of other procedures which develop scales. Canonical correlation, however, provides a measure of relationship as well as two scales.

It should be kept in mind that canonical correlation is subject to the same basic assumptions as ordinary regression, applied to *both* sides of the equation.

These assumptions are least restrictive when the variables on both sides are dummy variables, i.e. when linearity in the sets of variables is actually not assumed. Indeed, perhaps the most useful application of canonical correlation is as a measure of association in cross-classification. One thinks of each category of one class as a dummy variable predictor and each category of the other classification as a dummy variable dependent variable, and computes the canonical correlation, the *size* of the coefficient indicating the extent to which one can predict the distribution of one knowing the distribution of the other. As was pointed out earlier, when most or all of the predictors in some multivariate analysis are classifications (ordinal scales), then this becomes an effective way of displaying the pattern of intercorrelations among the predictors, in the form of the canonical correlations among the sets (age, occupation, sex, etc.), though Cramer's V is equivalent and easier to compute, being based on chi-square.[25]

Structural Models: As analysts attempt to develop models of situations in which large numbers of variables are relevant, it frequently becomes inappropriate or impossible to describe the model in a single equation or even focus on one dependent variable at a time. The variables may be regarded on theoretical grounds as subject to a system of relationships. In the development of econometric theory Frisch and Haavelmo criticized the single equation approach of Moore and Working on the ground that it would lead to biased estimates when the appropriate model is a system of simultaneous equations.[79]

In much econometric work the method of working with sets of simultaneous equations has been used. This approach is commonly used, for example, in aggregative models of the American economy, such as that initiated by Klein and Goldberger and revised by Suits.[80] In the analysis of survey data, the reliance has mostly been on a special type of simultaneous system, the recursive system.

In recursive systems development up to time t-1 determines values at time t. Also, the variables at time t are obtained one by one. A recursive system may have the following form:

$$X_1 = e_1$$

$$X_2 = b_{21} \ X_1 + e_2$$

$$X_3 = b_{31} \ X_1 + b_{32} \ X_2 + e_3$$

$$X_k = b_{k1} \ X_1 + b_{k2} \ X_2 + \ldots + b_{k, \, k-1} \ X_{k-1} + e_k$$

Thus X_1 is endogenous; X_2 is a function of X_1 plus an error term; X_3 is a function of X_1, X_2 and an error term; and so forth. It should be understood that the relationships in a recursive system need not be linear and additive as in the above example. What is required is that the variables appear in successive equations as shown. For example, X_3 might depend upon the product of X_1 and X_2. Recursive systems can be fitted by ordinary least squares. They can exploit the flexibility of the survey method in using information about timing to assist in the analysis of causal patterns.

In setting up recursive systems economists tend to rely to a considerable extent upon a priori reasoning concerning the relationships. There has been work recently by Blalock on the problem of how to use correlation coefficients to discover the nature of recursive systems.[81] Blalock argues that the correlation coefficients can be used in such analysis rather than regression coefficient since what is at issue is whether or not a variable belongs in a certain equation. If the correlation coefficient is zero, the regression coefficient is also zero, and vice versa. Blalock develops each equation by testing to see whether the data are consistent with a model in which certain variables do appear in that equation while others drop out. In other contexts, however, Blalock argues that regression coefficients are better for making comparisons across populations.

The great contribution of econometrics to aggregate analysis was to point out that in a system where there were feedback loops, one could not derive unbiased estimates of any of the parameters without estimating the whole structural model. To what extent do these same problems arise with survey data?

Clearly if we had sufficiently dynamic data about individual households over time, such problems arise. Much survey analysis to date, however, has been dynamic only in a limited sense, incorporating all the past in certain measures of initial state (beginning of year assets, debts, housing and location, durable stocks) and certain "demographic" data such as age, education, where grew up, past mobility, etc. Even here there are feedback problems. For example, one may use initial assets to help explain saving behavior, but the accumulation of those assets resulted from past saving behavior and their stock reflects both a current influence and a representation of "personality" or past behavior which should also continue to affect current behavior. Clearly we do not have the data to untangle this, until we secure long-run data on individual families. We might, however, do better if we knew more about how the assets were accumulated, i.e. if we had even a retrospective history of income and asset accumulations from memory.

It is not surprising then, that there have been no instances where a realistic structural model has been fitted to actual survey data. More static models of causal inference have been attempted, mostly with recursive systems, where at each stage any or all of the variables of the preceding stage can have an effect, but the reverse is not true. These are particularly easy models to deal with, essentially because they do not really have dynamic feed-back loops, but are decompositions of chains of causation. And if one is willing to select some particular model, assume that the effects are linear and additive, then it is possible to estimate path coefficients which allocate the explanation of any variable in the system among the variables that precede it in the system.[82]

One must also assume that the laws governing the system specify the causal priorities in an undebatable way, that the disturbances of the dependent variables are all uncorrelated (i.e., that all system inputs are entered explicitly into the analysis), and that the usual assumptions of multiple correlation are met: independent units, homogeneous variances, additivity, linearity and no serious multicollinearity). If a theory happens to come closer to being a complete recursive system (each variable used in all the following stages) it will usually do a better job of reproducing the correlation matrix, even though it may be further from the truth. And the more paths one adds in the model, the more likely that the modified theory will reproduce the empirical correlations regardless whether the redefined model is more nearly valid.

Hence, one pays for the elegant analysis by being forced to specify the structure of the real world, when for most researchers, that is the prime question—what that structure really looks like. When one admits the possibility of interaction effects, the number of possible causal models explodes.

Are we left then with the policy of shaking the data to see what the structure looks like, with the intention of selecting a model out of the data? If so, we are left with little or no evidence of the reliability of our conclusions. One cannot develop a hypothesis from a set of data and test it with the same data. The problem is, do we have hypotheses worth testing, i.e. such that the suggestion that an alternative hypothesis would fit the data better would not upset us? In most of the social sciences, economics being no exception, we doubt that our theoretical structures and our substantive knowledge are good enough to move us from the data searching stage to the hypothesis testing stage.

Simulation: There is, however, a possible approach for dealing with structural and feedback problems, and for using the results of survey data in dynamic models which tell us something about the dynamic properties of the economic system. It relies on simulation with a model where the time periods used are so short that one can ignore the possible feed-back problems. If one can also assume that the relationships between initial states and subsequent actions (during a month, for instance) are stable, then the system is a set of Markov processes. The inputs are the kind of micro-data easily derivable from surveys, and the computer can, each "month" add up subtotals, to provide an output describing aggregate dynamic changes in the simulated system.[83] It is not necessary for the computer to keep track of each one of sixty million households and many firms. The system can be aggregated to the extent of having a thousand or so "representative" types of families, and similarly with firms. And where not all do something, the computer can use a built-in random number table or "jiffy randomizer" to assign the right proportions.

The procedure requires the initial specification of a set of households with the characteristics of the individual households specified in such a manner that the households represent the population. For example, the proportion of households with head within a certain age range should agree with the proportion for the population. The income distribution of households with head of that age should agree with the population distribution etc. (Note that representativeness is needed at this stage even though relationships may have been estimated using experimental designs.)

During each pass-through, the assigned relations impinge on individual households in the sample. The characteristics of the household to be affected in different ways are determined by relationships built into the model; which specific units in the representative sample are affected are determined by random numbers. For example, a relationship may be built in that a certain proportion of households containing married women of certain ages will add members through births. Individual households, randomly selected, each will have their numbers increased by one infant. How many births are to occur will depend on the length of time represented by a pass—Orcutt chose a period of one month. A complete demographic model obviously requires other events in addition to births—deaths, marriages, divorces. A complete economic model of household behavior must also contain relationships to determine income, expenditure, saving etc. Orcutt reports in his book actual development only of a demographic model, but the methods set forth are designed for economic relationships as well.

The first test of the model is whether the dynamic output is reasonable. Basic uses of the method are for prediction and analysis. It makes possible the working out over an indefinite number of passes, i.e. an indefinitely long period of time, of the implications of the initial conditions plus the relationships specified. Thus, in principle, a demographic model can be used to simulate the demographic processes affecting the population of the country.

A related use of the model is for the assessment of the effects of choice of policy. Alternative assumptions can be made about policy decisions, and runs of the model can trace the probable course of events which may be expected to follow. And, in the same way, simulation can explain outcomes in the sense of demonstrating how they can result from the inputs of the model.

A basic limitation on the possible uses of this method is that the requirements for data can be formidable. The quality of the inputs, including especially the inputs of estimated relationships, will be reflected in the results. It is further necessary for good results that the inputs be mutually consistent even when they come from diverse sources. There is the possibility that the random elements in the simulation may by chance lead to peculiar results especially if the number of households included in the simulation is limited—as it may be limited by the capacity of the computer being used. Yet it remains true that this method is at present the only technique which anyone has seriously attempted to develop for handling anything like the full complexity of the relationships which are appropriate to analysis of household behavior.

Actually the use of simulation models has proceeded most rapidly in subareas such as population models, for people or livestock. For instance, one can start with a model which assumes that people's output depends on their level of education, that taxes depend on output, and that a fraction of taxes will support the school system and determine the level of tuition fees to cover the rest of education costs. Such simulation models are actually complex to implement. One simple livestock model set up by the staff at the World Bank requires some 2500 computer cards of instructions merely to instruct the computer on the relations.

Summary on Analysis

It may be useful to summarize the main steps in analysis, since we have brought in so many special problems and possibilities:

First, one must look carefully at the dependent variable or variables. Extreme cases may be actual errors, or reveal conceptual problems. If they must be left in, they can be truncated to avoid undue distortions of least squares procedures, or the whole distribution can be transformed by taking logs or square roots (provided there are no zero or negative numbers).

If the dependent variable is a yes-no dichotomy, or has little variance one may want to consider building a more complex dependent variable with more variance to be explained. If it is a joint decision, one may want to transform it into a series of sequential or conditional decisions, such recursive models being easier to handle than complete systems of structural equations. Finally, one may want to analyze separately the forces pushing people into the top third of the dependent variable, and those pushing them into the bottom third, since the second set may not be the mirror image of the first.

As for the explanatory variables, one may want to compress them by building indexes, even arbitrary additive indexes. This provides a speedy way of getting rid of a lot of hypotheses at once, or else an indication in which set to search further. And if an additive index has a linear effect, one can rest with the additivity, but if not one knows to look for interactions. Where intercorrelations are too high, one may also want to build indexes, or orthogonal components, such as the average age of husband and wife, and the difference in their ages.

One may want to test whether the very economical assumption of additivity of effects is justified, by comparing an additive regression with the variance explained by subcells of a k-dimensioned table where there are k sets of predictors. Or one may prefer to proceed to some search process which does not assume additivity.

And if there is one variable, dominant because of its power, or its theoretical importance, or its likelihood of changing in the future, then one may want to move to a covariance search process, looking for subsets of the population which differ in their response to it.

Once one has a clear view of the structure that seems to fit the data, it can always be written as a linear model in a new set of complex variables, and one may want to fit the data to such a model, in preparation for fitting the same model to some other set of data, in more of a hypothesis testing operation.

In all this, one must steer a middle course between too little theory and structure on one hand, and too much on the other. What is needed is a working theory which indicates the kinds of variables to be tried, and reasonable ways they might fit together. This guides the selection of variables and the analytical approach without binding it, or binding it to alternative interpretations of the same data. The fact is that none of the social sciences, certainly not economics, have theories so well based that one would be comfortable testing them against the data without ever asking whether some other theory might explain the world better.

Finally, one must move to more complex models than the single-stage analysis of one dependent variable at a time. There are, first, stages in the causal process, and secondly, feedback problems, and the need for some more complete structure. It is simpler if the model can be made recursive. Even if the full model cannot be investigated, it may be useful to work it out as a guide to what analysis can fruitfully be done.

The authors feel that many of the mathematically elegant procedures attack the wrong problems, e.g., spelling out the implications of a model rather than selecting among several different ones, and place much too heavy a load of assumptions on the nature and quality of the data and the relationships. At the same time, the power of computers can seduce us into rank empiricism—trying everything and running everything, without imposing any judgment, limitations, or theoretical structure. Throwing all the variables into one big multiple regression often leads the analyst into embarrassing problems of interpreting the results. The middle course seems best: Some general theoretical structure, attention to what causal directions can be specified, but within those limits, a focus on the most powerful variables and models using them, in order to select the most promising explanatory structure.

Organizational Aspects and Practical Problems of Analysis

A parody of the *New York Times* once changed its famous motto to "All the News, Printed to Fit." Even a casual glance at the kinds of analysis done with survey data over the past twenty years will reveal a certain domination by the computer technology available at the time. This meant not only avoiding things that were difficult or impossible to do, but overdoing things that were easy to do. Once an efficient program is available for turning out tables, particularly percentagized tables, there is a temptation to run "everything by everything." And the availability of multiple regression programs subsequently led to an over-enthusiastic use of that. The problem is accentuated by our temptation to overlook the hidden costs of something whose direct costs look cheap. It may seem easy to turn out a lot of tables, but analyzing them, keeping track of them, and avoiding duplication, are not easy.

If the most common practical problem of analysis is the proper balance between selectivity and allowing a little serendipity, the next most common is documentation. Particularly when many people are working, or will be working, on a set of data, it would seem elemental that proper documentation was essential. It often happens that errors are discovered and corrections made after some new variables have been generated, and even some analysis tabulations done. Unless every step has been carefully dated, when completed, not when ordered, it may prove difficult to know whether some variable was created with components before certain errors were found in them, or whether some analysis run was done before or after certain corrections were made. With modern technology, it is easy to re-do certain steps, but careful attention to the disposal of the early output and referring the later searcher to its replacement, is less certain. What is even more likely, if tables have been made from the earlier output, without careful notation *on the table* as to the tabulation request which was its source, more trouble will ensue.

As tables and other analysis results go through many drafts, their connection to the basic data will become even more difficult to maintain unless there is preserved at the bottom of every one the serial number of the computer run and perhaps also the original code numbers of the main variables involved.

It may seem a trivial point, but the ability to go from a table back to the original code definition of the variables in that table and the computer instructions that produced it, is important. When work decks of computer cards tended to multiply, it was necessary to produce full code descriptions of each of them, rather than attempt to work back through a series of translations to the original (col. 75 came from col. 63 of card 15, which came from col. 59 of card 10, which came from col. 40 of card 7, where it was created by combining columns 5 and 23). With data tapes, it is not even possible to keep most of the material in the same positions, the tape locations change, and we have found it expedient to have a dictionary of variables on each tape which is automatically transferred when a new tape is built, and which, in naming each variable, also gives its original variable number on the first tape where it appeared, so that all variables can be referred back to a single master code, made up of the originally coded material, and any subsequently added variables.

The names given to variables are themselves a problem, together with a natural but lamentable habit of resorting to abbreviations and even acronyms which are utterly confusing to anyone but their creator, and often after a few months even to him. The only true definition of a variable is a reference to its detailed code which should include a frequency distribution (or mean and list of extreme cases), and a clear description of whatever process generated it, if it was a variable created from others (for instance, what was done with missing information, or extreme cases, or negatives). The labeling problem becomes even more difficult with panel studies, doubly so when the same "fact" may be asked more than once, in different waves of interviewing.

We have already pointed out that after a process of locating and correcting errors, new variables are often created, by recoding, combining, or simply bracketing variables into classifications. Checks on the distribution of these new variables are extremely important, not only to make sure the creation was properly done, but also to provide basic information about the distributions and to uncover additional errors. Even if one decided that missing information did not need to be assigned—on the argument that it was illegitimate to assign dependent

variables, using later variables to explain them, and that it was unnecessary to assign explanatory variables since a separate dummy variable for "Not Ascertained"
can handle them—one has to know what to do with such cases when combinations of variables are desired.

In the rush to get data ready for analysis, the question of whether weights
are necessary, and how they should be developed, requires a tight strategy. Commonly when only varying non-response is at issue, weights turn out to make so
little difference as to be disposable, particularly if the main purpose is analysis,
not national estimates. But if and when weights are required, it is a strategy
problem whether to make them internal (the inverse of the sampling-times-
response rates) or external (blowing up to outside proportions in one or more
dimensions so that all weighted data are ratio estimates). If the latter is en-
visaged, then preparatory work preparing outside estimates of the number of
families or individuals in each of several subclassifications and preparing the
analysis sheets for calculating the weights, will avoid delays.

In keeping track of computer work, one can number every request serially,
or have ranges of numbers for various kinds of operations. The latter is sometimes used as an accounting device in order to estimate the costs of the separate
steps.

In handling large masses of data, one always has the basic questionnaires,
editing worksheets, and coding sheets, but as each step in the cleaning and
manufacturing of the data progresses, the costs of having to go back to the
original documents increase. Hence a strategy of back-up files has to be developed.

Finally, when the main analysis is done, and the data are to be made available to any potential user, proper documentation of the codes, the editing
process, the basic data source, and the way the data are physically on the data
tape, are essential. Since the research staff is often unfamiliar with computer differences in tape handling: header labels, bits or bytes per inch, seven or nine
channel tape, etc., they frequently find difficulties in sharing data. And potential users are frequently unaware of the costs of answering the questions.

But transferring data from one computer to another is simple compared
with the problems of transferring computer programs. The modern computer is
usually a constellation of components which differ from one installation to
another, and each one has its own internal control mechanisms and executive
languages. The rules of getting on and off are likely to be idiosyncratic, as well
as the list of special subroutines that are kept available and can be called and
used. The net result is that programmers can usually do better if they start from
scratch and rewrite a program than if they try to adapt it. This is partly because
most computer programs are inadequately documented. If they provide a logical
flow-diagram, it was made before many of the bugs were found and eliminated,
some by changing the design. Often the capacity limits have not really been

explored, nor have the speed and costs of tasks supposedly within the capacity but never really tried.

Another basic problem is that many statistical "package" programs, are written with so many options that the "set-up" instructions for using them become cumbersome and error-prone. A reference back to Chapter VI on data analysis shows that with a numerical dependent variable, the basic elements are the total variance of the variable, and the means and number of cases for variously defined subgroups—all that is necessary for one-way analyses of variance. Yet it is hard to find a fast, efficient, flexible program that will provide means for sample subgroups. Table-making programs are better, but even they are frequently inflexible when it comes to procedures for eliminating the irrelevant cases before percentagizing.

A final difficulty is the delay in billing so that the analyst may find his analysis costs exploding beyond his budget before he is aware of the problem. Interim checks on actual computer times help, provided one takes account of the aborted runs as well.

In sum, a great deal of complex administrative foresight is necessary in order to avoid errors, or at least to correct them before they get compounded through a series of subsequent steps. And some economy in using computers is essential, they are not free.

With card-programmed computers, there is a new problem of documentation: The instructions for building data files, creating new variables, selecting subgroups, and doing analysis, may not always be printed so that they can be saved. And the cards with the instructions on them are difficult to save, and to read. Someone searching back to check just how something was done may find it difficult to reconstruct. The moral is, any program cards used in file building or analysis should be printed and those listings kept filed by the tabulation request number as though it were the output, or together with the output if there was some. The cards should also be kept for a while, in case the task needs to be redone, but they are a kind of expendable back-up. It may also be useful to have a system for entering on this same paper the numbers of the tape decks (input and output if they are different).

In the haste of getting things done, and particularly in the frantic process of redoing things when the first pass was wrong, it is easy to forget the need for keeping records. This is one of the reasons why errors seem to compound themselves at times. It is also possible to overdo record keeping. More than two copies of the master code lead to situations where marginal notes do not get added to all copies. Attempts to keep track of every time a variable has been used, transferred, etc., tend to get cumbersome and break down of their own weight.

In view of the difficulties of keeping track of data, and the speed and ease with which new variables can be built, it is increasingly appropriate not to save anything but the original data, plus copies of the programs that generate other variables. In other words, it may be more efficient to generate a variable every time you use it than to store it. One stores the instructions necessary to generate it, rather than the secondary data themselves.

Examples of Analysis

It would require far too much space to provide detailed descriptions and evaluations of even a small sample of survey analyses. The reader who wishes to make use of what he has read in this book, however, is urged to select one or two reports of surveys, perhaps starting with a brief one in one of the journals, and to make his own assessment. Indeed, it would be a useful exercise to assess the whole survey design at the same time. The following cursory outline of questions might be helpful:

1. Is there a probability sample, from some reasonably adequate frame, and with good coverage?
2. Was the response rate sufficient, along with the treatment of missing information, to hold down biases?
3. What about the actual stimulus questions, and their order? Were they calculated to secure the right information?
4. Who was the respondent (in theory and in practice)?
5. What were the things being explained, the behaviors or situations, or attitudes?
6. Was there some operational model into which various sets of variables fit? How was the possibility of causal sequences treated? What about the possibility of alternative models?
7. How were the following statistical problems treated:
   a. Effects of differential errors or extreme cases on the selection of variables that "work," and on estimation of effects.
   b. Intercorrelations among predictors, and spurious correlation.
   c. Interaction effects (relations that differ from some, or do not exist everywhere).
8. Do the conclusions follow directly from the data, or require the author to bring in other information or value judgements? If other information is added, is it documented?
9. Is the study related to previous research, and are its implications for future research spelled out?

A warning is in order: It is often the better studies which provide enough documentation so that the reader can spot flaws in the design or analysis. The authors may even spell out their errors as a warning to others. It is unfair to compare such well-described studies with others where one cannot tell just what happened.

It is common for an analysis of survey data to be preceded by an elaborate theoretical model containing terms with no operational measures. The "assumptions and implications" of that model are then subjected to "test" in a subsequent analysis. But the analysis design bears little resemblance to the original model, and frequently what is tested is mostly the assumptions of the model, rather than its "implications." (Or those implications are themselves any reasonable man's assumptions.) Hence the original model served largely as window dressing. If the model served to direct attention to the particular behavioral parameters of greatest importance (because important economic implications would be sensitively altered in the model system when those parameters changed), then it would serve a useful purpose. Or if there were competing models (hypotheses) the choice between which required a particular statistical analysis, again the theoretical discussion would serve a useful purpose. But too much of the time unbelievable assumptions (requiring foresight or insight that people are unlikely to have) are tested rather than asking more broadly what really did determine behavior.

Summary

We have touched on a wide variety of problems and techniques in this chapter. Where does all this leave the economist desiring to analyze his survey data? Should he feel guilty if he has not worked out a formal structural model, hopefully just identified? Should he feel compelled to conduct factor analysis or least space analysis or some other procedure in developing a reduced set of explanatory variables? Our feeling is no. What is needed is a more flexible general statement of the behaviors or statuses to be explained, and their relation to one another, a listing of the explanatory factors that are to be examined, and a discussion of the relation of the things measured to those explanatory factors. Some attention must be paid to the relative accuracy of different variables, since one may refuse to throw out a variable with weak influence, if that weakness may be due to poor measurement, not lack of effect. And for economists, one needs to ask which of the explanatory variables are of significance in dynamic economics, i.e. are likely to change for substantial groups at the same time in the same direction, or at least to influence the effects of things that do change.

Economists are unlikely to be unaware of problems of spurious correlation, or the necessity for multivariate analysis. We are perhaps less likely to be aware of the possibility of important relations (effects) existing only for a subgroup of the population, even though that is exactly what marginal analysis would predict. But most important of all, the tradition of multiple regression has made us under-sensitive to interaction effects of all kinds. We carry over the truth that non-linear relations can be treated as linear to a first approximation, especially for small changes, into the non-truth that non-additivity can be treated with additive approximations.

Finally, and perhaps most important, we are all too casual about the relationship of what we measure to our theoretical constructs, and about the possibility of many alternative hypotheses. The basic problem of behavioral science is not the testing of elaborate deductive hypotheses, but the selection among competing hypotheses. The final test of analysis, then, is whether it really allows one to select among the competing hypotheses, by selecting among competing explanatory variables, perhaps in different structural forms.

Footnotes to Chapter VI

1. See on this point the discussion in Hubert M. Blalock, Jr., *Causal Inference in Nonexperimental Research,* The University of North Carolina Press, Chapel Hill, 1964, Ch. 1, "Introduction," pp. 3-26. See also H. M. Blalock, Jr., "The Measurement Problem: A Gap Between the Languages of Theory and Research" in H. M. Blalock, Jr. and A. B. Blalock, Eds., *Methodology in Social Research,* McGraw Hill, N.Y., 1968, pp. 5-27. See also Herbert L. Costner, "Theory, Deduction, and Rules of Correspondence," *American Journal of Sociology* 75 (Sept. 1969), pp. 245-263.

2. Milton Friedman, *A Theory of the Consumption Function,* Princeton Univ. Press, 1957.

3. J. Lansing and E. S. Maynes, "Inflation and Saving by Consumers," *Journal of Political Economy,* Vol. IX, No. 5, Oct. 1952, pp. 383-391.

4. The following discussion draws upon "Theory and Methods of Social Measurement" by Clyde H. Coombs, in *Research Methods in the Behavioral Sciences,* edited by Leon Festinger and Daniel Katz, Holt, Rinehart, and Winston, New York, 1953, pp. 471-535. See also *A Theory of Data* by Clyde H. Coombs, John Wiley and Sons, New York, 1964; and Henry S. Uphsaw, "Attitude Measurement" in H. M. and A. B. Blalock, Eds., *Methodology in Social Research,* McGraw Hill, New York, 1968, pp. 60-111.

5. For a discussion of non-parametric statistics see H. M. Blalock, *Social Statistics,* McGraw-Hill, New York, 1960. See also Sidney Siegel, *Non-Parametric Statistics,* McGraw-Hill, New York, 1956.

6. Daniel B. Suits, "The Use of Dummy Variables in Regression Equations," *J.A.S.A.,* 52 (Dec. 1957), pp. 548-551.

Arthur S. Goldberger, *Econometric Theory,* John Wiley & Sons, 1964, pp. 218-227.

For one of the first uses in economic analysis, see T. P. Hill, "Analysis of the Distribution of Wages and Salaries in Great Britain," *Econometrica,* 27 (July 1959), pp. 355-381.

7. See Graham Kalton, *A Technique for Choosing the Number of Alternative Response Categories to Provide in Order to Locate an Individual's Position on a Continuum,* 3 memos dated Nov. 7, 1966; Feb. 10, 1967 and Mar. 10, 1967, Sampling Section, Survey Research Center, Ann Arbor, Michigan.

8. For an example see Daniel C. Rogers, "Private Rates of Return to Education in the United States: A Case Study," *Yale Economic Essays* (Spring, 1969), pp. 89-136.

9. H. S. Houthakker and John Haldi, "Household Investment in Automobiles: An Intertemporal Cross-Section Analysis," in I. Friend and R. Jones, Eds., *Consumption and Saving,* Vol. I, Univ. of Penna., 1960, pp. 175-224.

10. There are many introductory discussions of the subject. For example, see Chapter 6 of A. N. Oppenheim, *Questionnaire Design and Attitude Measurement,* Heinemann, London, 1966, or H. S. Upshaw, *op. cit.* For an intermediate level discussion prepared some years ago, see Helen Peak, "Problems of Objective Observation," pp. 243-299, in L. Festinger and D. Katz, editors, *Research Methods in the Behavioral Sciences,* Dryden, New York, 1953. For advanced treatments see W. S. Torgerson, Theory and Method of Scaling, John Wiley & Sons, Inc., 1958, and Clyde H. Coombs, *A Theory of Data,* John Wiley & Sons, Inc., New York, 1964.

11. See the discussion by Helen Peak, "Problems of Objective Observation," pp. 243-299, in Festinger and Katz, *op. cit.*

12. See Peak, *op. cit.,* p. 252. See also Rensis Likert, "A Technique for the Measurement of Attitudes," *Archives of Psychology,* 140 (1932), pp. 1-55.

13. For a clear description, see Oppenheim, *Questionnaire Design and Attitude Measurement,* Heinemann, London, 1966, Ch. 6. For careful assessment, see P. C. Sagi, "A Statistical Test for the Significance of a Coefficient of Reproducibility," *Psychometrika* 2 (1959), pp. 19-27 and L. A. Goodman, "Simple Statistical Methods for Scalogram Analysis," *Psychometrika* 2 (1959), pp. 29-43.

14. The account which follows is based on Clyde H. Coombs, "Theory and Methods of Social Measurements," pp. 471-535 in Festinger and Katz, *op. cit.* For a more elaborate treatment see his *A Theory of Data, op. cit.*

15. Coombs, *op. cit.,* pp. 515-516.

16. Alan C. Kerckhoff, "Nuclear and Extended Family Relationships: A Normative and Behavioral Analysis," in Ethel Shanas and Gordon Streib, Eds., *Social Structure and The Family: Generational Relations.* Prentice Hall, N.Y., 1965.

17. Harold Hotelling, "Analysis of a Complex of Statistical Variables into Principal Components," *Journal of Educational Psychology,* 24, pp. 417-441, 498-520 (1933).

18. See T. W. Anderson, *An Introduction to Multivariate Statistical Analysis,* New York, John Wiley & Sons Inc., London, Chapman & Hall Ltd., 1958; and Richard Stone, "On the Interdependence of Blocks of Transactions," *Journal of Royal Statistical Society,* Vol. IX, No. 1 (1947), *Supplement,* pp. 1-45.

19. Eva Mueller, "A Study of Purchase Decisions," in Clark, Ed., *Consumer Behavior,* New York University Press, New York, 1954.

20. See James Morgan, Ismail Sirageldin and Nancy Baerwaldt, *Productive Americans,* Survey Research Center, Ann Arbor, Michigan, 1966.

21. G. E. P. Box, "Non-Normality and Tests on Variances," *Biometrika,* 40, (Dec. 1953), pp. 318-444.

22. See any text on non-parametric statistics, e.g., William Hays, *Statistics for Psychologists,* Holt, Rinehart and Winston, New York, 1963; or Sidney Siegel, *Nonparametric Statistics,* McGraw Hill, New York, 1956.

23. M. Kendall and Stuart, *The Advanced Theory of Statistics,* 2 Vols. See also W. H. Kruskal, "Ordinal Measures of Association," *Journal of the American Statistical Association,* 63 (December, 1958), pp. 814-861; and for a brief exploration and proposed asymmetric measures, see Robert H. Somers, "A New Asymmetric Measure of Association for Ordinal Variables," *American Sociological Review,* 27 (December 1962), pp. 799-811.

24. See L. A. Goodman and W. H. Kruskal, "Measures of Association for Cross Classifications," *Journal of the American Statistical Association,* 49 (Dec. 1954), pp. 732-764; and Frederick Mosteller, "Association and Estimation in Contingency Tables," *Journal of the American Statistical Association,* 63 (March, 1968), pp. 1-28, who points out that correlations are affected by the actual frequencies, but that you may *want* a measure of importance in prediction which does that, rather than a pure measure of association. See also H. M. Blalock, *Social Statistics,* McGraw Hill, New York, 1960.

25. Orley Ashenfelter and Joseph Mooney, "Graduate Education, Ability, and Earnings," *Review of Economics and Statistics,* 50 (Feb. 1968), pp. 78-86; and K. S. Srikantan, "Canonical Association between Nominal Measurements," *Journal of the American Statistical Association,* 65 (March 1970), pp. 284-292.

26. See the discussion in A. S. Goldberger, *Econometric Theory,* John Wiley & Sons, Inc., New York, London, Sydney, 1964, Chapter 5, "Expansions of Linear Regression."

27. Guy H. Orcutt, et al., *Microanalysis of Socioeconomic Systems,* Harper and Brothers, New York, 1961. See Chapter 11, especially pp. 224-231.

28. D. J. Finney, *Probit Analysis,* 1952 (second edition), Cambridge, at the University Press.

29. Joseph Berkson, "Application of the Logistic Function to Bio-Assay," *Journal of the American Statistical Association* 39 (Sept., 1944), pp. 357-365.

30. Stanley L. Warner, *Stochastic Choice of Mode in Urban Travel: A Study in Binary Choice,* Northwestern University Press, Evanston, Illinois, 1962; Henri Theil, *Logit Specifications in the Multivariate Analysis of Qualitative Data,* Report 6944; *Conditional Logit Specifications for the Multivariate Analysis of Qualitative Data in the Multiple Response Case,* Report 6956; and *The Explanatory Power of Determining Factors in the Multivariate Analysis of Qualitative Data,* Report 6946, all October 1969, Center for Mathematical Studies of Business and Economics, University of Chicago.

31. James Tobin, "Estimation of Relationships for Limited Dependent Variables," *Econometrica,* 26 (January, 1958), pp. 24-36.

32. See the discussion in T. W. Anderson, *An Introduction to Multivariate Statistical Analysis,* New York, John Wiley & Sons, Inc., 1958, Chapter 6, "Classification of Observation."

33. George W. Ladd, "Linear Probability Functions and Discriminant Functions," *Econometrica,* 34 (Oct. 1966), pp. 873-885.

34. C. Radhakrishna Rao, *Advanced Statistical Methods in Biometric Research,* Wiley, 1952, especially Chapter 8.

35. Eva Mueller, "The Savings Account as a Source for Financing Large Expenditures," *Journal of Finance* 22 (Sept. 1967) 375-393.

36. For examples of criticisms based on considerations of these types, see *Consumption and Saving,* edited by Irvin Friend and Robert Jones, Philadelphia, University of Penna. Press, 1960, 2 vols.; comments by Guy Orcutt, Vol. I, pp. 155-519, and by Milton Friedman, Vol. II, p. 192.

37. M. Ganguli, "A Note on Nested Sampling," *Sankya,* 5 (1941), pp. 449-452. See also, George W. Snedecor and William A. Cochran, *Statistical Methods,* Iowa State University Press, Ames, Iowa, 1956, p. 274; and R. L. Anderson and T. A. Bancroft, *Statistical Theory in Research,* McGraw Hill, New York, 1952, p. 327.

38. S. J. Prais and H. S. Houthakker, *The Analysis of Family Budgets,* Cambridge, University Press, 1955. See Chapter 5. See also J. Durbin and G. S. Watson, "Testing for Serial Correlation in Least-squares Regression," *Biometrika,* 37, 409 and 38, 159 (1950 and 1951).

39. For a discussion of alternatives and results with actual data, see Lawrence R. Klein and James Morgan, "Results of Alternative Statistical Treatments of Sample Survey Data," *Journal of the American Statistical Association,* 51 (December 1951), pp. 442-460. For an example of three different ways of estimating the wealth-elasticities of components of wealth, see Dorothy Projector and Gertrude Weiss, *A Survey of Financial Characteristics of Consumers,* Board of Governors of the Federal Reserve System, Washington, D.C., 1966.

40. Harold Guthrie, "Propensities to Hold Liquid Assets," *Journal of the American Statistical Association* 55, (Sept. 1960), pp. 469-490.

41. J. Johnston, *Econometric Methods,* McGraw-Hill, New York, 1963. See Chapter 6. See also, M. Kendall and Stuart, *The Advanced Theory of Statistics,* Vol. 11, Chapter 29, "Functional and Structural Relationship."

42. Hans Theil, Economic Forecasts and Policy, 2nd revised edition, North Holland Publishing Co., 1961, pp. 225-231, 334-344; see also R. L. Basmann, "A Generalized Classical Method of Linear Estimation of Coefficients in a Structural Equation," *Econometrica,* 25 (Jan. 1957), pp. 77-83. See also A. Goldberger, *Econometric Theory,* John Wiley, New York, 1964, who proves that two-stage least squares is identical with an instrumental variable estimation, p. 332.

43. See Louis H. Bean, "Simplified Method of Graphic Curvilinear Correlation," *Journal of the American Statistical Association,* 24 (Dec. 1929), pp. 386-397.

44. For a detailed discussion of multiple regression using categorical or dummy variables, see Frank Andrews, James Morgan and John Sonquist, *Multiple Classification Analysis,* Survey Research Center, Ann Arbor, Michigan, 1966. See also Daniel Suits, "The Use of Dummy Variables in Regression Equations," *Journal of the American Statistical Association,* 52 (Dec. 1957), pp. 548-551.

45. See Eva Mueller, "The Savings Account as a Source for Financing Large Expenditures," *Journal of Finance* 22 (Sept. 1967), pp. 375-393, cited earlier, where the forces leading to large decreases in savings accounts were not the mirror image of those leading to above average increases.

46. Richard Barfield and James Morgan, *Early Retirement,* Survey Research Center, The University of Michigan, Ann Arbor, Michigan, 1969, pp. 25ff.

47. See Morgan, Sirageldin and, Baerwaldt, *Productive Americans,* Survey Research Center, Ann Arbor, Michigan, 1966, p. 128.

48. See John Sonquist and James Morgan, *The Detection of Interaction Effects,* Survey Research Center, The University of Michigan, Ann Arbor, Michigan, 1964.

49. James N. Morgan, "The Achievement Motive and Economic Behavior," *Economic Development and Cultural Change,* 12 (April, 1964), 243-267.

50. Grover C. Wirick, James N. Morgan and Robin Barlow, "Population Survey: Health Care and Its Financing," in Walter J. McNerney, Ed., *Hospital and Medical Economics,* Vol. 1, Hospital Research and Educational Trust, Chicago, 1962, pp. 61-357, and James Morgan and John Sonquist, "Some Results from a Non-symmetrical Branching Process that Looks for Interaction Effects," *Proceedings of the Social Statistics Section.*

51. James Morgan, Ismail Sirageldin, and Nancy Baerwaldt, *op. cit.,* p. 128.

52. Robert Hermann, "Interaction Effects and the Analysis of Household Food Expenditures," *Journal of Farm Economics,* 49 (November 1967), pp. 821-832.

53. See the discussion in S. J. Prais and H. S. Houthakker, *The Analysis of Family Budgets,* Cambridge Univ. Press, Cambridge, 1955, Chapter 7.

54. Prais and Houthakker, *op. cit.,* Chapter 9.

55. Martin David, *Family Composition and Consumption,* North Holland Publishing Co., Amsterdam, 1962. As we noted earlier Hermann has found that not only are there different income elasticities of food expenditure according to family size, but that these differences differ depending on whether the families live in rural areas or not. Hermann, *op. cit.*

56. Compare Eisner's comments on Crockett and Friend, in Friend and Jones, ed., *Consumption and Saving,* Vol. I, *op. cit.,* p. 162.

57. Edwin Kuh and John R. Meyer, "How Extraneous Are Extraneous Estimates?" *Review of Economics and Statistics,* 39 (November 1957), pp. 380-393.

58. Gerry Miner, "Consumer Personal Debt: An Intertemporal Cross-section Analysis," in Friend and Jones, eds., *Conference on Consumption and Saving,* University of Penna. Press, Philadelphia, Penna., 1960, Vol. II, pp. 400-461. See also James Morgan, "Analysis and Interpretation of Cross-National Surveys," in *Interdisciplinary Topics in Gerontology,* 2 (1968), pp. 106-110, where the problem is the same.

59. For additional comparisons over time see John B. Lansing and Dwight M. Blood, *The Changing Travel Market,* Institute for Social Research, University

of Michigan, Ann Arbor, Michigan, 1964; and John Lansing and Gary Hend-ricks, *Automobile Ownership and Residential Density,* Survey Research Center, University of Michigan, Ann Arbor, Michigan, 1967.

60. Lewis Shipper, *Consumer Discretionary Behavior,* North Holland Publishing Co., Amsterdam, 1964.

61. See H. S. Houthakker and John Haldi, "Household Investments in Automobiles: An Inter-Temporal Cross-Section Analysis," in I. Friend and R. Jones, eds., *Consumption and Saving,* Vol. I, University of Penna., 1960, pp. 175-224.

62. Philip Cagan, "The Use of Wealth to Compare Household's Average Saving," *Journal of the American Statistical Association,* 59, Sept. 1964, pp. 737-745.

63. See James Coleman, "The Mathematical Study of Change," in H. B. Blalock, Jr. and A. B. Blalock, eds., *Methodology in Social Research,* McGraw Hill, New York, 1968, pp. 428-478, especially pp. 441-444.

64. "1948 Survey of Consumer Finances, Part I, Expenditure for Durable Goods," *Federal Reserve Bulletin,* June 1948, pp. 634-643.

65. Ronald Bodkin, "Windfall Income and Consumption," in Friend and Jones, *op. cit.,* pp. 175-187.

66. George Katona, *Private Pensions and Individual Saving,* Institute for Social Research, University of Michigan, Ann Arbor, Michigan, 1965; Philip Cagan, *The Effect of Pension Plans on Aggregate Saving,* Columbia Univ. Press, New York, 1965.

67. This point is strongly made by Robert Eisner, *Determinants of Capital Expenditures: An Interview Study,* Bureau of Economic and Business Research, University of Illinois, Urbana, Illinois, 1956.

68. For a good treatment of this, see Hubert M. Blalock, Jr., *Causal Influences in Nonexperimental Research,* University of North Carolina Press, Chapel Hill, 1961.

69. J. G. Kemeny and J. L. Snell, *Mathematical Models in the Social Sciences,* Ginn, New York, 1962; and Patrick Billingsley, *Statistical Inference for Markov Processes,* Univ. of Chicago Press, Chicago, 1961.

70. J. Morgan, M. David, W. Cohen and H. Brazer, *Income and Welfare in the U.S.,* McGraw Hill, New York, 1962.

71. Sherman J. Maisel, "Rates of Ownership, Mobility and Purchase," *Essays in Urban Land Economics,* pp. 76-108, in honour of the 65th birthday of Leo Grebler, University of California, Real Estate Research Program, L.A., 1966.

72. See Arthur Goldberger, "Stepwise Least Squares: Residual Analysis and Specification Effort," *Journal of the American Statistical Association,* 56 (December, 1961), pp. 998-1000, and Arthur Goldberger and D. B. Jochem, "A Note on Stepwise Least Squares," *Journal of the American Statistical Association,* 56 (March, 1961), pp. 105-110.

73. For the best statement, see David R. Heise, "Problems in Path Analysis and Causal Inference," in Edgar F. Borgatta, ed., *Sociological Methodology,* Jossey-Bass, San Francisco, 1969, pp. 38-73. For a discussion of the impact of errors in measurement (or imperfect proxy variables) on the interpretation of causal structures, see Herbert Costner, "Theory Deduction, and Rules of Correspondence," *American Journal of Sociology,* 75 (Sept. 1969), pp. 245-263.

74. Herbert Simon, "Spurious Correlation: A Causal Interpretation," *Journal of the American Statistical Association,* 49 (Sept. 1954), pp. 467-479.

75. See A. Goldberger, *op. cit.* For examples of residuals analysis, see J. Morgan, I. Sirageldin, and N. Baerwaldt, *Productive Americans,* Survey Research Center, University of Michigan, Ann Arbor, Michigan, 1966.

76. J. Morgan, M. David, W. Cohen and H. Brazer, *Income and Welfare in the United States,* McGraw Hill, New York, 1962.

77. For a systematic discussion, see T. W. Anderson, *op. cit.,* Chapter 12. The subject is also treated in M. H. Quenouille, *Associated Measurements,* London, Butterworths Scientific Publications, 1952, pp. 203 ff. Canonical correlation is not usually discussed in introductory textbooks on statistics.

78. John B. Lansing and Nancy Barth, *Residential Location and Urban Mobility: A Multivariate Analysis,* Institute for Social Research, University of Michigan, Ann Arbor, Michigan, December 1964.

79. See the discussion by Herman Wold and Lars Jureen, *Demand Analysis,* Wiley and Sons, New York, 1953.

80. Daniel Suits, "Forecasting and Analysis with an Econometric Model," *American Economic Review,* 52 (March 1962), pp. 104-132. See also J. Johnston, *Econometric Methods,* McGraw Hill, New York, 1963; and Lawrence R. Klein, *A Textbook of Econometrics,* Harper and Row, New York, 1953.

81. H. B. Blalock, Jr., *Causal Inferences in Nonexperimental Research,* The University of North Carolina Press, Chapel Hill, 1961, 1964, and his "Theory Building and Causal Influences," in H. M. Blalock, Jr. and A. B. Blalock, eds., *Methodology in Social Research,* McGraw Hill, New York, 1968, pp. 155-198.

82. For a clear explanation, see Otis Dudley Duncan, "Path Analysis: Sociological Examples," *American Journal of Sociology*, 72 (July, 1966), pp. 1-16. For a clear statement of the restrictions and limitations, see David R. Heise, "Problems in Path Analysis and Causal Inference," in *Sociological Methodology*, Edgar F. Borgatta, ed., Jossey-Bass, San Francisco, 1969, pp. 38-73.

83. Guy H. Orcutt, et al., *Microanalysis of Socioeconomic Systems*, Harper and Brothers, New York, 1961.

Chapter VII

THE FINANCING, ORGANIZATION, AND
UTILIZATION OF SURVEY RESEARCH

Introduction

Survey research is expensive, particularly if it is well done. Since knowledge is a "social good" not really salable in the market place, the problem of how an optimal quantity of survey research focused on the right topics is to be financed is a difficult one. Given some level of financing and general focus there is a problem of how to select individual projects and organize them so as to keep the information/cost ratio high. And finally, given some information, there is a problem of how to achieve an effective diffusion of the results so that the social benefits/information ratio is high, and hence the social benefits/costs information as well. We shall discuss these three topics—financing, efficient organization, and effective diffusion of the results, in order.

Financing of Survey Research

All research output is not marketable at its full value, hence its financing must be based on social rather than market criteria. But surveys are expensive, particularly as compared with dissertation fellowships, or small-scale projects using aggregate data or micro-data that are already collected. Nor can they compete for national funds now devoted to the collections of large scale data sets by government, because there the pressures for information about local areas or individual industries require censuses or huge samples, and put severe limits on the type and amount of information that can be collected on each unit.

The financing of survey research comes largely from private foundations and from government agencies which have provisions for research funding, like the National Institutes of Health, the Department of Health, Education, and Welfare, the Office of Economic Opportunity, and the National Science Foundation. Occasionally financing comes from business corporations or trade associations or non-profit organizations.

Since funding is on a project basis, it is impossible to separate the problem of total funding from the problem of the selection of projects. It is common to ask whether the dependence on financing by "clients" does not make the researcher the handmaiden of whoever has money. A counter charge is sometimes made that researchers insist on tackling trivial projects that intrigue them or build their reputation with their professional colleagues, ignoring the great social needs of the day.

The real situation, of course, is more complex and less extreme than either of these views. Following are the sequences by which survey research projects get developed, financed, and reported:

Foundations or government agencies may initiate the process by announcing the availability of funds, describing the research areas for which they stand ready to fund proposals, or even issuing requests for proposals in rather narrowly described areas. They may, if they have their own research staff, design a study and look for a survey organization to do the field work.

In general, however, the research groups have rather wide latitude in formulating proposals, interpreting, altering, or implementing the concerns of the fund sources. There have been occasions when offers of research funds for research projects in specific areas, have had such little interest that the funds could not be used, presumably because no one thought the research was feasible, or worth doing. And, of course, researchers find some of the research they think most crucial is not fundable.

There is often some mutual adaptation, so that the ultimate question of who initiated the design, or who really had the power to decide what was to be done, has no simple answer. It is not true that the researcher has more flexibility and freedom with research *grants* than with research *contracts,* it all depends on the particular situation. Some foundations have quite firm notions what they will support, and quite actively coerce researchers into redesigning their projects. Government mission-oriented agencies, and even private corporations, on the other hand, sometimes make grants or contracts for very broadly specified research which the researcher is free to design, analyze, and publish without restraints.

The complex process does not end with the submission of a formal proposal, since the proposal must then be evaluated and compete with other proposals. Frequently this involves formal committees set up by, but somewhat independent of, the source of funds. These committees may merely rank and evaluate, or they may make the final decision. There are problems of conflict of interest here, of course, since the more the evaluators know about the research area in question, the more likely they are to have strong feelings about what should be done and who should do it. On the other hand, those with no research experience may not be able to provide adequate evaluations.

The practice has been much better than the suspicious might think, though it leaves much to be desired. Perhaps the best procedures have been those of the National Institutes of Health, whose evaluation teams are encouraged to make site visits, and actually communicate with the researchers who may even respond by altering a research design. In other fields, it has often been difficult for the researcher even to know about and respond to the criticisms and comments of an evaluating committee or their consultants. In fact, this lack of two-way-communication can lead to uncorrected misunderstandings of the purpose or method of a project, since writing out a study design unambiguously and clearly is not easy.

One criterion for evaluating any research proposal is, of course, the past performance of the principal researchers. This implies that there should be not only prior evaluation of proposals, but later evaluation of what came out of each research project. There is little evidence that this evaluation is being systematically done either by the sources of research funds, or by the professional associations. There is a relatively high turnover in the staffs of fund-giving organizations, and so much pressure to allocate the new grants, that little time seems left for asking what happened to the old ones. The professional associations have not been very active in attempting any systematic assessment of survey research projects, particularly in economics, perhaps because they are often so large and complex, but partly because survey research in economics is relatively new and alien to the main traditions of analytic analysis and macro-dynamic research.

In spite of everything, however, there is some selective process, and some feedback from past results to future capacity to secure research funds. The total support for survey research is partly the result of the total support for social science research, and partly the result of the proportion of those funds allocated to survey research in economics, presumably based on the quality and relevance of the research proposals advanced.

The total research support for the social and behavioral sciences is not determined on any broad national basis, particularly since it comes from many sources. Presumably it should bear some relation to the total social benefits likely from such research, which, as any economist knows, requires adding utilities (themselves not usually quantifiable) vertically, not horizontally. The more people there are who use the results, the more the total social benefit. And the benefits are partly contributions to better decisions by government agencies, legislators, businessmen, private organizations, or individuals, and partly contributions to a body of scientific knowledge of human behavior, or of research methods. Those of us engaged in economic survey research are convinced that an increase in such research of several orders of magnitude would be clearly justified. But it is difficult to prove it.[1]

Financing on a project basis has developed out of the desire to see to it that the allocation of funds was effective, and the desire to achieve accountability, not just of the expenditures, but of the results. Such financing does introduce some uncertainty, and some costs, not so much because of the need to justify each project, even if it is part of a sequence of studies, but because of the short duration of most grants and the inability of researchers because of this to make long-term plans. We shall see shortly that there are not only economies of scale for a survey research organization, and for each project, but also economies from a steady flow of work and a long planning horizon.

It seems unlikely that these problems would be reduced by institutional grants. What is needed is a much longer time period for grants for survey research, realizing that it takes two to three years to design, conduct, analyze and report, a piece of survey research. Hence, studies need to overlap, too. One of the problems is that the gestation period for other kinds of economic or social research may be shorter, but a more important reason is that Congress in its desire to keep control of the budget, does not allow its agencies to make long-term commitments, unless the funds have already been appropriated. (And the agencies hesitate to set aside their present funds for such future commitments, restricting the number of things they can start this year.)

It seems likely that the future will not differ much from the past. That is, there is likely to remain a number of different and hopefully competing sources of research funds available for economic survey research, a balancing of interests in the design of projects, a selection process among competing proposals, and ultimately some evaluation of the outcome. Perhaps the major long run improvement will come from better evaluation of the results, which will in itself improve the selection of new projects.

Institutional grants may increase the total funds available, but they raise problems of evaluation, since there is no explicit research attached, as with project grants. There will also be problems of accounting, with the change in overhead versus direct costs.

If there were to be some major increase in the support for behavioral science research at the National Science Foundation, or with a new Social Science Foundation, the decisions about the allocation of those funds might well require some new procedures which would represent the interests not just of the professions, but also of the potential users of the results—Congress, mission agencies, etc.

The main sources of funds for economic surveys have been:

The Ford Foundation
The Carnegie Corporation
The Rockefeller Foundation
The Board of Governors of the Federal Reserve System (mostly 1947-60 and 1963-65)
The National Science Foundation
The Social Security Administration
United States Office of Experiment Stations.

Given the difficult problem of assessing research needs in the social sciences, and the embarrassing position of those who want to do research and must tout their own product, some intermediaries have sprung up:

The Social Science Research Council, while it has some funds of its own, often serves as an allocating channel for funds from other foundations or the government. Its Board has representatives of the various professional societies, plus some "at large" members.

The Behavioral Science Division of the National Research Council, whose original and main purpose was to provide unbiased (unpaid) technical advice to government agencies, occasionally serves to allocate small research grants, and, more important, sets up ad hoc advisory committees which recommend directions in which research support should go. It also is made up of official representatives of the various professional societies and some others "at large."

The Russell Sage Foundation also, while having some funds of its own, often secures funds from other foundations for projects which it deems worthy.

Foundations are understandably reluctant to support research which seems fundable by government agencies. Yet occasionally an agency without funding capacity, such as the Council of Economic Advisers, will induce a foundation to support some timely research project. And the Ford Foundation made large grants to the Brookings Institution for a program of studies in public finance, some of which supported survey research.

From a more historic point of view, the various sources of funds, the kinds of things they would support, and the various rules for applying, have been subject to a great deal of change, some of it rather sudden. Foundation boards will decide to change the whole focus of their interests, or Congress will make dramatic shifts in the amount of financial support in the budgets of agencies or for the National Science Foundation.

The variety of accounting rules, and demands for "local participation" increase the complexity and the real cost of securing research funds. The allowable "indirect cost" charges vary from ten percent of total costs with some foundations, to fifty-five percent of wages and salaries with some government agencies. Requirements to prove that the university, for instance, is providing part of the costs of a research project are good in theory, but clearly no university could engage in much research if each project was really a net burden on the university's teaching budget. And a state legislature providing research money for a university might resent having it supplement the funds of some Federal agency which was deciding what research should be supported.

Basically, however, all these confusions and costs of securing research funds would not be so bad if the process had to be endured only at infrequent intervals. When it must be done annually for each project, the sheer accounting burden and the burden on the time and energy of the researchers is formidable.

When research *contracts* are used, there is a general problem as to who "owns" the results of the research.[2] Clearly the survey organization must keep control of the sample books and, if there is any possibility of revealing individual responses, of the questionnaires as well. There is also a question about "clearance" of results before publication, and, in the case of research where the results relate to controversial reform proposals, the secrecy until a report is cleared. Actually the problem has existed more in prospect than in actuality, but the legalistic wording used in some federal contracts is enough to give a researcher pause.

For surveys conducted with federal funds, there is also a requirement that the questionnaires be cleared through the Bureau of the Budget.* Given the tight time schedules of many surveys, and the understandable reluctance to freeze the questionnaire until the last minute (and a desire not to change it after the last pretest), it is difficult for this process to avoid irritating and expensive delays. There have been instances of questionnaires taking long periods to clear, of demands for changes that implied real alterations in the research design, and of objections on minor and irrelevant points. Since there is no appeals procedure, a project can be held up so long that it has to be canceled. The original purpose was to avoid subjecting people to redundant questionnaires from different government agencies, or questions irrelevant and unnecessary for the legitimate purposes of the project, or to badly designed instruments. And this seems justified.

A recent ruling that questionnaires designed for research only, not for descriptive data, need not go through the Bureau of the Budget clearing process, remains to be interpreted. For those not exempted, the ruling that whenever more than six people are to be given the same questionnaire, it must be cleared, makes it difficult even to do pretesting legally, except by making minor changes in each set of six.

It is often argued that "applied" research directed to current social problems, does not provide any lasting basic findings. Our contention is that the distinction between "basic" and "applied" research in the social sciences is a false one. There are many real problems whose answers would be of real utility to people in making decisions, but which would also contribute to the basic body of knowledge in the behavioral sciences. Indeed, many economists have now come to the conclusion that further progress will require a much better data base, and better information about behavioral parameters, before the implications of the econometric models will be of real use in national policy.[3]

A more cooperative working relationship is required between the analytical economists working out the implications of systems of behavioral relationships, and the behavioral economists attempting to make the behavioral parameters in those relationships more realistic.

*Now Office of Management and Budget.

The Organization of Survey Research and the Search for High Information/Cost Ratios

In the true tradition of economic analysis, we can approach the problem of efficient organization of survey research both as a problem of maximizing the output of information per dollar spent, and as a problem of minimizing the costs of providing a given set of information. And we must also look at the total cost curve, that is, the economies of scale. There are also costs associated with instability or with short planning horizons.

Survey research, particularly good survey research, is expensive, particularly in comparison with the costs of econometric analysis of aggregate time series. The difference is several orders of magnitude. In addition it is labor-intensive, using large amounts of time of many highly trained specialists, and providing very little hope for mechanization or automation. But there *are* advantages and economies in specialization and division of labor, and there are heavy overhead costs (again mostly labor) so that there are economies of scale. The costs of survey research, per bit of information, start reaching their lowest possible levels only when the survey organization is regularly doing several million dollars worth of research each year. It may be worthwhile to provide some of the reasons in more detail.

Much of the overhead cost is in the training of specialists and coordinating their efforts. In addition to the researcher who is generally responsible for the design and the analysis of the substantive findings, there must be highly trained professional specialists in:

Field operations—the hiring, training, and supervision of interviewers and the improvement of procedures and continual research on methodology.

Content analysis—the hiring, training, and supervision of editors and coders and the improvement of procedures and research on coding error, coding drift, etc.

Sampling—the design of multi-purpose and special samples, the supervision of collection and processing of sample materials, the development of specific and general purpose approximate sampling errors.

Computer services—file management, data processing, statistical analysis, and improvement of archival and retrieval systems.

Bookkeeping, business management—the rapid provision of cost data required by sponsors and by the organization to avoid cumulative disasters, and the efficient procurement of printing and other services and supplies.

Editing and library—the conversion of reports into readable documents, the collection of relevant outside data, maintenance of archives and files, etc.

If people are assembled for a single limited project, they have neither the time nor the incentive to learn to work together, nor to cooperate. The difference is like the response of a plumbing firm to an individual who is building a single house and their response to a contractor who is building many houses. In the second case they have a long-term concern that the latter be satisfied, for he is a source of future business as well. It is for this reason that the authors have serious doubts about the viability of a survey facility available purely as a service to a rotating series of outside researchers for whom it collects data. Some collaboration between a specialist in methodology and a specialist in a substantive area of behavior is called for.

Not only does the training and assembly of staff represent a kind of fixed cost that needs to be spread over many surveys—and this includes hiring and training of interviewers—but since most of the capital is human capital, it deteriorates through non-use even faster than through use. The sampling materials get out of date, interviewers drift off to other jobs, computer software does not fit the newer generation of computers that come along, etc. This means that both a substantial flow *and* some regularity in its rate is required for efficiency.

Furthermore, given sources of financing which do not like indirect or overhead costs and put arbitrary limits on them, it is necessary to have cost systems which make as many things as possible into variable costs, chargeable to specific surveys. This is much easier with a continuous stream of work where, for instance, each survey can pay for some of the costs of updating the sampling materials in the field. The preparation of manuals, procedures, etc. also represents a cost which can be spread over many surveys, and indeed the development of conventions, standard procedures, etc. makes the work easier all along the line.

In order to achieve these economies of scale, it may be necessary for a survey research center to engage in a rather wide range of surveys in several fields. It is an interesting question just how much variety can be covered without difficulties. Interviewers trained to fixed-question open-answer interviews with heads of families may find it difficult to shift to other techniques. Very small samples have different computing problems from larger ones or panel studies. But the range can be rather wide, and indeed people who start out with rather widely different notions may converge somewhat as they learn from one another.

Problems arise as to the evaluation of individual performance necessary for the proper rewards and career development of the various individuals involved. The principal researcher can follow the usual path of articles and authorship, though even here the growing necessity for multiple authorship demanded by the staff needs of surveys, makes individual evaluation and recognition difficult.

More serious problems arise with the more specialized methodological skills involved, and with the sub-professional specialties. The heads of the specialized service sections such as sampling, field, etc., may have their own programs of methodological research and teaching, but still the demands of the

organization take their time and provide little recognition from their professional colleagues. The most dramatic case has been computer programming, a highly
specialized and demanding occupation. But a competent programmer finds himself solving other people's problems and seeing them get the glory. This, coupled
with the unwillingness or inability of many universities to provide monetary rewards, titles, or tenure for such people, has left many a magnificent computer
almost bereft of adequate software, or of programming service for those who
want to use the computer. Some professors have become programmers, or convinced graduate students to do so, in clear violation of the economist's law of
comparative advantage and the principle of specialization.

One major advantage of large, on going survey organizations, is that they
can provide tenure, titles, recognition, and evaluation of their own staff. They
can also provide career lines and promotions within the organization, allowing
people to upgrade their skills. The status of the specialists can also be enhanced
by their gradual "professionalization" and by separate authorship in study reports of methodological chapters by the specialists in sampling, interviewing,
coding, and data processing.

There is another way in which the scale of a survey operation affects its
efficiency or information/cost ratio. There is transfer of learning enthusiasm,
and criticism across different substantive programs. People studying one kind of
economic behavior learn from those studying another kind, and also from those
studying political behavior. Frequently one group borrows from the other, particularly in the development of measures of the explanatory variables which are
often interdisciplinary.

Effective survey research often requires cooperation with specialists in
more than one field. Economic surveys may require active participation by experts in law, medicine, public health, religion or philanthropy, city planning,
outdoor recreation, air transport, etc. And this cooperation should begin in the
early design stages and continue through the writing of the results.

In practice, securing funds for a piece of survey research involves working
out a design, getting cost estimates from the various specialists (sampling, field,
data processing, content analysis) estimating a total budget of time and money,
and summarizing all this in a research proposal. We now turn to some explicit estimates of components of survey costs.

We have already seen that there is another resource allocation problem in
designing each survey. It is usually stated in the form of maximizing the incre-
ment to knowledge from the utilization of a fixed total budget. The most common error is to invest so much in collecting data that there are insufficient funds
for analyzing and writing. The second most common is to devote so little to design and pretesting work that the data are not worth analyzing.

Within a topic there is a question whether to focus on a more limited area
and spend more time on it, or to cover several areas (usually on the grounds that

they are related anyway and hence must be studied together—like the components of saving).

And in the explanatory variables, again one has a choice of spending much time measuring a few very carefully, or whether to expand the range of explanatory variables with less attention to each.

There are also economies of scale in conducting a single survey, even in an organization doing surveys continually. The costs of many components are almost independent of the number of interviews: original design, pretesting, interviewers instructions, editing and coding procedures, programming the file building and cleaning of data on the computer, and writing the results. And other costs are less than proportionate to the number of interviews: printing, computer runs, interviewing. Hence, there are sample sizes below which it does not seem worth the investment for the little information that comes out. If a sample is designed with 50-100 primary sampling areas, and it is very costly for a single interviewer to take fewer than 10-20 interviews in any one study, this becomes a kind of restriction, unless there is a probability subsample which uses only half of the primary sampling areas (except for the self-representing ones). But the most important overhead cost is probably in design and development of the questionnaire and materials.

A Preliminary Analysis of Survey Costs

The purpose of this section is to present an elementary analysis of the determinants of survey cost as a contribution to the rational planning of sample surveys. In the design of a sample survey there are a large number of choices to be made about what is to be done. Comparisons of two surveys in which different options were selected can be of doubtful meaning, or, in the extreme, completely meaningless. Nobody would conclude that Fords cost more than Chevrolets from the comparison of two cars without taking into account the detailed characteristics of the particular vehicles. Surveys are, if anything, more heterogeneous than automobiles. It is important, therefore, to know the cost of the options.

A few general observations may be made at the start. Surveys are labor intensive. Hence, costs tend to move with wages and salaries, especially, for academic personnel, with university salary rates. In most aspects of survey work gains in productivity are not easy to achieve. In this respect surveys are more like live theatrical performances than they are like the manufacture of durable goods. The principal technological innovation now in process is the introduction of new and improved computers. The gain has been primarily in more and better tabulations for the same expenditure rather than in a reduction of cost for a given quantity and quality of tabulations. Even when the gain is taken in cost reduction, tabulating costs represent a comparatively minor part of the total cost of a typical survey. They may be ten percent of total costs, or less. Even cutting tabulating costs in half would not reduce total costs very much. In other aspects of survey work technical gains have been limited. Hence, there is a tendency toward upward pressure on survey costs over time.

Here we merely assemble information readily available at the Survey Research Center, primarily from the heads of the sections of the Center. The starting point is existing practice and observed costs on current financial surveys. In general, the greater the departure from existing practice at the Survey Research Center, the less certain the cost estimates. No attempt has been made to develop new knowledge of costs.

Table 1 presents estimates of the approximate total data collection cost for a recent financial survey conducted for the Office of Economic Opportunity.

This was an unusually large survey for the Survey Research Center, with a total of 4800 interviews taken in 1968. As Table 1 indicates, total direct costs were $47.60 per interview, the largest items being field salaries at $21.88 and field travel at $8.12, or $30.00 per interview for total field costs. On this study sampling, coding, supplies, and tabulating were all in the range of $3.50 to $5.00 per interview. Each of these components of the cost of data collection will be considered below. Information on research salaries will be presented separately in a concluding section.

Field Costs: It is possible to prepare tables showing long-run trends in direct field costs. Table 2 shows such a trend for selected "Omnibus" surveys conducted by the Survey Research Center in the period 1951-1952 to 1968. Note that this tabulation includes only interviewers' salaries and interviewers' travel, and excludes field supervisors' salaries and travel and costs in the Ann Arbor office of the field staff. Note, first, that there has been a major upward trend in cost per interview for interviewers' salaries and travel, from about $6-$7 in 1951-1953 to $16-$21 in 1967-1968. Note also that there has been variation from survey to survey in these costs. For example, the costs per interview fell from $20.05 in the fall of 1966 to $16.07 in the spring of 1967 but returned to $20.81 a year later.

The basic trend can be explained in considerable part by changes in hourly wage rates. Data on minimum and maximum hourly rates are available for the period, but weighted average hourly salaries are available only for the last year or two. They are shown in the lower part of Table 2. Since in 1952-1953 the spread between the minimum and maximum rates was only 20¢, we can assume that the average was about the mid-point, that is, $1.25 per hour. The average of $2.43 in 1968-1969 then is about double the rate paid in 1952-1953 for an hour of interviewer's time. Strictly speaking, the comparison of total costs should consider separately the shifts in reimbursement rates per mile of interviewers' travel, but they increased more or less in the same manner as salary rates over this period. If

TABLE 1

Approximate Data Collection Cost of a Financial Survey,

Based on First Wave of Interviews for

Study of Income Dynamics

(1968, n = 4800)

		Total	Per Interview
1.	Field salaries (interviewers and supervisors)	$105,000	$21.88
2.	Field travel (by interviewers and supervisors)	39,000	8.12
3.	Sampling	17,000	3.54
4.	Coding	21,000	4.38
5.	Supplies	23,000	4.79
6.	Tabulating	23,500	4.90
	Subtotal	$228,500	$47.60
7.	Fringe benefits, service personnel, at 10% of lines 1, 3, 4	$ 14,300	$ 2.98
8.	Indirect costs at 47% of lines 1, 3, 4, 7	$ 73,931	$15.40
		$316,731	$65.98

Note: This table includes no entry for payments to respondents
       which were made between the first and second waves of
       interviews on this study. This study was also unusual
       in using additional sample points and in these and the
       regular sample points in reinterviewing families previously
       interviewed once or twice by the United States Census
       Bureau.

TABLE 2

Long Run Trends in Direct Field Costs Per Interview

for "Omnibus" Surveys

Year	Interviewers' Salaries	Interviewers' Travel	Total
Fiscal 1951-1952 #601	$4.46	$1.16	$5.62
Fiscal 1952-1953 #607	6.26	1.52	7.78
Fiscal 1956-1957 #649	7.30	2.17	9.47
Fall 1962	10.02	3.97	13.99
Summer 1963	11.93	4.91	16.84
Fall 1963	11.08	3.47	14.55
Spring 1964	10.28	3.17	13.45
Fall 1965	11.45	3.73	15.18
Summer 1966	12.29	3.49	15.78
Fall 1966	15.99	4.06	20.05
Spring 1967	13.00	3.07	16.07
Summer 1968	15.02	5.79	20.81

Hourly Rates:	1952-53	1968-69
Minimum hourly rate	$1.15	$2.00
Maximum hourly rate	1.35	2.80

	1967	1968-69
Weighted average hourly salary	$2.16	$2.43

we take Study 607 in 1952-1953 as a starting point for a comparison, then that
study would have cost not $7.78 per interview but a little under $16 at wage and
mileage rates in 1968-1969. Actual surveys in 1967-1968 cost $16.07 to $20.81.
If we consider interviewers' salaries alone, then we may take $6.26, roughly
double it, to about $13-$14, and compare that figure with the observed $15.02
in the summer of 1968. It is clear that costs per interview have increased slightly
more than can be accounted for by changes in hourly wage rates.

What is lacking in this comparison are data on the characteristics of the interviews, It is entirely possible that the interviews have become longer and more
complex over this period. One way to reduce cost per unit of information collected is to collect more items of information in a single interview. Thus, cost
per unit information may have been constant while costs per interview increased.
Another difference between interviewing in 1968 and in 1952-1953 is that the
geographic distribution of the population in the country has changed. In general,
people have tended to shift into metro areas, where costs are higher, and also to
shift into spread-out suburban areas where travel costs are higher. Such changes
may have increased the amount of time interviewers spend in locating their respondents, thus increasing both the mileage costs for travel, and salaries while
traveling. We can only speculate as to the importance of these factors with the
data at hand.

Determinants of Cost Per Interview: In view of the importance of field
costs as a proportion of total survey cost it is not surprising that considerable attention has been given to the determinants of cost per interview. Information on
four factors has been assembled in Table 3 and additional historical data appear
in Table 4.

First, cost per interview depends upon the number of interviews taken by
a given interviewer employed on a survey. As shown in part I of Table 3, the
average cost per interview on a project for a given interviewer falls at a decreasing rate as the number of interviews taken increases. The shape of the relationship suggests the existence of some initial fixed cost which is being distributed
over an increasing number of interviews. This cost presumably is the time taken
by an interviewer to become familiar with the questionnaire and instruction
book for a particular project. There may also be some efficiency in actual data
collection in calling on different addresses if one has more addresses to cover
and, hence, more options open on a given trip into the field. In any event the
data show quite clearly that it costs more for interviewers to take less than ten
interviews on a given project. Yet, on comparatively small surveys, such as
Study #504, as many as thirty-six percent of the interviews were in fact taken
by interviewers who took one to nine interviews. On Study 763, the 1967 Survey of Consumer Finances, with a total of 3102 interviews, only four percent of
the interviews were taken by interviewers who took less than ten interviews a

TABLE 3

Four Determinants of Cost Per Interview for

Interviewers' Salaries and Travel

I. Size of sample and number of interviews per interviewer employed

Number of interviews taken per interviewer	Average cost per interview		Percent of interviews taken by interviewers with each "take"	
	#763	#504	#763	#504
1-9	$27.50	$24.28	4	36
10-14	19.70	18.79	17	37
15-19	18.98	15.08	18	12
20-29	17.40 ⎫		36	
30+	16.09 ⎭ 14.29		25	15
			100	100
overall	$18.13	$19.68	N= 3102	1496

Based on #763, 1967 S.C.F., and #504

II. Type of place--large cities versus medium sized cities and other areas

Size	Interviewers' Salaries		Interviewers' Travel		Total	
	#763	#750	#763	#750	#763	#750
Small towns, rural	$12.12	$ 9.87	$ 3.14	$ 3.20	$15.26	$13.07
Metro areas, not including 12 largest	13.20	10.85	3.96	3.42	17.16	14.27
12 largest cities	18.34	14.55	5.37	4.91	23.71	19.46

TABLE 3 - continued

III. Local vs. national surveys

A.   "Time Use" Study

                              Jackson, Mich.   National metropolitan
                              (n = 792)   sample

                              #471   #491

Interviewers' salaries $ 8.94 $14.62
Interviewers' travel   2.46   4.90

Total $11.40 $19.52

"Extra" 96 interviews taken at the end of the study in Jackson

Interviewers' salaries $ 6.70
Interviewers' travel   3.14

Total $ 9.84

B. #755 Living Patterns and Attitudes in Detroit, Data for Detroit
    Interviewers' work only (n = 1008)

                              #755 (Spring 1966)

Interviewers' salaries $ 7.52
Interviewers' travel   1.76

Total $ 9.28

C. Comparison between Detroit and Other Large Metro Areas (#763)

                         Interviewers'   Interviewers'
                           Salaries   Travel   Total

Detroit $15.93 $ 4.66 $20.59
All large metro areas   18.34   5.37   23.71

D. Study of Young Drivers (Pelz), Detroit area, n = 669 (Required
    screening at 6 addresses per 1 final selection included. Also,
    badly located for Detroit staff in western Wayne, Washtenaw, etc.)

Interviewers' salaries $13.48
Interviewers' travel $ 4.45

Total $17.93

IV. Cost of telephone interviews ("Omnibus," brief interview by phone)
     #757, telephone reinterviews, with personal interviews where
     no telephone

Interviewers' salaries $ 2.84
Interviewers' travel   .63

Total $ 3.47

TABLE 4

Historical Data on Interviewers' Salaries as a Function of

Length of Interview and a Breakdown of Interviewers' Time

I.   Relation between length of questionnaire and costs:
     costs of interviewers' salaries, for omnibus studies,
     1957-58 through 1962-63: I = $2.50 plus $.11 L,
     where L = length of interview in minutes
         I = interviewers' salaries per interview

II. Breakdown of time spent:

	Metro	Urban	Rural
Interviewing	17%	23%	23%
Calling	17	13	12
Editing	12	15	16
Training	5	7	9
Administration	7	10	7
Travel	35	22	19
Sampling*	7	10	14
Total	100%	100%	100%

*Estimated.

This table is based on data from day-by-day records
kept by interviewers as tabulated for a sample of
counties on one "omnibus" survey, #685, in 1960.

piece. It is not surprising, therefore, that the average cost per interview was $1.50 cheaper on Study 763 than Study 504.

While it is possible to consider this relationship in terms of administrative practices in the field, it is also possible to think of it in terms of sampling. If the number of primary sampling units in which interviews were taken on Study 504 had been reduced, no doubt the number of interviews taken per interviewer could have been kept at the level of the larger survey. There would have been a loss, however, in the form of increased sampling error.

A second determinant of field cost per interview is the type of place in which the interviews are taken. Data on cost per interview by type of place are shown in part II of Table 3 for Study 763 and Study 750. These results are typical. On Study 763, for example, costs per interview in small towns and rural areas were $15.26, and in the 12 largest cities, $23.71. The difference was $8.45 per interview. On Study 750 it was $6.39.

There are at least four underlying factors at work. First, wage rates are higher in large cities, and on the average interviewers must be paid more per hour. Second, interviewers in large cities spend more time traveling and less time interviewing than those in smaller cities and rural areas, as is indicated by Table 4.

Third, there is a substantial difference in costs between local and national surveys as shown in part III of Table 3. A direct comparison can be made in connection with the study of time use undertaken by Converse and his colleagues in which a national sample of people in metropolitan areas was interviewed on the same schedule as a cross-section of a small metropolitan area, Jackson, Michigan. Costs per interview for interviewers' salaries and travel were $11.40 in Jackson compared to $19.52 in the national sample, a difference of about $8. This comparison is complicated by the fact that some of the interviews in the national sample were taken in large metropolitan areas where as just noted, costs tend to be $5-$6 higher. There is still a cost advantage of $4 or so for the local study.

It is also of some interest to note the results of a special situation in the Jackson sample. At the end of the study an extra 96 interviews were taken which had not been planned for in advance, and the cost information about these interviews was kept separate. The cost per interview was $9.84, or $1.56 less than the average for the project in Jackson. This result is consistent with what was observed above about the effect of increasing the number of interviews per interviewer.

A second example of a study in a single area is Study 765, Living Patterns and Attitudes in Detroit, in which 1008 interviews were taken by Detroit interviewers in the Detroit metropolitan region. (We exclude a few interviews by non-Detroit staff.) Cost per interview was $9.28 for interviewers' salaries and travel. These results may be compared with the experience on Study 763, a national survey involving 93 interviews in Detroit, in which the total costs were $20.59

in Detroit. Note, however, that Detroit is a low cost city for interviewing by the Survey Research Center. On Study 763, in all large metropolitan areas combined average cost per interview was $23.71. Another recent local project in the Detroit area was a study of young drivers under the direction of Donald Pelz with 669 interviews. This project was unusually difficult in that it required screening interviews to locate people in the appropriate demographic group with about six screening interviews for one final·selection. Nevertheless, interviewers' salary and travel per final interview cost only $17.93.

Fourth, costs per interview can be drastically affected by changing from personal interviews to telephone interviews. The cost of telephone interviewing depends heavily on the length of the interview and on the procedures used to deal with people who do not have telephones. On Study 757, a brief telephone reinterview on an "Omnibus" survey, personal interviews were taken where no telephone was available. Even including the cost of these personal interviews, the total interviewers' salaries plus travel was only $3.47 per interview.

Information was collected about the length of interview on the average in the field as well as on costs for Omnibus surveys in the period of 1957-1958 through 1962-1963. Results are summarized in a simple equation shown in Table 4 part I. In effect, this equation assumes that all of the variation from one Omnibus survey to another is the result of differences in length of interview. The marginal cost shown of eleven cents per minute reflects cost levels in the period around 1960, and would have to be substantially increased for 1968-1969. It should be pointed out that the length of an interview influences the time actually spent interviewing and editing plus the number of interviews that an interviewer may be able to complete successfully on a single excursion into the field. If the interview is reasonably short, the chances are better that she can complete more than one interview on a given visit to a cluster of sample addresses. It may also affect the amount of non-response, the costs of which are spread over the other interviews.

The second part of Table 4 shows data from 1960 breaking down the amount of time spent in different activities by interviewers working in different types of areas. Note that in metropolitan areas on that study only seventeen percent of the hours of the interviewers were actually spent in interviewing, compared to thirty-five percent spent in travel. The reference to sampling is to work done in assembling information for sampling purposes by interviewers in the field.

Sampling Costs: The selection of the sample involves two stages, the development of a sampling frame, and then the selection of elements from that frame. A given frame may be usable for selection of several specific samples. The first question, therefore, in considering the cost of selecting a sample for a particular study is whether there is an existing sampling frame which is appropriate for this survey. If there is, a sample can be drawn quickly and economically.

In general, the sampling section has a well developed frame for national samples which makes use of a specific selection of primary sampling units. To include additional primary sampling units would involve an extension of the frame, but this expansion is not likely to be necessary except in the event that the one wishes to use a very large national sample for some purpose. Local surveys also require frames, and, in general, the sampling section does not have such frames available for most metropolitan areas in the country. There are a few exceptions: Detroit, Philadelphia, and a few other areas.

For a national sample using the existing frame the cost is a function primarily of the number of interviews. Some costs, such as the cost of selecting individual segments, are proportional to the size of the sample. Other aspects of sample selection do not increase very much as the size of the sample increases. For a sample of about 1500 interviews, expense for sampling salaries is about $6000-$7000, that is, about $4.00-$4.66 per interview. Doubling the size of the sample to 3000 interviews would roughly increase the cost by fifty to sixty percent, that is, to $9000-$11,000. Cost per interview would fall to about $3 to $3.66. For particular projects additional expense may be incurred if, for example, there are extensive calculations of sampling errors, or if there are special problems such as splicing two samples.

Samples located in a single metropolitan area are somewhat less complicated, and, therefore, somewhat more economical for a given number of interviews. In 1967 the sampling section drew a sample of about 1000 in the Cleveland metropolitan area. A total cost of $3,250 covered both these selections and a sample of union locals which was needed at the time. If roughly $650 of the total is allocated to the sample of union locals, and about $2600 to the area sample of the metropolitan area, then the cost per selection was about $2.60. (Cost per interview would be slightly higher owing to the usual losses from nonresponse and non-sample addresses.)

A sample is now being drawn for the Boston metropolitan area. Including the setting up of a frame with a capability for future use and actual selection of 800 addresses the total cost is estimated at $3,950 in sampling salaries. If the total amount is allocated to these 800, then the cost is nearly $5 per selection. The work has been done in such a manner, however, that an extra 2400 selections could be made at a very small additional cost, implying a cost per selection well under $2.00. The experience in Boston clearly illustrates both the economies in the full exploitation of a given sampling frame, and the difference in cost between a local and a national frame.

A final comment about sampling costs may be made for panel studies. There is little additional sampling work required on a "pure" panel survey after initial selection. If, however, the panel is to be used also as a cross-section of the population of dwelling units existing in the future, there is additional sampling work. It becomes necessary to develop and apply checking procedures designed to pick up the new dwelling units which may be created after the initial selections have been made.

Coding Costs: The estimation of the cost to code an interview may be described in a series of steps:

a) *Time to code a standard interview.* An interview from a study takes one hour to code and requires six to eight cards. A rule of thumb is to estimate the length of time an average interview takes in the field and estimate that the time to code will be the same. This rule applies to "standard" economic interviews, which contain twenty-five percent or less open-ended questions.

b) *Additional time.* Adding twenty-five percent to the time to code an interview to allow for training, check coding, and miscellaneous time. Thus, the result of these two steps is an estimate of time per interview in man-hours.

c) *Apply an average rate.* The average rate is now about $2.40 per hour. It varies depending on the rates for the coders assigned to a project. Currently the range is $1.90-$2.65, the latter level being that paid to people who have been coding for 1 1/2 years or more. Multiply the average rate by the number of interviews.

d) *Office time and supervision.* The cost of office time and supervision is now about $150 per week for a typical study, assuming that there are two studies in coding at the same time, which is typical. The length of time in coding is ordinarily comparable to the length of time a study is in the field.

In addition, although many surveys need no editing, a separate editing operation is required on complex surveys such as the Surveys of Consumer Finances. The cost may be estimated on the same basis as for coding, but obviously must depend on the complexity of the work to be done by the editors. On the 1968 Survey of Consumer Finances editing required an average of 0.8 hours per interview while coding required 1.1 hours.

Coding costs may be expected to vary depending upon the number of open-end questions. Elimination of open-end questions will cut coding time to roughly half of field time instead of the same as field time. Increasing to fifty percent open questions will increase coding time roughly to 1 1/2 times interviewing time. It should be understood that these estimates are approximate and depend on the complexity of the code for the open-ended questions.

Tabulating Costs: Tabulating and computing costs have two basic characteristics. First the technology is shifting very rapidly. Second, there is a close and complex interaction between the computing staff and the research staff. Functions may be shifted back and forth between these two groups of people. In addition, there is a tendency for the detailed knowledge of the computing facility by the analysis staff to become obsolete very quickly. Between the analysis of one study and the analysis of the next there may be major changes in the computer software. There are also important trade-offs between computing costs and research salary costs. An organization of the flow of work which is efficient from the point of view of minimizing tabulating costs may not be an organization which is efficient from the point of view of the utilization of the research staff. Compromises may be necessary.

The computing section at present is working with an organization of costs for their services into eight types of operation. As one proceeds down the list these costs become increasingly difficult to estimate. The available information may be summarized as follows. (Remember, however, that they depend heavily on the computer software available and require a heavy input of research staff time.)

1. *Transcription.* The cost of punching and verifying is now about ten cents per card. This figure is based on the rate of $5.50 per hour for the machine plus the operator. That rate, like other rates to be cited below, includes an allowance for the overhead costs of the data processing section. If we think of a hypothetical standard survey with a sample of 1500 and five IBM cards per interview, the cost of transcription works out to $750.

2. *File construction.* The data processing charges involved in file construction for a typical survey are $25 plus $15 per 100 cases. For the standard survey used as an example here the total amount would be $250. This process involves certain checking and matching operations as well as the conversion from card to tape.

3. *Cleaning.* This step involves the internal checking of the data for consistency and correction of any errors which are found. The amount spent will depend on the extent of the checking. A typical figure is thirty-five cents per interview, or, for the hypothetical standard survey, $525.

4. *Variable generation.* On an average in a typical survey 50 variables will be generated per 100 variables coded. The cost of the operation is thirty cents to fifty cents per interview depending upon the number of variables, their complexity, any errors detected in the process, and the number of passes through the computer which are required. The total cost for the hypothetical survey thus would be in the range of $450 to $750.

5. *Univariate analysis.* The typical first step in actual analysis is the preparation of univariate distributions. The cost is in the range five cents to fifteen cents per variable per 1000 cases. For the standard survey, it would be in the range of $33 to $100.

6. *Bivariate analysis.* The cost of bivariate distributions ranges from ten cents to twenty-five cents per table per 1000 cases. If we assume 1500 cases and 450 tables, which would not be unusual, the range would be $60 to $150.

Up to this stage in the analysis the standard survey has cost $1525 for steps 1, 2, and 3, plus $550 to $1000 for steps 4, 5, and 6, for a grand total of about $2000-$2500. Roughly speaking, the costs are in direct proportion to the number of variables coded and the number of interviews for a given level of effort in cleaning and variable generation. From this stage on costs depend on the complexity of the analysis which is undertaken.

7. *Analysis of interrelations.* Costs of this type of analysis depend on what is being done, whether it is missing data correlations, factor analysis, scaling, or whatever. Minimum costs are about $50 to $100 per run per 1000 cases with a limited number of variables, that is, 60 to 100 variables. Costs may be higher depending on what is required.

8. *Multivariate analysis.* The cost of multivariate analysis depends directly on the program and the complexity of the analysis.

It is prudent practice to add a safety factor to the above estimates. Unexpected developments and errors can add to costs, but they cannot reduce them. Experience with previous studies is often a better guide than estimates built from components, where errors can cumulate.

One approach has been suggested for handling the problem of how to estimate costs for the later, more complicated analysis of (7) and (8). Sonquist suggests using a rough estimate of $1000 per man-month of analysts' time. He has in mind estimating tabulating costs on the basis of the number of man-months of time of professional staff who will be making use of the computer in this phase of a project. All these estimates assume continuous operations and a lot of previous investment in human and physical capital.

Research Salaries: There are two broad choices to be made in planning or estimating research salaries: first, how large a total staff in man-years of different types of personnel should be assigned to a project? Second, how should the time of the research staff be distributed among the different phases of a project? It may be useful to distinguish five stages as follows:

1. *Planning.* This period extends from the initial conception of a project up to the time when data collection actually begins. Several months are ordinarily required, depending on the novelty of the project.

2. *Supervision of data collection.* This period extends from the data when materials are mailed to interviewers to the date when coding is completed and the cards have been keypunched. The lag between the completion of coding and the completion of keypunching is ordinarily negligible. It is standard practice for interviewing, coding, and keypunching to proceed simultaneously, so that the total length of time for data collection exceeds by only a few weeks the total time in the field.

3. *Supervision of data preparation.* The next phase is the supervision of data preparation, that is stages 2, 3, and 4 above: file construction, cleaning and correction, and variable generation. File construction ordinarily requires about

one week, and cleaning and correction and variable generation may proceed more or less at the same time. The total period required for the cleaning and correction (only) of the 1968 Survey of Consumer Finances was about two months. For the OEO study the total period was approximately three months for the Survey Research Center part of the study for the three steps. Of course, if little or no cleaning or variable generation is needed, these two steps can be reduced or omitted.

4. *Computing.* The next phase is analysis proper, in which computing proceeds through steps five-eight above, the statistical manipulation of the data. Some overlap is possible both with the preceding and following phases of the work.

5. *Report preparation.* Report preparation may well be commenced while computing is still going on. The usual experience is that computing gradually tapers off as the report is going through its final phases of preparation. This phase may be regarded as completed with the delivery of the final published report. This phase is the one most usually under-budgeted, and the part of the budget most often robbed by over-doing other things.

Supplies: The category "supplies" used at the Institute for Social Research includes four main components: duplicating and printing, postage, communications (toll calls), and general office supplies, including maps and other materials needed for sample selection. It is sufficiently heterogeneous so that it is customarily estimated simply as a percentage of total costs. That approach seems appropriate, for example, to handle variations in duplicating, which includes duplicating of drafts as well as final copies of memoranda, questionnaires, codes, worksheets, instructions, tables, reports, and so forth. Field work requires expenses for postage on completed interviews and toll calls to interviewers which are roughly proportional to the total volume of work.

An exception is the preparation of the final report or reports. The length of these documents, the number of copies, the use of graphic displays, and the type of reproduction vary substantially. Costs vary accordingly from small sums for mimeographed reports to several thousand dollars. However, for more than one hundred copies, printing (photo-offset) is cheaper than mimeographing or multilithing, because the paper is so much cheaper and the actual printing so much faster.

Concluding Comments: The preceding discussion has been based on the assumption that the basic research techniques required for a particular inquiry have been developed. Allowance is made only for a planning period and a standard type of pretest. It may be true, however, that the techniques needed for a particular project do not exist. If innovations are needed in sample design, questionnaire design, or analysis, appropriate allowance should be made in the budget. A pilot study may be required, particular measures may need development or validation, new computer programs may need to be developed, or some other special effort may be called for. This work may be thought of as "extra" in the sense that it is in addition to the basic costs of a standard survey, but it may be fundamental to the success of the research. The estimates also probably understate the amount of research salaries that ought to be provided if more attention is to be given to dissemination of the results, increasing their social benefits. The difficulties in financing and the natural tendency to collect adequate data in a historic context where they could not be improved later, have led to underspending on careful writing of separate interpretations for different audiences.

Although the previous estimates have looked at separate components, and to some extent built them up from subparts, it is often quite misleading to estimate the costs of a new survey in this manner. It is easy to omit things, and underestimate the total.

For example one might estimate the time an interview would take, multiply by the average interviewers' salary, and add some travel costs. But the interviewing costs also include the interviewer's salary while she is:

> travelling
> being trained
> reading instruction books
> doing pretesting of earlier questionnaires
> doing preliminary sampling work (listing addresses, checking for new construction, etc.)
> calling on not-at-homes
> making call-backs
> chatting with respondents during or after the interview to assure completion and satisfied respondents (interviews often take longer than pretests)
> writing afterwards to fill out shorthand and abbreviations, and adding a description of the situation
> filling out forms for non-response, for financial accounting, etc.

Furthermore, the total field budget may be expected to include the salaries and expenses of supervisors who hire, train, and supervise the interviewers, the salaries of office contact persons, typists and mailers, the salaries of the head of the field section and others who aided in designing the questionnaire, pretesting, etc. Someone has to check the sample books, and there are bills for telephone, mail, paper and printing.

Some functions fall between sections, so that the budget may inadvertently omit them because each section assumes the other will handle it, when that section is asked for an estimate of its costs for a survey. This is particularly true of sample book controls which may be done by the field section, the sampling section, or the analysis section, or of supervision of editing and coding which is often divided between the analysis section and the supervisors in the coding section.

It is also common to estimate how much each subcomponent would cost if little went wrong, multiply by the number of such components, and leave insufficient margin for errors and breakdowns. The tendency for building contractors to underestimate, year after year and house after house, how long it will take to finish the job, illustrates the kind of perceptual bias involved.

A major cost often overlooked is the cost of delay, since salaries are a major part of the cost, and many of them are paid even if the people cannot do their job because they are waiting for something. Hence proper scheduling and meshing of the parts are critical. This is true for each survey, and for a series of surveys. For instance, it is efficient to have interviewers starting their calls on a new survey while still attempting to find a few "not-at-homes" left from the previous one, particularly since the final sample clusters are located close together. For each survey some common instances of delays that keep staff "standing on their own shoelaces" are:

> Assembling and training editors before there is a sufficient supply of interviews to edit.
> Assembling and training coders before there is a sufficient backlog of interviews edited to assure a steady flow of work.
> Starting either editing or coding too late, so that problems in field interviewing or editing are not caught until a large number of errors have already been made.
> Failure to plan for the analysis, so that things stop while additional variables are generated, etc.
> Failure to enforce a deadline in the field, so that interviews keep trickling in.

Another cost-raising error is unnecessary complexity in the questionnaire, in sample design, in editing procedures, in codes, etc. Interviewers make costly mistakes if the instrument is too complex. Complex samples cause problems in the field, in weighting the data, in computation of sampling errors. Complex codes slow down coders and multiply the error rate. The use of several different questionnaires makes codes complex, exacerbates analysis problems, and often leads either to no differences in results, or unexplained differences. If some questions are asked of only half the sample and a different set from the other half, again the analysis and the data file management is more complicated. Combining samples and splicing them together is another example, though it may sometimes be necessary.

A major source of difficulty is that time and money budgeted run out before the study is finally cleaned up, archived, etc. Some procedure for reserving funds to be used for final editorial work, cleaning up files, providing a proper final documentation and lending library of data tapes, would vastly improve the archives of the future. Even the final costs of printing or typing derivative articles often come in long after the study budget is closed.

The implications of all this discussion on maximizing the information cost ratio is that what is required is a large, steady, well-planned program of surveys, efficiently organized with attention to costs as well as to amount of information. There are economies of scale for survey organizations, for each individual survey, and for sequences of surveys on one general topic area.

Diffusion of Results; the Social Benefits/Information Ratio

The benefits of research are a function of the extent to which the information is utilized. In so far as the responsibility for interpreting the research findings to a variety of audiences falls upon the researcher, the previously discussed problems in financing research are relevant. In the current state of short-run project financing, a survey research specialist must be simultaneously writing proposals, designing other studies, supervising the implementation of still others, and writing up the findings of earlier studies. Once the main report of a study is written, there is tremendous pressure to move on to the other projects at various stages of their development. This pressure is intensified by the overall under-financing of economic surveys, and the large number of things that need to be done. It is also made dramatic by the fact that research is in a historical context, and findings relate to major events in the economy. Data not collected at a point in time cannot be collected later, and every economic event whose impact on the economic actors is unstudied, is one more chance lost forever. The mere calendar limitations on budgets also make it difficult for a researcher to continue writing and speaking on past studies, while charging his time to a budget supporting other, later studies.

Excuses aside, it is worth looking at the problem of how the results of economic survey research might be put to use more effectively, making their potential social benefits a reality. Any presentation, the communications experts tell us, must know its audience. There are several audiences: respondents, interviewers, the general public, professional colleagues, and perhaps most important the various groups whose decisions may be affected by the information: sponsors, legislators, government agencies, private organizations.

Whatever the audience, there is a real problem how the results should be presented—with precision or with passion. All the professional training of academic researchers stresses precision, detailed care as to the accuracy of the results, presentation of the methodology, and not making statements that cannot be backed up by the data. This makes for dull reports and difficulty in finding what really matters. On the other hand, colorful writing is frequently inaccurate, or at least misleading, and may well combine the survey results with (a) other knowledge and (b) value judgements, explicitly or implicitly.

A few examples may be useful. Peter Townsend wrote a book on his studies of old people's homes in Britain, so dramatizing the plight of the people in them that the book led to Parliamentary action. Is it unscientific to put photographs of desolate looking old people in a report supposedly based on probability sampling?

A reverse example was a study in Michigan of the outcome of lump-sum settlements under the Workmen's Compensation law. An injured worker receiving medical care and weekly subsistence payments could settle his total future claim against his employer for a lump sum, if the hearing examiner approved. Some argued that this merely took the insurance company and the employer off the hook, let the man pay his back debts (including welfare, which demanded repayment), and that he would end up on welfare again. Others argued that the end of the gravy train and any future claims would miraculously cure bad backs and get people back to work. The study showed conclusively that people who settled for a lump sum payment were mostly not back at work, even the cases of injured backs, but the report did not go into the whole issue of reform of the workmen's compensation law. The immediate result was that the examiners made it very difficult for workers to get settlements, but inflation had so eroded the value of the weekly payments that they could hardly live on them. It was a number of years before the schedule of payments was raised so that the situation was genuinely improved.

A similar example occurred with studies of auto accident costs and compensation where studies show gross inequities, but a series of alternative reforms have been proposed. What obligation does the survey researcher, whose expertise is in research and perhaps also economics (but not law or insurance) have to enter that battle?

In between the active support of particular policies, and the refusal to go beyond the survey findings, there may well be a broad no-man's land of opportunities for making clear the implications of findings. Consumers' ignorance of effective interest rates, or their inefficient purchasing practices have relatively obvious importance to the effective operation of a market economy, and should not be buried in dull complicated reports.

To some extent the problem reflects a general tendency for researchers to allocate too little time and funds to both ends of the process. The design, pretesting, and development are often skimped in the haste to get into the field, and then the careful writing, and development of alternate presentations for different audiences, are skimped in the desire to get at the next piece of research. Most people dislike giving up the chance for more statistical analysis and finally putting a finished report on paper, until they are about to run out of time and money.

As the complexity of the analysis and of other survey procedures increase, the problem of reporting *simply* what the results were also increases. One interesting exercise is to see whether one can state in one sentence what a table shows and, if so, whether it is necessary to produce the whole table to show it. Another main issue in presentation is whether to present in detail all the negative findings—the variables that did *not* explain behavior and, if so, whether to first give the positive findings, and then separately the negative ones, so as to make the presentation simpler.

We discussed in the previous chapter some of the problems of presenting data. Even the titles given to variables can cause difficulty for readers, if they do not clearly indicate the operation that developed them. It is useful for the reader to have easy access to the actual question which elicited the information. Where a great deal of complex analysis is done, it is a great help to the reader to have, perhaps in an appendix, a complete list of questions, with numerical distributions of the answers by categories. Where many additional variables are created, their definitions and distributions (or means and variances) should also be easily accessible. In addition, where many complex terms are involved, for variables or procedures or units of analysis, a glossary of terms is frequently useful. Most United States Census Bureau publications are models in this respect.

When complex analyses are done, particularly such multivariate analyses as multiple regression, it is important to give the reader the univariate relations as well. When dummy or dichotomous variables are used, this means that the reader should have the unadjusted mean of the dependent variable for each subgroup (for whom some dummy variable is 1 rather than 0).

In addition it is extremely useful for the reader to know the degree of intercorrelation among the pairs of predictors used in a multivariate analysis. When they are numerical, this implies a table of simple correlation coefficients. When they are categorical, it is the association among sets of them which matters (age and education, for instance). The two-way tables would help and, if computers allow, Kendall's Tau Beta or even the canonical correlations between the sets of dummy variables, or Cramer's V.

Finally, and perhaps most important, the number of cases on which any estimate is based, together with some general procedures for approximating sampling errors, need to be provided, even if the analysis carefully discusses only results which are clearly statistically significant.

Research on communication (and persuasion) seems to indicate that written word is much less effective than personal communication, particularly if the latter allows two-way communication. While most people can read much faster than they can listen, they prefer to listen, and can often save a lot of time if they can ask a question. The questions also reveal problems in communication. Hence verbal communication, particularly with concerned people, may vastly improve the quality of a written report. It may also reveal complexities with policy implications, or new policy implications, that would not have occurred to the researcher.

In a broader perspective, one can think of the output of a survey research project as a lot of printed paper, plus some verbal presentations. The output serves many audiences, however, and must be tailored for them: They have some vested interest and a right to information. Most of them will be asked for further cooperation in the future, too.

1) *Respondents.* They may not be called on for reinterviews, but their neighbors will be interviewed in future studies. They gave time and energy and deserve some expression of thanks. They do not want the complex details, but may be interested in very simple things such as how many other people use their seat belts, or approve of installment credit. They need a report rapidly, before they forget all about the interview, and most such reports are based on the straight runs of questions likely to interest them, with perhaps a few comparisons among regions, or people of different ages.

2) *Interviewers.* They like to know not just some of the overall answers but reports on how the field work went, stories of unusual cases, and perhaps some notion what difference the study will make on issues of public policy. They also like to know a little about how the data get processed and how one goes from a series of questions to an index of, say, "risk avoidance."

3) *Specialists in the survey center itself.* They are most likely to be interested in a broader picture of the whole process, of which their work is a part, and in the implications of the study for science and for public policy. They usually get their feed-back personally, or in meetings which include the next group:

4) *Professional colleagues in the center and in the university.* These are busy people, often not much interested in the technical details (unless they suspect deficiencies) but concerned with how the material relates to a larger picture both of research and theory. They usually serve as a trial audience for papers and presentations designed for a larger national or international audience of professionals. But they are more crucial, in the sense that it is important that other parts of a university are sufficiently well informed to be reassured as to the quality and the importance of the work. Even if there is a national advisory committee, there needs also to be a local university committee which is kept well informed about the findings and the new research plans of a survey center.

5) *Colleagues in the professional associations.* This is the traditional audience, the one to which most research reports are directed, and the least interested in many cases. They have learned that it is necessary to be very selective about additions to the body of knowledge for which they are responsible, and those whose main interest is theory tend to be impatient with empirical findings

unless they are directly related to a particular theoretical structure. In economics, for instance, it is mainly income and price elasticities that are of interest to the profession. Reports which show the importance of other variables are not very interesting, unless it turns out that they actually account for differences (over time or between groups) in their dynamic responses to changes in income or prices. In the process of developing such information, the researcher must also generate a lot of other information, if only to remove "noise" in the estimates of interest to economists. And there is a great temptation to present all the ancillary information, to the distress of the readers. Some of it belongs in the professional journals of sociology or psychology, or statistics and methodology. The difficulty, of course, is that it is not easy to present only the findings of interest to one audience, without describing the whole study. Hence, there must be a full report available which gives the full methodology and most of the findings. The difficulty is that this main report usually exhausts the staff and the budget, leaving most of the audiences unsatisfied.

6) *Legislators and administrators.* People responsible for making or implementing public policy are again selective in what they want from a survey. They want the findings relevant for their decisions, and yet they do not want the researcher to try to make their decisions for them. For one thing, he often does not know a lot of other things essential for wise decisions. For another, it is not his responsibility, nor will he be called to task for the results. This puts the researcher in the position of trying to find out what the connection is between his findings and the problems of legislators or administrators, and making clear the relation of his findings to those problems, without attempting to go on to the next logical step (and an attractive one to anyone interested in problem solving) of working out the implications for action.

In underdeveloped countries this temptation is even stronger, and research experts frequently give advice (often bad) without realizing the extent of their ignorance about problems of implementing it, or other considerations. The more restricted contribution of providing continuous feedback on how programs are going and why (by interviewing people whose actions the government is trying to influence) would be far more useful.

7) *Reform groups.* Perhaps we should think of reform groups as another audience, and make a special effort to see that they understand the research findings in designing their reforms.

8) *The general public.* They indirectly support survey research and may be affected by the influence of its findings, so they deserve to know what is going on. Popularization of research findings is perhaps the most difficult of all, and often done by professional writers who may put too much emphasis on what is sensational or sexy, or jump too fast to generalize or draw policy implications. Press releases, issued by the survey center itself, can go a long way to close the gap and, when they are really well written, tend to be published almost verbatim

by newspapers. Once again, this obligation tends to be forgotten or delegated to someone with many other duties or little knowledge of the study or both.

Relation of Survey Research to the Universities

We have already argued that survey research can attack important current problems and still be contributing to the permanent body of scientific knowledge about human behavior. There is the danger, of course, of pressure to attack very much ad-hoc problems with little basic scientific interest. Another danger is that even if basic knowledge is created, it is a long time getting into the body of material being transmitted in the educational system. For this reason it seems important that survey research centers be closely attached to teaching institutions and that the researchers themselves do some teaching. It is not that status and titles still go with teaching, but that there is a symbiotic relation between teaching and research. Teaching material forces one to organize it, be prepared to defend it against criticism, and relate it to larger bodies of knowledge. The inevitable criticism from students and colleagues often points up the optimal next steps in a program of research. At the same time, a university is then teaching the best new knowledge, not material that is well-organized but out of date (or even wrong).

This, of course, benefits the individual university where there happens to be a survey center. National advisory committees can serve the function on a broader scale of alerting professionals all over the country of the available findings, and of data sets that can be used for further analysis. Such a committee also gives the survey center advice and counsel about the direction of research and even about specific research designs.

The other alternative, panels of readers and critics asked to judge designs and manuscripts, has not worked well, perhaps because it expects too much work and involvement from people who may be interested in the results and in future designs, but not in details.

In general the history of independent, isolated research groups or groups totally imbedded in administrative or action agencies has not been good. It is interesting to note that two national commissions have recently come out in favor of a number of university-based multi-disciplinary research organizations on a relatively permanent basis.[41] The advantages of such an arrangement seem clear, including some competition among them. What is not clear is how to assure that they will be responsible to the really important problems of the day and see to it that both legislators and administrators receive feed-back as to the implications of the research.

There are two main problems of large scale research organizations within universities, including survey research organizations. They are: titles, accreditation, and the maintenance of standards on the one hand, and financing, tenure, perquisites, and reserve funds on the other.

A university depends on its teaching departments for awarding titles and promotions, and maintaining standards of academic excellence. Professors see the results of their colleagues' teaching, and of their published scholarship, and are competent to judge it. It is not so easy for them to judge the competence of those engaged largely in research of a new, interdisciplinary, large-scale kind. Yet there is reluctance to see the title "Professor" awarded without some systematic accreditation and judging process, even if it is a title like Research Professor. One consequence is a second-class status for all but a few top staff in a research institute in terms of titles and some non-economic perquisites. "Teaching" titles also imply voting rights in the department on curricular matters, new staffing, etc. on which a department might justifiably feel that it would not want to be outvoted by a large group of part-time teachers. When it comes to maintaining the quality of the research, that monitoring is actually done within the research institute itself, but it has been found salutary to have an executive committee widely representative of interested segments of the university, approving the general policies and even each new proposal of the research institute. Not only can such a group warn against slipping standards, or unwise shifts in emphasis, but it can also communicate to the university a better sense of what is going on.

The issue of titles and standards is usually included in the discussions with the other, financial, issues. Joint appointments always raise questions of equity in the distribution of time and payments. More important, universities generally provide tenure to their senior faculty, in order to assure academic freedom. But they wince at the thought of providing such guarantees to personnel engaged in research with outside funds, outside the teaching budgets that is, which are seen as capable of withering any time. The history of oscillations in government and foundation support, particularly if one looks at individual areas of research, makes such fears credible. Since professional titles usually imply tenure, the two issues easily get mixed up.

Another economic issue has to do with indirect costs, and the extent to which there are hidden subsidies, in either direction. Foundation grants with limited "indirect costs" allowed, may be charged with adding to the university's general budget some of the total real costs of the research they support. After all, the university administration has to spend some part of its energies on these matters, and the university may be providing buildings, library services, etc. On the other hand, if a university takes all the indirect cost allocations in research contracts, it can easily use the funds to support other research or even some of its teaching functions.

One sensible solution to both these financial problems is to allow the research institute to keep nominal control of its own reserve funds, accumulated out of indirect charges on grants and contracts. With such funds it can provide tenure for its own staff. It can also take care of many of its own administrative functions and cost accounting. Perhaps more important, the research institute is then vitally concerned with its economic efficiency, since that builds its own security and capability for pioneering in areas otherwise unfinanced.

Conclusion

The future of economic survey research depends on adequate financing with long time horizons, judicious selection of the important areas of research, adequate evaluation of the benefits of past projects, efficient organization of research centers to maximize the information per dollar spent, and the wide diffusion of the results. A group of writers capable of interpreting the results of economic survey research, or a system of cooperating with specialists in producing separate statements of the action implications of studies needs to be developed. In the meantime, a major increase in the social benefits from economic surveys could come from clearer, and perhaps more specialized, reporting of the findings.

Not only is there need for greater total support for economic survey research, but a need for several research centers which can compete with one another and for an accompanying expansion of support for methodological research and for training of personnel. It has been difficult to convince people to learn economic survey methods when the total support for, and jobs in, the field were limited. It has been difficult to finance methodological research, when its benefits would be too late to help the current sponsors of individual substantive studies. And potential rates of expansion of economic surveys are hampered by shortages of personnel and inadequate development of methodology.

Hopefully, we are on the threshold of an era when analytical economists will be explicit but reasonable in their needs for behavioral information, and when the behavioral economists will focus survey research on these needs, so that the gap between what we hypothesize about behavior and what we seek to know, is narrowed.

Footnotes to Chapter VII

1. See the 1969 Budget Hearings and Testimony on the National Science Foundation, for example.

2. For a dramatic history of supression of research findings in another area (forestry) see Ashley Schiff, *Fire and Water,* Harvard University Press, Cambridge, Mass., 1962. Classified research supported by the government has usually not been survey research, except for some state department studies some years ago.

3. Guy Orcutt, "Data, Research, and Government," *American Economic Review,* 60 (May 1970), pp. 132-137.

4. Behavioral and Social Sciences Survey Committee, *The Behavioral and Social Sciences, Outlook and Needs,* National Academy of Sciences, Washington, D.C., 1969. (Committee under the auspices of the Committee on Science and Public Policy of the National Academy of Sciences and the Committee on Problems and Policy, of the Social Science Research Council; and Special Commission on the Social Sciences of the National Science Board, *Knowledge into Action: Improving the Nation's Use of the Social Sciences.* National Science Foundation, Washington, D.C., 1969.

   See also Gene M. Lyons, *The Uneasy Partnership,* Social Science and the Federal Government in the Twentieth Century, Russell Sage Foundation, New York, 1969.

BIBLIOGRAPHY

PUBLICATIONS AVAILABLE FROM THE INSTITUTE

Listed below are books and articles published by the staff of the Economic Behavior Program of the Survey Research Center. They may be ordered by author and title from the Publications Division, Department B, Institute for Social Research, The University of Michigan, P.O. Box 1248, Ann Arbor, Michigan 48106.

Barfield, Richard and James N. Morgan. EARLY RETIREMENT: THE DECISION AND THE EXPERIENCE. 1969. $6 (paperbound), $8 (clothbound), 289 pp.

Barfield, Richard. THE AUTOMOBILE WORKER AND RETIREMENT: A SECOND LOOK. 1970. $1.75 (paperbound), 60 pp.

Dunkelberg, William C. and Frank P. Stafford. The cost of financing automobile purchases. REVIEW OF ECONOMICS AND STATISTICS, 1969.

Katona, George, James N. Morgan, and Richard E. Barfield. Retirement in prospect and retrospect. TRENDS IN EARLY RETIREMENT (Occasional Papers in Gerontology No. 4). Ann Arbor: The University of Michigan Institute of Gerontology, March 1969, 27-49.

Katona, George. On the Function of Behavioral Theory and Behavioral Research in Economics. AMERICAN ECONOMIC REVIEW, LVIII, March 1968, 146-150.

Katona, George. Consumer Behavior: Theory and Findings on Expectations and Aspirations. Proceedings, AMERICAN ECONOMIC REVIEW, LVIII, 2, May 1968, 19-30.

Katona, George. Consumer Behavior and Monetary Policy. In GELDTHEORIE UND GELDPOLITIK (Festschrift for Guenter Schmoelders). Berlin, Germany: Duncker and Humbolt, 1968, 117-132.

Katona, George. PRIVATE PENSIONS AND INDIVIDUAL SAVING. 1965. $1.50 (paperbound), $2.50 (clothbound), 114 pp.

425

Kosobud, Richard F. and James N. Morgan (Editors). CONSUMER BEHAVIOR OF INDIVIDUAL FAMILIES OVER TWO AND THREE YEARS. 1964. $5 (paperbound), $6 (clothbound), 208 pp.

Lansing, John B., Robert W. Marans, and Robert B. Zehner. PLANNED RESIDENTIAL ENVIRONMENT. 1970. $5 (paperbound), $7 (clothbound), 270 pp.

Lansing, John B., Charles Wade Clifton, and James N. Morgan. NEW HOMES AND POOR PEOPLE: A STUDY OF CHAINS OF MOVES. 1969. $5 (paperbound), $7 (clothbound), 136 pp.

Lansing, John B. and Gary Hendricks. AUTOMOBILE OWNERSHIP AND DENSITY. 1967. $3 (paperbound), 230 pp.

Lansing, John B. and Eva Mueller. THE GEOGRAPHICAL MOBILITY OF LABOR. 1967. $5 (paperbound), 421 pp.

Lansing, John B. RESIDENTIAL LOCATION AND URBAN MOBILITY: THE SECOND WAVE OF INTERVIEWS. 1966. $2.50 (paperbound), 115 pp.

Lansing, John B. and Eva Mueller. RESIDENTIAL LOCATION AND URBAN MOBILITY. 1964. $2 (paperbound), 142 pp.

Lansing, John B. and Nancy Barth. RESIDENTIAL LOCATION AND URBAN MOBILITY: A MULTIVARIATE ANALYSIS. 1964. $2 (paperbound), 98 pp.

Lansing, John B. THE TRAVEL MARKET, 1964-1965. 1965. $4 (clothbound), 112 pp.

*Lansing, John B. and Dwight M. Blood. THE CHANGING TRAVEL MARKET. 1964. $7 (paperbound), 374 pp.

*Lansing, John B., Eva Mueller, and others. THE TRAVEL MARKET 1958, 1959-1960, 1961-1962. Reprinted 1963 (originally issued as three separate reports). $7 (paperbound), 388 pp.

*Lansing, John B. and Ernest Lillienstein. THE TRAVEL MARKET 1955, 1956, 1957. Reprinted 1963 (originally issued as three separate reports). $10 (clothbound), 524 pp.

*Package of three available for $20.00.

Lansing, John B., Eva Mueller, William Ladd, and Nancy Barth. THE GEO-
GRAPHIC MOBILITY OF LABOR, A FIRST REPORT. 1963. $3.95
(paperbound), 328 pp.

Morgan, James N. and staff. A PANEL STUDY OF INCOME DYNAMICS, Vol.
I-III, 1968-1970. $4 (paperbound), 331 pp.

Morgan, James N. Family Use of Credit. JOURNAL OF HOME ECONOMICS,
60, January 1968.

Morgan, James N. Some pilot studies of communication and consensus in the
family. PUBLIC OPINION QUARTERLY, 32, 1, Spring 1968, 113-121.

Morgan, James N. The supply of effort, the measurement of well-being, and the
dynamics of improvement. AMERICAN ECONOMIC REVIEW, 58, May
1968.

Morgan, James N. Survey analysis: applications in economics. In INTERNA-
TIONAL ENCYCLOPEDIA OF THE SOCIAL SCIENCES, 15, New York:
Macmillan, 1968, 429-436.

Morgan, James N., John A. Sonquist, and Frank M. Andrews. MULTIPLE
CLASSIFICATION ANALYSIS. 1967. $3 (paperbound), 211 pp.

Morgan, James N., Ismail Sirageldin, and Nancy Baerwaldt. PRODUCTIVE
AMERICANS: A STUDY OF HOW INDIVIDUALS CONTRIBUTE TO
ECONOMIC PROGRESS. 1966. $5 (clothbound), 546 pp.

Mueller, Eva. TECHNOLOGICAL ADVANCE IN AN EXPANDING ECONOMY:
ITS IMPACT ON A CROSS-SECTION OF THE LABOR FORCE, 1969.
$5 (paperbound), $7 (clothbound), 254 pp.

Mueller, Eva, Arnold Wilken, and Margaret Wood. LOCATION DECISIONS
AND INDUSTRIAL MOBILITY IN MICHIGAN, 1961, 1962, $2.50
(paperbound), $3 (cloth), 115 pp.

Sirageldin, Ismail Abdel-Hamid. NON-MARKET COMPONENTS OF NATIONAL
INCOME. 1969. $3 (paperbound), $4 (clothbound), 127 pp.

Sonquist, John A. Problems of getting sociological data in and out of a computer. Paper read at the American Sociological Association, Boston, August
1968. 22 pp.

Sonquist, John A. and James N. Morgan, THE DETECTION OF INTERACTION EFFECTS. 1964. $3 (paperbound), 292 pp.

Stafford, Frank P. Concentration and labor earnings: comment. AMERICAN ECONOMIC REVIEW, 58, 1, March 1968, 174-181.

Stafford, Frank P. Student family size in relation to current and expected income. JOURNAL OF POLITICAL ECONOMY, 1969.

Data collected by the Economic Behavior Program are available on either punched cards or computer tapes, together with a detailed code describing the content of the cards or tapes. Thus, interested scholars or other parties may obtain or prepare further analysis byeond that presented in this volume.

SURVEY OF CONSUMER FINANCES SERIES

1960 SURVEY OF CONSUMER FINANCES. 1961. $4 (paperbound), 310 pp.

1961 SURVEY OF CONSUMER FINANCES. G. Katona, C. A. Lininger, J. N. Morgan, and E. Mueller. 1962. $4 (paperbound), $5 (cloth), 150 pp.

1962 SURVEY OF CONSUMER FINANCES. G. Katona, C. A. Lininger, and R. F. Kosobud. 1963. $4 (paperbound), 310 pp.

1963 SURVEY OF CONSUMER FINANCES. G. Katona, C. A. Lininger, and E. Mueller. 1964. $4 (paperbound), 262 pp.

1964 SURVEY OF CONSUMER FINANCES. G. Katona, C. A. Lininger, and E. Mueller. 1965. $4 (paperbound), 245 pp.

1965 SURVEY OF CONSUMER FINANCES, G. Katona, E. Mueller, J. Schmiedeskamp, and J. A. Sonquist. 1966. $4 (paperbound), $6 (cloth).

1966 SURVEY OF CONSUMER FINANCES. G. Katona, E. Mueller, J. Schmiedeskamp, and J. A. Sonquist. 1967. $4 (paperbound), 303 pp.

1967 SURVEY OF CONSUMER FINANCES. G. Katona, J. N. Morgan, J. Schmiedeskamp, and J. A. Sonquist. 1968. $5 (paperbound), $7 (cloth), 343 pp.

1968 SURVEY OF CONSUMER FINANCES. G. Katona, W. C. Dunkelberg, J. Schmiedeskamp, and F. P. Stafford. 1969. $5 (paperbound), $7 (cloth), 287 pp.

1969 SURVEY OF CONSUMER FINANCES. G. Katona, W. C. Dunkelberg, G. Hendricks, and J. Schmiedeskamp. 1970. $5 (paperbound), $7 (cloth), 340 pp.

OTHER BOOKS BY MEMBERS OF THE ECONOMIC BEHAVIOR PROGRAM

(Published by commercial publishing houses or University presses. Available only from publishers or bookstores.)

ASPIRATIONS AND AFFLUENCE: COMPARATIVE STUDIES IN THE UNITED STATES AND WESTERN EUROPE. George Katona, Burkhard Strumpel, and Ernest Zahn. McGraw-Hill, 1970.

CONSUMER RESPONSE TO INCOME INCREASES. George Katona and Eva Mueller. Brookings Institution, 1968.

TRANSPORTATION AND ECONOMIC POLICY. John B. Lansing. Free Press, 1966.

THE MASS CONSUMPTION SOCIETY. George Katona. McGraw-Hill, 1964.

INCOME AND WELFARE IN THE UNITED STATES. J. N. Morgan, M. H. David, W. J. Cohen, and H. E. Brazer. McGraw-Hill, 1962.

AN INVESTIGATION OF RESPONSE ERROR. J. B. Lansing, G. P. Ginsburg, and K. Braaten. Bureau of Economic and Business Research, University of Illinois, 1961.

THE POWERFUL CONSUMER. George Katona. McGraw-Hill, 1960.

BUSINESS LOOKS AT BANKS: A STUDY OF BUSINESS BEHAVIOR. G. Katona, S. Steinkamp, and A. Lauterbach. University of Michigan Press, 1957.

CONSUMER ECONOMICS. James N. Morgan. Prentice-Hall, 1955.

CONTRIBUTIONS OF SURVEY METHODS TO ECONOMICS. G. Katona, L. R. Klein, J. B. Lansing, and J. N. Morgan, Columbia University Press, 1957.

PSYCHOLOGICAL ANALYSIS OF ECONOMIC BEHAVIOR. George Katona. McGraw-Hill, 1951. (Paperback edition published in 1963.)

ECONOMIC BEHAVIOR OF THE AFFLUENT. Robin Barlow, H. E. Brazer, and J. N. Morgan. Washington, D.C.: Brookings Institution, 1966.

LIVING PATTERNS AND ATTITUDES IN THE DETROIT REGION. John B. Lansing and Gary Hendricks. A report for TALUS (Detroit Regional Transportation and Land Use Study), 1967, 241 pp. (Available only from TALUS, 1248 Washington Blvd., Detroit, Mich. 48226—$5 to nongovernmental agencies.)